Praise for John Demos's

THE HEATHEN SCHOOL

Longlisted for the National Book Award

"This splendid reconstruction of everyday life ... describes what happened at Cornwall as a story of 'high hopes, valiant effort, leading to eventual tragic defeat.'"　　　—T. H. Breen, *The American Scholar*

"Absorbing.... The men and women in [Demos's] stories come alive across the centuries."　　　—*The Wall Street Journal*

"John Demos ... has gifted us with a historical opus.... The book is outstanding in many ways. Primary among them, it is beautifully written—the mixing of Demos's craftsmanship and early melodious borrowed quotes.... [W]onderfully executed impressions of his personal sojourns around today's Cornwall and Hawaii."
　　　—*The Providence Journal*

"Much-needed.... Demos shows how the founders' dreams fell victim to racial bigotry within both the student body itself and in the greater Cornwell community.... This brilliant work is highly recommended."
　　　—*Library Journal* (starred review)

"A poignant, well-researched historical vignette of how changing the world weighs on the individual shoulders bearing the task." —*Booklist*

"Demos manages a sly, significant feat in this historical study/personal exploration.... In 'interludes' alternating with his historical narrative, Demos chronicles his visits to the places involved—e.g., Hawaii, Cornwall—in order to impart a personal commitment to this collective American tragedy. A slow-building saga that delivers a powerful final wallop."　　　—*Kirkus Reviews* (starred review)

"[Demos's] research is characteristically prodigious, his writing disarming, and his story captivating and of national resonance."
—*Publishers Weekly*

"The masterful account of a utopian nineteenth-century experiment in education—one that goes painfully awry. A splendidly nuanced, wholly absorbing tale; patiently, brilliantly, John Demos coaxes unexpected lessons from a singular collision of enlightenment and assimilation."
—Stacy Schiff, Pulitzer Prize–winning author of *Cleopatra: A Life*

"This moving, engrossing history of an early American experiment in multicultural education charts the collision between soaring aims and human limitations. . . . Demos weaves a compelling tale that invites us to reflect on the meaning of the nation's struggles toward equality."
—Richard D. Brown, author of *The Strength of a People*

"The global meets the local as rarely before in *The Heathen School*, an eye-opening story about a stunningly cosmopolitan community in the heart of early national New England. John Demos uses his powerful literary gifts and insight to animate the experiences of people brought together by love, learning, and loss, across dramatic cultural divides. Imaginative, compassionate, and exquisitely written, this book will change your understanding of America's founding project to make a difference for the world—and to make our different peoples into a national whole."
—Maya Jasanoff, author of *Liberty's Exiles*

"Demos, a consummate storyteller, has written a parable about the nature of the American experiment itself: the hills and valleys of our dreams."
—Jill Lepore, author of *Book of Ages: The Life and Opinions of Jane Franklin*

JOHN DEMOS

THE HEATHEN SCHOOL

John Demos is the Samuel Knight Professor Emeritus of History at Yale. His previous books include *The Unredeemed Captive*, which won the Francis Parkman Prize and was a finalist for the National Book Award, and *Entertaining Satan*, which won the Bancroft Prize. He lives in Tyringham, Massachusetts.

∾ THE ∾
HEATHEN SCHOOL

~~~ THE ~~~
HEATHEN SCHOOL

A Story of Hope and Betrayal
in the Age of the Early Republic

JOHN DEMOS

VINTAGE BOOKS
A Division of Random House LLC
New York

FIRST VINTAGE BOOKS EDITION, DECEMBER 2014

Copyright © 2014 by John Demos

All rights reserved. Published in the United States by Vintage Books,
a division of Random House LLC, New York, and in Canada by
Random House of Canada, Limited, Toronto, Penguin Random House
companies. Originally published in hardcover in the United States by
Alfred A. Knopf, a division of Random House LLC, New York, in 2014.

The Cataloging-in-Publication Data is on file at the Library of Congress.
Library of Congress Control Number: 2013956402

Vintage Trade Paperback ISBN: 978-0-679-78112-7
eBook ISBN: 978-0-385-35166-9

Book design by Maggie Hinders
Author photograph © Michael Lionstar

www.vintagebooks.com

147429898

To Carter Umbarger

After such knowledge, what forgiveness? Think now
History has many cunning passages, contrived corridors
And issues, deceives with whispering ambitions,
Guides us by vanities. Think now
She gives when our attention is distracted
And what she gives, gives with such supple confusions
That the giving famishes the craving.

—T. S. ELIOT, "Gerontion"

Contents

~ THE ~
HEATHEN SCHOOL

Prologue

Just a piece of local history . . .

More than any of my previous projects, this one began with serendipity.

Summer 1996. I have gone with my wife for an evening visit to the home of
an old friend in the town of Cornwall, Connecticut. Before supper we chat
with other guests, one of whom begins to tell us a story from Cornwall's
past. It is, he says, "just a piece of local history"—but interesting all the
same. In fact, it's *very* interesting; as the details unfold, I'm transfixed.

A "heathen school" specially designed for indigenous youth from
all parts of the earth . . . Young men and boys from Hawaii, Polynesia,
India, China, plus a smattering of European Jews, and quite a few Native
Americans, too, all brought together in little Cornwall during the
opening decades of the nineteenth century . . . Educate them, "civilize"
them, convert them to Christianity, then send them back to help start
similar projects in their various homelands, and the entire world will
be "saved" in the shortest time imaginable: thus the goal of the eminent
Protestant ministers in charge . . . High hopes and strong claims of initial
success, followed by unexpected crisis . . . They court, and marry, our
daughters! . . . Families torn apart, public outrage at fever pitch: the
school shut down in disgrace . . . And then, in the aftermath, two of the
heathen "scholars" back in their own nation, leaders now, charting a

painful "removal" process, along an infamous "trail of tears . . ." Until, at
the very end, comes violent death . . .

   At home later that night, I cannot sleep; what I've heard at my friend's
house goes around and around in my head. The next morning, I get up
early and drive straight to the library. I'm anxious to discover how much
this story of the heathen school has been known, and written about,
previously. The answer is: not a lot. There are passing mentions in several
books, and a chapter or so in at least two, but no full-fledged treatment.
I drive home, and ponder. A book project is a major commitment; does
this clear the bar? Is there more here than "a piece of local history"? It
doesn't take long to decide.[1]

Remembered now from many years later on, that moment is still vivid
in my mind. The research, the thinking, the writing: All is done; only
publication awaits. The process has not been easy, but I have no regrets.
The story of the heathen school is "local," yes, but it's also a national
story, even an international one. And it has taken me into some very
deep layers of the American past.

   One of these is the enduring legacy of "American exceptionalism."
At their best, our national traditions have fostered a generous spirit
of outreach toward neighboring peoples and nations, a feeling of
obligation—not to say "mission"—to make the world as a whole a better
place. (Think the Marshall Plan, after World War II. Think the Peace
Corps. Think the ever-ready offers of American-driven relief following
disasters all around the globe.) "For we must consider that we shall be
as a city upon a hill. The eyes of all people are upon us," John Winthrop famously declared while leading the first band of Englishmen
and women to colonize Massachusetts (1630). And that idea—America
as a "redeemer nation," showing others the way to broad-gauge human
improvement—has been with us ever since. To be sure, exceptions to
this exceptionalism intrude. Generosity may slide into arrogant presumption, helpfulness into imperialism. All of our country's wars
fought in my lifetime had, as their declared purpose, something more
than national aggrandizement. Most were, in one way or another, meant
to protect and advance humane values thought to be characteristically
American—freedom, democracy, opportunity. Yet some of them, in
hindsight (or even at the time), have a markedly downside look.[2]

   In short, it's been part of America's history—this redemptive project,
this crusader mentality—all along. It's been creative and destructive,

glorious and tragic, noble and ignoble, by turns. Inevitably, attitudes toward it will differ, but there is no doubting its power as a key historical theme. It both frames and suffuses the story of the heathen school.

A second large theme at the story's center is what the critic Tzvetan Todorov calls "the discovery *self* makes of the *other*." How do we deal with others who are manifestly different from ourselves? This, of course, is not a specifically American question, nor is it only a history question. Rather, it has a broadly existential grounding; it's generic; it's part of the "human condition." It takes many forms (difference of race, of class, of gender, of culture, of religion, of age, of sexual orientation, and so on); each one of us confronts it, in our private lives, every day. Yet in America—the United States of America—it has acquired a *public* depth and coloration; for the bedrock fact of human difference has shaped our collective experience from the start. The three-way encounter of our colonial period—Indians, Europeans, and Africans—was extraordinary; the Old World across the Atlantic had nothing like it. And this was only the beginning. The magnetic force of our national project has continued to draw into our midst people of every stripe and condition. The heathen school was a microcosm of the struggles rooted in this part of our history.[3]

There is a third key element to mention up front; it may sound counterintuitive, but no matter. This is a story of failure. Its dark, tragic end lies far from its bright beginning. As such, it's not the sort of thing writers and readers of American history commonly look for. The national narrative we favor has a triumphalist score; progress is its central note. Yet our history is strewn with failures, large and small: projects gone awry from poor planning or bad luck, ideas missing their mark, emotions running amok, and—especially in an "exceptional" country—the hubris of overreaching. Many of these are forgotten almost as soon as they conclude; often, a feeling of shame attaches to them. Sometimes the groups most directly involved acknowledge them only to claim a lesson learned, and a reason to "move on" as fast as possible. Yet most failures do, at the very least, tell us something about who we are as a people; we ignore them at our cost. Of course, every individual life knows personal failure—moments of falling down, or falling short. From this, too, much can be learned. As Samuel Beckett has written, "Ever tried. Ever failed. No matter. Try again. Fail again. Fail better."[4]

In sum: America as a redeemer nation. The encounter of self with other. The shape and substance of failure. Plus the inherent drama of the story itself. Reasons enough for me to write this book, and—dare I hope—for others to read it.

And one thing more. Along with the serendipity that got me started came fate. My father, born of Greek parentage and raised in Istanbul, was educated just after the start of the last century at a place called Anatolia College, a missionary school in a remote part of central Turkey. Indeed, the college's original sponsor was the very same American Board of Commissioners for Foreign Missions that played a key role in the story of the heathen school. Anatolia's students were a mix of Eastern Orthodox Greeks and Armenians, and Turkish Jews, the staff (for the most part) Protestant Americans. It was, then, itself a heathen school.

> Summer 1997. I'm a year into the project, and have a full day of research ahead; notes are piled high on my desk. At lunchtime I take a break to fetch the mail from our village post office. Included in the deliveries is a fund-raising brochure from Anatolia College. (The college goes on, though now relocated to northern Greece.) I am about to toss it aside, and go back to my work on the heathen school, when my gaze is drawn to an image on the brochure's front; it's an old photograph of the college orchestra taken many decades previous. And there, looking out at me from the middle of the photograph, is my father (age about eighteen), yet another heathen youth marked for salvation. In his left hand he grasps a trumpet.

A trumpet? Is this a summons? Serendipity *and* fate: Maybe the two together "make history"?

Final prefatory note: The book has a somewhat unusual architecture. Each of its four parts contains two chapters: The first is brief, designed to provide context for what immediately follows; the second unfolds the narrative. The parts, in turn, are separated by "interludes" about places central to the story. Occasional indented passages are vignettes presenting up-close views of specific events and people.

Tyringham, Massachusetts
May 2013

~ PART ONE ~

BEGINNINGS

CHAPTER ONE

American Outreach:
The China Trade

With their Revolution completed, their Constitution written, their nation established, the self-styled Americans faced the world in a fundamentally altered posture. Throughout the preceding two centuries, they had been colonists—and thus, in a broad sense, dependents. They had absorbed from elsewhere regular infusions of migrants, of "goods," of cultural nourishment and guidance.

But henceforth the currents would flow, also, in reverse direction. The new United States would increasingly—sometimes aggressively—turn *out* toward other groups and places. It would proudly proclaim its republican credo as a "beacon of freedom" for political reformers around the world. It would proffer its "go-ahead" spirit as the key to social development. It would urge its highly charged version of Protestant Christianity on all sorts of "heathen" unbelievers. Moreover, its people would rapidly multiply their physical contacts with the rest of humankind. Especially after about 1800, their travel and commerce would extend, quite literally, to the farthest corners of the earth.

The acme—the epitome—of this remarkable outreach was the so-called China Trade. To be sure, Americans were followers, not pioneers, here. Britons, Russians, and Spaniards (among others) had preceded them along the route to "Cathay," since at least the beginning of the eighteenth century. The Portuguese had claimed the island of Macao (just south of Canton) in 1557. And occasional Europeans had been voyaging that way, singly or in small groups, from far back in the Middle Ages. The American colonists, meanwhile, had been expressly forbidden by their imperial masters to join in most forms of international exchange.[1]

Yet once independence was achieved, American traders hastened to assert claims of their own; within little more than a generation, they gained for themselves a leading role. From Boston and Salem, Massachusetts; from Newport and Providence, Rhode Island; from New York and Philadelphia and Baltimore, the ships poured out—by the dozens each year. Canton was their chief, but far from their only, destination. For the China Trade was just one piece of a still larger "East India" (Asian) connection. Calcutta, Madras, Sumatra, Batavia, Port Jackson, Manila: These places, too, figured heavily in the traders' itinerary. The eventual outcome would include some astonishing individual fortunes, and a burst of capital formation to fuel the first phase of American industrial development.[2]

Even within itself, the China Trade was complex, many-sided, ever changing.

It was a clutch of prosperous merchants—gathered on summer afternoons in a massive glass-domed structure called the Boston Exchange Coffee House—dressed in ruffled nankeen shirts, seated at finely turned mahogany-and-bamboo tables, sipping tea from china cups, exchanging choice bits of financial gossip, and looking out across the nearby harbor for the return of long-departed ships. (Some voyages lasted for as long as four years.)[3]

It was twenty-odd Yankee farm boys turned "tars," the crew of a trim three-masted schooner—becalmed in the midst of a glassy tropical sea—mending ropes and sails and nets, whittling scrimshaw figurines, catching sea turtles, counting the spouts of a passing whale, cursing the endless, windless horizon, and dreaming all the while of the "shares" they would one day carry home to stake a claim in their native countryside. (Most sailors in the China Trade would make just a single voyage, and then return to the land.)[4]

It was a gang of sea-hardened hunters—young men bent on adventure, set ashore for months at a stretch on a rock-rimmed beach along the outermost of the Falkland Islands, deep in the lower Atlantic—methodically clubbing to death hundreds of bellowing fur seals, whose skins would then be scraped and dried on nearby pegging grounds prior to stowage en masse for shipment to the Orient. (Fur seals were taken from islands and atolls across a broad arc girdling the entire southern quadrant of the globe, including large sections of the Atlantic, Pacific, and Indian Oceans. Within a scant few decades, the hunt had rendered them nearly extinct, almost everywhere.)[5]

It was another group of Yankees—but this one a resident colony, and numbering in the hundreds—living as "alone men" on the Spanish-owned isle of Mas Afuera, off the west coast of South America, huddled in dank wooden huts, with scruffy little vegetable plots set alongside, struggling against ceaseless storms, insects, and disease, drinking, gambling, fighting, and gathering their own stash of skins for the arrival of the next season's trade fleet. (Mas Afuera was a seal hunter's El Dorado. It is estimated that three million skins were taken from this one little site, before a Spanish naval squadron evicted the hunters, and burned their settlements, in 1805.)[6]

It was yet another group, with another trading target, in another place: Fiji, far out in the South Pacific—where a transient population of foreign "beachcombers" mingled with native islanders, in love and war and occasional rites of cannibalism—all to the end of securing the highly aromatic bundles of sandalwood that would later fetch huge sums on the Canton market. (The Chinese turned sandalwood into a fine powder that, for centuries, they had used as incense in elaborate religious and funerary ceremonies.)[7]

It was a wholesale assault on another ocean fur-bearer—the charming, hapless sea otter—in the waters off the coast of present-day Alaska. And thus, too, it was a meeting ground for white and native North Americans—the latter including Tlingit and Haida, Salish and Tsimshian, Nootka and Chinook, with their powerful warrior traditions, their water skills, their swift dugout canoes, their totem pole–fronted, stilt-raised villages, their potlatch and other complex cultural practices, all achieved within a productive system that did not (and could not) include agriculture. (The Northwest Coast would quickly become a vast adjunct to the China Trade. Sea otter pelts, informally dubbed "soft gold," were especially prized by merchants from the cold climes of north China; a fully loaded trade ship might thus expect triple, quadruple, or even better, returns on its investment.)[8]

It was a mile-long train of pack animals (llamas, horses, mules, and their attendant herders) laden with bags of silver newly mined from the *cerro rico* (rich hill) at the great boomtown of Potosí high in the Andes mountain range, threading its way week after week along precipitous trails in the descent to ports on the coast of Spanish Peru. From there most of the precious cargo would go in one of two directions: westward in ships known as "Manila galleons" through the Pacific via the Philippines to Canton, or north by boat to Panama, overland on the jungle-shrouded isthmus, back on the sea for transfer in Havana (Cuba) to Spain's annual "treasure fleet," and then across the ocean, to be unloaded, finally, at the imperial hub of Seville. Sooner or later, some might be procured by American (or other) merchants and sent on to the Far East. (*Specie*—Spanish silver dollars—was rated above all else in the China Trade. Indeed, the Potosí mines, by far the world's leading source of bullion, fueled the entire system.)

It was also, of course, Canton, the only Chinese port of entry open to foreigners. Here, at its eastern terminus, the trade was subject to elaborate regulation and protocol: gift exchanges; the engagement of pilots, interpreters, provisioners, and stevedores; the payment of taxes, duties, and outright bribes; the inspection and rating of all imported products (sea otters, for example, were divided into ten carefully delineated categories). There were dangers to avoid, ranging from Malay pirates lurking outside the port entrance, to the sudden onset of Pacific typhoons, to local sharpers who packed shipping chests with wood chips or paper instead of tea and silks, to overindulgence in *samshew* (a potent Chinese whiskey). There were restrictions to obey, especially those that confined all *fan kwae* ("foreign devils") to a narrow waterfront warren of streets and alleys set apart from the city proper. There was an intricate commercial system to master, with *hoppos* (customs superintendents) and *cohong* merchants (those formally licensed by the emperor), coolies (day laborers) and *chinchew* men (local shopkeepers), "chops" (official seals and marks) and *hongs* (warehouses), and the widespread use of Spanish dollars. Finally, there were "goods" to buy and carry home—the point of it all—starting always with tea and silks, but also including nankeens (hand-loomed cotton fabrics), crepes, and grass cloth; porcelain tableware ("china") of every conceivable description; lacquered furniture; elegant oil, watercolor, and reverse-glass paintings (portraits, landscapes, garden scenes); carvings in ivory, jade, and soapstone (chess sets, for example); sewing and snuffboxes in mother-of-pearl; silver flatware sets that mimicked Western styles; brightly painted handheld fans of both "screen" and folding varieties (exported literally by the thousands, and considered de rigueur for genteel American ladies throughout the nineteenth century); elaborately filigreed tortoiseshell combs (also by the thousands, also wildly fashionable); umbrellas, window shades, straw mats, wallpapers, feather dusters, horn apothecary spoons, and numerous other bits and pieces too humble to have been included in the surviving records. In short: a kaleidoscope of (what came to be known as) chinoiserie, on a scale almost impossible to comprehend. (Virtually every "middling" household, in or near American cities of the period, would have had at least a few China-made objects. And in those with direct connections to the trade, the total might easily have risen into the hundreds. Moreover, tea was a beverage of choice for people of all classes.)[9]

It was, even beyond the terminus, the various people who made these things—in towns and villages stretched far across the interior of the Chinese mainland. First, the tea farmers in the eastern provinces above Canton who harvested the remarkably bountiful shrub three times a year, in dozens of varieties and grades. (Americans preferred green tea, especially the so-called young Hyson, which came principally from Kiangsi and Chekiang.) And also the merchants who brought the tea to market, mostly on rivers and streams in small, shallow-hulled junks. And the silk growers in the lower Yangtzee Valley who tended both the precious fiber-producing caterpillars (*Bombyx mori*, aka silkworm) and the equally essential caterpillar-sustaining mulberry trees. And, not least, the painters, carvers, carpenters, silversmiths, porcelain workers, and other anonymous craftspeople whose handiwork would grace the homes, and lives, of strangers half a world away.[10]

It was—most importantly here—Hawaii. Set roughly in the middle of this entire web, and known then as the Sandwich Islands, the Hawaiian archipelago served as crossroads, as refitting and provisioning stop, as vacation spot, as pleasure garden, as commercial entrepôt, as hiring station, as escape hatch, and (beginning about 1820) as key target for American missionaries. Ships arrived from several directions—Sitka Bay, the coastal towns of Peru and Chile, other parts of Polynesia—reflecting the different segments of the China Trade. Most stayed for intervals of from two weeks to two months before proceeding on across the Pacific. Officers, crew, and supercargoes alike described the islands in paradisiacal terms—"designed by Providence," wrote an admiring visitor, "to become . . . a place for the rest and recreation of sailors, after their long and perilous navigations." All praised "the genial climate, the luxurious abundance, and the gratifying pleasures" to be found there. All enjoyed the remarkable variety of fresh food and drink, especially pork from the hogs that ran more or less wild onshore, fowl of several types, tropical fruits and vegetables such as breadfruit and taro, and coconut, with its delicious milky contents. Most partook of the freely flowing liquor in the form of locally distilled rum and gin. And, perhaps inevitably after the long months at sea, many sought the company of lissome *wahines,* native women described as wonderfully "complaisant" and "amorous." (By one account, similar to many others, "they would almost use violence to force you into their embrace." But much of this activity was simple prostitution.)[11]

It was, finally, a host of impressions—thoughts, feelings, wishes—that grew, and spread, and palpitated in the hearts and heads of the innumerable throng whose lives it touched. Widened eyes, expanded horizons, a lifted gaze, a new sense of possibility and potency: thus its impact across the length and breadth of what was then called "Young America." For the China Trade was indeed a key part of our national youth. "China," wrote a pioneer sea captain who had seen for himself, "is the first for greatness, richness, and grandeur of any country ever known." (Might America rise one day to become its equal?)[12]

As often as not, there was some reshuffling of personnel while the trade ships stood at anchor in Hawaiian harbors. Some sailors would decide to remain in the islands—would jump ship to become, in effect, deserters. Others were discharged by their captains for insubordination, incompetence, or failure to perform their duties. (Men from either category might subsequently put down roots in native communities; a few actually rose to the status of chiefs, or trusted advisers to the royal family.)[13]

The process also went the other way, with Hawaiian men hiring on as crew for the remainder of a voyage. Known as *kanakas* (the islanders' word for themselves, modified in shipboard parlance to "knackies"), they would then sail to Canton, to London, to New York or Boston— and, in some cases, might begin a long career at sea. Most of these men led difficult, unrecorded lives, on the margins of organized society.[14]

One, however, would become a famous exception. He was called Obookiah, with "Henry" added in front. Even today, he is much remembered in Hawaii. And, across a large swath of nineteenth-century America, few names were more well and widely known than Henry Obookiah.

· CHAPTER TWO ·

"Providence unquestionably
cast them on our shores"

Who was Henry Obookiah? In the legend that would come to surround his life, one scene anchored all the rest.

On an autumn afternoon in the year 1809, at the main door of Yale College, in New Haven, Connecticut, a stream of undergraduates flows steadily in and out. Off to one side, a rather odd-looking young man—of "dusky" complexion and in ragged apparel—stands watching, and quietly weeping. After several minutes, his presence is noticed and acknowledged by some of the students. When asked the cause of his distress, he replies, haltingly and in broken English, "that nobody gives me learning."[1]

Should we believe this as historical fact? Perhaps not; when set in the context of the entire Obookiah legend, it seems almost too good to be true. Still, it can be taken as a kind of capsule of much that did happen— in this place, with these people, at around this time. For Obookiah did reach New Haven at some point during the summer of 1809, following his arrival in New York, with a certain Captain Caleb Brintnall, aboard a China Trade ship called the *Triumph*. And he did take up residence, together with his friend and fellow "knacky" Thomas Hopoo, in the captain's own home. And he did then become acquainted with a large number of Yale students. And the students did offer him some of the "learning" he craved.[2]

At first, however, he was discouraged by his "ignorance" and difficulties with the English language. Hopoo seems to have done better; according to Obookiah's later recollection, "friend Thomas went to school to one of the students in the College before I thought of going to school." At this point, Obookiah was inclined to return home, having "heard that a ship was ready to sail from New York . . . for Owhyhee." But after staying another week, he was invited by a particular undergraduate—Edwin W. Dwight—to begin regular lessons "to read and write," and soon became a frequent visitor to Dwight's college room. Years later, Dwight recalled Obookiah's initially "unpromising" appearance: his "rough sailor's suit," his "clumsy form," his seemingly "inactive . . . mind." As time passed, however, he began to display "an unusual degree of discernment," a trait that belied "the dulness which was thought to be indicated by his countenance."[3]

One senses here a complicated mix—of appreciation and condescension, of closeness and distance. There was, too, some genuine camaraderie. Obookiah proved himself "dextrous as a mimic," and, from time to time, delighted his new friends with suggestive and satirical "imitations." Walking strangely and flapping his arms, he would ask pointedly, "Who dis?" When once the pattern was reversed, and he was mimicked by another, "he burst into a roar of laughter and fell upon the floor, where he indulged his mirth until he had exhausted his strength." In fact, this little picture is laced with ambiguity; Obookiah appears something of a buffoon. Other descriptive bits reflect his struggles in learning, his fondness for petty mischief, and his sense of the "ludicrous." English, in particular, came to him slowly. (Long afterward, in a letter to Dwight, he recalled "one morning [when] I came into your room in College, and . . . *you say, 'what c.a.p. spell?' Then I say, 'c.a.p. pig.'*") Sometimes he would mock his own "heathen" religion: "Owhyhee gods! they *wood, burn.* Me go home, put 'em in a fire, burn 'em up. They no *see,* no *hear,* no *any thing.*" Not surprisingly, his Yale tutors saw him very much as an exotic.[4]

Yet, in some ways, Obookiah's reception was remarkably full and positive—even generous. When he tired of living with Captain Brintnall, or perhaps when the captain tired of him, he was quickly invited into the household of Yale's president, Rev. Timothy Dwight (a distant relative of young Edwin). There he stayed put for several months, while continuing his education. The president himself, and perhaps dozens of sympathetic undergraduates, sat with him to guide his lessons.

The president's home was a stately Georgian-style building of three stories and fifteen rooms, closely abutting the college grounds. Its occupants at that point included members of Dwight's immediate family—his wife and two youngest sons—plus a couple of indentured house servants. The duties of a college president meant that both students and faculty would be frequently dropping in. Moreover, Dwight cut a large figure well beyond the boundaries of Yale (and New Haven). His eminence among the Protestant clergy led to his being widely, if informally, known as "Pope Dwight"; he was a writer, poet, and naturalist, as well. No doubt, therefore, his home was open to important visitors from near and far. What his young Hawaiian guest might have thought of all this, we can only imagine—likewise what the others thought of the guest. But the bare fact of being invited, and accepted, into such a household is itself noteworthy.[5]

If President Dwight or any of the interested students had asked Obookiah about his origins, what might he have said? Later biographical accounts offer a riveting story.

When he is just "a lad of about 12 years . . . two parties [are] contending for the dominion of the island [on which he lives]." A battle ensues. There is a "dreadful slaughter." His father is directly involved. The other side emerges victorious. His family then flees to the mountains and remains hidden for several days. Driven by thirst, they go looking for a spring and are promptly surprised by enemy forces. The father escapes, but the mother and children are taken and "put . . . to the torture." At this, the father returns—whereupon he, "with his wife, [is] cut in pieces." Obookiah takes up an "infant brother upon his back" and attempts to run away. But the brother is speared from behind and dies soon after. Obookiah is caught "and saved alive, because he [is] not young enough to give them trouble, nor old enough to excite their fears." He is then held captive together with an aunt, whom he considers "the last individual of his kindred." At one point, he gets free "by creeping through a hole into a cellar." But his aunt is condemned to die and "taken to a precipice, from which she [is] thrown and destroyed." Obookiah, "feeling himself more than ever alone," runs to the same spot and tries also "to throw himself over," but at the last moment he is caught and brought back. Thus is he preserved "by a kind interposition of Providence"—for reasons that will be revealed only by the subsequent course of his life.[6]

This, too, was part of the legend; its details cannot now be confirmed. (Nor could they have been in New Haven in 1810.) But some of the timing and structure does conform to known elements of Hawaiian history, and even to independently established facts of Obookiah's life. We can be quite certain about his birth—in the village of Ninole, Ka'u district, on the eastern shore of the Big Island of Hawaii, in about the year 1787. We know, too, the names of his parents and their own points of origin: Keau (father), also from Ka'u district, and Kamohoula (mother), from Napo'opo'o, on the island's western shore.[7]

The entire Hawaiian archipelago was then undergoing a major, and violent, transformation. The leading islands had long been divided into numerous separate chiefdoms. But a process of unification had recently begun, with one particular chief—later to be known as King Kamehameha I—leading the way. Starting in 1782, and continuing for a full decade, the islands were convulsed by a succession of civil wars. By 1792, Kamehameha had gained control nearly everywhere. However, sporadic local resistance continued for some while longer, culminating in a final, failed rebellion, on Hawaii itself, led by a subchief named Namakeha.[8]

This last, which ended in August 1798, may have been the war to which the Obookiah legend refers. And his father could have been a partisan of the defeated Namakeha. In any case, there followed a period of peace, with the islands joined under the rule of Kamehameha and his court. Here, then, was the setting for the next stage of Obookiah's life, some of it described in his own words.

"The same man which killed my father and mother took me home to his own house." Though he seems "amiable" enough (and so, too, his wife), Obookiah does not "feel contented." After another year or two, he finds "one of my Uncles who was a priest among them." The uncle "wished me not to go back . . . but to live with him" instead. However, Obookiah's captor is for a time unwilling; long negotiations ensue. Finally, they reach an agreement: The boy will be transferred from the one household to the other—"and I lived with my uncle a number of years." The uncle is indeed a native priest (*kahuna*), at a site called Hikia'u near Napo'opo'o; he decides that his young nephew should be trained "for the same

service." Thus Obookiah is "taught . . . long prayers" and given the task
of repeating them daily in the "temple of the idol." Eventually, he will
assume personal charge of "three important gods."⁹

In short: As Obookiah passed through childhood, he was himself
marked for the life of a *kahuna*. Ironically—in light of what became
of him later on—indigenous Hawaiian religion was entering a period
of decline. Christian influence had begun to seep into the islands even
before the arrival of missionaries, with the rise of the China Trade. Traditional practice was sometimes neglected and core principles flouted (a
trend that Kamehameha tried to reverse by executing a number of viola-
tors). There is no evidence that young Obookiah was affected by any of
this while going about his duties as an apprentice priest. But something
was making him feel restless. As he remembered much later: "I began to
think about leaving that country to go to some other part of the globe.
I did not care where I shall go to. I thought to myself that if I should get
away . . . probably I may find some comfort, more than to live there [in
Hawaii] without father or mother."¹⁰

The process that would lead to Obookiah's departure was long and
tortuous. Captain Brintnall and his ship the *Triumph* had reached Hawaii
in 1807 and "tarried some time." While there—and after having "completely gained the confidence" of Kamehameha—the captain agreed to
take one of the king's sons back to America "to receive an education."
As part of the same arrangement, two more Hawaiian youths were
chosen to accompany the prince as "attendants"; this pair, apparently,
was Obookiah and Hopoo. The king, however, soon changed his mind,
"influenced by the fears of his subjects, that some evil would befall the
Prince"; his son would remain at home after all. Meanwhile, Obookiah
and Hopoo, "having their expectations excited, and a strong curiosity
to see America, were unwilling to relinquish the voyage." But now the
problem was Obookiah's uncle, who—acting in loco parentis—refused
his permission. An elaborate struggle ensued. At one point, Obookiah
was confined to a room as a virtual prisoner, and obliged to hear out
the tearful pleas of "my old Grandmother." (She "asked me what was
my notion . . . [to] go with people whom I knew not. . . . She said that I
was very foolish boy.") Eventually, he escaped and swam out to the ship,
with his uncle in close pursuit, only to be again "brought forth." Now the
uncle offered a compromise: "[H]e would not let me go . . . unless I paid
him a hog for his god." Whether or not this condition was fulfilled, the

parties at length agreed, "and I . . . bid them farewell." (Hopoo seems not to have experienced similar difficulties.)[11]

At last they were on their way, and enrolled as members of the *Triumph*'s crew. From Hawaii, the ship sailed to an island off the Northwest Coast (present-day Alaska), to retrieve a group of "twenty or thirty men" previously left there "for sealing business." No doubt, too, it took aboard a full cargo of sealskins. En route, Obookiah made an important connection with one Russell Hubbard, "a son of Gen. H. of New Haven [and] . . . a member of Yale College." Hubbard had gone to sea following his graduation in 1806, hoping that a change of air and climate would resolve some (unspecified) health difficulties. He was deeply pious—in Obookiah's phrasing, "a friend of Christ"—hence, in due course, he began teaching his Hawaiian shipmates the rudiments of Protestant belief. Obookiah would long, and fondly, remember this "very desirable young man"; perhaps, indeed, the Hubbard friendship helped smooth his way when he fetched up, a year or so later, at Yale.[12]

By now, it must have been at least the summer of 1808, but a considerable journey still lay ahead. Upon arriving in China, the *Triumph* was seized by a British warship, with the crew confined to quarters and Captain Brintnall jailed in Macao. Released after a few days, crew and captain continued to Canton, sold their cargo of skins, and filled the ship with a quantity of tea, cinnamon, silk, and other goods. Sailing home past the southern tip of Africa, they ran low on provisions; daily rations per man were reduced to "one biscuit and one pint of water . . . [which] the cook put in our tea." Just in time, they encountered another ship, outward-bound from Boston and able to supply their needs. There were frightening accidents, too: Hopoo fell overboard and was barely saved "after being several hours in the water." (Still faithful to Hawaiian religious practice, he cried out from the sea "to his god Akoah," and afterward consecrated his jacket as a gift of thanks "to the Great Spirit.") At another point, while rounding the Cape of Good Hope, Obookiah and Hopoo were the targets of an elaborate prank—in effect, a sailor's initiation rite—in which a crew member impersonated a supposed sea god called "Old Neptune." These and like adventures would be vividly remembered years later when Obookiah composed a "relation" of his life.[13]

Eventually (April 1809), the ship arrived at New York; its cargo was sold, its crew dispersed. Obookiah and Hopoo, however, remained with the captain, saw the sights (including a stage play), met "two gentlemen" who invited them for a home-cooked dinner, were astonished by the crowds ("a great number of people, as I ever saw before"), and pondered how "strange [it was] to see females eat with men." From there, they traveled to New Haven, still for a while longer in the care of Captain Brintnall. Thence to the steps of Yale College, and to the ministrations of the various students, and, finally, to the household of President Dwight.[14]

Dwight's home was the starting point for a second Obookiah odyssey—an eight-year wander that would take him into three states, eight different towns, and at least a dozen separate families scattered across the New England countryside. The first in this chain of removals came following a visit to Yale by an especially ardent young clergyman-to-be named Samuel J. Mills, Jr. Obookiah encountered Mills "sitting with Mr. D[wight] my instructor" one evening in the fall of 1809. At once, the two began a friendship, and Mills became "deeply interested in this heathen boy." (The "boy" was now about twenty-two years old.) Some weeks later, Obookiah ended his stay at the president's house, and was temporarily at loose ends. Mills and Dwight worried that if he remained in New Haven, he might "be exposed to bad company . . . [or even] be treated as a slave." (*Treated as a slave?* In short: This particular person of color must be exempted from the pattern that shackled so many others.) The result was an invitation to visit Mills's home in the town of Torringford, Connecticut, where his father (Samuel, Sr.) was resident minister. Obookiah lived with this family for much of the following year, and would frequently return later on for visits of varying duration. Indeed, he would come to regard the Mills household "as my own home." The Millses, for their part, treated him as they would a blood relative. According to a somewhat later account, they made a practice, in church on the Sabbath, of "seating him in their own pew at a time when a strong prejudice existed against any person having a dark colored skin."[15]

While in Torringford, he continued his study of English, and also worked at various "kinds of business that pertain to a farm." This would become a pattern for his subsequent stays elsewhere: lodging, board, and "learning" received, with labor given in return—a straight-up exchange. In fact, farmwork was also part of his education, something else to be used and "improved" should he go back one day to his native islands. Rev. Mills noted his unusual aptitude in such matters: "He had never mown a clip until he came to live with me. My son furnished him with a scythe. He stood and looked on to see the use he made of it, and at once followed, to the surprise of those who saw him. . . . It was afterward observed by a person who was in the field that there were not two reapers there who excelled him."[16]

After several months Mills, Jr. left home to pursue his own studies at Andover [Massachusetts] Theological Seminary, and decided to take his Hawaiian protégé along; thus began another stage in Obookiah's journey. For the next two years, he was in and out of Andover, spending some periods in a room shared with Mills, others in the home of the seminary steward (a certain "Mr. Abbot"), and still others with local farm families. As before when at Yale, he was much noticed by the students and "taken under their care." Some gave him lessons, and he "had a right to go to any room . . . to recite." (By one later account, "he roamed over the buildings like a common pet.") Perhaps, however, these arrangements seemed a little too scattered. For Mills concluded that he should "leave Andover and go to some school" where his time might be employed more efficiently. As a result, he enrolled for several months at nearby Bradford Academy. There he lived with yet another "most pious family"; but his own piety suffered from exposure to "unserious company [presumably, academy students] talking many foolish subjects."[17]

Returning to Andover and the home of the steward, he managed to regain his spiritual "concerns." Meanwhile, too, he sought to extend his knowledge of practical matters. The steward would later recall his "very inquisitive" attitude, which was "peculiarly observable during an eclipse of the sun, concerning which he asked many troublesome questions, and also with regard to many kinds of public business." There was a particular morning that he devoted to "measuring the College buildings and fences." When asked the reason for this, "he smiled, and said: 'So that I shall know how to build when I go back to Owhyhee.' "[18]

At some point, he left Andover again and moved on to Hollis, New Hampshire, apparently at the urging of a seminary student who came from there. In Hollis, he lived with three more families, including that of the minister, Rev. Daniel Emerson. In Hollis, too, he was "taken sick of a fever" for over a month. This made him the focus of much tender concern—and of anguished prayer sessions with his hosts and interested neighbors "while I was upon my sickbed." His sense of religious conviction deepened; he declared himself "willing to die and leave this world of sin" if God so willed it.[19]

In fact, he recovered—and, in the spring of 1813, returned to the parsonage at Torringford. His friend Mills, Jr. was away on a missionary tour in the western states, but he was able to reconnect with his first teacher, Edwin Dwight, living now in nearby Litchfield. That fall, he received another invitation, from James Morris, Esq. (also of Litchfield), "to spend the winter in his family, and attend the public grammar school, of which for many years he [Morris] has been Preceptor." This second experience of formal schooling pushed him to make "very considerable progress . . . [in] the study of English Grammar, Geography, and Arithmetic."[20]

When his teachers and mentors considered the reasons for Obookiah's success in learning, they stressed his "great inquisitiveness," his "industry," and his capacity for imitation. In effect, they were saying that he was an unusually eager pupil, one anxious "to discover whatever was within his reach." But equally important was his strong motive to connect himself with others. "To families in which he had lived, or to individuals who had been his particular patrons," wrote Dwight some years later, "he felt an ardent attachment." His own self-descriptions repeatedly stressed his orphaned condition—something he experienced as an agonizing gap, a void to be filled in his new surroundings. Once, upon seeing a particular "patron" after a period of separation, he pointedly declared: "I want to see you great while. You don't know how you seem to me: you seem like *Father, Mother, Brother, all.*" With the Mills family, including "my father" the minister, these feelings were especially strong. Moreover, their force carried over into his religious life. At one point, under questioning about his faith in God, he replied "I have neither a father nor a mother . . . but He. But O! am I fit to call Him my father?"[21]

In March 1814, the younger Mills wrote on Obookiah's behalf to leaders of the American Board of Commissioners for Foreign Missions (ABCFM), the nation's largest missionary organization, headquartered in Boston. Though focused on overseas missions, the board had already involved itself with nearby "heathen" converts by supporting the education of a singular Indian youth named Eleazer Williams. Born of Mohawk parentage in Canada, Williams had been sent to school in New England, where, as the great-grandson of Eunice Williams, a famously "unredeemed captive" taken a century before from Deerfield, Massachusetts, he had a claim to family connections. Board members would have known this about him, and their actions in his case (1811) prefigured their subsequent sponsorship of Obookiah. About "poor Henry," Mills offered the following: "I believe his improvement has been as great as could be reasonably expected, with his advantages. . . . He speaks the [English] language with considerable propriety. He can read different Authors intelligibly. . . . He likewise writes a very decent hand. He has considerable acquaintance with Agriculture. . . . His Christian friends have hope of him that he is pious." This summary of Obookiah's progress to date must have seemed convincing, for soon thereafter the board approved a plan by a "consociation" of Litchfield County ministers to "superintend his education." Three men from Newburyport, Massachusetts, volunteered "to put into the hands of Mr. Mills one hundred dollars this year . . . for the purposes of defraying the necessary expenses of Henry's education."[22]

Clearly, there was a building tide of public concern with Obookiah and his prospects; from now on, his tutelage would assume a more organized form. A year after the Litchfield group took him in charge, the board offered its direct sponsorship and support. The heart of this sequence—and the chief motive for these gestures of aid—was, of course, Obookiah's promise as a convert to Christianity. Increasingly, his admirers and patrons "saw . . . the hand of God in bringing him hither." His achievements in school, his growing fluency in English, his mastery of farming and related pursuits, his attention to public affairs: All were linked to his remarkable "growth in Christ."[23]

Obookiah's spiritual progress closely tracked the pattern for Protestants throughout the region. He felt, by turns, "hopeful" and "despairing"; he was "active . . . in the faith," then "prayerless and thoughtless." This stop-and-go pattern was entirely typical; no one would have expected otherwise. And through it all he was repeatedly—often fervently—coached and prodded by his associates. When asked at one point by Dwight, "How does your own heart appear to you?" he replied bleakly, "Oh, black, all black." Yet on other occasions, in response to similar inquiries, he described his thoughts as being "in Heaven—all [the] time [and] then I very happy."[24]

Finally, he reached a point of culmination, and felt himself ready for baptism and full church membership. He engaged in long and prayerful consultation with his "good friend and father [the elder Mills] concerning my case." Mills then endorsed his "profession," and arranged to present him to the congregation at Torringford. On the appointed day, Obookiah arrived, feeling "that I was going home to New Jerusalem—to the welcome gate." So it was—as he solemnly recorded later on—that he entered "into the Church of Christ . . . on the ninth day of April, in the year 1815." Mills used the occasion to preach from an obviously pertinent biblical text: "I will bring the blind by a way that they knew not; I will lead them in paths that they have not known." Its meaning must have seemed powerfully important—and visible—to all present.[25]

Curiously, the moment was, for Obookiah himself, crossed with disappointment. He had asked Mills beforehand for a chance "to speak a few words to the people," and the preacher had "readily consented." But when the time came, he "did not recollect . . . Henry's request, and it was neglected." Afterward Obookiah approached Mills with a "broken heart" and blurted out, "[Y]ou no let me speak, sir—I sorry." Mills acknowledged his oversight, apologized, and then inquired, "What did you wish to say, Henry?" To which his young convert replied, "I want to ask the people—what they all waiting for?—they live in Gospel land—hear all about salvation—God ready—Christ ready—all ready—why they don't come to follow Christ?"[26]

This last was a mark of Obookiah's growing confidence in his own religious vocation. From the position of object, he was moving now to that of subject, from proselytized to proselytizer, from recipient to giver. His personal story of rising from "heathen" origins to the status of a "civilized," Christianized young gentleman was deeply compelling—for himself no less than for others. And he drew on it to issue a challenge to native New Englanders. *They* lived in a "Gospel land" surrounded by religious influence, in sharp contrast to the situation of his own land and people. (The contrast would be dramatically evident whenever he spoke to them in his still-imperfect English.) Their failure, in many cases, to achieve full conversion was thus doubly culpable: They had all the necessary advantages, with few of the expected results. Obookiah's admission to the Torringford church was the capstone of his own spiritual (and spatial, and cultural) pilgrimage: how fitting, then, to use this chance "to speak a few words to the people." Except the minister forgot. (Was there something a bit too jarring, even for Mills, in such blatant turnabout: a dark-skinned, personally exotic, formerly "pagan" youth exhorting—and at the same time upbraiding—a churchful of birthright parishioners?)

In other cases, Obookiah would act directly on his own. He was tireless in urging his "friends" toward greater and greater religious exertions—sometimes in person, but increasingly, too, by way of long impassioned letters (many of which were subsequently preserved and published). To one, he would implore, "Do not forget to pray for me with our heavenly Father when you are alone." To another: "We cannot conceive the consequences of one sin." To still another: "Oh, what a wonderful thing it is that the hand of Divine Providence has brought me here, from that heathenish darkness where the light of divine truth never had been." He would say, and do, no less in meetings with complete strangers—with "a sick woman lying upon a sick bed," with an "aged man" encountered in the course of "a walk for exercise," with an "old grey-headed man [found] next to the road, hoeing corn." Sometimes such opportunities seemed virtually to seek him out; for example, in visits paid by "two young gentlemen," or "five pious young men," or "a pious and good [minister], Rev. Mr. H. of L."[27]

As his confidence rose, Obookiah was gradually forming a plan for the future. The story of his arrival at Yale underscored his misfortune as an uneducated heathen; its key line was his expression of sorrow that "nobody gives me learning." The flip side of the same theme appeared in his wish to confront the members of the Torringford congregation: Their fortunate circumstances should (but often didn't) enable them to achieve true godliness. As early as December 1812, he was writing to an unidentified friend in the following terms: "I hope the Lord will send the Gospel to the Heathen land, where the words of the Saviour never yet had been. Poor people, worship the wood and stone and shark, and almost every thing [serves as] their gods; the Bible is not there, and heaven and hell they do not know about it." A similar preoccupation with relative advantage and disadvantage—with good and bad fortune, with "learning" and ignorance—echoed through much of his subsequent correspondence. The heathen were simply "poor people," who for unknown reasons had so far been excluded from the outreach of God's grace. They were not to be condemned for what they could not escape; to the contrary, they must be pitied—and, above all, assisted. In this project, as it specifically embraced his own people, Obookiah might cast himself in a leading role. Thus he would, with increasing frequency, tell auditors (and correspondents) of his aim to return home "to preach the Gospel to my Countrymen."[28]

As part of his plan, he set himself the ambitious task of "reducing to system his own native language." Since it was "not a written language, but lay in its chaotic state, every thing was to be done." (The description is Dwight's.) By linking the English alphabet with "the different names and different sounds" of Hawaiian, he began to create a spelling book, a grammar, and a dictionary. These, in turn, he could use in translating key biblical texts. Indeed, as part of the same process he undertook to learn also "the Hebrew language, and from its resemblance to his own, acquired it with great facility."[29]

From all this, his reputation spread, both locally and beyond. Ministers, in particular, exchanged ideas and information about him, even as they passed him along from one community to the next. Expressions of interest came from many parts of New England, from New York and Pennsylvania, and (in one case at least) from even farther south. No doubt, too, there was a kind of lore that grew up around him, including striking (sometimes amusing) details of his everyday behavior. Mr. Abbot, the steward who had been his host in Andover, noted his "playfulness," as evidenced in a trick he liked to try with puppets (presenting the image of "two little gentlemen dancing—shaking their feet and fists"). In Hollis, New Hampshire, "one time having the toothache (the tooth was a good sound one) . . . he got . . . a stone and knocked out the tooth." Also at Hollis, he showed himself to be "fond of the narcotic weed"; thus he "kept a tobbacco [sic] patch back of the barn." But "the turkeys would visit . . . [and] he would drive them away [saying] 'Shew you there get out of my terbacker yard.'" (These details were a matter of local remembrance nearly one hundred years after their occurrence.)[30]

His physical appearance, his character, and his personal style would also invite comment. He was "considerably above the ordinary size": nearly six feet tall, and "in his limbs and body proportionably large." His posture and bearing, which upon his arrival in New Haven appeared "awkward and unshapen," had become "erect, graceful, and dignified." His facial expression had lost its previous aspect of "dullness" and now seemed "sprightly and intelligent." He had "a piercing eye, a prominent Roman nose, and a projecting chin." His complexion was olive, his hair black ("dressed after the manner of the Americans"), his features "strongly marked." Considered overall, he cut a distinctly imposing figure. Years later, a Cornwall resident described, from personal memory, the power of his charm and charisma: "the lineaments of his countenance . . . when lit up, as in addressing an audience . . . [made him seem] almost divine. 'Lovely man!' they would whisper, as they gathered around him to see how a poor heathen could preach to them Jesus."[31]

His "disposition . . . was amiable," his "temper . . . mild." Moreover, his mind "was such that, with proper culture, might . . . become . . . of the first order." He consistently exhibited "sound common sense" and "keen discernment." He had a "clear sense of propriety" and fine judgment of people. His manners were "grave and reserved," yet his conversation was lively and occasionally spiced by "a fondness for humour." For all these reasons he was a born leader, someone whose "counsel was sought . . . and regarded as decisive . . . by his companions." Indeed, "few young men it is presumed command so much respect from persons of every age and character."[32]

As time passed, his spiritual mentors sought his active participation in a variety of "social religious meetings." He spent the period from 1814 to 1816 living first in Goshen, then in Canaan, Connecticut—in each case at the home of the local minister. He began to keep a diary, and (evidently at the urging of his hosts) composed an account of his previous life. The circle of his correspondence widened; his hortatory tone grew louder, more insistent. He "made it his habitual practice, to converse as he had opportunity, with persons whom he supposed to be destitute of grace." In "several instances" he succeeded in promoting "an apparent conversion of the soul to God." In short and in sum: His public profile was rising impressively. It would continue to rise—even more so—in the months ahead.[33]

Obookiah ranked as the most famous Hawaiian emigrant of his time, but there were others. His friend and shipmate Thomas Hopoo had, after living "for a season" in New Haven, chosen to resume "the life of a sailor." Hopoo served on "several privateers during the late war [the War of 1812]," and, when that was over, he worked as a coachman for a family in "the interior of the country." A year later, unemployed and increasingly despondent, he wandered back to New Haven in hopes of finding passage home to the Pacific. But here he was intercepted by "Christian friends" and persuaded to "stay and obtain an education." Soon thereafter, he joined Obookiah at the minister's house in Goshen. William Tennooe reached Boston in 1809 in a group of six "knackies" aboard another China Trade vessel. (Four of his companions would soon leave. The fifth, his brother, died some years later in Rhode Island.) Like Hopoo, Tennooe went to sea to fight on the American side in the War of 1812. Upon returning, he found work in New Haven as a barber's apprentice (and "became very expert at his new occupation"). He attracted the attention of Yale students eager to instruct him—and also of some "pious females" who prayed for his soul and raised money for his upkeep. In due course he, too, joined the little band at Goshen. John Honoree, yet another Hawaiian seaman, reached Boston in 1815. Almost at once he gained local patrons, who passed him along to New Haven and "very generously gave one hundred dollars toward the expense of his education." A few months later, he was taken into a minister's home at Guilford, "where he began to learn the first rudiments of the English language."[34]

Perhaps the most colorful of these stories featured a youth named George "Prince" Tamoree.

Born the son of an island chief (Kaumuali'i of Kaua'i, northernmost of the island chain), he is indeed a prince of sorts—and is also, by some accounts, in line to succeed to the kingship of Hawaii as a whole. His original name is Humehume, but at some point early on he is given the additional name George, after the king of England. (Later, when he enters the Mission School, he will become known also as Tamoree, an Anglicized rendering of his father's name.) The father, "being a man of considerable information . . . [and] a manifest partiality for the Americans," arranges with a visiting sea captain, James Rowan, to take the boy to Massachusetts "to receive a finished education." His evident goal is to prepare his son for a role as adviser on foreign trade and related matters, for these are the years when Kaua'i, like all of its sister islands, is being suddenly swept up in worldwide commerce.

Since the boy is barely four years old, the plans with Captain Rowan include a generous "bequest" (said to amount to several thousand dollars) to defray the expenses of his care and schooling. However, the captain gives up seafaring, resettles his family in the countryside near Worcester, squanders the money entrusted to him, and ultimately hands George off to one Samuel Cotting, a local "preceptor" (teacher). The latter, in turn, "soon [leaves] the business of school keeping," takes up carpentry, and makes his young charge into an assistant. Several years pass, and George grows "discontented." Being now of an age to look after himself, he runs off to work for a farmer in the town of Fitchburg. But there he receives "much harsh treatment," and so removes again—this time to Boston, to enlist "on board an American armed vessel." For the next two years, he endures "all the hardships attendant upon the life of a common sailor," including naval battles in various corners of the Atlantic basin. He takes part in a famous victory of the American brig *Enterprise* over the British *Boxer* (1813); he also serves on the frigate *Guerriére* and fights (as he later puts it) "the barbarous Turks of Algiers." At one point, he is badly wounded by a boarding pike; but he recovers, and sees further duty along the coasts of North Africa, Italy, and Spain. At war's end, he returns to Boston, "ragged, dirty, and in want." Eventually, he hires on as manservant to an officer at the Charlestown Navy Yard, where Rev. Jedediah Morse, the minister of a nearby Congregational church, discovers him. At this point (1815), he seems a "good-looking" youth of "about 18 years," who speaks fluent English but has "almost entirely forgotten his native tongue." When asked if he would like an education—which was, after all, the original purpose of his coming to America—he says "he would be glad with his heart." Morse arranges his release from service and his further transfer to New Haven. Like Obookiah before him, he lives for a time in the home of Yale's President Dwight, and enjoys "everything that could render him contented and comfortable." He is said to be "much noticed here—is put into good clothing & looks like a new man—his countenance is brightened—& his dejection gone." Indeed, by this point George Prince (as he is generally called) has become a known figure; his link to Hawaiian royalty is much discussed. He is briefly considered for admission to the national military academy (West Point); President Madison is one of his sponsors. But instead, he is "sent to join his countrymen" at the minister's home in Goshen.[35]

It is clear that the trade ships brought still more young Hawaiians to New England—for example, a certain Benjamin Carhooa, resident at Boston "several years" and "highly esteemed by his acquaintances"; another youth "recently arrived with Captain Edes . . . [and] said to be very promising"; a boy at school in Catskill, New York. Indeed, one account places the total of these arrivals at "fifty or sixty." But it was Obookiah, Hopoo, Tennooe, Honoree, and Tamoree who gained, and held, the public eye. Their stories, though different in detail, showed a number of common elements. All had spent time as sailors on American trade ships. (Three had served, at sea, in the War of 1812.) Most had experienced periods of extreme hardship after reaching New England. (According to later accounts, they were "destitute," or "in want," or "under great depression of spirits.") All had sooner or later found sponsors, teachers, and spiritual guides. All had been moved through a kind of missionary pipeline, centered in New Haven but reaching out well across the Connecticut countryside. Gathered together in the summer of 1816—closely watched over by a cadre of Protestant leaders, already launched into various kinds of secular instruction, and pointed as well toward religious conversion—this little group was about to become the founding nucleus of an institution unlike any previously seen on American soil.[36]

The idea of a special school for "heathen youth" emerged sometime during these same months, though its specific authorship is unclear. Certainly, it built on the hopes of Obookiah (and others) for a mission to the Sandwich Islands. Likely, too, it seemed a natural extension of the piecemeal instruction that several of the Hawaiian émigrés were already receiving from ministers, Yale students, and local schoolteachers. And, obviously, it incorporated an impulse of giving that was gathering strength all across New England.

A letter dated May 13, 1816, from a New York philanthropist named Ward Safford to Jeremiah Evarts, the corresponding secretary of the American Board of Commissioners for Foreign Missions, includes the earliest surviving formulation. Safford urged decisive action for the sake of "our Owhyhean & other Heathen youths." As soon as possible, "they should have a permanent residence & a permanent instructor." This, in turn, might "grow into a great institution at which should be assembled heathen from any part of the world."[37]

During the weeks that followed, a new "board of trust" was established in Litchfield County to assume "the more particular charge of these youths." Meanwhile, money was beginning to accumulate for their support. An evangelical journal, *The Religious Intelligencer,* noted the increasing "liberality of the benevolent [toward] . . . these young men," and then described one especially affecting case. A "pious lady" from Savannah, Georgia, while on a visit to New Haven, had "heard the story of three of the Owhyhee lads" and formed "a lively interest in their welfare." Upon returning home, she told friends about them and began to "solicit contributions . . . in their behalf"; the upshot was a gift of $335 from "the citizens of Savannah . . . for the very purpose of educating [them] . . . as missionaries to Owhyhee." In fact, the Savannah gift would set a pattern for many others in years to come. (The *Intelligencer* did offer an important caution: Monetary gifts should be sent only to the "trustees," not to the "lads" directly, since they "are not considered competent to manage . . . pecuniary or other concerns" by themselves.)[38]

In late August, the three trustees submitted to the officers of the

American Board a long memorandum, laying out in abundant detail the case for founding a mission school. Their reasoning was carefully measured, their tone restrained, their diction quite formal, not to say officious. Yet their excitement, their sense of importance in what they were about, comes through every line even today.

They began by noting "the hand of Providence" in directing particular young men to America—and thus identifying "the Sandwich Isles . . . as an important missionary field." As a result, a process was already under way—and was already proving itself—since the various efforts to teach and convert "these heathen youth . . . have been singularly blessed." Some, indeed, showed strong signs of being "endued [sic] with the special grace of God," and all were "ardently wishing to be qualified to present the Gospel to their perishing countrymen." If this outcome should actually be achieved in Hawaii, it might then inspire "youths from other heathen countries, in relation to a mission to their respective nations." Appropriate candidates might "with little difficulty be obtained from China, from the different Nations in India, from Africa, from the Islands of the Sea, from Nootka Sound and the various tribes on the western coast of North America, from South America, and from among the Jews in various parts of the world." The basic goal would be the same in every case: to create a class of native "laborers" ready to serve as "instruments of civilizing and Christianizing their countrymen." (The term *laborers* seems nonspecific, but their primary focus would be one or another form of mission-centered work.)[39]

Here, then, was the end in view—leading the trustees to the further, and crucial, question of the most suitable "means." One possibility was the creation of schools in each of the separate mission "fields." But this would involve much duplicate effort and cost, since "the expense must be repeated whenever a new field is occupied." Missionaries would have to be trained as teachers prior to leaving, with buildings bought on-site, and equipment transported. Better by far to concentrate the preparation here—in America—at a school that "can successively receive youths and educate them from all parts of the world." Not only would the expense be less; the process itself would go more efficiently. The "heathen youths brought to this country" would be placed "at once under a regular government and have their business systematized." This, in turn, would quickly make them "inured to habits of industry and regularity," and teach them "the art of government and subordination."[40]

Moreover, the salutary effects of an American-based education would extend well beyond the school setting (in and of itself). For the students involved would be "brought into the midst of light." They would learn "not only . . . from the instructions of their teachers . . . [but also] from what they see and hear every day" in the surrounding environment, and would emerge well attuned to the "habits and customs of civilized life, which they could never be taught in any other way." Indeed, the benefits of the proposed scheme went further still—for example, to clergymen who might be preparing for work in overseas "fields." From mission-school students, such trainees could gain both "useful information" and firsthand experience with "heathens"; perhaps they might even "learn something of the language of the country to which they are going." Moreover, the work of "such an institution would [aid] . . . the cause of missions generally in our country." Official accounts of its progress would "rouse attention and call forth the resources of our country," and, quite likely, "effect more for the support of missions than many sermons." This last expectation, the trustees noted, came directly "from our own observation." For, in the case of Obookiah and his companions, "we have found the public greatly interested in their state and concerns"; indeed, "many generous donations have, unsolicited, poured in upon us." It seemed very likely, therefore, that "such a school [would] . . . be a powerful auxiliary" to the fund-raising arm of the American Board itself. The proposal concluded on a glowing—not to say grandiloquent—note: "We feel confident that this thing is from God . . . [and] will, among others, be a means of evangelizing the world."[41]

Case closed; point made. And all signs suggest that it was immediately persuasive with the officers of the American Board. In fact, the way had been well prepared during the preceding weeks and months— quite specifically, in the Safford letter of mid-May, and, more generally, in a burst of both public and private exchanges among many of the mission-minded clergy. All parties agreed that the building ferment conformed to divine wish and plan—and, with specific reference to the recent arrivals from Hawaii, that "Providence unquestionably cast them on our shores." Furthermore, all agreed that the goal should be nothing less than "evangelizing the world." An official statement from the leaders of the board described this as "a long neglected work of immense extent and importance," since 600 million of the world's people "are yet without the gospel"; nonetheless, "the energies of Christendom, if wisely directed," would surely be sufficient to meet the challenge. In fact, it could all happen quite rapidly. With skill and effort Christ's message might reach "every dark corner of the earth . . . within the short period of a quarter century."[42]

By late September, a slightly reshuffled "agency" had taken charge of the school-founding project; one important change was the addition of John Treadwell, a former governor of the state of Connecticut, as its chairman. Soon thereafter, the agents convened in an official way at the home of President Dwight in New Haven, and produced a full-blown "constitution" in fifteen "articles," comprising the main elements of their plan. These included governance (by the agents themselves); staffing ("a Principal . . . with such Assistants as the Agents . . . shall judge necessary," including a steward who would "superintend the agricultural interests of the School," and provide the students with their board); physical plant ("such buildings as the Agents shall deem necessary"); curriculum ("spelling, reading, and writing the English language . . . English Grammar, Arithmetic, Geography, and such other branches of knowledge as shall be deemed useful"); calendar (two vacations each year, three weeks in May and six in September and October); and daily schedule (including "morning and evening prayers . . . accompanied by the reading of Scriptures and the singing of psalms or hymns," with special allowance for Sundays, when the principal would "instruct the pupils in the great truths of Christianity"). Its formal name would be the Foreign Mission School. (However, in the everyday parlance of both sponsors and local residents, it would soon become known simply as "the heathen school.") In addition to promulgating their overall plan, the agents decided to locate the school in the town of Cornwall, Litchfield County, Connecticut, "near the south meeting-house." And they recommended Rev. Joseph Harvey, then the pastor at nearby Goshen and himself an agent, for the position of principal.[43]

Finally, in publishing all this, they "proposed to subjoin a few remarks on the importance of the proposed institution," and thus to add their own piece to the steadily widening rationale. "Natives of almost every heathen country," they noted, were being drawn away from their homes by "our commerce" and then "conveyed to this land of gospel light." When they arrived, they felt themselves to be "strangers"; invariably, too, they were utterly baffled by "the arts and employments of civilized life." Left to their "evil propensities," they would turn to vagrancy, gravitate to "the vilest class of society," fall into "abominable practices," and "thus too often come to an untimely end." Worst of all: Those who somehow survived and later got back to their homelands would further "corrupt their fellow countrymen," sow "prejudice against Christianity," and "thus become obstacles in the way of spreading the Gospel."[44]

Yet it need not come to that. Let them be "placed in religious families . . . and required to perform the various acts of religious worship," let them "have the prayers of the whole Christian community," and they, too, can become "the children of God and the heirs of salvation." Moreover, this was not simply a matter of "individual good," for when they were subsequently "employed as instruments of salvation to their benighted countrymen," they would "possess many advantages over Missionaries from this or any other part of the Christian world." They would know the "manners and customs, the vices and prejudices" of those they must convert. They would have an especially powerful motive for the work, "being united . . . [to] their countrymen . . . by the ties of blood and affection." They would be "free from suspicion" of the sort that most heathen people feel toward even "enlightened" foreigners. They would be well adapted to the local climate. They would know the languages needed. (This last often proved an "exceedingly difficult" obstacle to foreigners.) In elaborating their case, the agents did not wish to downgrade the importance of missionaries from among "our own countrymen"; quite the contrary. Just as "some . . . advantages . . . are peculiar to natives," so, too, "our Missionaries . . . possess many advantages, which they do not." The point was to find ways of "uniting both"; thus would the "success of our exertions" be assured.[45]

The agents concluded by reasserting the importance of broad-gauge education for the "natives" to be enlisted here. Conversion was their ultimate goal, but "Christianity and civilization go hand-in-hand, and ever have been, and ever will be mutual helps to each other." Therefore: The youths taken into the Mission School must be fully "instructed in the arts of mechanism, agriculture, and commerce." Some, moreover, should be "educated as physicians," since heathen people will be especially grateful for "relieving their bodily sufferings." Still others might be "usefully employed in teaching the arts and sciences." In this way, and this alone, could all become "powerful auxiliaries, in the work of spreading the Gospel."[46]

Throughout these critical months of planning and preparation, the five young Hawaiians—now clearly designated as future Mission School pupils—had been living in two separate locations: Obookiah and Hopoo in Canaan with Rev. Charles Prentice; Honoree, Tennooe, and Tamoree at Guilford with Rev. Herman Vaill. All, presumably, were continuing their individual studies and their striving for spiritual and moral improvement. Some of their thoughts and doings can be gleaned from letters they sent to one another and to various patrons. They, too, seem to have sensed the rising tide of interest and excitement.

As the fall began, the five were brought together in the town of Litchfield, there to await the actual opening of the school. Litchfield was the largest community in northwestern Connecticut—and a cultural and commercial hub. Its main street was lined with the spacious residences of local merchants; its interior parts were home to prosperous farmers. The town was also the site of the nation's first law school and a well-known "female academy." (Named "Miss Pierce's School," after its founder, this was a pioneering venture in women's education, roughly parallel to the numerous all-male academies begun throughout the country during just those years.) Litchfield made, then, a fine stage for the arrival of the young Hawaiians.

The entire group was temporarily enrolled in James Morris's "grammar school," but with a kind of special status (and possibly in a separate building). One account states that "they were under the care of Rev. W. Weeks," another that "their instructor was Rev. A. Pettingill [who] keeps them in his own family." At some point Rev. Elias Cornelius of the American Board came down from Boston to provide more regular supervision. He established rules of conduct, set "the boys" (most of whom were in their mid- to late twenties) to a six-hour study day, and described them as "very happy and content . . . jabbering English very often & to some effect." In March, Edwin Dwight (Obookiah's original mentor) was asked to "take them in charge"; by now, he and others were already referring to these arrangements as a "Heathen School."[47]

Meanwhile, the school's agents had turned to the matter of building popular support and raising money. Part of this involved publicity: telling the story of the "heathen youths" already on hand, and describing the plans for obtaining more. Local newspapers, and especially religious periodicals, were peppered with writings about (and by) the several Hawaiians. Typical was a letter from Tamoree to a "Dear Madam" who had befriended him during a stay in New Haven. Rev. Vaill sent a copy to *The Religious Intelligencer,* where it was printed along with a "testimonial of its genuineness." Vaill assured the editors that he had "corrected nothing except the spelling," and pronounced himself "astonished at . . . the ingenuity of his [Tamoree's] pen." From such evidence readers might draw conclusions favorable to plans for the school, and to the cause of missions generally.[48]

Yet publicity—not to say celebrity—brought its own complications. In a private note to a fellow clergyman, Rev. Lyman Beecher (of Litchfield) argued that "we must leave off printing Owhyhean letters, or the boys will be ruined." Indeed, "all of them but Obookiah are injured by the noise that is made about them, & feel very big." Tamoree was becoming an especially difficult problem. Having announced in a newspaper interview his expectation "of being king of all the islands," he began to "put on princely airs" and thus to antagonize his companions by "thinking to reign over them." In particular, his original sponsor, Rev. Jedediah Morse, should be urged to "discontinue his correspondence with the prince who is already as great a man in his own estimation as the Dr. [that is, Morse] himself." (From here on, the name "Prince" may have carried a double edge.) Thus, Beecher concluded, "we must cease puffing them."[49]

But a degree of "puffing" could not be avoided when the "boys" were so useful as an advertising tactic. A different part of this campaign—but presumably open to the same objection—involved a "manuscript account" of their lives and prospects, written some months before by parties unknown and circulated by hand in the interim; the agents were eager to arrange its publication "for the information and excitement of the Christian public." Entitled *A Narrative of Five Youths from the Sandwich Islands, Now Receiving an Education in This Country,* it was printed in New York in the last weeks of the year (1816). Its contents were as suggested by the title: narrative biographies, one after another, starting with Obookiah's and concluding with Tamoree's, to which was appended the school's new constitution. The authors declared at the outset their fervent hope "that the contemplated school may take an eminent station among those great objects which at this day engage the attention of the people of God." Unspoken but clearly felt was a related hope that God's people would open their hearts—and purses—for the school's benefit. In fact, the *Narrative of Five Youths* was perfectly timed to catch a rising wave of public interest in "heathens" abroad (as opposed to nearby American Indians, among whom the results of missionary work so far had proved disappointing). Moreover, education was increasingly seen as the best way of achieving success in these endeavors—meaning schools that could be expressly designed to join the goals of conversion and "civilization." Not coincidentally, donations to the ABCFM would soar—from just over $12,000 to nearly $30,000—in the year of the Mission School's founding.[50]

Still another part of this process was active soliciting by individuals. Even before their crucial October meeting, the agents had chosen four men to lead in this task, each to cover a separate area—New Jersey and New York City, the rest of New York State, "the Atlantic states south of New Jersey," and Massachusetts, respectively. In addition, several Connecticut ministers were asked "to collect funds as they shall have opportunity"; in particular, they might find strong support among "wealthy farmers in Litchfield county." The most striking of these fund-raising ventures was the one in Massachusetts. For the clergyman in charge there, Rev. Nathan Perkins of Amherst, was joined by none other than Henry Obookiah. Together, the two ranged across the central and western parts of the state, and Perkins himself credited Obookiah for the "highly liberal" results of their appeal. Their method was to hold special meetings devoted to issues of "missionary service." In visiting the various towns, Perkins wrote afterward, "it was my practice to gratify the people by calling on Obookiah to address them on the subject of Christianity." He was always "appropriate, solemn, and interesting," and his comments elicited "many flattering remarks." Indeed, it was "truly astonishing to see what effects . . . [were] produced on the feelings of the people by seeing Henry and hearing him converse." Years later, Perkins would recall having "repeatedly witnessed great numbers in a meeting melted into weeping . . . and several sobbing, while he [Obookiah] stood before the throne of God, filling his mouth with arguments and pleading for Christian and heathen nations."[51]

In a much broader sense, too, Obookiah's work performed an "essential service to the cause of foreign missions." For it refuted "the weak but common objection against attempting to enlighten the Heathen, that they are too ignorant to be taught." On this point, Perkins offered a grim historical perspective. Having "enslaved . . . [and] degraded . . . people of color" from far-off lands, having "deprived them of the means of mental improvement," Americans had quite generally "hastened to the irrational conclusion that all the heathen are a race of idiots." But the example of Obookiah went powerfully against such prejudice. "The proof he gave of talent, as well as of piety, carried conviction to many that the Heathen had souls as well as we, and were as capable of being enlightened and christianized."[52]

Wherever such conviction became well established, previously "slumbering energies" could be directly mobilized on behalf of missions; thus "many have become interested for the benighted Heathen." A "spirit of prayer" was now widely diffused, and "benevolent efforts . . . [had become] more numerous and more liberal." In particular, there was an "increase of fervency and holy wrestling in the addresses of Christians . . . for the unevangelized nations." And, as some induced others to join the cause, they pointed to Obookiah as "an instance of the propriety and practicability of Missionary exertion." *Propriety* and *practicability:* These would become watchwords in the story of the Mission School all the way to its end.[53]

Even as some were raising money for "this Great Cause," others were deciding how to spend it. Morris, Prentice, and Harvey had been appointed as a committee to make "all necessary contracts . . . for property" to be used by the school. And the choice of Cornwall as its site was made, in part, because the townspeople gave it "a very liberal donation." In fact, Cornwall had been obliged to outbid "sundry [other] towns in this county . . . [seeking] to have the School established in their town." Initial plans envisioned the purchase of "two dwelling houses" and the use of "an academy school house." (The schoolhouse was offered at no cost.) Moreover, land would be needed for a farm to "enable the students by their labour in a great measure to support themselves." The planning group estimated that a sum of "about four thousand dollars" would cover all necessary expenses, and thus "place the establishment on a very comfortable footing."[54]

As autumn turned to winter, local excitement built and built. "There are," wrote one correspondent, "in several towns . . . female associations formed and others forming," with aims that included "aid [to] the foreign mission School." Gifts to the school from Cornwall residents included "clothing [made] by females," valued at $100 overall, and $74 worth of "farmer's produce." Permission was granted by the Connecticut General Assembly for the school to "hold real estate . . . and furnish buildings for the accommodation of the preceptor and students" free of regular taxation, considering that its "benevolent designs . . . will be of incalculable benefit to mankind." The agents addressed a number of legal and logistical problems, such as the fact that two of the prospective students were still officially enlisted in the U.S. Navy. Tapping Reeve, founder and principal of the Litchfield Law School, was asked to examine the details of certain school-related land "conveyances." (He pronounced them valid.) Ministers and others continued to discuss questions of operating procedure. There was broad consensus that the students should be kept apart from the regular school system, since "mingling promiscuously" with local youth might "expose them to be corrupted in their moral principles." (The "them" in this phrasing seems ambiguous.) At the same time, the school should include at least a few American-born pupils, so as to provide "intercourse with the right sort of Civilized Society." Indeed, were the foreigners to be "shut up in a school by themselves," they would undoubtedly "remain Savages still, as it respects their manners and all those things which our children learn insensibly by being brought up in a society which is highly improved." As to pedagogy, the agents favored the currently fashionable "Lancastrian system," which meant "employing the scholars to instruct one another," with the older and more advanced among them tutoring the others. This would be "admirably suited to their natural turn, which is to learn by imitation rather than by reflection."[55]

Even in places well removed from Litchfield County reports of the plan "for establishing a school for . . . pagan youth" circulated widely, and sparked vigorous discussion. For example, a group in Andover, Massachusetts, debated the question of instructing such students "in their own, or in the English, language," and concluded that "proven experience" favored the former alternative. After all, "the Hottentots of Africa, whose language & manners are represented as sinking them into the lowest classes of the human race, are now successfully instructed by missionaries in their own tongue." And Sandwich Islanders ranked well above Hottentots.[56]

The prospective students themselves were both looking ahead to weigh their chances and looking back to settle accounts. Obookiah, for instance, wrote a new round of letters to his various benefactors, offering fulsome thanks as well as loud spiritual exhortation. Tamoree, for his part, managed to reestablish contact with his father, the "King of Atooi, one of the Sandwich Islands"; a long letter, sent in late October, recounted his various adventures "since I left your habitation," and expressed the hope of returning home "in a few years." Tamoree also wrote to Samuel Cotting, one of his former "protectors"—he used the word here with obvious irony—in astonishingly angry terms. "You did not let me attend the schools as I had ought. . . . You used me like a dog more than a human being. . . . You are a base, dirty, mean, low, shameful, poor, avaricious rascal. . . . I have always said that if you ever come within my reach, I would level you to the face of the earth." This explosion reflected a darker side in the experience of the visitors, something that may have been more prevalent than the surviving record suggests.[57]

There was, finally, the matter of staffing the school, most especially in the vital position of principal. Rev. Harvey remained the agents' strong preference, and it seems he wanted the job. He was obliged, however, to withdraw when the members of his local congregation, in nearby Goshen, refused to "dismiss" him. The next man proposed was Rev. Herman Daggett, a preacher and schoolteacher from Long Island. Daggett accepted the agents' offer but could not begin work until after completing a previously made engagement to serve for a year as minister at New Canaan. Thus the duty of actually opening the school fell to a third choice, Edwin Dwight, the same man who had first befriended Obookiah at Yale, and who was currently an assistant pastor at Litchfield. No doubt it helped that he was already nearby—and was closely attuned to the project of educating the "heathen."[58]

Indeed, much in Dwight's previous life seemed to point toward this moment. He was born in the Berkshires village of Stockbridge, Massachusetts, in 1789, the son of Henry and Abigail (née Welles) Dwight; his bloodlines were impeccably "Puritan," reaching back across several generations to distinguished forebears in the first cohort of New England settlers. His childhood consisted in work on the family's substantial farm, tutelage at a local "dame school," and an early inclination toward religion. At seventeen, he left home to begin his further education at Williams College; there he remained for three years. He transferred to Yale just before Obookiah's arrival. He took two degrees (B.A., M.A.) and then began a nineteenth-century version of a career search. He served for a year as "rector" (principal) of the Hopkins Grammar School in New Haven, had several intervals of study with Protestant ministers, became a special protégé of Lyman Beecher, was certified as a "licentiate . . . recommended to the churches . . . for the gospel ministry," toured New York State as an itinerant preacher to frontiersmen—but still a settled position eluded him. Finally, he returned to Connecticut for another several months under Beecher's wing. At that point—after such wanderings and so many preparations—came the Mission School invitation.[59]

On April 1, he wrote at length about the matter to his mother in Stockbridge. He had not yet given his official response, and wished for some parental advice, but evidently was eager to accept. He explained the time-limited nature of the appointment, and described its terms ($500 in annual salary). And he offered a kind of snapshot of the school as envisioned just weeks before its start. The first group of students would include "six Owhyheans," the five made known in the recently published *Narrative* and another whom he did not identify. There would also be "one of our own Indians, a young man who has been brought up amongst white people and appears promising." In addition, "there are others from Owhyhee & other Heathen countries, already known . . . & expected to join the School when it is opened." Thus: While "the number yet is small . . . the Institution is undoubtedly to be a very growing one & not long hence to have a very important connexion with all our plans & efforts to spread the Gospel."[60]

Eight years had passed since the moment of Obookiah's appearance at Yale College and the start of his connection to Dwight. Hundreds, perhaps thousands, among "the benevolent" had seen the opportunity—and the challenge—presented here. Now they were poised on the threshold of a new project, whose aim was nothing less than to save the world.

Hawaii

For people in New England, Henry Obookiah's home (also that of his fellow Hawaiian "scholars") was a mystery. If they carried any image at all in their minds, it might have come from a much-celebrated book by Rev. Jedediah Morse, published in several editions, starting in 1812, and carrying the grandiloquent title *The American Universal Geography, or, A View of the Present State of All the Kingdoms, States, and Colonies in the Known World.*

A brief section near the end described the Sandwich Isles (as Morse called them). "The climate appears to be temperate . . . [with] rain inland, while there is sunshine on the shore." The wildlife was rather sparse: "The kinds of birds are not numerous . . . [principally] large white pigeons, plovers, owls, and a kind of raven"; moreover, "the quadrupeds . . . are few, only hogs, dogs, and rats being discovered." He had a bit more to say about the people. "The natives are of a darker complexion . . . but the features are pleasing." They dress in "narrow" garments made of "coarse cloth," and "tattoo their bodies." They are "a mild and affectionate people . . . [who] have even made some progress in agriculture and manufactures; yet they still sacrifice human victims, but do not eat them like the people of New Zealand." Their food "consists chiefly of fish, to which are added yams, plantains, and sugar canes." They are ruled by "a supreme chief called Eree Taboo"; below him stand "inferior chiefs . . . a second class of proprietors, and a third of laborers, all of these ranks seeming to be hereditary."

In conclusion, Morse noted that "a number of very promising youths from these islands . . . are now in Cornwall, in Connecticut, at a school established there by the American Board of Commissioners for Foreign Missions, for the education of heathen youth from different parts of the world. . . . They have good natural talents, are easily taught and governed, and of amiable disposition." He had, in fact, been directly involved in the school's founding; about that, he could speak from direct experience.

About Hawaii as a whole, however, *The American Universal Geography* was a disappointment. After all, Morse had never been there; what little he knew came from the scattered writings of travelers. Today, of course, Hawaii is a widely favored destination—for tourists, long-term visitors, retirees, or even for a wandering historian.

It is a long journey from my home in the New England countryside. By jetliner, over the broad middle of the continent and halfway across the Pacific, through the busy airport at Honolulu; then, in another, smaller plane, to the Big Island of Hawaii and the handsome seaside town of Hilo.

At Hilo, I pause. I will spend the coming week on the trail of Opukaha'ia. (This, I have only recently learned, is the proper phonetic spelling of his name; "Obookiah," its rough Anglicized equivalent, dates from around the time of his arrival in New England.) I hope to see the place where he was born and passed through childhood—in effect, to walk in his tracks. I have the name of his village, Ninole, which no longer appears on any map. I ask around, in Hilo, and presently locate three Opukaha'ah descendants. (Theirs must be a collateral line, for he had no children.) One of these, a local hotel manager, knows the entire family history. She knows, too, about the vanished village, and the route to get there. Soon I am on my way again, this time by car, along winding roads, through a bleak lava-strewn landscape, then down toward the shore, to arrive finally at a place now called Punalu'u, in Ka'u district. Two centuries ago, this was the site of Ninole.[1]

I park and walk a few yards to a narrow, black-sand beach, on the inner edge of a U-shaped cove. Along its sides are rocky points of land reaching out several hundred yards into the water—fingers at the end of a long armlike volcanic rift. Between these points, the sea churns fiercely, fueled by spring-fed rip currents from below; here and there, thick green seaweed breaks the dominant gray of the surface. Ragged clouds spit raindrops in occasional bursts; a salty wind rises in the east. The air itself seems to sag under the weight of a sodden heat. Two large hawksbill turtles, their marbled shells glistening, nap at water's edge; gulls swoop and dive overhead. Otherwise, I am alone.

I turn and face inland. Immediately to the rear stands an irregular line of coconut palms, mixed with patchy scrub growth. On one side, near a cluster of low dunes, lies a small pond, in which a few ducks are languidly swimming. Farther back, the land rises gradually for perhaps a mile—through a tangle of jagged lava flows—to reach the base of several dome-shaped bluffs. Above the bluffs, merging at the top with the sky, looms the enormous mass of the ancient (but still active) volcano, Mauna Loa.

I roam the beach and its immediate surroundings but find only the bare foundation lines of a large *heiau* (temple) where local people once worshiped. The rest is gone, swept away long ago in one or another of several historic tsunamis. From here on, I must imagine.

Fortunately, there are aids to start this process. In 1823 (some two decades after Opukaha'ia left for good), a missionary named William Ellis toured the region and wrote about it in his journal. Ninole was at that point a thriving place, "celebrated on account of a short pebbly beach . . . the stones of which were reported to possess very singular properties, amongst others that of propagating their species."[2]

To hear Rev. Ellis tell it, Ninole was all about the stones. Some were used in "making small adzes and hatchets." Others would be separated into black and white piles, to serve as "pieces . . . in playing at *konane*," a native board game. Still others held special importance in times of war, "as the best stones used in their slings were procured here." But "most particularly," it was from such stones that "the gods were made, who presided over most of the games of Hawaii." These last involved elaborate religious ceremonies in the *heiau*, leading to a remarkable feat of lithic reproduction. Stones were arranged in pairs to represent "one of each sex . . . [and] wrapped very carefully together in a piece of native cloth." In due course, "a small stone would be found with them"; this, in turn, "when grown to the size of its parents, was taken to the *heiau* or temple, and afterward made to preside at the games." (Ellis, of course, was appalled by such "nonsense"—and tried both "argument and ridicule . . . to make them believe it could not possibly be so." They, however, clung to their "opinion . . . with tenacity.")[3]

Stones, stones, stones. As I stand on the same beach, two hundred years later, I see nothing extraordinary under my feet. But surely, as a young and impressionable boy, Opukaha'ia was pulled into this part of the local culture—with its convergent links to spiritual belief, *heiau* ceremonies, and the island's public "games." I think I can picture him, together with other village youths, darting about, eyes on the ground, stooping to grasp an especially "singular" stone.

What else? In fact, archaeologists and historians have succeeded in re-creating a surprisingly detailed view of Ninole and its environs during the period of Opukaha'ia's childhood (the last years of the eighteenth century). The village served as a "royal center" for Ka'u district, the seat of a regional high chief named Keowa. A hundred or more home sites were strung around the cove and nearby pond. The usual building pattern, found throughout Hawaii, was a triangular shell, set with upright poles, beneath a steeply pitched, heavily thatched roof. In addition to residential housing, there were canoe barns, cabins for religious worship and burial rites, storage huts, and other ad hoc construction. The *heiau* just to the south covered an expanse of at least three acres and was bordered by rock walls up to nine feet thick and nearly as high; its interior was paved with the famous beach pebbles. The buildings, the *heiau*, the beach, the sea, the great volcano at the rear: All this would have been the prospect on which the young Opukaha'ia looked out every day.[4]

But the shoreline community was just one part of it. The land immediately around the cove was rocky and infertile, the annual rainfall quite low. As a result, Ninole's people depended for food on agricultural fields well inland and higher up. There the soil was relatively deep, and rain was reliable; in addition, streams with year-round flow could be tapped for irrigation.

The whole territory was divided into several extremely long rectangular units (called *ahupua'a*), extending from near the shoreline to far up on the mountainside. Each one would encompass a variety of environmental conditions—forest, grassland, exposed rock; wetter and drier; warmer and cooler. In the topmost sections, taro was the preferred crop; a bit lower down, sweet potato; lower still, breadfruit and banana. Along its borders, each would be marked with walls of piled-up rock and sometimes a line of cultivated sugarcane. Internally, there might be additional walls and, wherever the grade was steep, a stepped arrangement of small plots supported by stone terracing. Every *ahupua'a* was controlled by a single chief (*ali'i*) and worked by as many as a dozen households. Typically, there were small dwellings within or alongside the fields to supplement those found down at the shore. Well-established trails ran the length of the entire system.[5]

Meat played only a minor part in the island diet. Pigs, dogs, and fowl might be consumed on festive occasions (mostly by the chiefs and their families), but not otherwise. However, the sea and the life within it supplied a wide range of important staples: fish, mollusks, crustaceans, seaweed. Men were regularly out in their canoes, setting nets and traps, casting long spears with sharp stone points, and dropping lines fastened to delicately fashioned hooks. (Fishhooks are to Hawaiian archaeology what ceramics are to archaeological study in other parts of the world; fine details of their style mark key points of historical change. Hawaii has no ceramic tradition of its own.)[6]

If I proceed with my imagining of Opukaha'ia's early life, I may place him in the fields, learning to cultivate taro and other essential foods, or on the water, mastering marine skills such as spear fishing. Perhaps, at the same time, he was being tutored in one or another of the more specialized crafts: building canoes from the wood of koa trees, fashioning twine and rope from forest vines, forging hand tools from hard chunks of basalt (rock), or shaping the ubiquitous fishhooks out of animal bone.

Always, too, there was the enveloping presence of Hawaiian spirituality, Hawaiian religion. Opukaha'ia, like every child, would have learned at an early age about the four "major gods," or "high heads": Ku, god of war; Lono, god of fertility and health; Kane, god of agriculture; and Kanaloa, god of death. (To be sure, these designations oversimplify the actual, highly complex set of meanings attached to each one.) In addition, there were numerous lesser deities, linked to specific aspects of everyday life—fishing, craft work, landscape features, and the like. For example: Pele, goddess of volcanoes, was a particular focus of dread and veneration; the period of Opukaha'ia's childhood brought at least one major eruption of nearby Mauna Loa. (In fact, the stones venerated at Ninole—as described by the visiting missionary—were considered to have come from Pele; hence their sacred character.) Finally, individual households would commemorate the spirits of key ancestors. All members of this pantheon, from lowest to highest, required regular acts of propitiation, especially sacrifice. For the major gods, *kahunas* (priests) would conduct dramatic public ceremonies in the *heiau,* with offerings of animal and, at least occasionally, human victims.[7]

Religious belief and practice expressed a vast array of prohibitions (*kapu*, the source of our own word *taboo*); these, in turn, were inter-woven with an elaborate hierarchy of social rank. Hawaiian society was rigidly graded: king and high chiefs at the top; the various *ali'i* a level or two below; *maka'ainana*, "commoners," or, literally, "dwellers on the land," far beneath. (According to some estimates, this latter group com-prised approximately 95 percent of the total populace.) The chiefs were thought to have descended from the gods, and thus to possess special *mana* (spiritual power). Great emphasis was placed on proving these specific connections; hence genealogy acquired deep cultural signifi-cance. Encounters across category lines were scrupulously regulated. For instance, a commoner must avoid throwing his shadow on the person of a high chief; punishment of infractions could extend to death. The king should not even be seen by others, except on special ceremonial occasions.[8]

The commoners, too, enforced deep differences within their own ranks—most conspicuously around gender. Men dined separately from women, to whom certain foods were entirely forbidden (pork, coconuts, bananas). Moreover, with foods permitted to both sexes, men would perform a ritual separation—reserving "sacred" portions for them-selves, while consigning the remainders to women. They also maintained "men's houses," for their use only; the equivalent spaces for women were identified by the "pollution" of a menstrual *kapu*. The underlying prin-ciple, throughout this system, was purity (or the obverse, contamina-tion), and the point of its specific parts was to separate the sacred from the profane, the elevated from the lowly, the noble from the common.[9]

All this Opukaha'ia would have begun to absorb while passing through his earliest years. Those same years were, however, shadowed by something else: the mounting series of island wars. Their beginnings preceded the time of his birth; their end would open a new chapter in his young life (and in Hawaiian history as a whole). How he experienced this progression of events, we have no way of knowing—except for its final sequence. His family's belated flight to the mountains, in retreat from invading armies led by Kamehameha, fits well with other, firmly established facts. The residents of villages like Ninole did indeed make that sort of escape. And the exotic, volcano-scourged hinterland high above the coast offered many forms of refuge: caves, lava tubes, dense forest. (Today some of these are tourist attractions.)

The eventual violent death of his parents was personally catastrophic; it could hardly have been otherwise for a ten- or eleven-year-old boy. His subsequent placement—first with his captor, the man who had killed his father and mother, then with his uncle, "a pagan priest"—offered little consolation. In fact, the uncle's residence—not in Ka'u district, but, rather, in Kona, seat of power for the newly victorious King Kamehameha—implies a link with the enemy side.

Kona, too, must be part of my search; there, Opukaha'ia spent most, perhaps all, of his later childhood. (On his arrival, to join his uncle, he seems to have been around twelve years old; when he left on Captain Brintnall's ship, he was approaching twenty.) Exiting Punalu'u, the route takes me along and above the shore, skirting the southwest flank of Mauna Loa, passing numerous little inlets and a host of rather unprepossessing villages. From the mid-nineteenth to the mid-twentieth century, this was a region of vast plantations raising sugar and pineapples for the export trade. More recently, the emphasis has shifted to coffee growing; indeed, Kona coffee has become famous worldwide. But most of the activity is higher up; views from the roadway are of very bare, very brown rock fields.

After somewhat more than an hour's drive, I approach my goal, the great coastal amphitheater of Kealakekua Bay. In centuries past, this was considered to be a sacred place; its name means "pathway of the gods." A short detour leads to the water's edge and the site called Napo'opo'o. At once, stunning views open up—huge in scale, and full of sharply contrasting contours. The land surface is a mix of brown rock fields and many-shaded green forest, the sea a liquid turquoise. Tall cliffs loom overhead; from these, the god Lono was believed to have descended to earth. Higher still, the verdant slopes of another volcano, Hualālai, stretch toward a cloudless sky. Directly to the north, a long, sharply angled ridge projects far out into the bay. On its lower edge, clearly seen from my viewing point nearly a mile away, stands a thin white obelisk commemorating the death of Captain James Cook. It was Cook who famously "discovered" these islands for the rest of the world in 1778. And it was here at Kealakekua, a year later, that he fell victim to a native warrior's spear. (Greeted at first as the embodiment of Lono, he was soon recast as a dangerous intruder.)[10]

My main interest in coming to Napo'opo'o is its ancient *heiau*, named Hikai'u and dedicated to the god Lono. Located just yards up from the shore, it presents today an immense, though somewhat degraded, stone platform, over 100 feet wide by 160 long, and raised eight to twelve feet above ground level. On its interior surface lie the remains of various additional structures—what might once have been worship huts, altars, benches, scaffolds. Fortunately, there is a vivid period description from the hand of Captain Cook himself. "The top," he wrote after a personal visit with some of his crew, "was flat and well paved, and surrounded by a wooden rail, on which were fixed the skulls of the captives sacrificed on the death of their chiefs." At the center stood "a ruinous old building of wood, connected with . . . a stone wall which divided the whole space into two parts." On one side, facing inland, "five poles upward of twenty feet high" supported an "irregular kind of scaffold"; on the other, front-ing the sea, stood "two small houses" linked by a covered passageway. Near the entrance, Cook and his men "saw two large wooden images, with features violently distorted," their base "wrapped round with a red cloth." Beneath the scaffold, twelve more images were "ranged in a semi-circular form," in the midst of which, on "a high stand or table . . . lay a putrid hog, and under it pieces of sugar-cane, cocoa-nuts, bread-fruit, plantains, and sweet potatoes." The visitors inferred that a sacrifice was about to begin but did not stay for the actual performance.[11]

In this magnificently situated and culturally important spot, Opu-kaha'ia went about his life as an apprentice priest. His particular duties were focused on "a small pen enclosed by a rude stone wall," adjacent to the main complex. There he would conduct worship ceremonies that might last "the whole or the greater part of the night." There, too, he is said to have planted "by his own hands" a coconut tree, which, in turn, would grow, and flourish, and be sought out by adoring visitors all through the nineteenth century. Indeed, its fruit "was given to none but us missionaries," according to one unidentified source. (I pause to reflect on this highly ironic turnabout. A formerly "pagan" temple becomes a virtual pilgrimage site for later generations of Protestant Christians.) After he reached America, Opukaha'ia would occasionally intone parts of his "heathen prayers . . . to gratify the curiosity of his friends." Their content—according to his own account—was "the weather, the general prosperity of the Island, its defense from enemies, and especially the life and happiness of the King."[12]

Where did he live—sleep, eat, and otherwise maintain himself—during the years of his apprenticeship? It must have been in the house of his uncle, whom he described as holding "the rank of High Priest of the island." Typically, such men (for they were invariably men) resided close to the temple in which their work and their authority were centered. I find no visible remains of this on the ground around Napo'opo'o, but once again Captain Cook comes to my rescue. Near a pond just north of the *heiau,* Cook and his companions observed "the habitations of a society of priests . . . Their huts . . . were surrounded by a grove of cocoanut trees, which separated them from the beach . . . and gave the place an air of religious retirement." Another early visitor mentioned one house in particular, located "nearest . . . to the morai [temple]" and belonging to "the priest who was the lord of this beautiful recess." (This would, at least for some period, have been Opukaha'ia's uncle.) The same writer described a verdant landscape, including numerous "cocoanut [*sic*] and other trees . . . a pond . . . [and] grass plots intersected by several square holes with water in them, which were private baths." All were "most delightfully situated." Farther out stood a substantial village, presumably for the commoners, with farm plots, small clearings, and stone terraces. The village, for its part, was oriented toward the uplands high above the shoreline cliffs, where large walled fields yielded the taro and other foods required for basic sustenance.[13]

If I close my eyes, I can picture Opukaha'ia settled in the home of his uncle, directly adjacent to the *heiau.* He would easily have moved back and forth while attending to his various duties. The setting was "beautiful," the atmosphere one of "retirement," the life comfortable by the standards of the time. But the work itself was unpleasant and unrewarding. (Or so he would claim later on. Was its downside perhaps exaggerated in the memories he carried into his life as a newly converted Christian?) Most difficult of all for this youth of still tender years was his sense of isolation, the complete absence of immediate family. As he recalled much later on, "I was now brought away from my home to a stranger place, and I thought of nothing more but want of father or mother, and to cry day and night." Under these circumstances, "I must go and see the world, and see what I can find."[14]

My search is finished. I lean back on the *heiau* wall, steadying myself against the heat, and look around yet again. The softly swaying sea, the thin line of the far horizon, the bold promontory with the Cook memorial, the cliffs behind, the brilliant sky on every side, the withering sun directly overhead, the massive presence of the *heiau* itself: This very place, my final destination, was Opukaha'ia's starting point. I have reversed his route: Hawaii to New England, then; New England to Hawaii, now.

What a distance between them! And how much more so for him than for me! Not simply the many thousands of miles. Also the climate and landscape: from tropical to temperate, from maritime to landlocked, from smoldering, sometimes explosive, vulcanism to hard, granite-based terra firma. The culture, too: from lush, life-centered, polyvalent spirituality to spare, otherworldly monotheism, from ritual to metaphor, from collective to individualized. In one way after another, a looming, immeasurable distance.

~ PART TWO ~

ASCENT

CHAPTER THREE

American Mission:
The World Savers

The impulse to save the world, and thus to arrive at a perfect "millennium," has a history that is wide, deep, and (in its later parts) distinctively American. Elements of it are embedded in the three great providential religions, Judaism, Christianity, and Islam. In some versions, it includes a search for worlds already perfected—for example, the tradition of the "lost Atlantis," celebrated from classical times to the late Middle Ages.[1]

World saving gained additional strength during the so-called Age of Discovery (the fifteenth and sixteenth centuries). "New-found lands" in Asia and the Americas served Europeans as a virtual fantasy screen on which to project some hugely inflated goals. The myth of gold-rimmed El Dorado, the legendary Seven Cities of Cibolla, Ponce de León's fabled "fountain of youth": Such dreams of personal and social excellence lured explorers again and again to the farthest corners of the globe.[2]

Meanwhile, too, world saving was present, and prominent, in the Protestant Reformation. Victory over the papal "beast" would (supposedly) propel history toward the long-awaited Second Coming of Christ, and the start of His thousand-year reign on earth. This, in turn, would lead directly into full realization of God's everlasting kingdom.[3]

England was one of the first places to feel the full impact of these forces. English leaders in colonization promoted broad goals of social betterment, embracing both the metropole and its several "plantations."

The economy would be stimulated through the development of new resources and trade lines; excess population would be drained off overseas; vagrancy, crime, and poverty would disappear as a result. English Protestants, dubbed "Puritans" by their opponents, pursued a program of religious reform that included, at its outer edge, fully millennial expectations. An intense focus on Old Testament prophecy drew these groups to the theme of "latter days," of "last things," of "end times," an apocalypse that would usher in the kingdom of God.

Then, in the revolutionary turmoil of the 1630s and 1640s—and especially in the overthrow of the Stuart monarchy, followed by the founding of a republican "commonwealth"—some saw the actual start of that moment. Indeed, this period brought a fusing of Christian millennialism with a spirit of civic (and secular) utopianism that would echo in other revolutionary movements for centuries to come.[4]

At roughly the same point, the Puritan form of world saving was carried across the Atlantic to (what became known as) New England—first by a little band of "pilgrims" settling at Plymouth, then by a larger group clustered to the north around Massachusetts Bay. In fact, these particular migrants were embarked on an "errand into the wilderness" meant to shape the future everywhere. (This "errand"—both phrasing and theme came directly from Scripture—would be endlessly elaborated in their religious devotions.) Here was nothing less than a root-and-branch experiment in spiritual, and social, regeneration; if successful, it would serve as a compelling model both for their "dear mother" England and, by extension, for other lands, as well. Their sense of divinely inspired purpose infused the opening decades of New England history with a uniquely exalted spirit; hopes were high, feelings were high, people were high (in a spiritual sense). And intimations abounded of things yet more wonderful to come.[5]

Of course, it couldn't—and didn't—last. By mid-century, New Englanders realized that "the eyes of all people" were not upon them after all, and that "mother" England gave them hardly a glance. So they drew back and began a process of soul-searching in which they increasingly blamed themselves; their own moral "declension" had, apparently, betrayed them. Yet all was not lost; through prayer, repentance, and redoubled striving, they might yet reclaim their mission. Overtly millennial yearnings receded but by no means vanished. For example, in 1710 the Boston minister Cotton Mather declared that, while only God could know for certain when His kingdom would begin, "I believe . . . it is at hand." Mather went on to emphasize America's special destiny; his masterwork, the *Magnalia Christi Americana,* extolled "the Wonders of the CHRISTIAN RELIGION, flying from the Depravations of Europe, to the American Strand." This premise helped establish the bedrock historical theme described (nowadays) as American exceptionalism. Succeeding generations would pick it up, and recast it in various ways, but always with an underlying constant: America is different from every other place—is special—is, in fact as well as in self-concept, exceptional. And world saving would become an abiding American goal.[6]

Its power was greatly augmented in the mid-eighteenth century by the extraordinary series of religious revivals known thereafter as the Great Awakening. Millennial ambitions sprang once more into open view as preachers like George Whitefield and Jonathan Edwards spread their message of spiritual renewal throughout the colonies. At one crucial juncture, a document entitled *The Testimony and Advice of an Assembly of Pastors* (nearly seventy in all) expressly linked the revivals to the efforts "of such as are *waiting for the Kingdom of God* and the coming on of the . . . Latter Days." Individuals might go even further. As early as 1741, a Presbyterian minister in Pennsylvania published a sermon proving that "the Kingdom of God is come unto us at this day." Edwards himself viewed the revivals as "the dawning, or at least the prelude" of the millennium; moreover, he found in the Bible specific geographical references suggesting "this work will begin in America." Significantly, too, Edwards associated the approach of "end times" with the advance of civil and religious freedom. And this connection would open a new track for world saving once the Awakening had run its course. Human history might then be understood as a struggle to overcome "tyrannous authority," in its political as well as ecclesiastical guises.[7]

The 1750s brought a mood of post-revival retrenchment, and even of despair. Yet events furnished at least some ground for continued millennial anticipation. A series of devastating earthquakes, including one in New England, seemed to express God's intent to "shake up" the destiny of His human creatures. The Anglo-French wars in Europe, with offshoots in North America (the British colonies versus French Canada) served to sharpen the struggle against the Catholic "anti-Christ." In particular, New England's triumph over French forces at Louisburg in 1745 encouraged Edwards (among others) to think anew of the approach of God's kingdom. And when, some years later, the larger conflict concluded with a British-American victory, the future seemed brighter than ever. Ministers and political leaders alike envisioned a coming American "kingdom" that would be a "perennial source of strength and riches" for the empire as a whole. This included a dazzling panorama of rapid expansion across the continent, with "mighty cities . . . commodious ports . . . happy towns and villages." It included, as well, the expectation of dramatic moral and spiritual improvement, amounting finally to "a new heaven and a new earth."[8]

Post-Awakening and postwar attitudes made special place for the conversion to Christianity of "heathen" Indians. This element was not unfamiliar—witness the official seal of the Massachusetts Bay Colony, dating to 1629, which showed a scantily clothed native figure uttering a plea to "come over and help us." In fact, a good many seventeenth-century clergymen had attempted some form of preaching to native people. And one, Rev. John Eliot of Roxbury, Massachusetts, had become celebrated for his creation of at least a dozen "praying towns" in which Indian converts (and would-be converts) were gathered on an organized basis. Meanwhile, schools for Indians had emerged here and there throughout the colonies, and colleges like Harvard and William and Mary had offered instruction to at least a few native students.[9]

However, it was not until the mid-eighteenth century that such activities gained larger—even cosmic—significance. For only then did millennial-minded clergy stress the conversion of Indians, alongside the conversion of Jews, as a necessary precursor to the millennium. The result was a sudden spate of mission organizing and school founding aimed directly at Indians: by Congregationalists in New England, by Quakers in Pennsylvania, by Methodists, Moravians, and Anglicans farther south.[10]

To this point, American world saving had remained closely tied to the "mother country" and empire. But during the 1760s, when anti-imperial protest developed in earnest, Britain was recast as the bugbear of the millennial project—the enemy, the "beast." From then on, the claim of exceptionalism would be America's alone. At the same time, and as part of the same process, *liberty* became a key word of millennial hope and destiny. Looking back across the preceding decades, one clergyman could declare that God "has always owned the cause of liberty in North America . . . and will continue to own it." Looking forward, another could foresee the coming of a "great and mighty empire . . . which shall be the principal Seat of that glorious Kingdom which Christ shall erect upon Earth in the latter Days."[11]

Journalists, literati, and political leaders were no less enthused. Philip Freneau and Hugh Henry Breckenridge, composers of a fulsome *Poem on the Rising Glory of America* (1776), invoked the image of "a new Jerusalem sent down from heav'n," a place where "paradise anew shall flourish." Future president John Adams, in the days immediately following the patriot victory at Yorktown, wrote to his wife, Abigail, that "the progress of society will be accelerated by centuries by this revolution," which, in turn, reflected nothing less than "the great designs of Providence." In another, equally expansive comment, Adams described American history as "the opening of a grand scene . . . for the illumination of the ignorant, and the emancipation of the slavish part of mankind all over the earth." David Ramsay, a patriot leader in South Carolina, reached for the same heights with a series of rhetorical questions: "Is it not to be hoped that Human Nature will here receive her most finished touches? . . . That religion, learning, and Liberty will be diffused over this continent? And in short, that the American editions of the human mind will be more perfect than any that have yet appeared?" The same sentiments echoed at the level of common folk. Thus "a soldier," writing in the *New Jersey Journal,* was moved to "rejoice that the ALMIGHTY Governor of the Universe hath given us a station so honourable, and planted us [as] the guardians of liberty, while the greatest part of mankind rise and fall [as] undistinguished as bubbles on the common stream."[12]

But perhaps the biggest single contributor to this extravagantly sanguine viewpoint was Timothy Dwight—first during his years as a Yale student, tutor, and budding poet, later as Yale's president and a major Protestant eminence. In 1771, while still an undergraduate, Dwight authored a long work entitled *America: or a Poem on the Settlement of the British Colonies, Addressed to the Friends of Freedom and Their Country,* in which he showed how the entire course of history pointed toward an America-based millennium. Moreover, the same theme figured prominently in his subsequent "epic" *The Conquest of Canaan* (1783), in a collection of his poems, *The Columbian Muse* (1794), and in his best-known writing, *Greenfield Hill* (1794). "O Land Supremely Blest"; "Here Empires's brightest throne shall rise"; "Hail, Land of Light and Joy"; "Here truth and virtue shall find their home" (and so on): thus the recurrent strains in Dwight's rapturous hymn to his country's future.[13]

Such effusions—from many hands, across the entire Revolutionary era—served to energize the American people for protest, for war, for independence. But the "progress" they anticipated would not come easily; and the immediate post-Revolution years brought another sag in morale. Hard economic times (with commerce virtually at a standstill) and political disarray (under the loosely framed Articles of Confederation) made millennial prospects seem a good deal further away. Moreover, their center shifted from the transforming effects of liberty to the imperative need for moral regeneration.[14]

Accordingly, the 1790s brought a renewed interest in scriptural exegesis of "end times." Ministers debated questions of sequence—would Christ return before or after the inauguration of His earthly kingdom?—and some offered elaborate calculations about His timing. At the same time, the outbreak of the French Revolution helped to reinvigorate the political dimension of all this as (in Thomas Paine's words) "the beacon of liberty began revolving from West to East." First America, now France, eventually the world.[15]

Then, in the very last years of the century came a new round of religious revivals—what some called "showers of grace"—beginning in New England and spreading rapidly south and west. Within a decade or so, the showers had become a torrent, indeed a "Second Great Awakening." Few places would remain unaffected, and virtually all Protestant denominations were drawn in as wave after wave of religious excitement spread out across the land. Millennial hopes shot up once again and resumed their earlier, more spiritual emphasis.[16]

Still, the principles of "freedom"—American freedom—might remain a valuable adjunct in the march toward millennial change. A Massachusetts preacher, typical of many, asked, "May we not view it, at least, as probable that the expansion of republican forms of government will accompany that spreading of the gospel . . . which the scripture prophecies represent as constituting the glory of the latter days?" And, in neighboring Connecticut, the eminent Lyman Beecher framed a similar question: "From what nation shall the renovating power go forth? What nation is so blessed with experimental knowledge of free institutions?" What nation indeed! This and similar reflections led Beecher to conclude—echoing Edwards eighty years before—that "the millennium would commence in America." In some formulations, this idea assumed an openly imperial tone. Thus the president of the Massachusetts Missionary Society could write, "There is great reason to believe that God is about to transfer the empire of the world from Europe to America, where he has planted his peculiar people. . . . This is probably the last peculiar people which he means to form, and the last great empire which he means to erect, before the kingdoms of this world are absorbed into the kingdom of Christ."[17]

World saving was always a many-sided project, but in this latest version one aspect stood out above all others: the spreading of "gospel truth" to peoples and places where it was not yet known. In short, missions had again become *the* fundamental concern, both for their own sake and as a precondition for the arrival of the millennium. An initial focus was "unchurched" settlers along the western frontier—together with their Indian neighbors. But then, in very short order, those horizons expanded dramatically. By the second decade of the new century, religious leaders were boldly vowing to convert all of "the world's 600 million heathen." (This widely accepted figure was the result of some necessarily loose, but not unthinking, calculation.) A quite representative sermon, published in 1820, declared: "The objects of missionary work . . . are chiefly savages . . . [who] must be elevated, purified, and enlightened . . . [and] converted, *in order to* make the kingdom come [italics in original]."[18]

Indeed, the moment seemed uniquely propitious, for already "great preparation has been made." For example: "The English language, which contains more of the elements of civilization and moral reformation than all others united . . . [is now]widely diffused." And: "[H]eathen nations, to a great extent, are subjugated to Christian nations." And: "[T]he right of mankind to govern themselves [*sic*] has begun to be understood," a point which "our own country has had the honour of teaching." And: "[L]ove to the Heathen and to Christ have increased brotherly love among Christians." And: "Revivals of Religion have been greatly multiplied, particularly in our own happy country." Finally, and most importantly: In the work ahead "the church in America . . . is pre-eminently qualified. . . . She alone is able to furnish in the requisite number the Missionaries of the Cross. . . . Her flag whitens every wave, and visits every shore. On her the Spirit of Life has been poured out; and thousands of her youth have been just called into the Kingdom of Christ." Another sermon, by a different minister, condensed the missionary project into a single, supremely confident sentence: "Our object is to effect an entire moral revolution in the whole human race." As a result, declared a third, future generations "would look upon us of the nineteenth century as the most enviable of the whole race, who have lived from Adam downward."[19]

Of course, it was one thing to announce such goals, and quite another to carry them into practice. But missionary organizing would develop in a remarkably vigorous way. In fact, as all parties conceded, British clergymen had already taken the first key steps by establishing a mission in India in 1792, and another, a few years later, in Ceylon. Their American counterparts were close behind. The earliest state-level "missionary society"—in effect, a support group—was begun in Connecticut in 1798. And soon thereafter similar organizations appeared in many local communities, as well. Another founding moment occurred in 1806 when a group of uncommonly pious students at Williams College gathered—supposedly behind a haystack, in the midst of a ferocious thunderstorm—to form a secret "brotherhood" dedicated solely to the cause of foreign missions. (This would subsequently be remembered, and mythologized, as the "Haystack Prayer Meeting.") Then came the start of the organizations that would put actual missionaries into the field. The most important of these was the American Board of Commissioners for Foreign Missions (with its predominantly Congregationalist ties), founded in 1810, with headquarters in Boston, and managed by a "prudential committee" composed mostly of eminent clergymen. Within two years, the ABCFM had dispatched missionaries to India; inside of a decade, its reach embraced Burma, Greece, Turkey, Argentina, and Palestine, as well as several different Native American groups. Similar missionary "boards"—of Baptists, Presbyterians, Lutherans, Methodists, and Episcopalians—took shape in the years immediately to follow.[20]

Thus events seemed to be moving toward a glorious convergence. A long and rich tradition of world saving—and of preparation for "end times"—was steadily ripening; its fulfillment was almost in sight. In 1813, a Boston minister, Rev. Edward Dorr Griffin, preaching at the town of Sandwich, Massachusetts, put it this way: "If the church . . . is to rise from this day forth, where is it more likely to rise than in the United States, the most favored spot on this continent . . . And if in the United States, where rather than in New England? And if in New England, where rather than in Massachusetts, which has been blessed by the prayers of so long a succession of godly ancestors? And if in Massachusetts, on what ground rather than this, which among the first received the footsteps of the pilgrims?" Sandwich had been part of the original Plymouth Colony; thus Dorr's allusion to "the footsteps of the pilgrims." But if he had been speaking a few years later, the same rhetorical zoom lens—from the world, to the United States, to New England, and so on—might well have led him a hundred miles farther west, where, in the Connecticut village of Cornwall, the Foreign Mission School was about to open its doors.[21]

It was a time—and a place—of intense interest, keen anticipation, and utterly surpassing hope.

CHAPTER FOUR

"A seminary for the education of heathen youth"

Cornwall in 1817 was a sprawling expanse of some twenty-seven square miles, backed into Connecticut's most remote corner. Along its west flank flowed a large river, the Housatonic. The rest was a bumpy patchwork of hills, crags, and "cobbles," little valleys and dales, marshland, brooks, and ponds—all encircling a broad L-shaped "plain" in the middle.[1]

At this point, the town was three-quarters of a century old. Its "ancient" forests survived, albeit to a somewhat reduced extent. Especially conspicuous were several thick stands of pine that topped out at over one hundred feet aboveground. The wildlife native to the area was also reduced, though bounties might still be claimed for kills of wildcat and rattlesnake.

Farmland predominated, most of it in irregular little plots scattered through at least a dozen different hamlets and neighborhoods. There was the Center, the Bridge, the East and West Villages, Yelping Hill (where coyotes once abounded), Swift's Valley, the Barracks (the site years before of a small military encampment), Bear Swamp, Puffingham, Hardscrabble, and more. The names themselves evoked for residents bits and pieces of town history. The land's yield included wheat, most importantly, but also corn, rye, hops, hemp, and garden crops of every variety. Cows and sheep grazed the upland meadows.

At the same time, the town supported a surprising array of small-scale industries. A census from 1819 listed an iron forge, gin and cider distilleries, carding mills, gristmills, a woolens factory, and no fewer than twenty sawmills. (Logging had been, for many years, a major local enterprise.) Most of these operations were water-powered—hence their location near the numerous dams and falls that dotted the town's streams.

The inhabitants of early-nineteenth-century Cornwall numbered around sixteen hundred. Nearly all were of English stock; many could trace direct lines of descent from the earliest settlers, spanning three or four generations. The previous Indian population had largely disappeared from a combination of causes (disease, the pressure of white settlement, voluntary withdrawal), though a significant Indian community—the Schaticokes, housed in "sixteen wigwams"—could be found in the neighboring village of Kent. Native people did still visit Cornwall with some regularity, to work as day laborers or to show and sell their handcrafted baskets, mats, and brooms. Indeed, one or two Indian families remained as full-time residents. The most significant population change of this period was a growing outward migration, mostly of young folk headed west in search of more fertile land and a wider field of opportunity.

Local governance followed the time-honored New England model, with annual town meetings to set policy, and day-to-day management in the hands of a small group of "select" officers. The focus was almost exclusively on matters of immediate, and parochial, concern: the building and upkeep of "highways" (dirt roads), of bridges, of the "commons" and other public properties; the appointment of committees to deal with special problems (as these might arise); church-related affairs; schools; and occasional disputes with the neighboring communities.

Social experience had a similarly local flavor. There were endless rounds of visiting, often involving entire families. The weekly Sabbath began at sundown Saturday and continued through lengthy church services on Sunday. With Sunday evenings came a feeling of release and a chance for "merriment," especially among the young. Funerals were solemn occasions, with long processions through the Center and church bells tolling the number of years the deceased had lived. "Sports" included summertime swimming at local water holes and boisterous winter sleighing parties. Thanksgiving and Independence Day (July 4) were the chief holidays. (Christmas remained a relatively muted affair, following Puritan traditions from long before.)

Household gardens served purposes both practical and decorative.

Flower beds featuring roses, tansy, myrtle, and lilies sat alongside rows of herbs, legumes, and berries. Fruits might be spread out on rooftops or hung on sidewalls to dry in the sun. Residents cut their own firewood and stacked it in enormous piles beside doorways. Rail fences separated individual house lots and served also to bound the town fields.

The look of the whole was pleasant and prosperous, if not especially tidy. In springtime, mud was everywhere, and no one really minded. Offal might accumulate in roadways, to be cleaned up whenever nearby residents found the time. Housing, especially chimneys, would occasionally fall into disrepair. Outdoor privies conveyed an unmistakable odor into the adjacent air.

Such was the "visible world" of early Cornwallites. But none of it matched the importance, in their minds, of the invisible one. God and Satan, angels and devils, plus legions of previously departed "souls": These and related supernatural forces framed their lives. Organized religion, in its several Protestant guises, was a source of both deep consolation and recurrent "controversy." In the late 1770s, the First Church (first in the sense of originating with the town's founding) became bitterly divided. Months of wrangling and failed efforts at reconciliation led finally to a formal split, with a large group of "Separates" hiving off to form a second, and rival, spiritual community. The points at issue were partly doctrinal; the Separates espoused an especially strict, old-style version of Congregationalism. But personal enmities also figured in; the minister himself was a flash point. The separation would never be healed, for (as a town historian wrote later on) "the fighting spirit had been aroused." Soon, in fact, there would be still more churches: Baptist, Methodist, Episcopal. Divided or not, Cornwall parishioners experienced a marked upsurge of faith just after the start of the new century, with major revivals coming in 1801, 1806–7, and 1811–12. Each time, a wave of excitement swept through the ranks of the several congregations. Long, emotionally charged Sabbath-day services, combined with midweek "lectures," added scores of previously "unsaved" individuals to church membership rolls. The result was an increasingly straitlaced local atmosphere; one of the leading revival preachers would later claim, with evident pride, that social dancing had entirely disappeared from within the town's limits.[2]

Picture, then, the beginnings—in this place, at this time—of a unique evangelical and educational project designed to foster (as one supporter put it) "the ingathering of the heathen and the conversion of the ends of the earth."[3] Though its ambitions were grand—not to say grandiose—its outward appearance was modest enough.

Picture its physical arrangements. The chief "Academy building," a gift from the local citizenry, stood athwart the "green" in the town's Center. This simple boxlike structure, twenty feet wide by forty long, held a gambrel roof, clapboard siding, a chimney, and a little bell tower on its east end. The inside included a large ground-floor classroom and an upstairs loft adaptable for use as sleeping quarters. Already more than thirty years old, the building was in need of repair; hence the sponsoring American Board was obliged to send $1,000 to put it into proper condition.[4]

A second building, bought from a local resident and hard by the first, would become the boardinghouse. Here a steward would live and provide meals (along with other everyday "necessities") to the school community. This, too, was a wood-framed structure, two stories high and with a "well-painted" exterior. Attached to it stood a barn and a cluster of outbuildings, on five acres of land suitable for cultivation.[5]

The principal would need his own residence—hence the purchase of a third house, as yet just partially built, for $600. The agents proceeded to have it finished at a nearly equivalent additional cost. Also included in the initial layout were seventy-five acres of "arable" and a large plot of woodland about a mile and a half to the north; from the latter, the school might obtain timber for fuel, fencing, and occasional carpentry.[6]

Picture, too, the arrival of the first group of "scholars" (as they were invariably called), all five of whom hailed from the Sandwich Islands (Hawaii). To the townsfolk, these young men must have seemed different in every possible way—appearance, mannerisms, body language, speech. Some had visited Cornwall the previous year while staying in nearby South Farms (Litchfield); Obookiah was already well known, indeed a celebrity. But to have the lot of them fully installed right in the town's heart—walking the roadways, nodding to curious passersby, lingering by the town green—was a new experience. To be sure, it was one the townspeople had actively sought through a wide range of public and personal donations: from the Academy building itself, to cash gifts in varying amounts, to repeated offerings of construction materials, clothing, food, and labor. Cornwall had worked hard to meet competition from other nearby communities—all eager to become the chosen venue—and now it had succeeded.[7]

Admittedly, some of this picturing is conjectural; few records have survived from the school's earliest days. Even the timing is uncertain; apparently a start was made around the first of May.[8] Was there a formal ceremony to mark the moment? Did local residents have a sense of triumph, perhaps even a kind of millennial hope? Or, alternatively, did they feel some doubt, some anxiety, about the strangers suddenly landed in their midst? (Maybe these were not alternatives, but coexisting opposites uneasily yoked together.)[9]

Whatever the nature of local reaction, news of the school was spreading. The *Hartford Courant* (Connecticut's leading newspaper) printed a brief account in early June: "We rejoice to learn that in this state there is . . . a Seminary for the education of heathen youth, at which there are twelve of this description from different countries." Elsewhere, too, notice was taken. For example, far away on the opposite side of the state, a Ladies Education Society in the town of Hadlyme gathered "a collection" and then "appropriated [it] to the use of the Heathen School lately established at Cornwall. . . . The cheerful unanimity which pervaded the meeting seemed to evince that each one felt she was contributing for the emancipation of her fellow creatures from sottish ignorance and heathen idolatry." This same spirit of "contribution" would set a pattern for pious folk all across New England—and beyond—in the months and years to come.[10]

Rapidly, during the opening weeks, the roster of participants filled out. There was Dwight, the interim principal and chief instructor, and Henry Hart, newly appointed as steward and "farm superintendent." Moreover, because the school's agents (and main fund-raisers) were not locally based, the First Church minister, Rev. Timothy Stone, assumed the special role of "superintendent of donations," Philo Swift, another local resident, became the treasurer, and Rev. James Harvey the official "accountant." There was growth, too, within the ranks of the scholars. The original core group—Honoree, Hopoo, Obookiah, Tamoree, Tennooe—was quickly supplemented by two more Hawaiians: William Kummooolah, yet another refugee sailor from the China Trade, described as "a pleasant and lovely youth," and George Nahemah-hama Sandwich, a resident of Enfield, Massachusetts, for a full decade before his Mission School acceptance, "a professor of religion" (i.e., a convert), and "a good farmer." Also arriving at around the same time were a pair of "Yankee" New Englanders, James Ely, of Lyme, Connecticut, and Samuel Ruggles, of Brookfield, Massachusetts; their goal was to prepare for missionary work overseas through up-close contact with "heathen" colleagues. (At first, they were taken only on trial, but when they demonstrated "great usefulness," their status was soon upgraded. School leaders hoped that by modeling "exemplary behavior," a smattering of local recruits might "exert a salutary influence" on their fellow students from overseas.) Another in this first cohort of scholars was Simon Annance, an Abenaki Indian from Canada. And yet another was a Bengali man named John Windall, who had "followed the seas in vessels of different nations" before turning up "somewhat advanced in life" at Cornwall. (His age by then was at least thirty.)[11] Rounding out the group was one John Johnson, also a native of India. Johnson's story, as recounted in the missionary press, made an extreme case of the zigzag dislocations that marked the course of many Mission School pupils prior to arrival.[12]

He is born around the year 1800 in Calcutta. His father, a merchant there, is the mixed-race son of "an English gentleman" and "a Hindoo woman," his mother "a Jewess of the race of black Jews." (This means a line of native Bengalis, anciently converted to Judaism.) The father, having decided that young John must have an English education, sends him off to London; he is, at this point, perhaps twelve years old. The ship on which he travels is captured by an American privateer, retaken weeks later by a British frigate, and then "carried to Halifax [Nova Scotia]." After some refitting, it sets out again, but, amazingly, is soon captured for a third time—again by Americans—and sent on to New York. There the boy and ship's crew are prepared for return to England in a prisoner exchange. (All this is happening in the midst of the War of 1812.)

En route they stop in the West Indies, at the island of Grenada, where Johnson is suddenly stricken with yellow fever. When his case seems hopeless, he is wrapped in blankets and left to die on a beach. Fortunately, he is found by "a gentleman . . . taking an evening walk . . . with his lady," carried to their home, and nursed back to health. Eventually, he secures passage on yet another American ship, and debarks in the town of Derby, Connecticut. From there he removes to the neighboring village of Woodbridge, is hosted by the local minister, and is eventually referred to the agents of the Mission School. He is admitted despite (or because of?) pronouncing himself "a Mahometan [sic] by habit," and seeming "very bigoted, saying his prayers to the prophet four times a day." This is but a prelude to Christian conversion; within days he begins "to doubt the divine mission of Mahomet," and to feel "great reverence for the

Scriptures." His teachers find him to be "diligent and studious." And the fact that he speaks both Hebrew and Arabic makes them regard him as "an important acquisition." Indeed, considering "the remarkable leadings of Providence" that brought him to Cornwall, they feel certain of his destiny "to be an instrument of good in some station." (Another legend? Perhaps—in some parts. But the weave of the Mission School story would include such strands over and over again.)

Thus the total number of students by summer's end was an even dozen: seven from Hawaii, two from India, one Native American, plus the two Yankees. Their ages spanned a range from mid-teens to early thirties. Their prior experience was enormously diverse: seafaring, most especially, but also military service, farming, barbering, cooperage, "academy" schooling. Their educational levels, and their language skills in particular, were equally varied; one or two were nearly illiterate, while others had been tutored for months or years in Latin, Greek, and Hebrew. (And John Johnson, as noted, spoke Arabic.) Perhaps the first, most pressing problem their instructor would face was finding common ground among them.

Within the full cast here, Henry Obookiah was clearly the star—the leader and emblem of the entire project for the world at large. In a long letter sent to one of his erstwhile "patrons" in early June, he began by applauding his fellow scholars' "great progress in their studies"; the latter included English grammar, geography, and arithmetic, together with reading, writing, and spelling. (Some, however, "were just beginning to read.") The daily program centered on classes "from nine to twelve, and from two to five." School rules forbade visits "to any house or . . . any family in town." Moreover, none may "go to a store (unless they have a liberty)." By the same token, "no visitor or friend should call to see any that is in the school." Even within the grounds, there were restrictions. The "study hour," for example, was sacrosanct; at such times, "no student shall come into another's room." Finally, all must "take part in laboring . . . two [and] ½ days . . . a week . . . two at a time." This last referred to work on the school's agricultural property, something Obookiah considered "as important . . . as to learn to read and write." His opinion was not widely shared among his fellows, some of whom had "very little acquaintance with farming business . . . and so they . . . [do] not delight in it." (Most, he noted, "understand [more] about the sailor's business," having previously served for long periods at sea.)[13]

Obookiah's description sets a kind of frame; additional details lie scattered here and there in missionary writings. From the start, the focus of school authorities—both teachers and agents—went as much toward conversion as toward standard pedagogical fare. Sometimes religious faith lapped over directly into the classroom. A text entitled *The Missionary Spelling Book and Reader,* said to have been "prepared at the Foreign Mission School . . . and designed especially for its use," combined language training with key articles of faith. The latter included such familiar homilies as "We shall all die"; "Angels will come and take the souls of good men up to heaven"; and "The souls of wicked men will go to hell . . . [where] they will dwell with devils and be miserable forever." Cornwall's First Church was the one place where scholars might meet on a regular basis with the local populace. Their attendance each Sabbath was expected, indeed assumed. They were assigned a special "bench . . . in the [church's] southeast corner." One imagines them seated in close array, decked out in their Sunday finest (most of it garments donated by school supporters), and enduring—perhaps enjoying, perhaps embarrassed by—the inevitable glances thrown their way. For certain, they were on display.[14]

Obookiah was the lone scholar previously qualified for full church membership; according to one account, "he appears to grow in grace, and more and more to evince the reality of his new birth." But several of his fellows were pointed in the same direction. Hopoo, in particular, had "for about two years entertained a hope in Christ"; hence, in midsummer, he was "admitted to the church, and received the ordinance of baptism." Tennooe and Honoree showed promising signs of "having passed from death unto life." Sandwich had "become deeply impressed with the concerns of his soul." Kummooolah appeared to be "the subject of religious exercises of some kind," though "from ignorance of our language he [was] . . . unable to give an account of them." The same "concerns," the same "exercises," the same accompanying language of pious hope would infuse reports of Mission School life virtually to its close.[15]

At the other end of a long spectrum—from God to mammon—lay pressing concerns with money. Many of the start-up costs, such as those to enable the purchase of land and buildings, had been covered by the American Board, but that source would not suffice for regular operations. Instead, the school must develop a full-scale fund-raising program, to tap the rapidly mounting public interest in missionary outreach. Already some steps had been taken. Several regional canvassers were in place and at work—for New England, New York, New Jersey, and points farther south—and Rev. Stone stood ready to coordinate their efforts from Cornwall itself. During the course of the school's first summer, a sum of $1,400 was raised in eastern Massachusetts; in the town of Newburyport alone (as a local reporter proudly noted), "two hundred and thirty-two dollars and fifteen cents were contributed in one evening, besides several articles of jewelry." There and elsewhere "female societies," even "societies of children," were forming "for the promotion of the same object." "Missionary fields" were planted in many communities— farm lots set aside to yield produce for consumption (or sale) at the Mission School. Collection plates, "charity boxes," "concerts of prayer," and other such stratagems were also noted on the lists.[16]

In the months to come, fund-raising for the school would mushroom astoundingly. Thousands of ordinary folk would come forward to contribute—most at quite modest levels, but with no less commitment for that. Stone would arrange the printing of lengthy "donations lists" in missionary periodicals. And these, in turn, were meant to prompt additional swelling of the ranks. Read today, they are affecting documents; more than anything else, they limn the shape of evangelical fervor at ground level.[17]

Many of the gifts were in cash. Some came from named individuals:

Esq. Battle of Norfolk (Con.)	$ 5.00
Mrs. Battle, of the same place	5.00
Moses Woodruff, proceeds of a garden	1.40
Gratuities of the public house, of Mr. T. Cowles, New Hartford	1.75

Some were anonymous:

A Friend to the School	10.00
A widow's mite	0.55
Avails of Cider Collected by Several Persons and Sold	4.80
Avails of Gold Leaf, saved by a few Young Ladies in Terry's clock manufactory	30.00
From three little boys	0.12½

From a Lady in New Fairfield, the avails of a prize ticket   05.00
A highly respectable clergyman (Episc.),
    when visiting the school   5.00
From the colored people in Utica and New Hartford, N.Y.   12.00

Some came from organizations:

The Owhyean Society of Young People in Augusta, N.Y.   2.00
A Female Charitable and Praying Society in Westford,
    Otsego County, N.Y.   Cash twenty dollars

Some might set a little scene:

Mr. H. N. Crosby of N. East (N.Y.) is thanked for his
    generosity to the scholars of the institution, at the time of his
    exhibition of a number of interesting, living animals at
    Cornwall. . . . . he giving of   340 cents

Many were in-kind gifts, not cash:

Mr. Samuel Street of Goshen: 4½ bu. of potatoes, 50 lbs of veal
1 bushel of white beans from a missionary field
9 bushels of garden vegetables estimated at 2 dollars
One shirt given on his deathbed by William R. Hawley
Scaghticoke tribe of Indians, Sophia Rice: one sailor coat
A quantity of straw hats
Cloth for a pair of pantaloons
Quills, 1 ream of paper
1 bureau, 1 breakfast table, 1 doz. candle snuffers
Rollins Ancient History in 8 handsome volumes
Tyringham, Mass., a few ladies of the society of the Rev. Mr. Dow,
    1 bed quilt, 1 shirt, 1 vest, 2 pair of socks, also 1 blanket from
    Miss Thankful Brown

Some were given as labor performed:

Sewing $ 1.12
Tailoring   3.00
Grinding 3 new axes

These bits—they are no more than that, and just a tiny fraction of the whole—suggest how deeply interest in the Mission School would permeate everyday life in the outside world. Towns and villages in at least a dozen different states; taverns, factories, churches, private homes; farming, cider making, weddings, holiday celebrations, circus exhibitions, prize lotteries; individuals of every rank and station, from gentlemen dubbed "Esquire," to penurious widows and small children, to Indians and colored folk: All were represented here. Moreover, "innumerable local societies formed for the aid of the enterprise." Variously called "Owhyhean [Hawaiian]," "Ladies Aid," "Dorcas," "Young People's Mite," and so on, all would serve to funnel valuable assistance directly into school coffers.

As news spread, the range of donors widened steadily—including, among others, the new president of Yale College (Timothy Dwight had recently died), a large group of "concerned students" at Princeton, and "the girls of Miss Pierce's School at Litchfield." A collection in Charleston, South Carolina, raised nearly $400. Overseas contributions came from "a Liverpool gentleman" and another in Cuba. Sometimes a published list would conclude with a special plea from Stone, designed to shape the *next* round of donations. For example: "Shoes and boots of a strong texture, and hats also are wanted more than any other articles." Or: "As the colder season will soon commence, cloth and garments suitable for winter are solicited." The "friends" and supporters would read, would take to heart, would respond accordingly.[18]

Alongside the accounts of donations, so carefully recorded one by one, were others that periodically summed the receipts. One such, from a year and a half after the school's founding, was focused on bedding and "vestitures" (clothing); its forty-four categories included the following: "13 feather beds [mattresses], 63 linen sheets, 66 quilts, 135 pillow cases, 31 coats (partly worn), 61 pantaloons (partly worn), 137 vests (partly worn), 270 pairs of stockings, 79 shirts, 49 cravats, 6 surtouts [overcoats], 5 pairs of suspenders, 58 towels, 4 shaving soaps." (One special curiosity here: 2 buffalo skins.)

The various lists, taken together, afford a glimpse of life inside the school. The furnishings they included—bureaus, breakfast tables, and the like—suggest a domestic environment closely fitted to mainstream American models; likewise the accessories, right down to lowly "candle snuffers." The clothing, too, expressed local taste and preference. (Some may have come literally off the backs of previous wearers—for example, the shirt given by a man "on his death-bed.") The foods—meat, pota-toes, beans, garden vegetables—were staples of New England diet. Noth-ing at all acknowledged an alien element. To visit the school would mean encountering things known and familiar, with the crucial exception of the *persons* of the scholars themselves. But these, too, could be remade in time—which was, of course, the point of it all.

Indeed, the entirety of school operations conformed to well-established precedent. The curriculum described in Obookiah's early letter—English grammar, geography, arithmetic, together with reading, writing, and spelling—would be augmented as time passed. Additional subjects would include rhetoric, composition, natural philosophy, astronomy, and the classical languages, all of them standard fare in a typical academy education of those years. Another traditional element was the schedul-ing, at appropriate intervals, of public "examinations" or (as they were also called) "exhibitions." These were times for the scholars to give for-mal demonstration of their prowess in front of staff, sponsors, and other concerned parties (such as Cornwall townspeople). First, they would be examined in their various "academical" subjects; then they would pray and sing; finally, they would enact skits, speeches, and other little dra-mas that exemplified the "savage" ways they were leaving behind and the "civilized" ones they were seeking to embrace. These performances would be long remembered by all who witnessed them. As one admir-ing onlooker wrote some years later, "The students spoke on stage, first in their own tongue, then in our language. . . . The Indian pupils [in particular?] appeared so genteel and graceful . . . that the white pupils appeared uncouth beside them. . . . When they prayed, they knelt, clasped their hands together, and held them up. When they sang, they sat in a row, and all waved their hands simultaneously." Typically, the program would culminate with a sermon by a locally prominent minis-ter. As much as possible, this should be a bravura performance, lavishly underscoring current accomplishments and inspiring high hopes for the future. Inspiration was a currency on which the school relied for emo-tional and moral—as well as financial—sustenance. Thomas Gallaudet, founder of the Hartford Deaf and Dumb Asylum, would say of one par-ticular exhibition: "[I]t was more interesting . . . than a hundred college commencements." And on the same occasion John Treadwell, governor of Connecticut, "was completely carried away . . . & thought it beyond everything he had seen or ever expected to see here."[19]

The first of these events was announced for a certain "Wednesday in September [1817] . . . at 9 o'clock a.m." Barely four months had passed since the beginning; however, there was pressure to show quick "improvement" to the public—to disarm skeptics and rally supporters. According to a subsequent report, the audience that day included "several of the neighboring clergy, and a number of ladies who have taken an interest in these youths." (There is something unwittingly ironic, and prophetic, about the wording there—*ladies who have taken an interest in these youths*—given all that would follow in the history of the school.) Apparently, the proceedings went well; at least "the students acquitted themselves to the satisfaction of those present." They proved especially adept with grammar and arithmetic; they also produced some "handsome specimens of penmanship." Their "greatest difficulty" was in spelling.[20]

These "exercises" filled the morning. In the afternoon, the entire assemblage adjourned to the First Church to hear a sermon offered by "the Rev. Mr. [Charles] Prentice" (one of the school's governing agents). Only its biblical text is known today—Matthew 13:16–17—but this was admirably suited to the moment: "Many prophets and righteous men have desired to see those things which ye see, and have not seen them, and to hear those things which ye hear, and have not heard them." In other words: *What you have witnessed today is utterly special; you are fortunate and privileged beyond the lot even of holy men of old.* The effect was to underscore the performance of the scholars, its meaning and significance for God's plan. *These youths, so recently reclaimed from heathen darkness, are the carriers of a transcendently important change in human affairs.* Nothing could have been better calculated to lift the spirits and refresh the souls of all who listened.[21]

The program concluded with the reading of a "register of behavior" and the award of "premiums" (prizes) to the two "highest" named there. The first premium went to George P. Tamoree (which may have been quite a surprise, given his previously spotty record), the second to Hopoo. It was noted also that Obookiah and the two Americans were omitted from consideration, since they had been gone—presumably on fund-raising trips—for part of the summer. Of the others, who were not similarly honored, impressions were still very favorable. One was deemed "eminently useful," another "steady and free from vicious habits," still another "remarkably amiable and affectionate."[22]

All in all, the agents felt confident of still greater success ahead: "We can have students as fast as we can accommodate them and support them. Several are now waiting for permission to join the school." More-over: "[T]he plan of the school meets with such universal approbation, and the conduct of the students has been so regular and respectable, as to gain the affection not only of the people of Cornwall but of all the sur-rounding towns." Finally came this most ebullient flourish of all: "The Lord hath helped us. His hand has been conspicuous in every stage of the institution. And when we look forward, the most encouraging prospects are presented. We hope ere long to see this small stream become a river which shall make glad the city of our God." From now on—the world would know—the school was on its way.[23]

With the initial examination concluded, things moved into a quieter, more routine phase. A short vacation may have allowed the scholars to scatter—some on visits to their former "patrons" and benefactors in other towns nearby—but by early fall their studies had resumed in Cornwall. Despite the agents' assurance that new applicants were standing by, ready and eager for admission, enrollment seems to have remained at around a dozen through the end of the calendar year 1817. Times were hard throughout rural New England, with "scarcity of provisions both for man and beasts," high prices for "food and forage," and a general feeling of "want." Still public interest—and tangible support—was holding up nicely as winter began.[24]

Then, right after the New Year, came an event that would powerfully shake "this infant institution." Though its long-range effects were posi-tive, even enhancing, it played initially as tragedy. At some point in early January, Henry Obookiah fell ill, with what was quickly diagnosed as a case of typhus. He was moved from the schoolhouse into the home of Rev. Timothy Stone, where he could expect "the kindest and most judicious attentions." Stone, of course, was a close participant in school affairs (in more ways than simply his official role as donations "superintendent"), and the members of his large family were also quick to respond.[25]

Herman Daggett—who, as principal in waiting, was fully cognizant of Obookiah's special importance—received the alarming news from Stone. On January 12, he wrote from his pastorate in nearby New Canaan to "my dear young friend," expressing deep concern about "the feeble state of your health." He prayed that "the Lord will spare your life . . . that you may be instrumental, in due time . . . in planting the banner of the CROSS in your native isle, now covered with spiritual darkness." Still, he acknowledged that it might not be so, and urged submission to "the high will of Jehovah, who . . . accomplishes His purposes, ofttimes, by events which to us appear dark and appalling."[26] This was a standard form of religious counsel for people with potentially mortal illness; doubtless, too, Daggett was preparing himself for the possibility of crushing disappointment. If the school were a kind of "stream" destined one day to encircle the earth, Obookiah was its source point—and then its strongly flowing central current. Obookiah, first among the various "heathen" carried to America for Christian conversion! Obookiah, protégé of "pope" Dwight, of Mills, of Harvey, of Beecher, and of other towering figures in the Protestant establishment! Obookiah, already an important proselytizer in his own right—and inspiration to people of faith all across New England (America? the world?)! Obookiah, careful translator of the sacred Scriptures into his own native tongue! Obookiah, prepared in so many ways to assume a leading role in the "great cause" of foreign missions! What, then, if he should not survive?

As soon as his illness began, Obookiah was placed in the care of a local physician and started on a course of medication. For a time, his condition appeared to improve, and "confident expectations were entertained for his recovery." But then the "wasting . . . [of] his constitution" resumed, a process that would stretch over several weeks to its ultimate "heart-breaking," yet also triumphant, conclusion. Remembrance of this would later join with the story of his arrival at Yale (a decade previous) to bookend the larger Obookiah legend. Even the smallest details would be recounted—embellished—savored—by tellers and listeners, by writers and readers, for generations to come.[27]

One version, in particular, set a kind of standard.

His sickbed becomes a virtual shrine. Visitors come and go; conversation, both personal and prayerful, is almost nonstop. The atmosphere is thick with emotion; at some points "loud sobbing . . . [is] heard throughout the room, and from persons little accustomed even to weep."

Mrs. Stone remains at his side, day and night, a "ministering angel" in his time of need. (Later she will declare herself "more than rewarded for her cares and watchings . . . by his excellent example. . . . She said it was her highest wish to die like him.") He clings for a while longer to hopes of recovery, and sends "a note to the meetinghouse, on the Sabbath, requesting prayers that his life might be preserved and he permitted to return and preach the gospel to his countrymen." He is visited by several from the clergy, including Rev. Mills—"whom he always called 'father,' " and who now offers "counsel" of special importance.

But chief among his attendants are his Hawaiian compatriots and fellow scholars; indeed, he largely choreographs their comings and goings, "insisting that some one of them be with him continually," and "calling very earnestly if they were out of sight." Of course, too, he prays with them, usually at great length and "in their native language." (The content is then translated for the benefit of those "who are not able to understand the Owhyhee.") His feeling for Hopoo is particularly strong; hence the two of them "often . . . prayed together, alone, as they had done for years."

All his words carry a special aura of authority. To some in attendance he offers earnest exhortation: "Above all things, make your peace with God." To others, a kind of ultimate reassurance: "If we put our trust in God, we need not fear." To still others, gratitude: "You have been very kind to me. I feel my obligation to you." Now and then he may voice a special request: "William [evidently, his friend Kummooolah], if you go home, remember me to my uncle." Or he reiterates his own belief: "I have strong faith in God. I am willing to die, if God design to take me." Or he expresses a measure of yearning and regret: "Oh, how I want to see Hawaii!" Occasionally, his words seem ambiguous and hard to understand: "I've lost my time! I've lost my time!" (Does he mean the time spent in preparing for his return home to realize the goal of "planting the banner of the CROSS" there?) Whatever he says, or does, draws intense interest from everyone present; he is completely in charge.

He maintains without fail an attitude of "cheerfulness, resignation to the will of God . . . and benevolence"—all of which become, in turn, "particular subjects of notice and conversation" for others. His physician remarks that he is "the first patient whom he . . . ever attended through a long course of fever that had not in some instances manifested a . . . degree of peevishness and impatience." The "tones of his voice" are consistently marked by "sweetness," his "countenance" by a look of "perfect peace."

By the middle of February, he has become greatly weakened; clearly the end is near. The friends around him strain ever harder to grasp the power of his "example" and lodge it firmly within themselves. On the morning of the seventeenth, "after a distressing night . . . [in] a bewildered state," his mind clears and he summons his "countrymen" once more. When they have seated themselves beside his bed, he begins a last "address"— entirely of a religious nature—which "under the circumstances . . . [is] affecting beyond description." (As before, he speaks in Hawaiian, with

English translation to follow.) Tears flow; sounds of anguish again fill the air. His homeland remains much on his mind; reportedly, "one of the last things he . . . said is 'I shall never go to Owhyhee.'"

Then, "as death [seems] to approach," he shakes hands with each of his companions and gives them "a parting salutation— Alloah-o-e" ["My love be with you"]. The actual moment of his passing comes "with ease and without a struggle." It is left to Hopoo to make the final pronouncement: "Obookiah's gone!" At that, the entire group solemnly converges around his "lifeless form. . . . The spirit had departed—but a smile such as none present had ever beheld . . . remained upon his countenance."

Finally, there is this, attributed to him by his close friend and mentor Edwin Dwight: "He said that he came to this country to teach Christians how to die." No one who is present that day would ever think otherwise.

Doubtless the feelings of loss expressed here were genuine, lasting, and deep. And doubtless, too, the school had gained something—a martyr, whose life (and death) might be useful in promoting its interests. Its leaders moved quickly to take advantage.[28]

Following local custom in an age before embalming, both funeral and burial would take place the next day, with major figures in the religious establishment eager to take part. Lyman Beecher rode up from Litchfield to deliver the eulogy. Student and protégé years before of Timothy Dwight, exponent now of the vibrant "New Divinity" movement, himself a founder (and agent) of the Mission School, Beecher was the obvious choice. One imagines him rising to his task, alongside a flower-draped casket, in a meetinghouse filled with stricken mourners. (The latter, surely, included a phalanx of scholars.)[29]

Beecher's theme was pertinent and pressing—nothing less than "the mysterious providences of the Lord." Clearly, the loss of "this dear youth" seemed mysterious, surprising, appalling. Yet, when properly framed, such mysteries might be resolved; evil might sooner or later yield good. For example, "the death of great and good men may awaken the fears, and excite the prayers, and increase the responsibilities . . . of so many . . . that the amount of useful exertion shall be ever increased" in the world at large. Just there lay the essential lesson of Obookiah's passing. To be sure, "we did not expect it, and we should not have ordered things thus, to glorify God and extend His cause." Consider, however, the entire sequence of his life: his escape from "the deep darkness of Owhyhee," his arrival in "this land of light," the subsequent "renovation of his heart," and the final ascent of "his immaculate spirit" to Heaven. All parts, separately and together, bespoke the "wonderworking hand" of providence.

In fact, there was more to it—far more—than Obookiah's individual salvation. Consider also the effects on so many others. "By means of his conversion . . . numbers of his brethren, wandering like lost sheep . . . have been brought also to the knowledge of [God's] truth." The same "instrumentality" had led to the founding of the Mission School itself, "the hope of Owhyhee and other heathen lands." Nor would "this usefulness . . . terminate with his life," for "his death will give notoriety to this institution . . . and give it an interest in the prayers and charities of thousands who otherwise had not heard of [it] or been interested in its prosperity."

In his conclusion, Beecher reached for the loftiest rhetorical heights. "Let there be no despondency!" he thundered. The "clouds" and "darkness" of the moment "announce the presence of our God." Thus: "Instead of being appalled . . . we are cheered; instead of falling under the stroke, we are animated by it to double confidence . . . and double diligence in this work, forasmuch as we know that our labor is not in vain in the Lord." These words, and this viewpoint, would be fully vindicated in the months and years to come.[30]

The funeral was followed by a stately procession to the town burial ground. There, according to a letter written by a participant, "the corpse was set down," a choir sang "in a solemn manner," and Edwin Dwight, in his role as the school's acting principal, offered remarks "on the glorious death of the dear young man whom they committed to the dust." Dwight emphasized "the rich reward [of] all who had interested and exerted themselves for his instruction." The effect on those who watched and listened, said the same letter writer, "you can conceive better than I can tell you."[31]

Finally, there was the matter of a grave marker and memorial, presumably to come somewhat later. The townspeople raised $23, a considerable sum for that time, to cover its cost. They aimed for something special, something that might express the extraordinary significance of the dead man's career. And they achieved no less; the monument raised over Obookiah's grave would be among the largest and most impressive yet seen in Cornwall's cemetery. An elaborately carved slate plaque, set on a bed of local fieldstones, told of his "journey" in phrases that would soon become incantatory: "a native of Owhyhee . . . once an idolator . . . by the grace of God . . . became a Christian . . . eminent for piety . . . prepared to return to his native isle to preach the gospel . . . God took to Himself . . . died without fear, with a heavenly smile on his lips and glory in his soul." Visitors began going there, in a spirit of pilgrimage, almost immediately—and have continued going ever since.[32]

Grave-site visits were not the only sign of Obookiah's "martyrdom." There were fulsome obituaries in the missionary press. There were special prayers, accolades, whole sermons even, in the churches where he had once worshiped and proselytized. There were occasional bits of writing—poems especially—printed in local newspapers. (Sample verse: "He came in his youth from the isles of the sea / 'My country,' he cried, 'will it never be free?' / For the isles that were reeking / In the blood of the slain / Obookiah was seeking / Release from the chain.") There were donations by the hundreds, made specifically in his name. A New Haven museum exhibited a wax figure of Obookiah on his deathbed, "peacefully resigning his breath into the hands of that Saviour he had so confidently trusted for salvation." And most powerful by far in the breadth of its influence was a book-length biography, begun within days or weeks of his passing, by Edwin Dwight. Quite possibly something of the sort was envisioned well before he took sick; he had himself composed a partial account of his life, which Dwight could then adapt to a different purpose.[33]

The *Memoirs of Henry Obookiah* was released by a missionary press in New Haven the following September. (Dwight's authorship was suppressed and would not be directly revealed for another twenty years.) Priced at fifty cents, the book sparked immediate, and intense, public interest; orders came in from all around the country. Its subsequent publishing history was remarkable; new editions appeared, totaling about a dozen, at intervals over the next five decades. According to a contemporary source, "pensioners and stationers mentioned it above the year's almanac. Ministers preached on it. Sunday School teachers read aloud from it, and young ladies sobbed over it." Estimates of copies printed have run as high as 100,000; if accurate, these would place the *Memoirs* among the top sellers of its time. Translations appeared in Hawaiian, in Greek, and in Choctaw. The impact on fund-raising for missionary work was huge (although incalculable with any precision). Anecdotal evidence mentions wills altered to include large bequests, gifts from "eminent persons" overseas (a Swiss baron, a French countess), admiring tributes by "potentates" such as the Russian prince Aleksandr Golitsyn. The Mission School itself was, from the first, a major beneficiary. And for many years to follow, the book and the life it inscribed would serve to inspire missionary-minded folk in every corner of the globe.[34]

Beecher's command to reject "despondency" and feel "cheered" following Obookiah's death seems to have set a course quite generally. A letter written by a school supporter in mid-March argued strenuously against the notion that "all the charity afforded him is now lost"; to the contrary, his "legacy" gave much ground for "rejoicing." Several months later, another correspondent put it this way: "God's infinite wisdom . . . devised that Henry, by now being raised to glory, should do more good, more promote the cause in which he was engaged, than he could have done by a long life of active exertion." And Rev. Joseph Harvey would add a special twist: "Having finished this work, and at a moment when he was becoming dangerous to our wavering hearts, ever ready to idolize the instrument, God took him away to be with Christ, which is far better." (This idea of "our" responsibility, and the concern with overvaluing God's "instrument," brought things nicely into line with traditional Protestant belief.)[35]

The same reversal of attitude—from sorrow to hope, from despair to confidence—seems also to have prevailed within the ranks of the school community. All were soon back at work, preparing for a "signal occasion" that lay just ahead. In the first week of May, Daggett would be officially inaugurated as principal, thus completing the yearlong founding process. Much was expected of him; though physically somewhat frail, he was thought to possess the requisite mix of moral and scholarly gravitas. Years later, Lyman Beecher would write of Daggett: "He was a mild, intellectual man . . . cheerful, but never known to smile, so it was said."[36]

As part of the inauguration, the school would stage another public examination and "exhibition." Its result was summarized in the boilerplate language of a leading missionary journal: "The evidence of success in the attainments of the youth from various heathen lands was most gratifying and interesting." Another writer added a few details. The program featured a "colloquy" staged by several of the Hawaiians in their native language. John Honoree, among others, spoke "with surprising force, and [in] a manner painful to the audience from the agitation of his countenance & whole frame and the unparalleled rapidity & vehemence of his utterance." Presumably they could not understand a word, yet the listeners were deeply—even "painfully"—affected.[37]

It was, in any case, the inauguration ceremony on the following day that served as the crowning moment (both literally and figuratively). This was also the anniversary of the school's opening, and thus a further cause for celebration. By midmorning, "a great concourse of people" had filled the pews of the First Church, creating an atmosphere of the keenest anticipation. The proceedings began with a lengthy sermon by Rev. Harvey, entitled "The Banner of Christ Set Up." Its tone was hortatory in the extreme; martial metaphors (for example, "evangelizing" as "another warfare"; "the pagan world" as "the fortified camp of Satan") were mixed with ringing scriptural quotation. The Mission School plan was reviewed in detail, but with goals that included a new (or at least previously unstated) dimension. Its initial focus on the Pacific Islands would "by no means [be] confined there." Rather, "these islands are but a threshold . . . a stepping stone to numerous heathen tribes scattered on the borders of the western ocean." From Cornwall, to Hawaii, to the Indians of the American West: thus the grand vision, the broad and bracing battle strategy.[38]

Harvey's sermon was just an opener; there was much else to follow. Daggett offered an address on the necessity of "doing good" and his personal vocation "to be useful in this sphere of duty." Like Harvey, he described the Mission School in the most exalted terms: "It is a work . . . which involves the highest interests of myriads of immortal beings—and which, in its effects and consequences, will endure when this earth and these heavens shall be no more." Next in order came Governor Treadwell, whose role it was to complete, and formalize, the inauguration. With a direct—indeed literal—handoff to Daggett, he intoned, "I do . . . by the delivery of these keys into your care and keeping induct you into the office of Principal . . . with all the powers, prerogatives, privileges, and emoluments thereunto belonging." Then Edwin Dwight, his duties as acting principal now at an end, delivered an "affectionate valedictory . . . to his pupils."[39]

Finally, the scholars themselves were reintroduced, in order to perform an impromptu skit of Christian salvation. Four of the Hawaiians spoke a "dialogue" in their own language, while two more sang "one of the rude, barbarous songs" of their homeland. At the same time, Thomas Hopoo began a "tender and animated apostrophe to the audience" on the plight of his "poor, ignorant countrymen." Such grotesque "amusements" as these, he declared, are their "sublimest joys." They know nothing of "that God who made the world. . . . They worship dumb idols, and chant their stupid hosannas to gods of wood and stone." He went on "in this pathetic strain" for a full fifteen minutes; by the end, his listeners were completely undone. According to an eyewitness account, "every heart beat high with sympathetic emotions, and every eye was streaming." (The same writer noted that "the exercises closed with a liberal contribution to the school"; purses as well as tear ducts had been opened.)[40]

If the story of the Mission School is seen as rapid ascent followed by gradual, eventually precipitous, decline, then the inaugural moment of May 1818 may qualify as the summit. With a year of apparently successful work completed, with Obookiah's death transmuted into glorious martyrdom, with public support on a strongly rising curve, the future seemed brighter than ever. And no dark shadows were as yet evident on the far horizon.

For one thing, the school was growing, as more scholars arrived, and an informal but effective recruitment network was rounded into shape in missionary sites around the world. Of the dozen who had entered at the time of its opening (or just after), nine remained: six Hawaiians, Hopoo, Honoree, Kummooolah, Tamoree, Tennooe, and Sandwich; the two New Englanders, Ely and Ruggles; and the Abenaki Indian, Annance. The three no longer present were Obookiah and the two Bengalis, one of whom (Windall) had been dismissed for "incompetence," the other (Johnson) for being "unhappily addicted to intemperance." Johnson's story, begun so auspiciously with his multiple rescues from piracy, his recovery from yellow fever, and his arrival at the school the year before hailed as "an important acquisition," would end in a downward spiral of despair. After leaving Cornwall, he was briefly taken into the household of Judge Tapping Reeve in nearby Litchfield; from there, he wrote to Daggett to beg for readmission, avowing his undiminished hope "to get learning and go and teach my poor father and mother and all my poor countrymen." He invoked the missionaries' own language of special pleading: "I am a poor heathen. God brought me among you. I done wrong. I hope I never do so no more in this world." But Daggett was unmoved. Months later, having parted from Judge Reeve, Johnson turned up as "a poor outcast wandering in the streets of New York"; after that, his trail would vanish altogether.[41]

Meanwhile, there were eight new arrivals during the winter and

spring of the New Year: a young man from Canton, brought by a merchant in the China Trade; a German Jew, recently convinced that "Jesus
Christ, whom his ancestors crucified, is the true Messiah"; a mixed-race
Pennsylvanian (part Delaware Indian, part white); two young Pacific
Islanders, from Tahiti by way of New Zealand, Australia, India, England,
and New York; a thirty-year-old man, born on the Malay Peninsula,
but kidnapped as a child, sold into slavery in China, "purchased" there
by an American consular agent, and brought to Rhode Island; another
"youth of our own country" bent on missionary work; and a boy from
the island of Timor (present-day Indonesia), most recently a house servant to a minister in Philadelphia. The yield from this group, for all its
far-flung origins, would prove disappointing. Half were gone within
months, for reasons that included "misconduct and disobedience," a
"frivolous . . . [and] obstinate" temperament, a lack of "the true missionary spirit," and, in one case, a preference to be elsewhere. (This last
was the Jewish man, a highly educated sort who left the school almost
immediately in order to board in the home of a local minister, where he
could exchange lessons in Hebrew for "instruction in divinity.")[42]

Even so, the current directing additional recruits to Cornwall continued its flow. And now it would embrace a major new venue. Indians of
the American Southeast had become, in recent years, a particular focus
of public attention—Choctaws, Creeks, and, most especially, Cherokees.
Missionaries, among others, were moving into the traditional homelands of these important native peoples, with high hopes of achieving
"glorious gains . . . [for] the cause of Christ." Moravian clergy had been
present in the region since the start of the century; among their projects
was a small school for Cherokee children at a site called Spring Place, in
north Georgia. The American Board would follow their example, opening a school of its own—named Brainerd, after a Protestant missionary of a half century earlier—in the spring of 1816. From these sources,
the Foreign Mission School would draw a new group of scholars in the
months and years just ahead.[43]

In the Cherokee heartland there are, at first, doubts and resistance; the
journey would be long, the destination unfamiliar. Parents must agree
about their own children, and "most are not willing they should go so
far away." Indeed, when the idea is broached at Brainerd in the spring of
1818, "not a single full Cherokee . . . is willing to permit his son to go out

and be educated among white people." But the teachers there persist, and some of the pupils appear "anxious for an enlarged education."

Eventually, sometimes quite rapidly, the families come around. Then begins a period of testing and preparation. The teachers are responsible for selecting, from among their native charges, those best able to manage the rigors and "enlarged" opportunities of the Mission School. In doing so, they envision a kind of pyramid. Its base at the Brainerd mission will consist of young beginners, who can be allowed to live at home with their parents while obtaining from day classes at least the "rudiments" of knowledge. The next level will include "the more promising ones [who may be] removed at the proper time to the mission houses," where the teachers themselves are lodged; this will enable a more concentrated mode of supervision. Finally, at the apex stand "some few of them," eligible to go "to our Foreign Mission School at Cornwall, Con. for a more thorough training." These will have to demonstrate both "promising talents" for academic work and "serious impressions" of religious faith. (In one notable instance, a young man's qualifications include the following: "[H]e is in the habit of admonishing the vicious among his people on all proper occasions. . . . His labors have been blessed by the reformation of at least two drunkards.")

The system will be administered from afar by officers of the American Board. Ideally, the scholars sent north can be matched to school "openings." Delays in securing the necessary "permission" must be avoided, lest a designated youth's parents and clansmen take offense and "through pride refuse to let him go." (Pride is regularly identified by missionaries as a stumbling block in all sorts of dealings with native people.) The entire process is fraught with chances for misunderstanding; more than a few of the initial decisions will later be reversed.

The next step is arranging travel. Most of those selected are between the ages of twelve and seventeen and lack experience in negotiating the white people's world; thus they require chaperones. Sometimes they may leave in the company of an itinerant missionary bound for New England, or perhaps with a "gentleman . . . on his way to New York [and carrying] a satisfactory recommendation from the mayor of said city." (Always in such matters, there must be careful vetting.) They will need cash, horses, and clothing sufficient for the journey; these, in turn, come either from parents or, if that source proves wanting, from government and missionary coffers.

Finally, when all is in readiness, relatives and friends gather to bid the departing youths farewell. In a typical case (as described by a correspondent to the American Board), a local chief "gave them instructions respecting their conduct when at the school." Later the same evening, "we had communion." Next morning "Dr. D. [one Dempsey, the chaperone] and the three boys met a little after sunrise, and Brother G. [a minister, probably Rev. John Gambold, from the Moravian mission at Spring Place] commended them to God. . . . They departed after breakfast."

The route followed will vary depending on the seasons and other circumstances. Sometimes they take ship from Charleston or Savannah; more often they go overland through North Carolina, Virginia, Maryland, Pennsylvania, New Jersey, and New York. There may be stops along the way to meet with missionary supporters or leading public figures. One group detours somewhat from the usual route in order to visit ex-presidents Thomas Jefferson and James Madison, then goes on to Washington, D.C., for an audience with the current president, James Monroe. Others endure considerable hardship; bad roads and weather conditions, for example, can take a heavy toll. The time elapsed from start to finish may easily amount to several weeks. Some of the travelers reach Cornwall in a "state of sickness," others "destitute" of goods and money. But whatever their experiences en route, arrival brings an abrupt change. Now, at long last, they can begin.[44]

Between August and December 1818, nine southeastern Indians enrolled at the Mission School: seven Cherokees and two Choctaws. In age, in family background, in previous preparation—not to mention race, ethnicity, culture, and language—this group differed hugely from its predecessors. Indian boys, still years short of maturity, would henceforth be living and studying alongside fully adult men from the Pacific Islands (and elsewhere). If this put them at some disadvantage, in other respects they stood well ahead. Whereas virtually all the islanders had reached Cornwall after years of deprivation, and utterly devoid of material resources, the Indians were plucked straight from the topmost layer of their communities. Some had a white parent; indeed, every one was (to a degree) of mixed blood. Their fathers were politically prominent, including at least three "primary chiefs," and were wealthy besides; several owned substantial plantations, raising cotton, grains, fruit, and other produce with the labor of gangs of their own black slaves. The same men operated taverns in major towns, ferryboat services across rivers, and stores that supplied hard goods to neighbors. They were said, moreover, to look the part of grandees; their houses were large (and mostly European in style), their clothes fine, their carriages opulent, their presence commanding. No wonder that some of their sons, upon arrival in Connecticut, were described as "appear[ing] to think much of themselves." The families, including the sons, were partially or fully literate in English. And they had, by this time, gained considerable familiarity with Christian religious practice, up to and including full conversion. In all these ways, the new Indian scholars were fit—were primed—for entry into the Mission School.[45]

The arrival of this Cherokee-Choctaw group would tilt the balance toward Indian scholars for good. Six more—three Oneidas, two from "the Stockbridge tribe," and one Tuscarora Iroquois—would join the school in the opening months of 1819. Among the Cherokees, it now became a "popular thing to send their sons to the north for education"; a missionary leader worried lest they be led to believe that "all may come who please." By the end of the year, with the school's total enrollment having risen to thirty-two, "aboriginal Americans" had become a majority (seventeen). Both in Cornwall itself and farther afield, people began to refer sometimes to "the Indian School."[46]

The timing of this shift was ironic, for the same months brought renewed emphasis on plans for an actual mission to the Sandwich Islands (Hawaii). This, of course, had been in prospect from the start, but only now did practical arrangements begin. The American Board's fund-raising operation would henceforth encourage donations directly for this purpose. Daggett, for his part, sought to promote the creation of books and primers "in the Owyhean language" to be used in island schools. And two of his Yankee charges, Ely and Ruggles, bent themselves to learning that language—presumably with the aid of their Hawaiian fellow scholars. Meanwhile, too, the latter seemed more and more "impatient to go on to Owhyhee." When, in the fall of 1818, the board was unable to set a date of departure, they grew "quite uneasy"; Daggett worried that at least one of them—George "Prince" Tamoree—might abscond and find his own "opportunity to return home."[47]

As part of the same preparatory process, Daggett and the board searched for firsthand information on the islands. Although they remained confident in general terms—Hawaii was sure to make "a fine field for Christian charity," with its "population . . . kindly disposed, desirous of civilization, and of excellent mental endowments"—they knew little about the everyday realities of living and working there. At one point, they heard from a certain "Mr. Dorman of New Haven . . . [who] spent 13 months" in the islands, visited with King Tamoree (ruler of Atoi, today's Kaua'i, and father of the "Prince"), and learned something of local politics. He had, moreover, enjoyed "a great degree of hospitality by the natives, wherever he went"; however, "their moral state, he says, is truly distressing."[48]

Then came an extraordinary opportunity in the person (literally) of one Archibald Campbell. Born and raised in Scotland, Campbell had, when still a boy of thirteen, gone to sea on a British merchantman. He had traveled to China, Japan, Siberia, several parts of northwestern North America, Brazil, and, finally, Hawaii, where he lived quite happily for over a year on the island of Oahu. (While there, he had, supposedly, "learned the native language.") Along the way, he endured shipwreck, near starvation, capture by pirates, and the freezing, and subsequent amputation, of his feet following weeks of wintertime tramping in the Alaskan wilderness. Upon his return home, he authored a short but compelling account of these adventures, entitled *A Journey Round the World Between 1806 and 1812;* published in Edinburgh in 1816, and quickly reprinted four times in the United States, the book would bring him at least a modicum of fame. By 1818, Campbell turned up with his recently wedded wife in New York. There he underwent hospital treatment of some as-yet-unhealed surgical wounds, and began to plan a return to Hawaii; in fact, he still owned property on Oahu, granted to him years before by the king. Just then, he was put in contact with members of the American Board, who eagerly proposed his entering the Mission School. They hoped to derive important benefits from his firsthand knowledge of the islands; he, for his part, wished to study "divinity" and then to join the group that would open the mission there.[49]

It was an ill-fated bargain; almost from the start, things went badly off track. Both Campbells were expected to provide "personal labor" in exchange for "a comfortable support." Thus Mrs. Campbell "can wash & iron, & . . . do any kind of kitchen labor"; her husband, "if his legs should be well, can do many things." But this was a vain hope. As events proved, Mr. Campbell, "being a cripple, can do no labour for the institution." Moreover, "his knowledge of the Owhyhean language is very scanty and imperfect"; hence "he can be of no [future] use to us in the mission." In other respects, he "appears to be a mere man of the world . . . [who] frankly acknowledges that he never prayed in his life." Mrs. Campbell, too, seemed "a low-minded, frivolous, thoughtless person," full of eccentric affectations; among the latter was her habit of "carrying about with her a cage of birds." The couple occupied valuable space in the boarding-house—the "only chamber . . . where there can be a fire"—which meant that would-be scholars awaiting admission must be "deferred." Worse yet was the effect on those currently enrolled. "Mr. Campbell is ingratiating himself into the favor of the Owhyheans & continually filling their minds with accounts of their native Islands"; this served only to distract them from "the great objects which we have in view" and sometimes to "unhinge" them more deeply.[50]

These comments formed part of a long letter by one of the agents, ending with a proposal for "their removal from the establishment." In fact, this is precisely what happened; in early December, the Campbells were sent packing. But by then the school had endured four months of a most bizarre turmoil—described, in one account, as a "paroxysm"— which appears to have left some residue. Daggett's next report to the board sounded a new note of discouragement. "The School which before seemed to have a preponderance of piety has evidently put on a different appearance." Many of the scholars had declined in "seriousness," while a select few felt "grieved, and come to me expressing their fears that the School will not prosper." Alas, the report concluded, "unsanctified nature will act like itself." In a private letter from about the same time, Daggett said more: "levity and bickerings appear to prevail in the School more than I have ever observed them to do before." As a result, a most unfortunate "down . . . tide" was running.[51]

Still: With the Campbells gone, with new scholars arriving, with Hawaii looming ever larger on the school's horizon, the stage was set for a bounce-back. By May, when the next examination day came around, morale had been largely restored. Most of the following year (1819) would be consumed by thoughts of the upcoming mission. If only it could be managed, this would bring the first real fulfillment of the founders' overarching goal: native scholars, shorn of heathenism and full now of pious intent, returning to their homelands to spread God's Word. As the mission planners looked ahead, they faced a variety of strategic questions. How, exactly, should they approach their task? With what methods and "instrumentalities"? Schools, they decided, would become their entry point, their "prime object," for these were the most "popular, and inoffensive, means of effecting the ultimate good intended." Teach the heathen children to read, to write, to count, and all else will follow, including an "effectual introduction to the Gospel." In taking this position, they were simply reinstating the principle that had guided their efforts at Cornwall (and elsewhere) from the start: educating in the service of "evangelizing."[52]

There was, moreover, another reason for this choice. In Daggett's words: "The youths who are to accompany the mission" will find, in schools, "immediate & suitable employment . . . & gain the confidence & esteem of their countrymen." He was referring, of course, to his own Hawaiian pupils, around whom lurked a certain anxiety. Might they not—when returned to their original surroundings—lose their faith, forget all they had learned of "civilization," and revert to "primitive paganism"? Better, then, to "employ" them right away in a solid and "suitable" occupation, such as work in mission-sponsored classrooms.[53]

Schools would require books, so Daggett and others redoubled their efforts in that direction. With assistance from some of the native scholars they created a special "Owhyhean, book" composed of Bible extracts, sentence translations ("including some account of Obookiah"), elementary instruction in spelling and arithmetic, plus "a short & familiar account of Creation." They decided to save its actual publication for Hawaii—a printing press would accompany the mission—since "it will be pleasing to the heathen to see the production of the book designed for their use." Additional books (in English) would arrive among larger "donations." One such included "2 setts of Morse's Universal Geography," several of "Scott's Bibles," plus "50 or 60" additional volumes; a second "36 copies of the Memoir of Obookiah . . . to send . . . to Owhyhee."[54]

In fact, these donations spanned a very broad range: from bolts of cloth, finished garments, and shoes to bedding, tools, dried apples, cheeses, and writing paper. A typical shipment required three wagons for transport from Connecticut to Boston. There were cash gifts, too (some from as far away as Virginia and South Carolina). And one more, of special significance, was "the watch of Henry Obookiah, which has been reserved with the expectation that Thomas [Hopoo] would have it when he left this country." There were also several things "intended as presents to the heathen" but considered "improper . . . [such as] ear drops, rings, feathers, &c."; these "would give them wrong expectations," and must be returned. Finally, there were gifts collected by Hopoo during "a little tour . . . into the western parts of Mass. & Ver." and meant specifically for island royalty—for example, Bibles for the "son & daughter of King Tam-a-am-a-ah [Kamehameha]," and "a common Testament" for the king himself. It made, all in all, a considerable stash.[55]

Of course, the single most important task for the organizers was lining up the people to be involved. Two young clergymen, Hiram Bingham and Asa Thurston, volunteered to lead the mission. Bingham had been raised on a farm in Vermont and attended Middlebury College and Andover Theological Seminary; he was drawn to missionary work by Obookiah's story and a site visit to Cornwall. Of the latter, he wrote in typically grandiloquent, and patronizing, terms: "I saw those dear youths whom God in his providence had brought from pagan lands . . . having caught . . . the spirit of the gospel, panting for an opportunity to publish its doctrines & diffuse its hopes and consolation among their dying countrymen, & looking anxiously around them for some one to take them by the hand & lead them forward in this great and good work." Thurston, for his part, was a Massachusetts native and Yale graduate. The group would also include five more New England men: a printer, a farm superintendent, a "schoolmaster and mechanic," another schoolmaster, and a "respectable physician." Only one of them was married when chosen; the other six, including the ministers, rushed to take wives just before departure, after the briefest of courtships. This flurry of weddings reflected a general belief that bachelor missionaries might be subject to unwanted "temptation."[56]

The choice of the "Anglo-Americans" (as they were identified in Mission School documents) seems to have gone easily enough; their Hawaiian colleagues presented more difficulty. Throughout the summer and fall, Daggett agonized over the possibilities: Which of the current scholars were best prepared for the "arduous duties" that awaited them? Hopoo had shown the greatest overall promise. Boon companion for so long to Obookiah, he did not possess the same "force of mind," but his piety and "seriousness" were beyond doubt. Honoree, too, was "honest and faithful." As for Tennooe, "there have been suspicious things" about him in the past, but more recently "he has gained upon our good opinion." Sandwich was of "good character" but had "almost forgotten his native language" (after living for a dozen years in America); this in itself seemed disqualifying. Kummooolah's "talents are not . . . above mediocrity"; at the least he would need more time in order to become "useful." That left Tamoree. Though possessed of much intelligence—he had gained some local fame by learning how to predict lunar eclipses—his behavior was often "disgraceful." His connections at home, as the son of an island king, gave him great potential value. Yet what to make of his "irritable & self-important" manner, his lack of "restraint," his freely expressed "rages," his talking "very improperly," his misuse of money, his occasional drunkenness? The problems went on and on—leaving Daggett at wit's end. Tamoree was, in any case, determined to return without further delay; Daggett was resigned to this, but feared "his doing some fatal mischief, or coming to a dreadful end." He would join the mission entourage—not with the blessing of his teachers, but, rather, with their anxious prayers for his "reformation and final good."⁵⁷

In the end, the roster would consist of nineteen Anglo-Americans— the seven men officially attached to the mission, their wives, and five children belonging to one of the couples—plus the four young Hawaiians. The latter were identified as "native teachers" or simply "assistants," terms that implied a subordinate role; their exact duties would not be determined until after arrival in the islands. (Tamoree, in fact, was excluded even from this modest designation.) Still, their symbolic importance was clear to all; thus, before leaving, they were invited to sit for a group portrait by Samuel F. B. Morse, a much-admired artist of the time (and the future inventor of the Morse code). Morse's painting would subsequently become the basis for a set of engraved prints, to be sold far and wide as a fund-raising tactic for the school.⁵⁸

In late September, the entire Hawaii-bound contingent would gather in the town of Goshen for the official ordination of the two ministers, Bingham and Thurston; they were joined by "a large concourse," including some from "distant parts of the country." According to an eyewitness, "the effect of the whole was increased by the presence of . . . nearly all the members of the Foreign Mission School, who had come over from Cornwall with the Reverend H. Daggett, their instructor." Among the latter group, most of all, this event must have occasioned great excitement and pride. The hopes they had nourished through so many months were about to be realized.⁵⁹

The final send-off came three weeks later in Boston, from where their ship would set out. There was another round of ceremonies, including two at the Park Street Church before a "very numerous and attentive audience." At the first, the departing group joined together, "with very impressive solemnities," to form a church congregation that could then be transferred to Hawaii; and Bingham preached on the theme of "benevolent action." At the second, announced as a "farewell service," Thurston preached and Hopoo followed with a powerful, "extempore address" of his own. "It was," wrote an eyewitness, "a most affecting spectacle to see a native of Owhyhee preaching the Gospel to the citizens of Boston." Collections taken at both services yielded "upwards of two hundred dollars." (The equivalent amount today would be several thousand.) On the morning they sailed, another "great crowd" gathered at Long Wharf, for yet more hymns, prayer, and "salutation." At last, "they took leave of their weeping friends"—and were off.[60]

Perhaps now the school could take a new view of itself; no longer an "infant institution," it had become instead a maturing one, with progeny of its own abroad in the world. Something of an expanded spirit was evident in its workings during the weeks and months after the launching of the Sandwich Islands mission. Thus Daggett would, on one occasion, pronounce the school to be "uniformly prosperous," on a second "altogether flourishing."

Then came another memorable observance of the annual school examination (May 1820). The sermon, delivered by Rev. David Perry (from the nearby town of Sharon), was perhaps the most exalted and uplifting of the many such delivered at the school. Perry began by conjuring a picture of the departed missionaries, just then—"perhaps while I am yet speaking"—on their approach to "the wished for shore." (In fact, the entire group had arrived two months before, but the news had not as yet gotten back to New England.) "Is it an illusion?" he asked. "Or do we see the wandering natives throng to welcome the heralds of salvation, and clasp, in fond embrace, their long lost children?" (Illusion or not, such was the heart-hope of all present that morning.) "For many ages," he continued, "though something was attempted, nothing was done." But he then added, "[H]ow is the scene now changed! These wild men come to our shores, and our firesides." (And none of those in attendance could fail to notice the cluster of actual living and breathing specimens of "wild men," seated just there—below the preacher—as he pushed on.) "They enquire for the Babe of Bethlehem; they listen to his story; they admire his life; they weep by his cross; they tremble for sin." (Who among the listeners would doubt this? They were themselves witness to it.) "These, and many other equally animating scenes, have so rapidly crowded on the view, that the mind has almost lost the power of astonishment." (They might well, by this point, be cast into a kind of trance. Such magnificent prospects could scarcely be imagined.)[61]

The sermon closed with a candid acknowledgment of "challenges" to face and "obstacles" to overcome. The "wild men" were, after all, "buried in superstition and guilt; the madness of paganism has become enwrought into the very structure of their minds." (Creating a new structure would be a long and arduous process; no one should underestimate its difficulties.) Still, the Mission School offered a uniquely auspicious approach: "It stands alone, in the Christian world, an original essay for doing good. It has not its like in Europe or America. . . . Few institutions have brought such an accession of zeal and interest to the Christian cause; and few . . . promise more extensive benefit to the Church of God in heathen lands." (They were riding now on a sea of high emotion— their eyes fixed on a distant but glorious horizon.)[62]

After reaching such a crest, almost anything else would be a come-down. But when the gathering moved over to the schoolhouse, the examination itself went very well. The scholars performed in their usual "creditable . . . gratifying" manner—offering fourteen "declamations," in six different languages, and concluding with a "dialogue," entitled "The Cherokee Council," on the subject of "the removal of the tribe to the Arkansaw [sic] according to the proposition of the American government." (Thus did the outside world begin to press in on the scholars, some of whom would later be engulfed by this very same "proposition.") According to subsequent press accounts, the entire sequence proved "highly encouraging to the friends of the heathen," especially those personally in attendance.[63]

By now the school had regained full strength, as the places vacated by the island-bound missionaries were filled with an equivalent number of new arrivals. In each of the succeeding years, there would be additional comings and goings, but the total number of scholars at any one time remained within a narrow range of thirty to thirty-five. Recruitment in a variety of far-flung venues—the Pacific, the Far East, southern Europe, and, most of all, the North American "Indian country"—continued to funnel likely prospects toward Cornwall; recommendations came from ministers, overseas merchants, sea captains, and others in the ranks of "the benevolent." By now, too, there was a regular admissions process, requiring advance communication and written "testimonials of [an applicant's] moral and Christian character."[64]

And what would successful applicants find when finally they reached the school? What were their impressions? Their feelings? How were they regarded by others, both staff and fellow scholars? Detailed evidence for answering such questions is scanty to nil, but some things can safely be imagined. Most of the newcomers had no prior experience of the New England landscape, New England climate, New England culture; hence they arrived as strangers through and through. (One commented pointedly on "the great extremes of heat and cold," and imagined his family "enjoying the warm clime of our native country . . . while, as I am writing I hear the cold Northern wind whistling above me.") A good many could barely converse in English, and some were entirely lacking that way. A certain number (especially among the Indians) had previously encountered the Christian faith, which loomed so large in the school's everyday life and practice; at least a few could be described as already "hopefully pious." But for many, this element, too, was unfamiliar. Though their teachers and "patrons" were not overtly rejecting, they encountered little interest or sympathy for whatever they might carry with them from their "primitive" and "pagan" past; indeed, the goal was to "reform" and remake them as quickly as possible. All this they must have sensed from the moment of arrival. As a result, some were actively upset—anxious, disoriented, homesick—during their first weeks in Cornwall. Daggett acknowledged as much when stressing to the American Board the value of the school's isolated location: "It is . . . a fact that foreign youths, on their first arrival, are frequently uneasy, and desirous of leaving. . . . Were facilities presented for them to depart, the Agents believe that many of them, in some fit of pique or discontent, would abscond."[65]

To be sure, this was not always the case; some came full of hopeful anticipation. David Brown, a young Cherokee previously schooled for several years at Brainerd and steeped in Christian devotional practice, wrote home in a cheerful vein in July 1820. "I arrived here the 13th instant from Boston. . . . I generally find everything as I expected when I left home. . . . I like Cornwall. . . . There are at present students from all different parts of the globe. . . . I was happy to find our Cherokee friends [his fellow scholars] all doing well; most of them, I hope, are truly pious." Even Brown, however, would go on to suffer periods of "gloom &

discouragement"; in particular, he was troubled by a recurrent "hesita-
tion in speech" (stuttering), which "appears to be more since I have been
in Cornwall than before." (Curiously, he had "no difficulty in speaking
in the Cherokee language," whereas "the intricate English idiom was not
designed for me.")[66]

As part of their introduction to the school, some of the newcomers
would be renamed—either for a personal benefactor or for one or another
"luminary" in the Protestant pantheon. Thus John Paru, from Hawaii,
became Samuel Mills, after Obookiah's clergyman friend of years before;
and A-to-kah, a Seneca boy from upstate New York, became George Fox,
after a prominent seventeenth-century Quaker; and Taw-a-hee-chy, a
Cherokee, became William Kirkpatrick, "after his patron . . . [in] Lan-
caster, Pa. . . . who had engaged to sustain the expense of his education." (In most, though not all, cases, there was this same sort of quid
pro quo.) One especially well-documented instance shows details of the
procedure involved. It began when a minister asked school authorities,
on behalf of his wife, that a "suitable subject" be found to take the name
of her first (now deceased) husband, Rev. John Cleaveland; in return, she
would pledge a gift of "$25 per year for four years." Daggett was wary
of this request, and indeed of the entire practice. What, he wondered, if
the person chosen should "prove . . . perverse" and have to be expelled?
Would that not mean a "gift . . . lost," an "endeared name disgraced"?
Even so, he proposed "a likely youth," John Irepoah (a Hawaiian), but
this time with the proviso that the patron "consent to his retaining his
present names, with the interposition of Cleaveland between them"—
hence John Cleaveland Irepoah. Eventually, as many as a quarter of the
scholars would carry such "Anglo-American" names. Changed in this
outward way, might they also be changed within? What better means of
symbolizing the larger project of which the school formed such a crucial
part? (And then, too, there was the money to be gained.)[67]

Happy or homesick, renamed or not, the new arrivals would soon be
swept up in the school's ongoing routine. David Brown's letters to his
family and friends (at home in the Cherokee Nation) offer examples of
its leading parts.

Lodging for the scholars is on the second floor of the Academy building,
a space subdivided into small cubicle-like "apartments." In Brown's case:
"I room with Mr. J. Ely, one of the members of this school, who expects to
spend his days in the cause of Christ." Their board comes from the school

steward; hence at mealtimes they repair to his house, which stands just a few yards north of the Academy. About the food, Brown says nothing; probably it seems an unimportant matter alongside "the cause of Christ." The beginnings and ends of their days are not strictly prescribed; Brown writes, "I generally go to bed about 10 o'clock, and rise at 5, & sometimes 6." The Academy tower holds a working bell, which "rings for breakfast about 7." Classes start at nine and run till noon; there is also an afternoon session from two till four. All the instruction takes place on the Academy's lower floor, a single barnlike room with desks arrayed in several long rows. Brown, though a strong student, finds the schedule challenging. He mentions "a library of good books for the Institution," many of which "I wish to read, had I time; but my attention to study, and being with a class, deprives me, at present, of reading any kind of book much, except the Holy Bible." The teaching is supervised by the principal himself, whom Brown and the other scholars "all esteem highly, & we cannot adore the Giver of every good & perfect gift enough, in favoring us with his good instruction." An assistant teacher is also closely involved, and from time to time outsiders are enlisted to help. But much of the regular classroom activity follows a "Lancastrian" model, with the most advanced students tutoring the others. The curriculum remains what it has been from the start: a broad range of a dozen or more subjects. Specific course content is designed to meet the particular background, needs, and talents of each individual scholar. In the immediate aftermath of his arrival, Brown reports: "I am, at present, studying arithmetic, reading, writing, catechism, etc." Six months later, his program comprises "Geography, Latin & English Grammar, Arithmetic, & other things." Later still, he will move on to the "higher branches"; these include Hebrew, Greek, rhetoric, natural philosophy, and astronomy. Religion is a ubiquitous presence. There are morning and evening prayers, at which the scholars read from the Bible—in rotation, a verse or two at a time— with questions from Daggett when they are done. Of course, the chief "devotions" come on Sundays. Thus (again in Brown's words): "[W]e have two sermons . . . preached to us every Sabbath, besides a lecture on Sabbath morning in the school-room, by the Principal." In addition: "[W]e formed what we call a Cherokee prayer-meeting . . . [at which] we pray, sing, & converse in the Cherokee language." Meanwhile, "others of the School meet, at the same time, for that purpose, in their respective languages." Every scholar is obliged to labor at stated intervals on the "agricultural fields"; at one point, Brown mentions that he has been "planting potatoes today," at another, "digging stones." This requirement, never popular, seems "often to unfit them for study for a day or two after they are called out." The twice-yearly vacations (May and September) do, of course, bring changes. In most (not all) cases, scholars are permitted to "go abroad." Brown describes his plans "next May . . . [to] visit some good people in Boston, for a short time, during the vacation." Others travel to nearby villages in Connecticut and Massachusetts (perhaps to homes where they had stayed before enrolling at the Mission School), to New York and Philadelphia, and even beyond.[68]

Inevitably, outsiders would wish to see all this from close-up; hence the school became something of a tourist attraction. By consensus, it was one of three leading "points of interest" in the state of Connecticut. (The other two were Yale College, in New Haven, and the Deaf and Dumb Asylum, in Hartford.) Daggett would periodically complain of the crowding created by "throngs of visitors, some of whom frequently tarry overnight"; his assistant kept a record, which at one point included "200 visitors, during a period of 5 months." David Brown noted that "many ministers come to visit this school, from different parts of the country," and certainly it held great attraction for members of the Protestant clergy. Their enthusiastic impressions lie scattered through the religious press for the pertinent years.[69]

Some of the visitors came with a particular purpose. Thus, for example, Thomas Gallaudet, the principal of the Deaf and Dumb Asylum, journeyed over from Hartford one evening in 1819 in order to meet with "several of these interesting strangers from the islands of the South Sea, and from different tribes of the North American Indians." His goal was to "ascertain how far a conversation could be conducted with them merely by signs and gestures." Gallaudet's work with deaf-mutes had led him to regard signing as a kind of lingua franca, "implanted . . . by the Author of nature . . . in the very constitution of our species"; now he would put this idea to a special test. The results were remarkably confirming. Thomas Hopoo, among others, fielded questions in sign language about his parents, his fellow countrymen, the Hawaiian climate, and "many inquiries of a similar nature, all of which he well comprehended, and to many of which he replied by signs." Sometime later, Hopoo made his own visit to the Deaf and Dumb Asylum, and communicated "by the same means" with the inmates there. All this was expected to be of "immense importance to the missionary to the unlettered heathen." More broadly, it served to link the Mission School with the spirit of human progress in "an age of wonderful experiment."[70]

There were foreign visitors, too. An Englishman named Adam Hodgson traveled to Cornwall—having previously "heard [the Mission School] mentioned with deep interest"—in early March 1821. His experience there, as described in his subsequent book *Letters from North America* (1824), included lengthy conversations with several scholars who "paid me a visit in my room." He was particularly impressed by their polite manners, their academic program (he was able to examine their "trigonometrical copy-books" in detail), and their "devotions" in prayer. He was astonished, too, by the sheer diversity of their cultural backgrounds. He interviewed Daggett, who showed him a handwritten lexicon of English names for "common objects . . . and opposite to them the corresponding names in the different languages of all the pupils who had ever been at the school." Moreover, he received from the principal, as a parting gift, "a copy of the 19th psalm in the language of the Muh-he-con-nuk, or Stockbridge tribe of Indians." All in all, he concluded, "it would be difficult to conceive a more interesting sight than was presented by this school."[71]

Visitors—including authors like Hodgson—were crucial to sustaining the school's base of outside support. And public relations, in a very nearly modern sense, would remain a central focus of its leaders. Time and again, they proposed the publication of "interesting papers," such as "letters passing between the students and their friends" or "an account of the experience of each scholar who is a subject of piety"; these and "other . . . scraps of personal history might be given to the public, and would be beneficial to the School." Christian-sponsored journals, such as *The Religious Intelligencer* and *The Missionary Herald*, formed the front line here; most appeared monthly or bimonthly, with scarcely an issue failing to include some mention of the Mission School. Networks of more informal contact joined the numerous members of local "societies" devoted to the same end.[72] Their task was more difficult than might at first appear, for a current of skepticism about all missionary work ran strong within some sectors of the wider populace. Indeed, this was a major counterforce that would grow alongside, and in close connection with, the Mission School. Supporters rarely acknowledged it—and then only with reluctance—until, at last, it began directly to undermine them.

Anti-mission attitudes brought together an odd mix of "the enlightened"—highly educated, prosperous folk, mostly Unitarians or "moderate" Congregationalists—with Protestant traditionalists from society's lower ranks. ("Swamp Yankees," the latter were sometimes disparagingly called.) Together these groups opposed what they termed "the great missionary delusion." They started with scriptural arguments. Nowhere, they said, did the Bible require massive efforts to assist the heathen; moreover, since God could do everything He might wish, conversion was "taking the work out of His hands." They went on from there to cultural and biological difference. The heathen, they believed, were incapable of "civilization" and genuine religious understanding; hence missionary projects were misconceived from the start.

Significantly, too, their position expressed deep social concerns. The work of the mission-minded they described as "priestcraft"—a sneaky way for "a certain class of our clergy" to gain power and influence, and perhaps eventually to roll back the recently achieved separation of church and state. Local fund-raising for missionary purposes (of a sort on which the Mission School placed heavy reliance) they regarded as "pious fraud, pious tricks," its individual "agents" as little better than itinerant hucksters. They regaled one another with anecdotes like the following: "[T]he other day, one of those privateering priests, who are sent about to beg for the Missions, called at my house and by some means or other worked on the feelings of my family until they gave him five dollars. . . . Now I consider myself swindled out of the money."

In many such stories, women were cast in an especially compromised role—as witless dupes, or enablers, or (in a sense) co-conspirators. One writer deplored the activity of "female societies" in supporting missions; "their tendency," he declared, "is to countenance and encourage mothers and daughters to take the government into their hands." Another asked, "Is it not a fact that in almost every parish . . . every clergyman of a certain class has four or five . . . ladies, some matrons and some maids, whom they have . . . spoiled, by making them believe that the salvation of the heathen principally depends on them . . . filling them with all manner of conceits, pride, vanity, self-consequence, haughty and domineering propensities?" Worse yet, the women involved were liable to conclude "that they can not only convert the heathen abroad, but . . . have a right to govern and give tone to society at home." (Missions, ministers, matrons, and maids: how dangerous that combination! And how much lay at risk: civil society and governance, religious liberty, family life, the racial and gender orders—nothing less. If made real, theirs would be a topsy-turvy world; hence right-thinking folk were bound to push back.) The Mission School, in particular, received some pointed barbs. For example, this: "It is said . . . that the scholars are luxuriously fed; dressed extravagantly; are lawless; learn nothing; and abuse by indolence the liberality of their patrons." Also this: "For what purpose are some of these young 'gentlemen' dressed up in the best attire that this country, Europe, or India can afford, or a rich treasury purchase, and annually brought onto a public stage for exhibition? Is this only to get more money from the public, by contributions when people come to see them?" And, finally, this: "How many wheels there are in this business! Have an Indian show, [and] collect fifty or a hundred dollars, from the public. . . . By the head of Tecumseh, if this wasn't a good plan, when laid!" (In short: It didn't work at all as claimed; instead, it amounted to a fraud on the good intentions, and pocketbooks, of uninformed supporters—in effect, a kind of confidence game.) For some at least, perhaps for a good many, the school seemed virtually to epitomize the fault found with all missionary endeavor.[73]

Against these doubters and dissenters, the school worked tirelessly to maintain itself. Appreciative tributes and, most important, "donations" arrived from around the country and overseas. A Swiss nobleman, the Baron de Campagne, was an especially generous benefactor; his two gifts to "his beloved Cornwall, on which the praying hearts of thousands in our Switzerland are firmly fixed" would enable the purchase of hundreds of books, globes, "mathematical instruments," and a two-year supply of stationery. Such marks of international recognition seemed especially gratifying to the agents, inasmuch as the school "embraces all nations and stands without a competitor in the world." There were other substantial gifts, as well, from ministers, from merchants, from "a nobleman of South Prussia," from the estate of Congressman Elias Boudinot (for whom a Mission School student had been renamed), from John Jay, the famed diplomat and first chief justice of the Supreme Court, from Lydia Sigourney, a celebrated poet and novelist, and (at $2,000, one of the biggest) from a certain Mrs. Lewis of New London, Connecticut. Meanwhile, humble, small-scale contributions—in both money and kind—continued to pour in from countless supporters nearby. These resources were supplemented, on a regular basis, from the funds of the American Board. Finally, the federal government provided subsidies to aid some (not all) of the Indian students; this was part of an official policy "to provide for the Civilization of the Indian tribes."[74]

Part of the local fund-raising involved a door-to-door, "horse and wagon" strategy, but the leaders acknowledged that "people in this region are tired of the solicitation of traveling Agents." Better results would come from "mission boxes" strategically sited in churches, "concerts of prayer" (special meetings organized to promote the cause), and, most of all, collections taken at the annual examinations or other major events. Publicity about the scholars and their various achievements remained central to all such efforts. And the leadership placed special hope on news expected soon from the Hawaiian mission: If that proved favorable, support for the school might increase dramatically.[75]

So it was that many in Cornwall had eyes and ears pointed far to the west during the spring, summer, and fall of 1820. In fact, the first direct reports from that quarter took a full year in transit. But when finally they did arrive, they were nothing short of astonishing. The old island king, Kamehameha, had died not long before. Something of a succession crisis ensued, with the king's son and heir, Liholiho, eventually taking the throne. Through the course of these changes, much in traditional Hawaiian culture—especially religious culture—was overturned. Thus, when the missionaries landed, they received "the interesting intelligence [that] . . . THE KING IS DEAD! THE TABOOS ARE BROKEN! THE IDOLS ARE BURNT! THE MOREEAHS ARE DESTROYED AND THE PRIESTHOOD ABOLISHED!" Nothing else could have given them such an enormous lift; it seemed, quite simply, providential—the work of "that arm alone which sustains the universe." Wrote one: "A great and important Revolution has opened the way for missionaries, and seems to insure their success." Said another: "Christ is overturning the ancient state of things, in order to take possession." Within mere weeks they had fanned out across the islands—founding little churches, beginning farm projects, establishing schools. The new king, his family, and the various satellite chiefs seemed quite ready to accept them and their mission. They felt fully—and literally—blessed.[76]

All this they would describe, in extravagant detail, for their like-minded "brethren" at home. Daggett himself began a many-sided correspondence with several of the missionaries and two or three among the island's native royalty. As a direct result, affecting tales of "accomplishment" circulated widely at Cornwall and elsewhere: of conversions "hopefully anticipated" and native rituals abruptly given up; of lessons "newly learned" and "ancient" beliefs renounced; of Christian chapels built and "pagan altars" torn down; of crosses raised and "idols committed to the flames." For example, one of the returned scholars destroyed a group of "stone gods" lining a path to a native shrine; he did this "in his pious indignation against such an insult to the God of the Christians." In another case, a different scholar approached "several huge stones . . . dignified with the appellation of gods . . . and rolled them into the sea." Indeed, such stories went on and on.[77]

But not all "idols" were treated so roughly; some would be sent back across the ocean to New England, to be set up there on public display. One, in particular, became the focus of extensive comment; hence its long and quite remarkable journey can be retraced even now. At some point in the summer of 1820, King Tamoree (of Atoi) decided to disown his previous religious practice. He reportedly declared (through a translator), "I believe that my idols are good for nothing. . . . I throw them all away." In fact, however, he kept at least a few for a while longer. Thus the following November, Samuel Ruggles, one of the newly arrived missionaries, wrote home to Daggett: "We send by . . . Capt. Bennett [master of a China Trade schooner] a small box containing two of King Tamoree's favorite idols, which he lately presented to us. One is for yourself, and the other is intended for President Day [of Yale College]." Daggett received his part of the shipment in mid-May (1821); he described it as "a piece of wood curiously carved nearly in the form of a human being, with very distorted and disgusting features, and stained black."[78]

This timing was especially propitious; the idol arrived "on the day of our public exhibition" and was immediately incorporated into the official program. Daggett's account continued: "We had, upon this occasion, an Owhyhean Dialogue, spoken on the stage, between Kummooolah, Irepoah, Kriouloo, Whyhee, Arohekaah, Popohe, & Zealand [all, save the last, being Pacific Islanders], during which one . . . entered, as a messenger, & reported the pleasing intelligence received from the Sandwich Islands; upon which the youths gave a shout of approval . . . after which the idol was exhibited, & such observations made upon it, as were thought proper. The Owhyheans then joined in a song, after their native manner, & closed the performance by repeating, in English, the Hymn 'Owhyhee's Idols are no more' . . . [which] was immediately afterwards sung by the choir [composed of local townsfolk], in the gallery." The same object may also have been the source of a $5.36 entry in the school's account, recorded as coming from a Cornwall "charity box . . . by the exhibition of the idol of King Tamoree."[79]

Daggett said nothing about audience reaction when "the idol was exhibited," but we may easily imagine. Excitement, horror, fascination, and, most of all, disgust: There lay the animating spirit of the entire missionary project, its fount of creative (and destructive) energy. On the visible surface, laborers in "the Great Cause" showed only the most giving, most affirmative of motives. But underneath they struggled with feelings of a deeply aversive sort. Heathenism, as they knew it (or construed it), was utterly ugly and loathsome. This attitude, in turn, reflected the binary world in which they lived, where right and wrong, good and evil, salvation and sin, Heaven and Hell, perfection and failure, glory and abomination, formed a set of tightly linked opposites: Be one, be the other, there was nothing in between. Always they sensed a danger that the boundary might blur, that a line might be crossed. Put differently: The good and glorious might somehow be ruined by its awful, toxic underside. Still, together with danger came opportunity; heathenism, and all its doleful accompaniments, could yet be undone. Missionary work was, at bottom, a vast program of cleansing, of purging, of root-and-branch decontamination.

The idol encompassed and sharpened this element, and brought it starkly into view; in Daggett's words, "distorted . . . disgusting . . . and stained black." (Other comments, on other idols, especially favored the word *hideous*. And the "stain," of course, went beyond the matter merely of color.) Moreover, the idol seemed to epitomize deeply held views, throughout the ranks of "the benevolent," about all of Hawaiian life and culture. These would be summed up, several decades later, by a Connecticut preacher in the course of a "commemorative address." Hawaiians, he declared—recalling the situation as of around 1820—"are on nearly the lowest level of social and moral condition. They are a nation of lazy, lying thieves and gamblers, reveling in beastliness. Infanticide sweeps away two-thirds of all children born. . . . The most shocking licentiousness prevails. Woman is a slave. Government is unrestricted tyranny. . . . A more revolting superstition under the name of religion is hardly to be found. Human sacrifices are not infrequent." Here, then, was a sinkhole of filth and rottenness. For mission advocates—in terms both metaphorical and more—it stank to high Heaven. And it begged to be cleaned up.[80]

. . .

Shorn of his idols, King Tamoree (in proper spelling Kaumuali'i) was primed to become a key benefactor—if not a hero—to the missionaries. First, though, he must be reunited with his son, the wandering, mercurial "Prince" George. The story of George's homecoming would be endlessly told and retold—at Cornwall, in the missionary press, and beyond. Perhaps more than any other "intelligence" received from the islands, it gripped, and enraptured, the hearts of school supporters.

The moment has been carefully prepared. The ship *Thaddeus,* the same one that had brought the entire group from New England, carries the "Prince" and a small retinue from Hawaii (today's Big Island) to Atoi (today's Kaua'i), his place of birth. His companions include a wife he has "selected" just days before and two of the missionaries. The ship anchors offshore. Its captain orders "a royal salute of twenty-one guns," which is promptly "returned by the same number from the fort" just opposite. The visitors debark and make their way through a "crowd of natives," aided by "men appointed to clear a passage . . . by beating them off with clubs."

In due course, they reach the palace of King Kaumuali'i. As young George enters, the king rises from a sofa for a "long embrace . . . [pressing] his nose to his son's after the manner of the country." The two of them weep together, unable to speak. Bystanders, too, are greatly affected; one would later recall that "there were no less than one hundred and fifty eyes flowing with tears, and though the house was so full, it was as still & silent as the grave. Not a word was spoken for the space of one half hour." Eventually, the king breaks the silence, but only to say that "his heart is so joyful . . . he could not talk much."

Later George will introduce the missionaries. His father showers them "with tears of affection . . . calling them . . . 'hicanee' (friends) . . . [and] frequently putting his nose to [theirs]." When told of their kindness to his son, the king responds, "'[N]ooe roah aloha America' (It is very good—very great love to America)." He wishes to be "as much a father [to them] . . . as the good people of America had been to his much loved Hoomehoome." (This last is George's birth name.) An elaborate feast is "soon provided . . . consisting of . . . hogs . . . several fowls and a dog cooked after the style of the island, together with potatoes, taro, bananas, cocoanuts, and watermelons, brandy, gin, wines, &c." All present partake "most liberally."

As the hours pass, the king expresses himself more fully. He uses a native interpreter, who learned some English many years before on a visit to New York. Of his newly returned son, he exclaims, "I love him very much, more than I do my other children. . . . I thought he was dead. I cry many times. . . . But he live—he come again—my heart very glad." He lavishes praise on the missionaries, and says to one, "I make you a chief." (However, this offer is politely declined.) They, for their part, attempt "to tell him something about God, but [since] the subject was entirely new to him, . . . he could understand but little." He bestows on his son "two large chests of clothing," control of the nearby fort, a "large and fertile valley in which to dwell," and the position of "second in command" over all the island's people. George is "much elated with his promotion." He finds himself "considered by his countrymen almost as a 'houra' (white man)"; that, too, he enjoys very much. Both king and prince are eager to "have . . . [the missionaries] settle there, and to have other missionaries come out from America by the earliest opportunity."

This account is quickly relayed back to mission headquarters on Hawaii—and from thence to America. The outlook could hardly have seemed brighter.[81]

To be sure, the news from the islands was not entirely positive. Tennooe, his Mission School training notwithstanding, had reverted to "dissipated" ways within weeks of arrival; these included "intemperance and sabbath breaking." Since then, wrote one of his supposed colleagues, "he shuns our society"; moreover, he had readopted "the native habit [clothing]" and thus become virtually unrecognizable. In due course, the nascent church there voted to excommunicate him. The missionaries greatly lamented his "defection," and made "earnest and repeated attempts . . . to reclaim him"—but to no avail. They were led by this to some "salutary reflection" on the danger posed to all their native charges "the moment the restraints of civilized society are removed." From now on, they would have to be ever vigilant.[82]

With others in the native contingent, things went much better. Hopoo, in particular, "was daily and laboriously engaged in the duties of the mission," while gaining "high favor" with King Liho-liho; indeed, the king "had built for him a house near his own." Honoree, too, was "very exemplary" in his endeavors. Moreover, the Americans in the group continued to get a largely sympathetic hearing. Obookiah's personal story held special interest for young islanders, some of whom were heard to remark "me want to be rike-rike (like) Obookiah."[83]

For many at home, these reports were more than enough to justify all the effort previously expended on behalf of missions—and to spur enlarged hopes for the future. At Cornwall, in the closing months of 1821, Mission School authorities planned the dispatch of a second group to the islands. Intended as a reinforcement, it went out the following year with a roster that included three more native scholars. There was even a sense that the little Hawaiian outpost might soon reproduce itself by supplying missionaries "to the neighboring continents and islands"; one supporter plaintively asked, "Are there no more Obookiahs there?" Meanwhile, too, several of Cornwall's Indian scholars—Cherokees and Choctaws, in particular—were preparing a return to their own tribal homelands; once there, they might easily be attached to missions already at work. And well outside the school's official orbit, missionary advocates were bent on establishing a new, interdenominational "fund for the education of heathen youth"—in effect, a fellowship program designed to benefit especially worthy individuals. The organizers aimed to place the recipients "at Cornwall, where the necessary buildings and instructors are already provided, and where, we must not neglect to say, the highest advantages are enjoyed for the formation of the character." In their opinion, "the Foreign Mission School . . . may yet benefit half of the nations."[84]

These goals, in turn, implied a considerable expansion of the school—something the agents had begun to imagine a year or two before. The Academy building, which the town had bequeathed them, felt "cramped and decayed" to many of its occupants. The second-floor dormitory, divided as it was into "crowded apartments," lay so close to the roof that "the heat is very oppressive in summer"; for the same reason, it was "too cold in winter for most of our heathen youth, who are from a warmer climate." It was, in any case, "just sufficient" to hold the current complement of thirty to thirty-five scholars; a larger number would require more space. Thus in the summer of 1822, school leaders proposed the construction of a new building "of two stories [and] . . . of sufficient length and width to accommodate, with lodging apartments, forty or fifty persons." The scholars themselves "might render much assistance in procuring materials." (The latter would include timber from the school's woodlot.) To make way for this, the original Academy could be moved to another location and "there converted to useful purposes." A portion of the requisite funds might be raised locally, but "perhaps $1500" would have to come from the coffers of the American Board. Pending official approval, "considerable might be done by the members of the F. M. School to forward the business, in the fall vacation."[85]

It was a bold idea, and an accurate reflection of the optimistic spirit then prevailing among school supporters. At around the same time, *The Religious Intelligencer* published an essay by "A Friend to the School," assessing its achievements to date and prospects for the future. Six years had passed since the formal adoption of its constitution and more than five since the start of actual operations. Within that period, the school had enrolled approximately fifty youths, sixteen of whom had completed some or all of its "course" and returned to their homelands. Of the latter, most were considered "hopefully pious," or at least "of fair promise"; several had since begun missionary work among their own people. (The outcome was clearest with the returnees to Hawaii, whose every action was observed, and recorded, by the "mission family" there. Their Indian counterparts seemed harder to track, once removed from the vicinity of Cornwall.)[86]

The writer's conclusion was emphatic: "The experiment has been tried, and has proved successful. Heathen youth can be civilized, and instructed, and prepared for extensive usefulness among their countrymen within a limited period and at a comparatively small expense.... No effort in behalf of the heathen world ... has ... resulted in greater benefit." To be sure, at the time of its beginning, "no institution similar ... in its object and plan, had ever before been known.... It was entirely novel, and original, and by many was considered doubtful as to the issue. But all doubts are removed. The plan is practicable and eligible, and what is more, it meets the approbation of the Great Head of the Church." Given such clear-cut results, it seemed plausible—indeed necessary—to move toward a much enlarged future: "Now what has been done for a few youths on this plan, may be done for many." Thus the writer was fully in favor of the proposal to construct a new building sufficient to accommodate "a considerable increase of the present number of scholars." He urged as well the purchase of more land for the creation of a substantial farm—this in order to strengthen the teaching of "the art of agriculture" while, at the same time, making the school more nearly self-sufficient. (He also recommended the hiring of a special "teacher of divinity," since Daggett's declining health no longer permitted him to provide a full measure of "theological education." Heathen pupils could not be transferred to "our common seminaries"; instead, they needed "peculiar treatment, and instruction in a peculiar manner, which is well understood at the Mission School.")[87]

Similar praise could be heard in many quarters both inside and outside Cornwall. Gifts would arrive with admiring tributes to the school's part in "evangelizing the world." Visitors would come away with "no words to express the gratification . . . afforded me," or a conviction that "it certainly proposes the best means of diffusing divine and human light where they are most needed." The annual examinations invariably produced a round of loud hosannas. And then there was the Baron de Campagne's assurance that "the praying hearts of thousands in our country [Switzerland] . . . are kindly fixed" on the school.[88]

Records internal to the school told a different, more complicated story. Read today, they disclose threads of difficulty dating back almost to the start.

One involved nothing less than the "academical" program itself. With scholars who spanned such a vast range—in age, cultural background, prior experience and training, not to mention individual mental endowments—it was hard to establish a common pedagogical center. Indeed, the exact opposite seems to have prevailed. As John Prentice, the school's assistant principal, put it in a letter to the American Board: "There are here, youths brought from each hemisphere and from various climates, regions, and nations, whose languages, habits, and customs are very dissimilar. . . . To manage them wisely, is no easy service. They cannot be placed in classes as it is with our own children. There must be almost as many classes as scholars."[89]

Mastery of written and spoken English, the necessary foundation of all their learning, presented an especially difficult challenge. Daggett complained very pointedly, with regard to the Pacific Islanders: "They come here where they associate & converse almost exclusively with their countrymen, & obtain only a smattering of very imperfect English. . . . They go through with their spelling book, & read for months and years in the Testament, with almost no advantage." Unless they could learn "the structure of the language," there was little chance "that it can be made the medium of conveying much instruction"; here, then, lay "an insuperable barrier between their minds & the efforts of their teachers." There were implications, too, for their spiritual development. When, at one point, several came to Daggett to profess their faith, he couldn't properly examine them because they "understand our language so imperfectly."[90]

Accordingly, the principal recommended that thenceforth individual youths "selected for education" while still "unacquainted with English" should be placed "in respectable Christian families" for up to three years, in order to gain a requisite level of language proficiency *before* enrolling at the school. Such was, in fact, the strategy tried in a few cases. Still, the problem was never truly surmounted. In the fall of 1822, when three of the Hawaiian scholars were readying to return home with the second mission group, Daggett warned that "friends of the cause will probably be disappointed in finding they have advanced so little in their English education." Unfortunately, he could "see no prospect that they would improve much more, if they were to stay here another 4 or 5 years." This comment squared with many others scattered through the school records, in which individuals were described as "dull," "insensitive," "indifferent," "incapable of learning," and so on. Indeed, as time passed, the frequency of Daggett's complaints increased and their tone sharpened. Eventually, he concluded that "a considerable portion of the scholars are not such as to intellect, as that we can hope they will *ever* attain an education to be distinguishingly useful."[91]

"Discontent" and "indiscipline" formed another area of concern. In offering general statements about the school, Daggett preferred to emphasize the positive; for example, "the scholars are, I believe, universally satisfied with their . . . treatment, respectful to their teachers, attentive to their studies, & give evidence of unusual seriousness." But when it came to particular "cases," his comments often went in the opposite direction. One student was "peevish, & fretful & troublesome," a second "fickle & boyish," a third "very obscene and indecent," a fourth "very obstinate & ungovernable," a fifth "vain, impudent, & extravagant"; a sixth "of very turbulent temper." (A list like this might be extended almost indefinitely.)[92]

Understood from the standpoint of the scholars themselves, these portrayals may well have reflected acute forms of personal distress. A considerable number were said to show "averseness" or, simply, "unhappiness." A young New Zealander seemed "extremely nervous and almost insane." One Cherokee youth was "so discontented & homesick that he has made very little progress in his study"; another "manifests a suspicious & gloomy disposition, which renders him unhappy & unpleasant."

(The same scholar sometimes exhibited "a considerable degree of mental derangement.") An Oneida boy had to be dismissed because he was "subject to a childish disorder (wetting his bed)." And one of the Hawaiians acted the part of "a poor exile, despondent and at times almost heartbroken."[93]

A suggestion, in the opening months of 1823, that the school be moved from its "retired" location in Cornwall to "a place of greater public resort," drew from the agents an unusually candid appraisal. By this account (sent privately to the leaders of the American Board), the scholars had shown such weak character that the proposed change would likely "prove fatal . . . [to] . . . their morals" and thus to "the institution" itself. They were, after all, "simple, uninformed, and inexperienced Foreigners . . . credulous, easily flattered, easily imposed upon, and unable to make much discrimination . . . [among] those around them."[94]

Weakness of character (if such it was) led, inevitably, to specific acts of misconduct. There was "the sin of drunkenness." One scholar bought a pint of brandy, "on which he drank through the day." Another "went away to a black family about three miles distant, and lay all night in a state of intoxication." Still others had to be expelled for chronic "intemperance." There were occasional incidents of theft. The worst involved three Cherokee youths whose money was taken "from their trunks and portmanteau . . . undoubtedly . . . by some of the students." After a careful search, some of the stolen dollars were found "under one of the beds," but the culprit was never identified. There was fraudulent dealing. Debts were incurred and not repaid, books or other property removed under false pretenses. There were bitter arguments between scholars and at least occasional outbursts of physical violence. Tamoree "raged" at a fellow islander, and reduced him to tears. A Malay youth stabbed another with a knife (fortunately without causing serious injury). A Chippewa boy wrote privately to the principal that certain of his Indian classmates were harassing him: "[T]hey kick me sometimes . . . and very soon I must be kill here if I stay here any longer." There was rank disobedience and failure of "subordination" to the will of the authorities. Examples included a large number of unauthorized absences, "truancy," and "keeping improper company." There were also times when "considerable uneasiness & disturbance was excited among the students" with respect to the school's internal "regulations."[95]

To be sure, these occurrences were spread out over several years, and some scholars—indeed a good many—behaved well enough to earn official words of approval. Still, the cumulative impact of so much disruption, taken together with the "academical" disappointments, brought Daggett to moments of near despair. At one point when Evarts admitted to his own "anxious thoughts respecting the F.M.S.," Daggett "most heartily sympathized," and added this: "I have long been convinced that something must be done to raise its character, or it must come to naught." A bit later he spoke of "a crisis with regard to the F.M.S., which demands, I think, some special exertions to be made by its friends."[96]

Health and illness presented an additional range of problems—different but no less worrying. School reports made frequent mention of these, most often with respect to particular individuals ("down sick," "very much out of health," "badly indisposed"), but sometimes in a more generalized way ("the School has been considerably interrupted this winter by sickness"). Specific illnesses included consumption, cold, dysentery, and, in one instance, a "dangerous . . . disorder prevalent among people destitute of moral restraint" (gonorrhea perhaps?). Seven youths died at the school, six of them Pacific Islanders—starting with Obookiah, and including each of three who came from the Marquesas. Presumably, those from tropical regions were especially vulnerable owing to New England's unfamiliar (harsh) climate.[97]

The authorities acknowledged some responsibility here, "endeavoring to do all we can, both by diet & exercise, for the health of the students." Whenever one of them fell seriously ill, he was moved into the steward's house for hands-on care. In an apparently typical case, a Delaware Indian boy contracted severe diarrhea; almost immediately he "was taken into the family by Mrs. Northrup [the steward's wife] who was directed to nurse him & give him a proper diet." He died anyway, prompting Daggett to write that "the health of the scholars ought to be taken up, this spring, as a very serious matter."[98]

Yet another potential source of trouble was the feeling created by ethnic and cultural difference. The most important divider within the ranks of the scholars involved Pacific Islanders versus American Indians. This was expressed in certain quite tangible ways. Money was one such; Indian students often arrived at the school with a roll of dollars in their pockets (or trunks). Daggett saw this as likely to have unfortunate consequences and urged that all private holdings be deposited with him. "A considerable part of the Scholars [i.e., the islanders] cannot have money," he wrote, "and for some to have it produces invidious & unpleasant feelings among them, & lays temptation before them." Clothing might also become a sore point, so, once again, the principal sought to level the field by creating a single school-wide standard—simplicity for all.[99]

More broadly, it was clear that like would mainly associate with like. And, in certain respects, the school actually encouraged cliquing. It was essential, for example, that every scholar should retain good command of his native language (whatever it might be); otherwise, his "usefulness" at the point of returning home would be compromised. Conversation among "fellow-countrymen" was an obvious means to that end; likewise the separate prayer meetings for the members of each natal group. At the same time, there was concern lest the boundaries between groups become too hard and fast—creating invidious, and tension-arousing, distinctions.

Meanwhile, alongside these now-familiar stresses and difficulties, a new chain of events had begun to unwind at the very heart of the school's life.

On April 12, 1823, Daggett sent a private letter to Jeremiah Evarts, secretary of the American Board, in order to "call your attention to a subject which appears to be deeply connected to the welfare of the F.M.S." The school steward, he noted, "has generally had a girl, or young woman, as cook in his family, who is, of course, much in the company of the scholars, when they go to their meals, work about the house, or occasionally visit the kitchen." Two years previous, there had been a problem (apparently unmentioned at the time) "of improper intimacy between the hired girl & one or two of the colored boys [i.e., the scholars] which gave us a great deal of trouble." The authorities had responded quickly and decisively by "sending the girl away"; that seemed to take care of it. But now, unfortunately, they faced "another case of this kind, which I fear may be of very serious consequences to one of our most promising Indian scholars and indeed to the reputation of the School." In the same letter, Daggett mentioned that "Northrup wants money . . . to settle all his accounts, before he resigns his Stewardship, which will be the first of May." (John Northrup had replaced Henry Hart as resident steward the previous year.) In fact, these two things—the troubling "case" and the steward's abrupt resignation—were directly joined. "One of our most promising Indian scholars" was a Cherokee youth named John Ridge; he and Sarah Northrup, the steward's fifteen-year-old daughter, had fallen deeply in love. By the standards of the time theirs was, for certain, an "improper intimacy"—and something that might well prove, in the principal's alarmed words, "of very serious consequences . . . to the reputation of the School."

As a later account would put it: "[A]mong all who came to the school from strange lands, the little heathen Cupid, entering uninvited, was the mischief-maker."[100]

Cornwall

Visitors to Cornwall today see a place both similar to and different from the Cornwall of the early nineteenth century. Its physical size and shape are the same: same boundaries, same hills and valleys, same rivers and streams, same central "plain" where the first of the "scholars" fetched up nearly two hundred years ago. Its population, in bare numbers, is also quite similar: 1,600 then, about 1,750 now. As before, the town is a collection of small settlements (villages) and more widely scattered homesteads. A few neighborhoods have shrunk, or vanished entirely; others have been enlarged. But, taken as a whole, what's there is roughly the old configuration.

At least outwardly. But look around for the inward dimension, and one finds much else that has changed. Many local residences are now second homes for city dwellers (mostly from New York City, a two-hour drive to the south), though the year-round folk are still a majority. There is a sense, too, of a divided community: "upstairs downstairs," to use the title of the celebrated television series. The second-home own-ers are well-off professionals and businesspeople. The year-rounders are largely middle and working class; indeed, some work *for* the other group—mowing their lawns and tending their gardens in summer, clearing their driveways of snow in winter. As one longtime resident explains, "Many of these folks just piece together a living, a little of this, a little of that."

·   ·   ·

I start my own visit with the village of West Cornwall, where the Housatonic River rushes through from the north. My entry point is a covered bridge, a hundred yards long, of boarded construction, and resting on a single stone pier—very picturesque, classic New England. First put up in about 1864, and subject thereafter to rot, storms, and recurrent floods, the bridge has been rebuilt several times. In the middle part of the nineteenth century, West Cornwall emerged as a commercial focus for the entire township—with a post office, a hotel, a school, a scissors factory, a smithy, a cluster of local stores, and assorted mills lining the river. No longer that sort of hub, it now sports a restaurant, art galleries, trinket shops, a bed-and-breakfast, and other tourist-themed establishments, while still retaining the look of an old mill village.

I drive farther in, turn north, and climb to the top of Cream Hill, where open views stretch as far as the Catskills in New York State. No less is true of other elevated points throughout the town, but most of the land is wooded today, and a good deal is actually state forest. Like all of the rural Northeast, Cornwall has gone through an ecological "succession"—from the dense wilderness encountered by the first settlers (1740s), to a predominance of cleared farmland (by 1800), to a gradual process of reforestation (beginning in the late nineteenth century and continuing throughout the twentieth). Old cellar foundations and crumbling stone walls, resting now in deep woods, are stark reminders of that different past.

Near the town's northern border sits a three-hundred-acre preserve, known as the Yelping Hill Association. Founded in the 1920s, it is owned as a corporation, with twenty-four leaseholds and a vaguely communitarian ethos. Its resident members are a special slice of Cornwallites; most are artists, academics, and other professional folk. Farther east lies Cornwall Hollow, a small cluster of working farms. In fact, farming has been coming back to these parts, after many decades of decline. Some of this has a niche aspect: dairying that produces unpasteurized milk, the raising of specialty beef cattle, food crops grown under strictly organic protocols. The Hollow also holds Cornwall's biggest single monument, honoring its most illustrious early resident, Maj. Gen. John Sedgwick. This doughty old soldier commanded an army corps in the Civil War; the monument includes a tall obelisk, a cannon, and several neatly stacked pyramids of large cannonballs.

From here, the road drops down through the lower part of North Cornwall, a wooded area partly held as a nature conservancy. The trees—evergreens such as hemlock, fir, spruce, and pine, plus deciduous oaks and maples—are typical of those found throughout the town. They are also subject to modest forays of logging. (No clear-cutting; "trimming" only.) Landowners contract the work out to interested residents; the product is sold both locally and elsewhere.

A short distance farther on comes Cornwall Center, the town's original point of settlement. But this is no center anymore; its housing is sparse and scattered, its roadways in need of repair. To be sure, its historical importance has not been forgotten. A tall wooden post, set just above a crossroads, carries the following inscription: HERE WAS SITE OF FIRST MEETING HOUSE, STOCKS AND PILLORY, PARADE GROUND. Religion, law, the military: the undoubted foundations of early New England town life.

Now I cut back to the south, on a good-size state highway. Along one side stands Mohawk Mountain Ski Resort—a cluster of brown buildings set beneath a swath of snowy trails (winter is on its way) that angle toward the top of a tall ridge. It's nothing fancy; no skier would trade Stowe, Vail, or Sun Valley for this place. However, Mohawk Mountain has been important, and integral, to the life of Cornwall for decades. Dozens of local people are employed there, local people enjoy skiing there, local people hold community events there—an annual rummage sale, a firemen's ball, family parties and receptions.

Still farther south, a rough dirt road climbs to a ghostly place called Dudleytown. This is Cornwall's internal frontier; the land is high, the forest especially dense. It still supports some local enterprise—logging, for example—but hardly any habitation. Several generations ago, it was a substantial, and quite distinctive, community. Its residents were considered outliers; most were poor, some were derelict, none were connected to the town's core families. On driving into it today, one sees few signs of life—at least of human life. It's a good place, however, to find the town's resident wildlife: deer, bear, raccoons, bobcats, fishers, coyotes, fox. And it's a reminder of the way Cornwall may have looked to the original settlers.

My tour has been tracing a circle: from northwest, to northeast, southeast, and southwest. This leads finally to the settlement known as Cornwall Bridge. (Outsiders sometimes refer to the entire town as "the Cornwalls"; I am learning why.) Like West Cornwall, the Bridge (as it's called locally) was once a commercial center—and, to some extent, remains so. There are logging offices, retail stores, gas stations, all within the narrow compass of barely a quarter mile. The actual bridge that identifies this place is an impressively arched construction, made from concrete and rising high above water level. The river, too, is impressive; at least once in the past, its flooding and ice jams entirely destroyed the bridge. Along its edges lie remnants of the iron foundries that once flourished here. Local schoolchildren still come to search for bits of slag tossed out a century or two ago from ancient blast furnaces.

This completes the rim of the circle, leaving only the midpoint—what today is called Cornwall Village. In previous eras, it was known, variously, as South Cornwall, the Valley, Cornwall Plain (or Cornwall Plains, or simply the Plain). The shifting nomenclature reflects both its geography—as the lone flat area of any size in the entire township—and its particular history. Once enshrouded in thick forest, it has passed through several stages: pasture and farming, satellite community, and for the past several decades civic center for all "the Cornwalls."

The logical place to begin this part of my tour is at the west end of Pine Street, in front of an attractive framed building painted white. Originally a carriage house, it serves at present as the home of the town's Historical Society. The society holds a trove of records and mementos from the Mission School; the curators serve as de facto custodians of its history.

A quarter mile to the east stands a stately old residence where, following his retirement as school principal, Herman Daggett moved with his wife. (They had no children.) The house presents a rambling arrangement of wings and dormers, some of which have been added in recent years; in the principal's time, it must have been a good deal smaller. (I'm told about one unusual feature of the interior: a door leading to the attic, with HERMAN DAGGETT boldly inscribed on one of the panels.) Behind the house, to the east, the land slopes up through broad fields to a craggy ridgeline. Indeed, all sides of this gentle valley (or "plain") are lined by twisted and convoluted landforms.

Continuing along, I reach a little crossroads; on the other side lies the village center. To the left stands the Town Hall, an impressive structure erected in the late nineteenth century of local stone, with broad Palladian windows spanning its upper story. Directly in front is a large sign presenting the headlines of the town's history: founded in 1740, part of what was then known as the "western lands," and so on. About now, I begin to notice a curious feature of the built environment; nearly everywhere there are cut granite stones, each approximately three feet tall, standing like stelae in carefully plotted rows. Some hold embedded iron rings, for tethering the horses that once traveled these roads. Most of the others are relics of fences whose inner sections (wooden pickets) have long since disappeared. Separately and together, they impart a certain solemnity to the entire scene.

Next comes the lower end of the town common. Tall shade trees mark its rim; the center is a true green. No buildings remain there now, but in several spots official markers recall the past. The southeast corner was the original location of the First Church, where so much Mission School activity once converged. Some of this I can easily imagine: the gravity of regular Sabbath-day devotions, with the scholars in their Sunday best arrayed on a special bench along one side; the excitement of the annual "exhibition day" programs, with a crowd of eager spectators looking on; the sorrow of Obookiah's elaborate funeral.

West of the meetinghouse, at the upper edge of the green, a bronze plaque rests on the site of the old Academy building, the school's literal center. I've brought along a sketch from that time, for help in conjuring its image: gambrel roof, with small dormers and a squared-off bell tower at the front; rows of shuttered windows lining each side; main entrance tucked neatly into one corner. In my mind's eye I can glimpse the scholars passing in and out, a medley of size, age, color, clothing, demeanor. I note also the "grave yet kindly" figure of the principal, and the earnest young men who serve as his assistants. I watch the steward and members of his "domestic" staff scurrying about to keep things in good order. I note the comings and goings of individual townspeople brought thither on some errand (or perhaps from simple curiosity).

Fifty yards to the south, another plaque, at another corner of the common, shows the location of Kellogg's General Store. There the school procured a range of "necessaries": foods not grown in its own fields, hard goods, stationery supplies. A short distance to the north stood another Kellogg building, what was once the storekeeper's home. Indeed, it's still there, converted now to the town clerk's office. Directly opposite, an imposing Federal-style building invokes still more of the school's history; this was the official residence of the principal. Set atop a small knoll, it commands a view of the entire green. Today it is larger, and grander, than was the case two centuries ago. A magnificent stonework facade rises above the lawn in front; a pair of lion statues guard the entrance. (Clearly, however, these are recent additions.)

Soon I'm back on the road, proceeding north. An impressive Congregational church, built in 1842 to replace the original one on the green, stands off to the right. Its entrance, framed by four large columns, its gleaming white facade, its rows of tall, evenly spaced windows, its pointed steeple, all shout Greek Revival. Just beyond lies another large building of similar form and vintage. This one is vacant today and in somewhat dilapidated condition; over the years, it has housed a succession of schools, the last of which supplied its present name, Rumsey Hall.

And then I reach another early house—a substantial framed dwelling, its architecture conforming to the boxy mode so characteristic of nineteenth-century New England. This was the home originally of the Mission School steward—John Northrup and family—during several critical years. The current owner, alerted to my interest, is ready and welcoming. A long driveway loops around in front, amid a spacious lawn, magnolia trees, and carefully laid out flower beds. I enter by the front door, crossing a large stone step, and find myself in a modestly appointed center hall. To the right, a doorway opens on the keeping room, which stretches the full north-south length of the house. ("Keeping room" is what the Northrups would have called it; today we would say living room.) On the east wall stands a chimney with fireplace; but both were added later on. There is simple wood paneling all around, and the numerous windows create an airy, expansive feeling. The room is large, roughly twenty-eight by fifteen feet; but even so, I wonder, Could it really have served as a dining space for some three dozen scholars? My eyes dart around; I try to reconstruct. A long table here? Some short ones there? Maybe benches or stools, instead of proper chairs? Whatever the arrangement, a very tight squeeze. Across the hall is a small space used now as a study. Of more importance is a somewhat larger room, on the northwest corner—now a parlor, once the kitchen. An ancient chimney, with stone-built base and hearth, dominates the south wall. The wide fireplace includes a beehive oven at the rear. Here, I imagine, the steward's wife and her "assistants" cooked for the entire school. And here, too, the space seems awfully cramped.

A rather narrow stairway with attractively fashioned railing leads up from the center hall to the second floor. There, near the front, are two similarly shaped bedrooms. Perhaps these were for the Northrups' children. I wonder, in particular, about their daughter Sarah, who would come to play such a key role in the larger story of the Mission School. Along the west wall, the layout becomes more complex. At one corner is a large master bedroom. For father and mother Northrup? At the very back is another hallway, and then, curled in behind, a tiny (ten feet by eight) utility room. I jump on this: What more likely spot for the "sick room" where young John Ridge was lodged for more than a year? Another crucial part of the larger story.

Nearby, a steep flight of stairs leads up to the large, entirely open attic, with its original beams and chimney stack prominently displayed. (The chimney turns here from stone to brick, so as to emerge above the roof in brick profile—evidently considered a more fashionable look.) The attic could well have been used as a sleeping space for servants; such, I know, was true of other houses built and occupied during the same period. It may also have served as an extra dormitory, for lodging a few of the scholars. While descending the stairs to regain the ground floor, I give one more glance into the keeping room. Used (during the school's lifetime) as a dining hall every day, it might also have hosted special occasions. Perhaps, for example, a wedding? Then I take my leave and am back outside on the street.

There are two more local houses with direct links to the Mission School. One was the home of Rev. Timothy Stone, where Obookiah was taken when sick—and where, eventually, he died. Unfortunately, however, a visit to this house is precluded by the illness of its current owner. The other is the original residence of the Gold family, a few hundred yards north of the green. As seen today, the Gold house has the same exterior look as the steward's: wood-framed, Federal-style, with double chimney and several dormers. But inside it has a more complex design. There is a center hall but no large keeping room. Instead, a parlor, a dining room, a large kitchen, plus a couple of small service rooms on the first floor, and three fair-size bedrooms on the second. From here "Col." Benjamin Gold performed many services at the behest of the agents: raised funds, gathered supplies, hosted important visitors. And here the family occasionally boarded a scholar or two—presumably, an overflow from the main school buildings.

The tour is ending; it has, for certain, lessened the distance between my own world and that of the school—between story and storyteller. Before

I leave, I spend a final hour with a local resident who speaks of something that draws the two worlds even closer.

Summer 2007. The owners of a fine home on Cream Hill have convened a meeting of their friends and neighbors to discuss a matter of rising public interest—rising in Cornwall, rising across the country. They begin the discussion on a personal note. During the past few years four members of their extended family, sisters and cousins, have come here in order to be married. Soon their own daughter will be visiting with her intended—but with a different prospect. This pair is no less bonded, no less in love; but for them marriage is legally impossible (at least at that time, in the state of Connecticut). The reason is simple: Whereas with previous couples the partners were of opposite sex, the hosts' daughter is betrothed to another woman. From this rather poignant starting point, discussion within the group ranges across a variety of conjoined topics—the law, religion, social mores, politics, civil rights. Apparently, those present share a similar perspective; they agree the law must be changed, so that all should enjoy the same opportunity for marriage. The question is: How to make this possible? How to create change? The meeting continues for most of an afternoon. Near the end one of the participants stands to add a different perspective—that of history. Almost two hundred years before, he notes, their town faced a similar "question of marriage." Then, too, it was about a couple—in fact, two couples—whose love went against traditional norms. The women involved were local and of "white" extraction (one of them ancestrally related to the hosts of the current discussion and their daughter); the men were Indians from the Cherokee Nation. Many in the community were opposed—vehemently, even violently, so. Marriage was for persons of the same race, they said; the Almighty had willed it so, and ancient tradition fully concurred.[1]

You must not do this! Then and now: The line between them stretches long and taut.

~ PART THREE ~

CRISIS

CHAPTER FIVE

American Paradox:
The Indelible Color Line

Intimacy across racial boundaries—love, sex, marriage—has a history reaching back to the earliest years of European colonization. In 1619, the Virginia planter John Rolfe famously courted and married the local Indian princess, Pocahontas. Because such liaisons were unusual— indeed, at that point unprecedented—Rolfe felt obliged to explain his choice in a long letter to the colony's governor, Sir Thomas Dale. Fellow colonists, he knew, would see him as indulging "a hungry [sexual] appetite, to gorge myself with incontinency"; they could imagine no other motive for attraction to "one whose education hath been rude, her manners barbarous . . . and so discrepant in all nurture from myself." In rebuttal, Rolfe avowed his "settled and long continued affection" for the princess, and his strong wish to "endeavor to make her a Christian." She, for her part, evinced both "great appearance of love to me . . . [and] the desire to be taught and instructed in the knowledge of God." In short, the match joined love and religion; hence it would gain the governor's blessing—and achieve, in due course, a lasting celebrity. Many eminent Virginians, down through Thomas Jefferson's time and beyond, would be proud to claim descent from it.[1]

Rolfe's letter also spoke to a prevalent English sense of superiority toward Indians. In fact, the same attitude shaped relations with many others: the Irish, the Jews, Africans, and, to a lesser extent, various peoples of the European continent.[2] But its basis was cultural, not biological.

Pocahontas was a case in point—scorned for her crude manners, her lack of education, her "paganism."

Such was the general pattern among the first generation or two of colonists, with Indians seen to fit the ancient concept of "the noble savage." They were admired for their "fine stature" and "clean-jointed" physique. Their skin color was taken as a variant of white, its "tawny" hue the result either of intense exposure to the sun or of their custom of rubbing their bodies with bear grease. Their manner seemed dignified, their physical courage beyond doubt. Their political organization—tribal chiefdoms, sometimes grandly mischaracterized by the English as "empires"—was freely acknowledged. Even their religious practice, including their worship of a "Great Spirit," could be understood, if not approved.[3]

Their everyday cultural ways were another matter. In "habit" (clothing), in housing, in diet, in many aspects of technology, in speech (and also in their lack of literacy), in the impermanency of their settlements, Indians seemed undeniably "barbarous." Still, these and other perceived deficiencies were not understood as fixed. Indians, no less than other peoples, were educable; with careful training and practice, they might sooner or later become "civilized." The English themselves had once been "backward," prior to being lifted toward their current lofty status through the help of invading Romans and Anglo-Saxons (among others). The native people of America could aspire to the same, with the colonists serving as exemplars and teachers.[4]

These hopeful expectations were framed by a belief in the underlying unity of mankind. Humans of every type were thought to have descended from a single act of creation (a theory that would later be known as "monogenesis"); differences among them reflected environmental pressures, not biology or genes. To be sure, humans—and the entire cosmos—presented, in full vertical array, a "great chain of being," stretching from the Almighty Himself at the top to the lowliest animate organisms on the bottom. As elaborated with increasing precision in the eighteenth century by (among others) the eminent Swedish naturalist Carolus Linnaeus, this idea placed white people above the tawny Indians, with the latter in turn outranking "Moors" and Africans. But, again, these positions could be changed over time. Indeed, all groups might eventually rise together—toward the pinnacle that was God's kingdom and the "end times" of His ultimate triumph.[5]

Under the circumstances, there was no explicit bar to Indian-white contact—up to and including "intimacy." Indeed, at least a few colonists openly advocated intermarriage. For example, William Byrd of Virginia, ever eager to advance the cause of Christianity, bantered that "a sprightly lover is the most prevailing missionary that can be sent among these, or any other infidels." And Robert Beverley, Byrd's contemporary and author of the first history of Virginia, sounded a similar note; if only his fellow colonists had tried intermarriage on some considerable scale, "in all likelihood many . . . of the Indians would have been converted by this kind method."[6]

In truth, the Rolfe-Pocahontas match was extraordinary; no similar case involving English persons of such prominence can be discovered through the entire span of the seventeenth century. Surely, there were some less formal liaisons—though the surviving records afford only an occasional glimpse. Colonists showed, from the start, a degree of sexual curiosity about their native neighbors—witness their fixation on Indian "nakedness." Some of them ran off "to take up their abode with the Indians in a profane course of life"; these, almost certainly, formed intimate relationships with Indian peers. Others were captured in the course of wars, were integrated into native communities, and acquired Indian spouses. The most famous of the latter group was Eunice Williams, daughter of a leading Massachusetts minister. Taken as a child from her home in Deerfield in 1704, she elected to remain with her Mohawk captors for the rest of her very long life. She married a Mohawk and became in all ways "Indianized." Her choices electrified—and horrified—colonists throughout New England and beyond. But it was the cultural, not the biological, aspect that especially concerned them—her preference for "savage" ways (and indeed for Catholicism, since her captors were part of a Jesuit mission community outside Montreal).[7]

On the whole, then, little, from the early years, seems to reflect feelings of a specifically *racial* revulsion among the "settler" population at large. However, revulsion would develop, more and more, during the early and middle decades of the eighteenth century. By then, colonists' perception of the Indians' color had begun to darken. No longer was it plausible to regard them as fundamentally white; instead, they were "red" or even, as some said, "black." In fact, it was Indians themselves who adopted—not to say invented—"red" as a mark of their own distinctiveness, and colonists would increasingly follow the same usage. Moreover, the growing presence of African slaves invested the whole matter of color difference with new and heightened meaning; pigmentation, behavior, social position, and inborn character were increasingly seen as linked. By this time, large numbers of Indians were themselves enslaved (mainly in New England, the southern colonies, and the West Indies). Some had been taken in wars—"enemy combatants," in the parlance of today—while others were sentenced to slavery by colonial courts following criminal prosecution and conviction.[8]

Hence the term *redskin*, rarely encountered prior to 1750, would now become (for whites) a stereotype conjuring a raft of negative images—degraded status, violence, deceit, shiftlessness, and, most pointedly, "savagery."[9] All of these were thought to characterize Indians *as Indians;* in short, Indians had become racialized, as never before. (So, too, had the colonists, though the meanings attached to their whiteness were diametrically opposed.)

The change was owing to a number of intertwined factors. The project to educate native people, such as it was, seemed to have borne little fruit, and parallel efforts at Christian conversion had also fallen short; most of the early New England "praying towns," for example, were languishing badly. The Indian—again, in stereotype—had supposedly rejected "civilization"; more and more, the two seemed antithetical. But, most telling by far, "Indian wars" had taken—and continued to take—a large toll in colonists' lives and treasure. (Never mind that most such wars were far more ruinous on the other side.) Anxiety, terror, and outrage rose in direct proportion. Especially along the ever-widening frontier, site of the bloodiest, most persistent conflicts, anti-Indian feeling reached new levels of virulence. In the 1760s, Sir William Johnson of New York, a preeminent trader and diplomat with Indians, described the deteriorating situation to imperial authorities in London. Throughout the backcountry, he wrote, colonists "murder, robb [sic], and otherwise grossly misuse all Indians they could find." Moreover, they treated the native population "with contempt much greater than they had ever experienced" before.[10]

Somewhat paradoxically, it was on or near the frontier that cross-racial intimacy also reached new levels. Warfare with Indians was regularly admixed with trade. And wherever there was trade, there were white traders. And wherever there were white traders, there were female Indian "consorts" and "bed-fellows." From these alliances, most of which were never formalized, came a growing population of mixed-race offspring. Both consorts and offspring would, in turn, play a vital role in the trade. They were translators, negotiators, facilitators, "intermediaries" in every possible sense; as such, they were conspicuous. So it was, on both sides, that the potential for racial "inter-mixture" became real.[11]

In the later part of the century, the Revolutionary struggle, the transatlantic cultural movement known as the Enlightenment (with its deep faith in human progress), and, not least, the "spirited resistance" of Indians to white dominance would together force a process of reconsideration around race. "All men are created equal," announced the Declaration of Independence, in starkly unambiguous terms. However, practice and experience would repeatedly contradict this principle—most obviously in the case of enslaved blacks. A nascent antislavery movement gained some ground in the immediate post-Revolution years, then faded under the weight of massive economic interest and anti-black prejudice; henceforth discussion of fundamental rights could ignore all so-called Negroes. With Indians, the case was different. White or red, noble or degraded, were they not "men"? And, as the land's original occupants, did their claims to recognition not equal, or even surpass, those of white citizens? Indeed, these claims could now be backed with impressive political and military might. What came to be known as the Old Northwest produced a series of tribal "confederacies" barring the way to white expansion. In the Southeast, the presence of five large and independent Indian nations—Cherokee, Choctaw, Creek, Chickasaw, and Seminole—had a similarly limiting effect.[12]

Meanwhile, some in the leadership of the nascent United States sought to breathe fresh life into the old plan to lift native people out of their "savage" state. President George Washington and his secretary of war, Henry Knox, declared the start of an official "civilization policy," in which the resources of government would be directly engaged. Its basic goals were threefold: to turn Indians from hunters into settled agriculturalists; to draw them fully into the orbit of Christianity; and to attach them to the principle of private, as opposed to communal, ownership of property. (No matter—regarding the first point—that many in the native population had long engaged in farming, something white Americans were unable, or unwilling, to see. What *did* matter, a great deal, was the way success with these plans might bring a drastic reduction of Indians' footprint on the land, and thus open vast new territories to white settlement.)[13] Specially commissioned agents were dispatched to Indian country, with plows, looms, cookware, livestock, and other equipage of "civilization," for general distribution there.

If the Washington administration took the first steps with all this, it was Jefferson who made the policy a special focus. Throughout his presidential tenure, the federal presence among the native population would steadily, and measurably, increase. Meanwhile, too, missionaries began to arrive with plans to found churches and schools. In time, these two elements—the one secular and governmental, the other religious and evangelical—would join in uneasy alliance. The educational program, in particular, achieved impressive growth; by the mid-1820s, the total of new Indian schools (mostly in the Southeast) had surpassed forty, with almost two thousand pupils officially enrolled. As part of the same general strategy, the households of resident agents and missionaries would serve as little replicas of "civilization"—modeling, for the native population, up-to-date farming, enlightened domesticity, and firm devotion to Christianity.[14]

All aspects were carefully rationalized; all were couched in the language of "improvement" and "assimilation." To one visiting Indian delegation, President Jefferson grandly declared, "The day will soon come when you will unite yourselves with us, join in our great councils, and form a people with us, and we shall all be Americans; you will mix with us by marriage; your blood will run in our veins and will spread with us over this great continent." To Benjamin Hawkins, a principal government agent among the southeastern tribes, he wrote, "The ultimate point of rest and happiness for them is to let our settlements and theirs blend together, to intermix, and become one people. Incorporating themselves with us as citizens of the Unites States . . . is what the natural progress of things will, of course, bring on."[15]

In practice, blending would necessarily entail procreation across racial lines. (*Amalgamation* became the term of choice here; *miscegenation* was a later, and more pejorative, invention.) The prominent Revolutionary-era physician Benjamin Rush believed that race mixing might improve the entire human species. "The mulatto," he wrote, "has been remarked, in all countries, to exceed in sagacity his white and black parent. The same remark has been made of the offspring of the European and the North American Indian." Rev. Jedediah Morse, author of a long and influential *Report on Indian Affairs* (1822) and staunch supporter of the Mission School, urged that education of the natives should have first priority, "and then let intermarriage with them become general." The American Board of Commissioners for Foreign Missions held to a similar position, and was pleased when one of its own field representatives took a Choctaw wife. Federal agent Hawkins, on coming to his post among the Creeks, favored "the idea of forming amorous connections with the women, [and] had in contemplation to set the example myself and order my assistants to follow."[16] (Apparently, he did not go through with it. However, his predecessor in the same post had married a Cherokee.)

Occasionally, too, there were policy initiatives along these lines. In 1784, in Virginia's House of Delegates, Patrick Henry introduced legislation to provide tax relief and other benefits to anyone who would marry an Indian. And a few years later, Secretary Knox urged that bounties be offered to induce white men to wed Indian women. (He also raised the reverse possibility, but only for white women who had "strayed from virtuous paths"; these—if no others—might reasonably take Indian husbands.) Several state governments considered similar proposals; in short, "amalgamation," as a means to "civilization," was in the air.[17]

To be sure, the project showed a certain one-sidedness: "your blood will run *in our veins*". . . . "incorporating themselves *with us*"—never the other way around. Evidently, *their* blood, *their* customs, *their* goals, values, and interests were of little account. Again, Jefferson exemplified this ambivalent pattern. On the one hand, whenever the native people were disparaged by European theorists eager to brand all things American as "degenerate," he came forcefully to their defense. The Indian, he assured the French general Chastellux, is "in body and mind equal to the white man." He was for many years an avid student of Indian culture (especially languages), and his mansion, Monticello, included a large space he called "Indian Hall," with an extensive display of native "curiosities." On the other hand, he made no effort—and expressed no desire—to keep that culture alive for the future.[18]

There was, too, a deeper irony here. The "civilization" offered to Indians was paired with a stark alternative: extermination. By standing firm and remaining true to their own traditions, they would seal their fate; their numbers, already much reduced from previous centuries, would dwindle to nothing. White society would insist on this; even without conscious intent, whites and their ways would prove overwhelming. It was, as Jefferson had written, "what the natural progress of things will, of course, bring on." *Of course!* Hence the "choice" presented was virtually a threat: Civilize or die. Yet "civilization" would entail another kind of death, a cultural death. Indians, and Indianness, would perish either way.[19]

It is impossible, moreover, to miss the paternalistic spirit that infused the entire script. Indians were cast essentially as children—lacking discipline and judgment, given to mischief, dependent on others for guidance, beholden to their "Great White Father." Even this was something of an abstraction; individual Indians, as living, breathing specimens of humankind, seem hardly to have entered the consciousness of many who wished most strongly to "improve" them.[20]

It is also impossible to overlook the way self-interest played into the mix, with Indian lands offering such an inviting target for "speculation" or outright appropriation. Jefferson himself was a large-scale land speculator (as were Washington, Benjamin Franklin, and other advocates of "civilization"). Displacement of Indians was a consistent thread in all his policy making; he repeatedly stressed the need "to familiarize them [Indians] to the idea that it is for their interest to cede lands at times to the US, and for us thus to procure gratifications to our citizens . . . by new acquisitions of land." It was, after all, Jefferson's administration that engineered the first major round of removals of native people to the Mississippi Valley and beyond.[21]

During the years when Jeffersonian philanthropy took center stage—roughly 1790–1815—other, much darker viewpoints retreated to the wings, but no further. Indeed, there were always doubters and scoffers about any plans to give Indians favorable consideration. For this group, their "savagery" remained a central, ineluctable fact; the very notion of "improving" them seemed absurd and pernicious. A British visitor to the American interior, in the 1790s, encountered "rancorous antipathy to the whole race of Indians." Indeed, he claimed, "nothing is more common than to hear . . . talk of extirpating them totally from the face of the earth, men, women, and children." That same talk now included the term *red nigger,* which effectively lumped native people with enslaved—and despised—blacks.[22]

A half century of particularly devastating warfare—stretching from Pontiac's War in 1763 to the end of the Creek War in 1814—served repeatedly to renew, and strengthen, anti-Indian feeling. Tales of dreadful "massacres" circulated widely, gaining notoriety as they went; even young children were among the hearers. "Which of us," asked Indian superintendent Thomas McKenney, recalling his own earliest years, "has not listened with sensations of horror to the nursery stories that are told of the Indian and his cruelties? In our infant mind . . . we have been made to hear his yell, and to our eyes has been presented his tall, gaunt form, with the skins of beasts dangling round his limbs, and his eyes like fire, eager to find some new victim on which to fasten himself, and glut his appetite for blood. We have been made to see . . . him striding amidst the bodies of the slain . . . his fingers dripping with blood, and his face disclosing a ferocious smile, as he enjoyed the sight of the quivering limbs and the agonies of the dying!" Other observers claimed to find in Indian psychology an inherent taste for violence, mayhem, and war—and especially for revenge, "which is the most distinguishing characteristic of these people." (This last idea contained a kind of ironic truth, for much Indian violence against whites was, at bottom, reactive—a response, that is, to the repeated depredations made on their own lands and security.) Where previously some had seen a noble savage now stood his antithesis, the vicious savage, "but a little way removed from a beast." The embellishments here were endless: "furious and deadly . . . desperate and rapacious . . . fierce and cruel . . . thirsting for blood . . . habituated to licentiousness . . . vagrant, lawless, and debauched." (And so on.)[23]

Joined to these horrific images was a widespread belief that Indians had consistently opposed the Revolutionary movement—siding with the British, and thus forfeiting any right to benefit from the achievement of national independence. From then on, in the eyes of many whites, they were indelibly branded as actual or potential traitors to the cause of "liberty." The truth of Indians' involvement with the Revolution was much more complicated. There was no single pattern; different tribal groups made different choices. Some fought valiantly on the patriot side. Others allied with the British. And still others tried to maintain a precarious neutrality. In virtually every case, their goal was simply to protect their own interests. But no matter what route they chose, nearly all suffered grievous loss as the war ranged deep into their own home territories. The War of 1812 would add to the same resentment, as many (not all) Indians supported the British side, in both the South and the Old Northwest.[24] (Again, Indians endured terrible devastation, including "massacres" such as the one inflicted by U.S. forces under Gen. Andrew Jackson on the Creeks in March 1814. Indeed, Jackson's rise as a political figure owed much to his reputation as a fierce Indian killer.)

There were also some countercurrents, channels of "sympathy" crossing racial boundaries, especially among reform-minded evangelicals (people often identified as "the benevolent"). *Sympathy* was indeed a key word here—both sympathy *for* a race thought to have been wronged, and ultimately doomed, by white encroachment, and sympathy *with* all that it seemed to stand for. The third and fourth decades of the nineteenth century witnessed the rise of a (so-called) Romantic movement, elevating emotion over reason, the natural over the artificial, human connection over personal striving. Accordingly, Indians might emerge as exemplars; their highly traditional, close-to-nature, communitarian way of life had supposedly resisted the corrupting influence of modern "civilization." Ethnographers, playwrights, novelists, and poets played endless variations on this theme.[25]

However, at around the same time, invidious racial feeling began to ramp up markedly. The immediate cause was heightened tension over slavery; this, in turn, followed from abolition of the slave trade, the Missouri Compromise (famously described by Jefferson as "a fire-bell in the night"), the start of an organized emancipation movement, and two substantial, though failed, slave rebellions (Denmark Vesey in South Carolina, Nat Turner in Virginia). White reaction bore down first and hardest on blacks, but Indians, too, were increasingly drawn in. Toward the end of the 1830s, leading public intellectuals had begun to develop a body of pseudoscientific race theories that would exert wide influence for years to come. Though somewhat different in emphasis, all were premised on the linked notions of absolute biological difference among the country's three main racial groups, the separate creation of each ("polygenesis"), and their profoundly unequal mental and moral "endowments." About Indians, in particular, learned opinion was now unequivocal. According to one prominent authority, "the intellectual faculties of this great family appear to be of a decidedly inferior cast when compared with those of the Caucasian or Mongolian races." (Sometimes "Caucasian race" might be smoothly elided to "American race"—a usage that, ironically enough, did *not* mean those most truly native to the land.)[26]

Moreover, as these lines were ever more sharply etched, "amalgamation" came to seem utterly repulsive—and, at the same time, fascinating. Novels, cartoon imagery, folklore, and learned discussion all testified to its powerful grip on the public imagination. In some states—Massachusetts, for example—laws were passed to prohibit marriage between persons of different race. In Georgia, a legislative committee recorded the widely prevalent anxiety that "constant intermarriages" would lead to "a sort of mongrel population . . . unfit for the character of citizens." Concern for "blood"—always a key marker, and supposed determinant, of racial inheritance—was everywhere; with respect to Indians, the older, relatively neutral term *mixed-blood* gave way to the highly pejorative *half-breed*. Under these conditions, hopes for Indian "civilization" necessarily ebbed. President James Monroe signaled the new climate when, in an official report to Congress, he declared, "It is impossible to incorporate them [Indians] in such masses, in any form whatever, into our system."[27]

Although these trends embraced the entire country, individual regions experienced them in different ways and to varying degrees. The South, of course, was most deeply imbrued in black-white relations (though the North was far from exempt). The western frontier was the flash point for whites and Indians; there would be found the most bitter of enmities—yet also the closest, most intimate, of connections.

New England, by contrast, was no longer a main stage for racial encounters. Its relatively small black population, consisting by now almost entirely of freedmen, struggled for space on the margins of white society—wherever work might be found in wage labor, household service, and small-scale entrepreneurship (barbering, tailoring, porterage). Indians, too, occupied the margins, or, in some cases, locations even farther removed. A certain proportion lived on specially designated "reserves"—enclaves of their own kind, operating under the supervisory arm of state-appointed white "guardians." Others were based in tiny encampments on the outskirts of the larger cities and towns.[28]

Some secured a bare subsistence from the soil and occasional hunting and fishing. A good many became "hired men" on nearby farms; more than a few worked as whalemen and mariners in the region's major seaports, or served in the military (when that opportunity arose). The women, for their part, became laundresses, domestics in white households, or occasional herbalists and healers. But perhaps the largest occupational group, and certainly the most visible to whites, was composed of itinerant craftspeople—producers and vendors of wood-splint bas-

kets, brooms, mats, and chair seats ("flags"). Their presence on the roadways was ubiquitous; few village households would not have witnessed
their comings and goings. Typically, they traveled in small clusters of
women and children, their wares strung on tumplines affixed to head
and shoulders, in bundles so large (one Massachusetts man would later
remember) "as almost to hide them from view."[29]

In fact, too, local Indians and blacks had been intermarrying for generations; from the white standpoint, they increasingly formed a single,
undifferentiated class of "coloreds." As such, they were subject to a quite
overt, and settled, racism. The hatred aroused by "savage" violence along
the frontier had no equivalent in New England, but racism was present,
and powerful, nonetheless. White folk contrived many reasons for scorn-
ing Indians: their "uniform sloth and stupidity" (so wrote Yale's president
Dwight), their propensity to alcoholism (so said almost everyone), their
"roving and unsettled life" (another nearly universal charge), and their
ramshackle neighborhoods, "where the vagrant, the dissipated, and the
felonious do congregate" (in the opinion of a leading Boston newspaper). The same parties were sure also about their imminent extinction.
In 1850, a careful history of Connecticut's Indians concluded with the
following judgment: "Nothing is left but a little and miserable remnant,
hanging around the seats where their ancestors once reigned supreme,
as a few half-withered leaves may be seen clinging to the upper branches
of a blighted and dying tree." Still later in the century, white residents of
many New England towns would take a peculiar interest—pride even—
in identifying the "last Indian" to have lived among them.[30]

The wretchedness of life under these conditions can be glimpsed in
a single case through the writings of the native author William Apess.
Of Pequot ancestry (admixed with some white and African-American
"blood"), Apess was born near the end of the eighteenth century in a
tent in western Massachusetts—there to begin an unremittingly bleak
childhood. He was soon abandoned by his parents, taken in by his belea-
guered (and violently abusive) grandparents, and shuttled between various white households in which he worked as a servant. He had a few brief
periods of schooling but was largely self-taught. While still a youth, he
served with the American forces during the War of 1812, held a succession of menial jobs, endured extreme poverty, succumbed at times to
"demon rum," was baptized as a Methodist, and eventually became a
circuit preacher to various New England Indian groups.[31]

In 1829, Apess published his autobiography—the first such by any

Native American—under the title *A Son of the Forest*. In this and subsequent writings, he poured out his anguish over "the calumny heaped upon us by the whites to an intense degree." He bitterly lamented his status as "a poor Indian"—the word itself was "considered as a slur"—and believed that "had my skin been white, with the same abilities . . . there could not have been found a place good enough for me." He recalled from his earliest years the humiliation of door-to-door peddling with his grandmother's baskets, the beatings he endured at her hands and those of white masters, and the way he was cursed as an "Indian dog." Deeply religious, he felt grievously let down by others of his faith in the white community: "In vain have I looked for the Christian to take me by the hand and bid me welcome . . . and if they did, it was only to satisfy curiosity and not to look upon me as a man. . . . And so all of my people have been treated, whether Christians or not." In particular, he believed that "missionaries have injured us . . . by degrading us as a people, in breaking up our governments, and leaving us without any suffrages whatever, or a legal right among men. Oh, what cursed doctrine is this! It most certainly is not fit to civilize men with. . . . We poor Indians want no such missionaries around us." (Did he know of the Foreign Mission School? If so, he gave no sign.)[32]

Considered as a whole, Apess's published work is a piercing cry of pain—nothing less. Here is his summation: "The land of my fathers is gone; and their characters were not known as human beings but as beasts of prey. We were represented as having no souls to save, or lose, but as partridges upon the mountains. . . . Thus, you see, we had to bear all this tide of degradation, while prejudice stung . . . every white man, the young as well as the old, to the very center of the heart." Apess was unusual in his literacy, authorship, and status as a minister; if his life was cruelly hard and unrewarding, how much more so the lives of average Indians in the same time and place?[33]

In the year Apess was born, Rev. Stephen Badger offered another summation—a white man's—of the same stung-to-the-heart prejudice. Since Badger had served for decades as minister at Natick—the first of the Massachusetts "praying towns" a century and a half before, now a mixed community with its Indian residents largely submerged and dispossessed—he knew whereof he spoke. Indians, he wrote, "are generally considered by white people, and placed, as if by common consent, in an inferior and degraded situation, and treated accordingly. Of that they themselves seem to be not a little sensible. This sinks and cramps their spirits, and prevents those manly exertions which an equal rank with others has a tendency to call forth."[34] Indeed.

President Monroe again: "It is impossible . . . to incorporate them . . . into our system."

The earlier "civilization" program, incomplete and unbalanced as it was, had opened a window toward a degree of racial inclusiveness not previously seen in American life. But now the window was closing.

It was closing among people throughout the country. It was closing in the halls of government. And it would soon be closing—pointedly, painfully—in Cornwall, at the Mission School.

After all, race mixing . . . *is impossible*!

· CHAPTER SIX ·

"So much excitement and disgust throughout our country"

Impossible? Not always, not at Cornwall anyway. In 1747, town officials recorded the marriage of a Narragansett Indian named Zephaniah Wix to Lydia Dibble, a white woman from a solidly respectable local family. This pair would go on to birth and raise thirteen mixed-race children, with no apparent resistance from others in the community.[1]

But the 1820s were a different time—hence the "very serious consequences" anticipated from the "intimacy" between John Ridge (Cherokee Indian scholar) and Sarah Bird Northrup (white daughter of the Mission School steward). What can be learned about these two?

Sarah first . . .

Her Connecticut pedigree was impeccable. Northrup, Prout, Bird, and other surnames on the branches of her family tree traced five or six generations of direct descent from immigrant "Puritan" ancestors. The Northrups, in particular, were counted among the founders of two of the colony's earliest coastal towns, New Haven (1637) and Milford (1639). Several decades later, they helped settle New Milford, forty miles inland on the upper Housatonic River.

Sarah's paternal grandfather, Dr. Joel Northrup, was a noted New Haven physician and surgeon during the decades before and after the year 1800; his wife's ancestral line included several Congregational ministers. Their son, John Prout Northrup, would be young Sarah's father.

Her mother, Lydia Camp Northrup, was also marked by long Connecticut ancestry, though without quite the same element of professional and social distinction. Her uncles included a prominent lawyer and a captain in the United States Navy. But her father's life followed a much more modest course. John Prout (as he was generally known) made his way as a hat maker and farmer, prior to becoming steward at the Mission School. He would be remembered later on as "eminent for integrity and piety"—and also for bearing "a remarkable resemblance to George Washington." Soon after marrying, he moved to his wife's hometown of Litchfield, where he and his growing family remained for roughly two decades. At the time of his appointment in Cornwall, his household included five children, ranging in age from seventeen years to three. Sarah, at fourteen, was the second eldest.[2]

The steward's duties were extensive. They began with supervision of the school's landed properties, and training the scholars in "the arts of agriculture"; thus John Prout's previous experience as a farmer must have seemed directly pertinent. This was an important responsibility, and one that engaged him every day; food for the school's table depended on it. There was also the matter of bookkeeping; the steward would perforce be much involved in managing accounts. He had other duties, too: maintaining various kinds of necessary "equipment" in good working order, ensuring a steady supply of firewood, buying and selling livestock, arranging travel for staff and scholars, hosting visitors—the list went on and on. Almost as much as the principal himself, a steward could make, or break, the successful operation of the school.[3]

A different part of the steward's duties extended to other family members. His wife was in charge of the kitchen—and thus of preparing "suitable repast" for the entire school. She worked also at keeping the scholars well outfitted: tending to their clothes, darning, mending, laundering. Finally—and crucially here—she, like other women of her time, played a special role in providing hands-on medical care; when one or another scholar took sick, he would be moved right into her household. Local physicians might be summoned to make a diagnosis and plan treatment, but day-to-day nursing fell largely to her. It fell also to her *daughters* (assuming she had some); as housewives in training, they would assist her on a regular basis. In the case of the Northrups, and specifically of young Sarah, this pattern was clear—and fateful.

About most parts of Sarah's early life, we can only speculate. Certainly her placement in the midst of a missionary-sponsored school was unusual—as was her day-to-day encirclement by several dozen boys and young men. Her youthful appearance would be remembered later as "beautiful," with "blue eyes and auburn hair"; surely, this was noticed at the time.[4] Most likely, she attended a local "district school." As the eldest daughter in her family, she would have had to assume important domestic responsibilities, including child care. In fact, in November 1822 a new child entered the Northrup household, her baby sister Eliza Alma. With her mother "lying in" after giving birth, Sarah's contributions—both at home and at the Mission School—may have increased significantly.

Now John . . .

His father, who would be known in later life as Major Ridge, held—still holds—a preeminent place in Cherokee history. Born around 1770 in what is now eastern Tennessee, this man claimed descent from a line of important chiefs. When, early on, he showed special aptitude for hunting and warfare, he acquired two Cherokee names, Nung-noh-hut-tar-hee (meaning "he who slays the enemy in his path") and Kah-nung-da-tla-geh ("the man who walks on the mountaintop"); the latter would be commonly rendered, in English, as "the Ridge." Long afterward, upon his death, a white acquaintance paid him the following tribute: "Those of us who knew his history from his own personal life are ready to agree that he walked along the mountain top in regard to integrity, high resolve, and purity of character."[5]

As a young man, the Ridge moved quickly toward leadership of his people, following the traditional route of exhibiting strength and success as a warrior. He participated in the Tennessee border conflicts of the late 1780s—when the Cherokees were striving to roll back the latest of many white incursions into their territory—and took his first scalp while still a teenager. After peace was restored, he returned to his home in the village of Pine Log. A few years later, he married a woman named (alternatively) Susanna Wickett or Sehoya. Though already renowned for his skills as a hunter, the Ridge decided at this point to devote himself to clearing land and creating a farm. He built a log house in the style of white frontiersmen and began a series of domestic improvements. In years to come, his fields would yield cotton, corn, and the produce of various fruit trees. He also raised livestock—and purchased "Negroes" (slaves) to do the estate's heavy work. Eventually, his lifestyle would mirror that of white plantation owners throughout the Old South. Meanwhile, Susanna embraced the role of genteel housewife, becoming adept at spinning, weaving, and other suitably "female arts." (In all these ways, the Ridge appeared to have become "civilized," just as Jefferson and like-minded white leaders wanted it.)[6]

An official of the American Board, who visited the Ridge home at some point later on, described his experience there in letters to the Boston office. He held lengthy discussions with his hosts on all manner of topics. (Presumably, these involved an interpreter, since "they understand some English, but do not talk.") Foremost was religion; thus, on one particular evening, "Mrs. Ridge desired to know what sin was, or what was displeasing to God. This opened . . . a long & pleasing conversation." On another occasion, they turned to astronomy, and "spent some time in viewing the stars. The Ridge inquired the [English] names of several," and was pleased to find that some had "a name signifying the same in both languages." On yet another, their focus was slavery, and "the Ridge called in his Blacks, 8 or 10, for me to talk & pray with." All in all, the visitor felt "most gratified" by what he found in this supposedly "uncivilized" environment.[7]

From quite a young age, the Ridge's importance in Cherokee governance was substantial. He became known as an especially effective speaker "in council," and during the first decade of the new century he was centrally involved in treaty negotiations with officials of the federal government. Then came the years of renewed war, 1812–15—the United States versus Britain, and a variety of (more or less related) Indian conflicts. In the summer of 1813, the Cherokees joined a federal force, led by Gen. Andrew Jackson, in subduing a rebellion by their Creek neighbors; the Ridge played a key role. A year or two later, he performed additional service, this time in the Seminole War (in Florida). Along the way, he was commissioned as a U.S. Army major—a rank that would subsequently become part of his name. All this cemented his reputation not only among fellow Cherokees but with whites, as well. The postwar era saw him again engaged in high-level diplomacy. He traveled several times to Washington and was received there with honor by President Monroe and other national leaders. Wartime collaboration had forged a special link with Jackson; the two would remain friends for years.[8]

John Ridge (or Skah-tle-loh-skee, his Cherokee name) was the second of five children born to Major Ridge and Susanna. One of the others died young; there were also two daughters and a mentally handicapped son. John seems from the start to have been marked for greatness— especially by his doting parents. His father, though wholly "untutored," was determined that the boy should have a white man's education. Thus, when John was barely seven, he was entered in the little school, recently founded by Moravian missionaries, at Spring Place, some thirty miles south of the Ridge estate. There he flourished, learning to speak and write English, mastering the fundamentals of drawing, arithmetic, geography, and other "academical" subjects, performing regular work on the school farm, and absorbing a heavy dose of Christian doctrine. He was joined in all this by his first cousin Gallegina (translated as "Buck"), an uncommonly "warm and loving" child. The two of them would remain allies and boon companions for decades to come—even unto death.[9]

John remained at the Spring Place school for nearly five years; toward the end, however, his life there was shadowed by illness. From time to time, he would suffer from "the scrofulous complaint," a glandular condition that caused both pain and lameness. Eventually, his parents decided to bring him home, where he could be watched more closely and schooled by a private tutor. Then, when his health improved, they enrolled him in the nearby Brainerd mission school; again he seemed to progress very rapidly. One incident, as recorded in the school's official journal, reflected his commitment to learning (and perhaps also something of his determined character). On a certain morning, his teachers proposed limiting the regular assignment because others in the class were having difficulty with it; John objected "in a hasty & petulant manner" and insisted that he "would not have such short lessons." When scolded for "disrespect" toward the teachers, he "burst into a flood of tears" and begged forgiveness. Soon thereafter, the matter was reported to Major Ridge, who hastened to visit the school. The missionaries were reassuring, but he left his son with a warning that henceforth "you must obey them [the missionaries] as you would me."[10]

From then on, John seems to have been a model student—so much so that he was among the first Cherokees thought ready for advancement to the Foreign Mission School. This led, in turn, to a series of family conferences—described in detail by a missionary eyewitness—at which "great desires were manifested . . . to have John sent to the North." His mother, always solicitous of his fragile health, worried that "accidents might befall [him] . . . on the way," but was persuaded nonetheless. In fact, John's trip was uneventful, except for his purchase of an expensive watch during a stop in Philadelphia. (This act of "indulgence" would subsequently bring frowns from his missionary sponsors.) His cousin Buck was similarly qualified for transfer to Cornwall; the two of them traveled separately but arrived at almost the same time toward the end of the year (1818). It was Buck who acquired, in the middle of the journey, the name of the elderly New Jersey philanthropist (and congressman) Elias Boudinot—by which he would become widely known thereafter.[11]

First impressions of the new Cherokee scholars were not especially favorable; Daggett noted that they gave "no appearance of seriousness" about religion.[12] But in the months that followed, their academic strength came rapidly to the fore; soon both were enrolled in the "higher subjects." John, in particular, struck others as "a noble youth, beautiful in appearance, very graceful, a perfect gentleman everywhere. . . . [He] was not dark and swarthy . . . [but] fine-looking." Indeed, according to later descriptions, he might easily have passed as white.[13]

Entries in his "commonplace book"—what we would call a personal scrapbook today—show John warming also to the spiritual side of school life. There he wrote out, in his own hand, copies of hymns ("The Goodness of Providence"), prayers ("The Christian Rapture"), inspirational nature poems ("The Falls of Niagara"), and pious homilies ("Procrastination Is the Thief of Time"). He also included a variety of geometric exercises, plus some brief verses entitled "Upon a Watch" (referring perhaps to the purchase he had made while en route to Cornwall). Taken as a whole, this assemblage suggests a young man of earnest intent, strong ambition, and a decidedly moral bent.[14]

At some point, John's old illness recurred, and he was confined to sickbed in the steward's house. Beginning in December 1820, Daggett's reports to the American Board made regular reference to his "unhappy situation." Though "improved very much in his conduct & in his learning," and now "seriously disposed" toward matters of faith, he "has, from a child, been feeble . . . and his complaints have rather increased . . . of late." In April 1821, "he continues to be ill"; in June "he is in a very feeble state of health"; in July "he continues to be very much out of health." In the latter month, Kellogg's General Store—the family-run shop supplying all manner of "necessaries" to the townsfolk—recorded a sale to the Foreign Mission School, "per Mr. N[orthrup] . . . 1 pr crutches"; surely, these were meant for John. Throughout the spring and early summer, he was under the care of Cornwall's local physician, Dr. Samuel Gold. However, in mid-July he was sent for several weeks to New Haven to receive a more specialized form of treatment. Daggett, meanwhile, repeatedly urged his return home to his own family—an idea that John himself resisted. (He "wishes much to stay & pursue his studies.")[15]

In the autumn, when reports of John's worsening condition reached

John Ridge (ca. 1802–39), a student at the Foreign Mission School (1818–22), became after his return home a leader of the Cherokee Nation—and eventually of the so-called Treaty Party favoring emigration. Around 1824 he sat for this portrait by the artist Charles Bird King. *(Permission and image from William Reese.)*

These portraits of Elias Boudinot (ca. 1801–39), a student at the Foreign Mission School (1818–22), and his wife, Harriet Ruggles Gold (1805–36), were painted by an unidentified artist, probably in the mid-1820s.
(Copyright 2012; used by permission of James Boudinot.)

This beach, photographed as it appears today, was in the late eighteenth century the site of the village of Ninole, where Henry Obookiah was born and lived during his early childhood.
(Diego Delso, Wikimedia Commons, License CC-BY-SA 3.0)

This image, from a print made in the 1770s, depicts a traditional Hawaiian shrine of the sort at which Henry Obookiah spent his later childhood years, apprenticed to a *kahuna* (native priest).

Another eighteenth-century print shows a group of Hawaiian priests in a longboat approaching the shore of Kealakekua Bay, where the young Obookiah lived and worked between (approximately) 1797 and 1807.

In 2010 the Cornwall Historical Society mounted an exhibition on the Foreign Mission School. It included this scale model of its "Academy building." *(Image courtesy of the Cornwall Historical Society, Cornwall, CT.)*

This house, as it appears today, was the residence of the Foreign Mission School steward John Northrup and his family. It was here that John Ridge was cared for during a long illness, in the course of which he and Sarah Northrup fell in love. *(Image and permission from Alec C. Frost.)*

This house was the home of Col. Benjamin Gold and family during the time when his daughter Harriet formed her "attachment" to Elias Boudinot. *(Image and permission from Alec C. Frost.)*

This was one of the many images of
Henry Obookiah that appeared in books about
the Foreign Mission School; it also was used
in circulars for fund-raising purposes.
*(Image courtesy of the Cornwall Historical Society,
Cornwall, CT.)*

Following his death in February 1818,
Obookiah was buried in the main Cornwall
cemetery; his gravestone was one of the largest
and most elaborate placed there. Visitors from
Hawaii have been traveling to see it, and to
pay their respects, for at least a century.
*(Image courtesy of the Cornwall Historical Society,
Cornwall, CT.)*

The 1993 removal of Obookiah's
remains from Cornwall to Hawaii began
with the opening of his grave, as shown here.
*(Image courtesy of the Cornwall Historical Society,
Cornwall, CT.)*

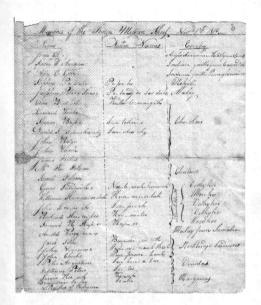

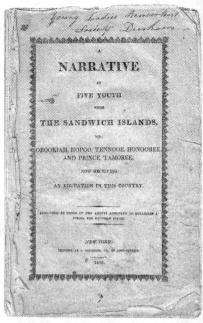

ABOVE, LEFT The leaders of the Foreign Mission School would periodically create lists of the "scholars" currently enrolled, complete with names and ethnic affiliations. This example shows the roster as of about two years after the school's founding. *(Image courtesy of the Cornwall Historical Society, Cornwall, CT.)*

ABOVE, RIGHT A carefully managed publicity campaign, just prior to the founding of the Foreign Mission School, included publication of this narrative tracing the lives of several of the young Hawaiians soon to be enrolled there. *(Image courtesy of the Cornwall Historical Society, Cornwall, CT.)*

ABOVE Henry Obookiah's *Memoirs,* ghostwritten by his friend and mentor Edwin Dwight, became an extraordinary publishing success; nearly a dozen editions appeared over several decades following his death. *(Image from the author.)*

Harriet Ruggles Gold Boudinot was buried in a tiny graveyard on the outskirts of New Echota, Cherokee Nation, following her death in August 1836. *(Image courtesy of the New Echota Historic Site, Calhoun, GA.)*

The courthouse, built at the time of founding the Cherokee capital, New Echota (ca. 1815–20), and later destroyed, has been reconstructed for present-day visitors to the site. *(Image courtesy of the New Echota Historic Site, Calhoun, GA.)*

Inside the print shop at New Echota (as seen in reconstructed form today), Elias Boudinot edited the *Cherokee Phoenix*, the first newspaper published by and for Native Americans. *(Image courtesy of the New Echota Historic Site, Calhoun, GA.)*

Major Ridge, Cherokee chief and father of John Ridge, was a close associate of Andrew Jackson and other leaders of the United States government. This widely distributed print image was based on a portrait, now lost. *(Courtesy of The Chieftains Museum, Rome, GA.)*

Maintained today as a museum (The Chieftains), this house was built and occupied by Major Ridge and his family prior to their removal to Oklahoma. *(Courtesy of The Chieftains Museum, Rome, GA.)*

This Cherokee council pipe was given by Major Ridge to S. W. Gold, one of his hosts on a visit to Cornwall in November 1821. *(Permission from James Gold; image courtesy of the Cornwall Historical Society, Cornwall, CT.)*

the Cherokee country, Major Ridge decided to undertake the long journey to Cornwall. His arrival there in mid-October was a local sensation.
His dress (including a "coat trimmed with gold lace . . . and white top
boots"), conveyance ("the most splendid carriage . . . that ever entered
the town"), and commanding personal presence ("a tall and athletic form
and noble bearing") made the deepest possible impression. He lodged
in the town inn, and stayed for a full two weeks. He called on Lyman
Beecher in nearby Litchfield and conversed at length with the famous
preacher, whose daughter Catherine described him as "one of the princes
of the forest." (Perhaps his son was present to serve as interpreter.) He
was cordially received in various Cornwall households, including that of
Dr. Gold. Decades later, the doctor's son would write that "no memory
of my boyhood is clearer than that of a visit to my home in my sixth year
of . . . John Ridge and his father, Major Ridge, the Cherokee chief . . . [in]
the uniform of a U.S. officer." The memory also included this: "My father
exchanged presents with him, giving him a small telescope and receiving in turn from him an Indian pipe carved in black stone." The same
pipe—nearly three feet in length, its surface burnished with the passage
of time—hangs today, enclosed in a glass casement, on the living room
wall in the home of a Gold descendant. Attached to it is an ancient label,
which reads "This pipe once belonged to Major Ridge, a distinguished
chief of the Cherokee nation. It was presented to S. W. Gold in 1820 with
the assurance of the giver that it had often been smoked in council."[16]

It was generally expected that John Ridge would return home with his
father, but when the time came, he remained in Cornwall. According to
some accounts, he was still too "feeble" to risk travel. But several months
later, Daggett declared, "He chose to stay, and still does." *Chose to stay,
and still does?* Why? Was it really because of his illness? Or was something else holding him fast to Cornwall—to the school—to the steward's
household, in which he would remain a patient for "about two years"?[17]
Reenter Sarah.

The story of their courtship was remembered decades later by a
woman with a personal connection to all those involved. Her account,
as dictated to her own daughter, remains the fullest we have.[18] Though
impossible to verify in every detail, it has the feel of authenticity. It centers on one particular occasion, and begins thus:

> *Mrs. Northrup had so much work and care that she would send her daughter
> Sarah into John's room to take care of him.* For a time John's condition

seemed to improve, so much so that *Dr. Gold said to Mrs. Northrup "I do not think it best to give him any more medicine, but he has some deep trouble, and you must find out what it is."*

On an afternoon when Sarah had left the house, *Mrs. Northrup, taking her stockings to darn for the students, went in to sit with John. She said to him, "John, you have some trouble, and you must tell me; you know, you have no mother here, only me, and you have always confided in me, as you would your own mother." He started up in wild amazement, and said, "I got trouble? No."* She replied, *"I can not leave until you tell me all."* John: *"I do not want to tell you."* Mrs. N.: *"You must tell me."* John: *"Well . . . if you must know, I love your Sarah."* Mrs. N.: *"You must not."* John: *"I know it . . . and that is the trouble."* Mrs. N.: *"Have you ever mentioned it to her?"* John: *"No, we have not said one word to each other; I dare not, but how could I help loving her when she has taken such good care of me these two years?"*

When Sarah returned home that evening, her mother was waiting. Mrs. N.: *"Sarah, do you love John Ridge?"* Sarah: *"Yes, I do love John."* At that, *Mrs. Northrup saw there was trouble in the camp.*

The Northrups decided that swift action was essential to prevent further dalliance between the two young sweethearts; they must send their daughter away. Thus, shortly thereafter *Mr. Northrup took Sarah to her grandparents [Dr. Joel and Mrs. Mabel Sarah] in New Haven, and told them why and what he had brought her for. [He] wished them to make parties and introduce her to other gentlemen, and try every way to get her mind off John Ridge.* Sarah would have none of it. She stayed three months, but *would take no notice of any gentleman or any company. [She] had no appetite for food, lost flesh, and they thought she soon would be [a] victim of consumption.* Understandably, her grandparents grew alarmed about her; there was nothing to do but send her home.

There were difficulties, too, on John's side. Major Ridge and Susanna expected their son to take a wife from within the Nation, preferably a chief's daughter. Thus when John wrote home of his wish to marry Sarah, they were surprised and dismayed. Susanna consulted with one of the resident missionaries, who warned that a white woman might feel superior to "the common Cherokees," and that her son would be more useful to his people "were he connected with them in marriage." She then had a letter sent to John, objecting strongly to his "intentions." But when he replied by reaffirming his love for Sarah, his parents were persuaded to yield.

It was clear now that their feelings could not be denied: *John was dying for Sarah, and Sarah was dying for John.* Sarah's parents weighed the possibilities and formed a new plan. *Mrs. Northrup told John to go home and stay two years, and if he could come back without his crutches he might marry Sarah.*

At around the same time, the prudential committee of the American Board voted that John "be permitted to leave the School, & that it be recommended to his father to procure . . . his return home, as soon as practicable." This was polite language for a forced removal, prompted (at least in part) by financial considerations. As Daggett noted, "he . . . [is] supported by the funds of the institution, but the expense and inconvenience which he occasions, is very considerable, without any prospect of advantage, to himself, or the cause [of missions]."[19]

Indeed, John himself had finally come around: "[I]t is now his wish to go." And go he did, together with three fellow Cherokee scholars who had completed their own time at the school. The group set out in mid-October. In deference to John's still-fragile health, they traveled by ship instead of overland; in early November, they debarked in Charleston, South Carolina. There, and later in Augusta, Georgia, they visited local churches, with John stepping forward as advocate for mission-based philanthropy. Addressing several "very numerous" congregations, he presented a somewhat divided message. On the one hand, he stressed "the wretched state of the Heathen, particularly of the aborigines of this country . . . [whom] the hand of charity can only pluck . . . from final extermination." On the other, he proudly recounted recent examples of "improvement" among his own people, the Cherokees, in order to refute "those who disbelieved in the practicability of Indian civilization."[20]

These appearances were notably successful; audiences responded each time by volunteering funds to support mission work. The same "liberality" would also assist "the Indian young men from Cornwall" in defraying the costs of their journey. While all were "warmly approved," John made an especially strong impression; one newspaper account applauded his "fine spirit and excellent talents" as a speaker. (However, it also regretted that "he is not a professor of religion"—that is, a fully converted Christian.) In early December, the group reached the Cherokee country, where they received something of a heroes' welcome. Once again, John was singled out for special praise. A white admirer would later comment that "from the time of his return from college" (meaning the Mission

School), he was considered "a leading man in the Nation . . . the idol of the half-breeds, and well respected by most intelligent Cherokees."[21]

All the while, knowledge of John's liaison with Sarah was confined to a small circle of Northrup and Ridge family members. It was not until the following April that Daggett's report of their "intimacy" reached the offices of the American Board in Boston, and even then the matter was described in confidential tones, without reference to named individuals. According to a bit of doggerel composed shortly afterward by a young "versifier" who is said to have been employed at the Mission School: "They kept it a secret and did not tell / How Sarah loved an Indian well / Nor was the secret thing made known / Till from his country he did return."[22]

That December, John published in the missionary press a bitter denunciation of race prejudice, "the ruling passion of the age." The Indian, he wrote, is "almost considered accursed . . . frowned upon by the meanest peasant" and compared unfavorably to "the scum of the earth." No matter how well educated, how "modest and polite . . . his conduct . . . yet he is an Indian, and the most stupid and illiterate white man will disdain and triumph over [him]." The phrasing here closely reflected John's own situation: well educated, modest, polite, the sum of his personal accomplishments. (Conversely, he must have known stupid, illiterate, disdainful whites.) This was, in any case, uncharacteristic—a new theme for him. All his previous comments on racial difference had looked toward linkage and cooperation.[23]

In the meantime, he remained at home with his family, presumably in poor health and (at best) in limited contact with Sarah. Still, their feelings for each other did not abate. Then, as another New Year approached, John's symptoms lessened enough to permit his return north to his intended bride. He set out in mid-December and reached Cornwall a month later. Evidently, Sarah's parents agreed that the terms of their previous stipulation had been met; though still somewhat lame, John could walk without crutches. In short order, the couple's intentions were "published" as banns in the local church, following long-established practice in such matters. Now, at last, the "secret thing" was fully exposed—and local reaction began to build. But John and Sarah were moving fast. On January 27, 1824, their marriage was formalized at a small gathering in the Northrups' home. Rev. Timothy Stone, agent of the Mission School and an obvious choice to perform the ceremony, declined—apparently to protect his own, and the school's, reputation. His colleague, Rev. Walter Smith, officiated instead.[24]

Though set to return to the Cherokee Nation, the newlyweds remained in Cornwall for some days longer. As was customary in that era, they would visit—and be visited by—friends and relations, in a kind of ritual acknowledgment of their "married estate." According to the report of a local resident, written several months after the fact: "On [the next] Sabbath morning . . . Col. Gold, a deacon in the church, called upon Ridge and his lady, and conducted them to the meeting house, and seated them with his family." Presumably, this was intended as a public sign of personal respect—all the more so as it meant moving Ridge from his former position on the "scholars' bench" to the deacon's pew at the front of the church. Additional gestures would follow. Thus: "Ridge and his lady were invited to visit at Capt. Miles', a wealthy farmer in the neighborhood . . . together with the aforesaid Deacon Gold and his lady." There they were "treated with that marked attention which has hitherto been given to the members of the Foreign Mission School, by some of the inhabitants residing in the vicinity." This, however, seems to have kindled resentment; the writer described it as "one of the causes . . . [of] the disgraceful affair," which, in the coming months, would bring "so much excitement and disgust throughout our country." (Indeed, his comment hints that some in Cornwall were already displeased with the "attention" frequently lavished on the scholars.)[25]

Whatever its source, John and Sarah soon faced "the highest indignation" (as another report said). Years later they would describe to a friend how "the papers proclaimed it [their wedding] as an outrage, and preachers denounced it in the pulpit." The news "flew with the wind"—from Cornwall, to the surrounding towns, to the rest of the state, and beyond. Threats were made by "the best and most respectable men . . . [to] drive the natives from the country . . . [and] heap indignity on the clergy engaged." According to a "gentleman" from Litchfield, "fifty men had signed an instrument in writing, promising to . . . go in a body to Cornwall, and not return till they had entirely demolished the building in which the school was kept." Sarah's parents felt obliged to accompany the couple on their way out of town lest they become targets of attack; even so, John "came near to being mobbed." At subsequent stops, as they traveled by stagecoach on the route south, they were met by "excited throngs, denouncing [Ridge] . . . for taking away as wife . . .

a white girl." He, for his part, readily acknowledged having entered the white world and "plucked one of its fairest flowers." But what of it? He was not, he insisted, "her inferior in any respect."[26]

As more time passed, the tempest they left behind in Cornwall would only strengthen. According to Isaac Bunce, longtime editor of nearby Litchfield's *American Eagle,* no "*white man* in town approved of that transaction, except their two clergymen, and two other families." Recriminations were hurled about, most of them centering on the bride's parents. It was said that her mother had "conspired" to promote the match, that the wedding had been performed in secret so as to deceive the public, even that her father, innocent of direct involvement, "was afflicted to distraction at the degradation of his daughter, has left the family and gone off, it [is] not known where." (One account, allegedly from a friend and eyewitness, confirmed the father's presence at the ceremony, but claimed that he "felt *like death*—felt dreadfully.") Newspapers throughout Connecticut—and in "nine or ten [other] states" besides—became channels for vehement fulmination. Bunce was an especially harsh critic; in issue after issue he decried "the affliction, mortification, and disgrace, of the young woman [who] . . . throwing herself into the arms of an Indian . . . has thus made herself a *squaw.*" (For many readers, the word carried a particular connotation of sexualized ugliness.) He linked this "criminal connection" with the reigning "missionary spirit"—and, more particularly, with the readiness of the Cornwall school to embrace intermarriage as "a new kind of *missionary machinery* . . . [for] christianizing the savages [italics in original]." It was, he declared, "one of their objects . . . to break down all objections of *colour,* and make our daughters become nursing mothers to a race of mulattoes [italics in original]." Another local newspaper, the *Litchfield Gazette,* stated simply: "The intermarrying with the Indians and Blacks of the Missionary School at Cornwall, now begun, is . . . not a subject for irony." To have Sarah "marry an Indian and [be] taken into the wilderness among savages, must indeed be a heart-rending pang." Other opposers were inclined to blame the participants directly; "some . . . said that the girl ought to be publicly whipped, the Indian hung, and the mother drown'd." Meanwhile, too, church leaders were reportedly "about to bring Mr. Smith to trial . . . for performing that marriage."[27]

Indeed, there was widespread expectation of more—and worse—to come. According to press accounts, "foreign scholars . . . have . . . been seen to walk arm in arm . . . [with] both married and unmarried ladies" from the town. Some of the stories passed around seemed truly "scandalous." One recounted a nighttime gathering at which "Cherokees and Choctaws were snugly seated with the ladies, in the parlour." Another told of a man who retired to bed, leaving his daughter "sparking it with an Indian." In this connection, the *American Eagle* noted a particular bit of racially charged colloquial speech: a woman's supposed request to a "tawny" suitor, "Indian, won't you Indian me?" Still another report had Sarah Ridge writing from her new home to Cornwall friends "that they must marry [their Indian sweethearts], and come on, AS THEY HAD AGREED!" (The capitalization appears in the original. A source claimed to have "seen the letter.") There were rumors that "other ladies there, being engaged . . . have got *scare* out of it"; more specifically, "a gentleman . . . informs us that three other marriages with these natives were supposed to be in treaty." If "the principle" of intermarriage should be allowed to stand, "does it not promise to hundreds of other respectable families in this county, a similar bitter and heartrending pang, that will cease only with death?" *Hundreds of other families!* The possibilities were dire—and limitless.[28]

To be sure, much of this was pure gossip and was rejected as such by many with close connections to the school. Moreover, public opinion was not all of a piece on the central question. A New Haven newspaper, having first declared its own "decided disapprobation of the unnatural union of different colours," then gave space to the opposite viewpoint. This allowed an unidentified correspondent to condemn the published attacks on "the late marriage of an Indian to a white girl" as "conceited ebullitions of spleen." In fact, the writer continued, "the man [Ridge] has a soul, and intelligence, and probably as much mind and refinement as the female; and when you have called him a man, your Bible tells you he belongs to your own species, and is made after the same Almighty image." If only "intermarriages with the aborigines" had been undertaken from early colonial times, they would have proved the best possible means of advancing Indian "civilization"; moreover, the country might have been spared "oceans of blood and mountains of crime."[29]

The same writer ridiculed the "pitiful strain in which it is lamented that the society of those young Indians is preferred [by local women] to that of the whites of the same sex and age." Yet the theme of racial insult was everywhere in public discussion; Litchfield editor Bunce returned to it repeatedly. One of his informants, apparently a Cornwall resident, declared it "a fact . . . that the Indians are treated with more attention and respect than the young white men of good standing." There is some possibility that Sarah had a second suitor—a white neighbor—whose interest she at first encouraged but later rebuffed in order to wed John. (Thus another bit by the previously mentioned versifier: "Upon her side it does look dark/To think how she used her neighbor Clark/He went with her both night and day/While her dear John was gone away/And unto him she did not tell/How that she loved an Indian well.")[30]

The larger point—about romantic competition—was vigorously challenged by certain "Bachelors of Cornwall Valley." In a letter to the Litchfield *American Eagle,* this group claimed to have met in "regularly convened" fashion, and then to have approved a series of sardonic "resolutions" explicitly denying "that the young ladies of this place show an undue partiality towards the members of the Foreign Mission School, and . . . that *we* are thus *cast into the shade,* and *eclipsed* by the intervention of these our *tawny rivals* [italics in original]." Additional letters to the same newspaper reviled its editor for espousing "the principles of an old hound Dog" and representing "the off scouring of the world"; Bunce, however, scorned them as unworthy of response, since their probable source was "some of the *red* pupils of the school." So it went with the "marriage controversy"—to and fro, thrust and counterthrust—through much of the following year.[31]

The school itself struck a studiously defensive pose. The members of its governing board composed an open letter, responding at length to the various "misrepresentations and groundless statements . . . by which the public have been abused." (Mr. Northrup had not gone crazy; the marriage was "solemnized in open day . . . with the consent of both parents"—and so on.) Their chief purpose was to disclaim all responsibility on the part of the institution. First and foremost, "neither the Agents nor the Principal have had any concern, directly or indirectly, in advising, aiding, or assisting, respecting this marriage." Second, the match had "not been the consequence of the ordinary operations of the School"; instead, it resulted from "peculiar circumstances, which can never be expected again to recur." (The letter went on to describe John's illness and his being kept for so long in the Northrup household; further, there had been no "intimation from the family" of his developing relationship with Sarah.) Finally, reports of "other, similar connexions, between the scholars and young ladies of this place" were groundless; school rules, including some very "particular restrictions . . . [on] intercourse with the inhabitants," ensured against any repeat occurrence. Thus, while not explicitly condemning the marriage, school authorities distanced themselves from it as much as possible. And they promised that nothing like it would happen again. Plainly, their greatest concern was to preserve the school's good name—and, more especially, to reassure its legion of loyal supporters. In this regard, they would soon be badly disappointed, as the flow of "donations" began a sharp decline.[32]

Some in the ranks of missionaries strongly disapproved of the school's evasiveness. One described a series of anguished conversations with colleagues at work among the Cherokees. "If I am not mistaken," he wrote to the American Board home office, "the President [Washington] and Secretary of War [Knox], but a few years since, recommended intermarriages with the Indians as a means of promoting their improvement." He knew John Ridge to be "a man . . . worthy of respect in any community"—though now "shamefully abused by some northern editors." The school's leaders, by focusing solely on the matter of "excusing themselves," had seemed to endorse the "objections" raised by critics. This would place other Cornwall scholars "in a very delicate situation." Henceforth they "must not look at a young [white] woman, lest they should conceive an affection for her which could never be gratified"; more broadly, they must accept being "viewed with suspicion & as a grade of inferior beings." Another missionary sent an account of recent "intermarriages" in the Cherokee country. These included two ministers with Indian wives, another "white man and a Cherokee girl," and "our Cherokee brother Joseph Crawfish [who] was lawfully married to a white woman." Why, he wondered, should matters be different in the North?[33]

As word of the Ridge/Northrup marriage traveled outward from Cornwall and entered the wider arena of national life, it sometimes assumed a very different aspect. Like Obookiah's "martyrdom" a few years before, it might easily transmute into romantic legend. For example: In 1825, the Maryland poet Edward Coote Pinkney wrote and published a long verse accolade to John and Sarah, entitled "The Indian's Bride." His tone was softly lyrical, his point the happy union of opposites. One stanza may stand for the rest:

> Behold them roaming hand-in-hand,
> Like night and sleep along the land.
> Observe their movements: he for her
> Restrains his active stride,

> While she assumes a bolder gait
> To ramble at his side . . .
> The one forsakes ferocity
> And momently grows mild
> The other tempers more and more
> The artful with the wild.
> She humanizes him, and he
> Educates her to liberty.[34]

Another poem, by a different hand, struck a similar note:

> Then, come with me, my white girl fair,
> And thou a hunter's bride shall be;
> For thee I'll chase the roebuck there,
> And thou shalt dress the feast for me . . .
> The olive is thy favorite hue,
> But sweet to me thy lily face;
> O, sweet to both, when both shall view,
> These colors mingled in our race.[35]

These lines—and these sentiments—showed that the ancient trope of the Indian as an uncorrupted, even "noble," primitive had not yet disappeared. Alongside the widely held, horrific fears of native "savagery" stood a different image, with which the American people at large might beneficially engage. Pinkney's pairing of "humanizing" (her contribution) with "liberty" (his) seems especially striking; likewise the balance between "artful" and "wild." Caught in the backwash of Romanticism, some Americans in the 1820s and 1830s would see their culture as too planned, too rational, too "civilized" for its own good. An element of wildness could thus be approved, and a "mingled . . . race"—the olive with the lily—might actually recommend itself.

It is difficult, from a vantage point of two centuries later on, to reconcile the disparate attitudes reflected in this range of public response—the racism with the romanticism, the outrage with the sober moral calculation. But a pair of factors seems to have been broadly operative in creating difference: spatial proximity and social class. The closer to Cornwall, the more likely (and more energized) the outrage; conversely, distance opened a door to romanticizing. Class division played a different, but convergent, part. The people categorized as "swamp Yankees"—those who were poorest in terms of wealth, education, and worldly experience—generally, even vehemently, opposed intermarriage, while their social "superiors" were (at the least) of more moderate, and divided, opinion. The former, for example, were eager consumers of the tirades published by *American Eagle* editor Isaac Bunce; the latter included preachers, professional men, and others in the leadership of the missionary cause.

In any case: The figures of the bridal pair, as depicted in sentimental poetry, were no more than florid stereotypes greatly at variance with reality. Sarah "a hunter's bride"? John preparing to "chase the roebuck"? Not a chance. In truth, Sarah was headed toward the life of a plantation mistress, presiding over a household full of enslaved "Negroes"—while John had already begun a career as an enormously "artful" diplomat and political leader.

What, finally, of the young couple themselves as these different currents of feeling swirled around them? How did they come, sooner or later, to regard the tumult aroused by their "connexion"? Yet another missionary, visiting the Cherokees almost a year afterward, described having "spent the night at Mr. J. Ridge's." Apparently, he was warmly received; still, he could see that "this young man is not altogether pleased with the treatment he received at the North, with regard to his wife." For one thing, "he says he was not dismissed from the school when sick at her father's, as the directors stated." For another, "he thinks his marriage was not a crime, for which they need make apologies." This reaction seems straightforward enough, if notably restrained. (John Ridge would always be remarked for his graciousness in personal relations.) Perhaps it helped that—as the same source also reported—"his wife appears quite contented and pleased with her situation."[36]

As the school struggled to right itself after this unexpected, and unwanted, imbroglio, it faced a mounting set of obstacles. Deep currents of resentment in Cornwall and the surrounding towns had now been laid bare. When the clergy on the school's board tried to defend its treatment of the scholars, the *American Eagle* responded thus: "You . . . [do] not deny that you have given them the highest seats in your churches—the highest honours of your table—the uppermost rooms in your houses. . . . You treat them better, and with more attention and affection than your own ordinary parishioners." No wonder, then, that "those people of *colour* feel above those whom they see you slight for them [italics in original]." Tales like the following, "related by . . . a gentleman of Goshen," sharpened the charge of favoritism. "When these Cherokees, &c. were first brought here, one of the principal characters in that town, happening to come late to meeting discovered two or three Indians in the parson's pew. Surprised at this, he beckoned and winked to them to go into the pew for the coloured people, in another part of the house, but all to no purpose, they still stuck to the pew. And after meeting the good man was informed that they were seated there by the parson himself." Another story making the local rounds charged Lyman Beecher with having placed several members of the Mission School "as principal mourners in the procession" at a local (Litchfield) funeral— surely an inappropriate choice. Meanwhile, too, the theme of romantic competition remained current, in spite of the strenuous denials published by Cornwall's resident "bachelors." Opponents of the school insisted that "females who would look down on the white hired maid [man?] or the plough boy and mechanic have been seen to walk out, or ride out with them [foreign scholars] in their airings."[37]

Moreover, far from Cornwall itself anti-mission sentiment was on the rise. Among the Cherokees, in particular—as one American Board member wrote in the summer of 1824—"there is now a very powerful opposition to missions." A second informant, writing from eastern Tennessee at around the same time, put it even more strongly: "The hatred . . . many express to the Gospel, & the boldness of many in this, gives reason to expect that missionaries will not long be safe in this land." Indeed, Cherokee leaders were discussing ways to forestall the arrival of new missionaries, and to control the activity of those already present.[38]

The situation was no more favorable among the white population; as a result, over the next several years, a heightened tone of defensiveness entered the pronouncements of mission leaders. One characteristic example—part of "an appeal to the enemies of missions"—began thus: "You said the natives would rise and destroy all who dared to meddle with their system of idolatry. . . . You said that missionary operations are draining and impoverishing the land. . . . You said that this work would come to nothing."[39] (Whereas, in each case, according to the writer, events had proved otherwise.) As before, the chief point of debate was the "practicability of . . . reform." Would it ever be possible to convert, and "civilize," heathen peoples? Could the results justify the enormous effort required? Might not the heathen prefer to remain as they were? To the latter question, John Ridge himself, in one of his public "addresses" in South Carolina, gave an especially pointed response. "Will anyone believe that an Indian, with his bow and quiver, who walks solitary in the mountains, exposed to cold and hunger or the attacks of wild beasts, trembling at every unusual object, his fancy filled with agitating fears lest the next step should introduce his foot to the fangs of the direful snake ... actually possesses undisturbed contentment superior to a learned gentleman of this commercial city who has every possible comfort at home?"[40]

The effects of anti-mission attitudes were felt, first of all, in a monetary way. At the Mission School, the total of donations dropped from roughly $500 per quarter in 1823 to $60 the following year. Moreover, there was a similar (though less extreme) trend at both the regional and national levels. Donations to the Foreign Mission Society of Litchfield County (which included Cornwall and a dozen other communities) fell from $2,450 to $1,670 per annum over the same period. In 1826, the Litchfield Society was forced to acknowledge that its "receipts ... have, for the last three years been constantly diminishing." Even the American Board, with its worldwide purview, was not immune. There, too, the sums received went sharply down—from approximately $68,000 in 1823 to just over $47,000 a year later. How much of this could be blamed on the Ridge-Northrup affair is impossible to say; but the date of their wedding—January 27, 1824—conformed precisely to the timing of the change.[41]

At any rate, the American Board decided now to reexamine the terms of its sponsorship of the Mission School. The official report of its annual meeting, held at Hartford in September 1824, included the following: "There appears to be some danger that this school would cease to be a mere instrument of good in the hands of the Board, and obtain a separate existence of its own, having its own interests, purposes, and resources; and yet sustaining such an inseparable connexion with the Board that each would be perpetually embarrassed by the other's movements." (A "separate existence" together with an "inseparable connexion": Here, indeed, was a formula for being "perpetually embarrassed"—if not for disaster.) Should, therefore, the board entirely disengage from the Mission School? In fact, it chose to take an opposite course, by creating new—and firmer—lines of control. From now on, the school would be required to submit "reports, at stated times, of the progress and character of each pupil." The language here had the same dry, fastidious quality of all such communications; clearly, however, the board was trying to fashion a blunt instrument. "[R]eports . . . of the progress and character of each pupil" meant the kind of close oversight needed to prevent any repetition of previous misadventure. Somehow or other, this runaway institution must be roped in, lest it imperil the progress of the entire missionary cause.[42]

The school itself would add one more statement to all that had already been said in the aftermath of these events. In June 1824, as part of their regular quarterly report, the agents defended their approach to "these strangers of different and distant climes and regions . . . [who] have a skin not colored like . . . [our] own. They have immortal souls; they have intellectual faculties, also, which . . . may be made eminently instrumental to the salvation of their pagan countrymen." They had every right to expect "kindness" from their "friends and teachers." Moreover, "it is not true that they are treated in such an improper manner as many have apprehended." The report made no reference to the recent "intermarriage." Instead, it affirmed the broad principle of racial equality, and addressed the charge of special preference accorded to the scholars— a harmful distortion created by "the tongue of slander." This was as far as the school's leadership would ever manage to go.[43]

In other respects, the school seemed to revert to familiar routines, familiar triumphs, familiar struggles and difficulties. Some scholars were making "pretty good progress," while others showed "mediocre talent," and still others proved "quite averse to study." Several became "professors of religion," but an equal (or greater) number gave "no sign of true piety." Some struggled with illness ("very much out of health") and injury ("had a fall from a horse, 4 weeks ago, & has complained much of his head since"). Many resented the labor required of them on the school farm: "After working one day, they are very commonly laid up the next with complaints of stiffness & fatigue." They complained, too, about newly imposed restrictions on travel. At vacation times, they "have an ardent desire to go abroad & visit," which frequently led to "trial & temptation"; hence the principal was unwilling to "grant . . . indulgence of this kind." Even so, from time to time two or three would simply disappear; for example, "these boys . . . took it into their heads to play truant, by going to Litchfield, & spending a week." Some engaged in mischief and foolishness. One, "nearly well" after a long illness, "went into cold water to bathe, improvidently & contrary to advice, & is now quite unwell again." But they also provided school leaders, like Daggett, with moments of reward: "the Lord's Day, Aug. 24 ... eight of my pupils were publickly [*sic*] baptised." And the annual examination days still brought a lift, though perhaps less so than in the school's earliest years. After one of these, the principal somewhat tepidly described his "satisfaction ... considering the character of the youths now in the school."[44]

The principal's health, always precarious, now took a turn for the worse. At one point, he was bedridden for six weeks and completely unable to carry out his teaching duties. In January 1824, just as the "marriage crisis" was unfolding, he informed the American Board of his intention to resign "on account of the state of my health." He rebounded briefly that summer, but in October his departure was confirmed, and a new principal—Rev. Amos Bassett, another Connecticut pastor with long-standing connections to missionary work—arrived to take charge. There were additional staffing changes at around the same time, including the hiring of two new assistant teachers. (Both were New Englanders who had previously been enrolled as students at the school.)[45]

There were comings and goings, too, among the scholars. This was especially true of the year 1823, when perhaps a dozen departed (most to fulfill the promise of return to their homelands, a few expelled for misconduct), while twenty-three were newly admitted. The latter showed a remarkable worldwide spread: Many were trailed by stories of great depth and complexity. Thomas Patoo, a native of the Marquesas Islands, far out in the western Pacific, had left home at an early age, had lived for a time in Hawaii as "one of the king's guards," and had served as a deckhand on several China Trade ships—all this prior to arriving in Boston in 1820. Sent to a "religious family" in the village of Coventry, Connecticut, he had "accepted Christ" after much inner struggle, and was then placed at the Mission School, only to be stricken with a fatal illness. His short but event-filled life would be remembered in a vivid Obookiah-like memoir published within a year of his death. Henry Martyn A'lan and William Alum, both from Whampoa, China, had traveled via northern Europe and a long ocean voyage to Philadelphia; there they endured several months of life on the street before coming to the attention of a "Society of females" bent on promoting "heathen education." Their arrival in Cornwall was preceded by a tour of New York and New England towns, in the course of which they appeared in "native costume" before "large assemblies" of curious onlookers, and raised "a handsome collection" for the school. Jonas Isaac Abrahams, born to Jewish parents in London, had attended three different British "academies" while undergoing a step-by-step conversion to Christianity, had clerked for a merchant uncle in Sicily, and had managed on his own to arrange ship passage to Massachusetts, from where he gained entrance to the Mission School. Along the way, he became a passionate advocate for the "ingathering" of fellow Jews. Photius Kavasales and Athanasios Karavelles were Greek boys from the island of Malta, brought up in the Eastern Orthodox Church. Channeled to New England by Protestant missionaries, they would be greeted with special fanfare by local philhellenes who viewed them as avatars of the then-ongoing Greek War of Independence from Ottoman Turkey. David Carter, a Cherokee youth of mixed-race background, could claim actual ancestral roots in Cornwall. His white grandfather had lived in the town for some years before moving to a frontier location in Pennsylvania, where, along with others of his large family, he was cut down in an Indian raid at the conclusion of the Seven Years' War. David's father, at that point just a child, survived and was carried off by Cherokee captors, and raised as a member of the Nation; thus David's coming to Cornwall completed what was, in effect, a three-generation cycle. Others in this newest group of arrivals included several more Pacific Islanders, Indians of various tribal affiliations (Choctaw, Seneca, Mohegan, Kahnawake Mohawk), a Mexican, and two Anglo-Americans (from Vermont and New York).[46]

The departures were no less noteworthy. A third missionary contingent, including two Cornwall scholars, set out for Hawaii at the end of 1822; more would follow a year later. By now, too, there were Indian returnees, chiefly among those from the Southeast. For them, travel home might yield significant public reward. Typically, they found lodging and other forms of assistance among mission-minded supporters along the way. (This, an American Board official noted, "saves us both embarrassment and expense.") Sometimes they were personally feted: given a formal welcome, treated to elaborate dinners, paraded from one church or religious gathering to another.[47]

All this was especially true in the case of the Cherokee youth David Brown. Considered "most promising" virtually from the moment of his arrival in Cornwall (1820), Brown sailed through the school's program and then went on for several months of additional training at the Andover Theological Seminary. His journey back to the Cherokee Nation, during the winter of 1823–24, became a carefully orchestrated, and extraordinarily successful, speaking tour—its progress closely tracked in both the missionary and the secular press. Its main purpose was to display another signal achievement in the matter of "civilizing," and Christianizing, "heathen" people. Obookiah himself had pioneered this role a decade earlier; with Brown, it would achieve new levels of public impact.[48]

He will travel in company with Jeremiah Evarts, Secretary of the American Board. Evarts will make all the arrangements, collect "donations" for the school (and for the larger missionary cause), serve as master of ceremonies whenever necessary, and send regular reports back to the home office.

The journey begins in late October. At the suggestion of a "patron," David offers, in the town of Salem, Massachusetts, "an Address . . . on the condition and prospects of his countrymen"; then, "on its being favorably received," he agrees "to deliver it in other places . . . when requested." Over the next few weeks he presents the same address in at least a dozen more New England towns (Newburyport, Marblehead, Boston, Charlestown, Cambridge, Dorchester, Reading, Bridgewater, Worcester, Springfield, all in Massachusetts; Providence and Bristol, in Rhode Island). Local newspapers describe "crowded audiences"; in Boston, for example, he has "3000 delighted hearers."[49]

The same reports attend closely to his personal appearance: "His complexion is lighter than most Indians, his features are . . . rather handsome than otherwise, and the expression of his countenance indicates great vivacity and intelligence." His speaking style "is appropriate, manly, and energetic." And most hearers are "astonished at the intimate acquaintance with our language which he evinced." As one of the newspaper accounts concludes: "It was a most interesting and gratifying scene; and we shall long remember the time when we listened with admiration and delight, to a chaste and eloquent address, in our own language, from the lips of an Indian of North America."[50] ("[C]haste and eloquent": exactly as it should be.)

David himself is more cautious in appraising the same events: "The people are ready to hear . . . [but] seem rather shy of me. . . . They have no knowledge of me or my nation. They think that I am one of the few [Indians] who still linger in this [region] . . . without ambition or native energy." If this is a disappointment, he doesn't show it; he also writes, "I could speak in public every day." He makes a short side trip to

Mount Hope [Westerly, Rhode Island], "the former seat of my illustrious ancestor King Philip." (He refers here to the Wampanoag Indian leader in a lethal race war in New England two centuries before. Since then Philip's reputation has been somewhat repaired. David, though no actual blood relation, feels a personal link, and wishes to pay homage.)[51]

In mid-December, they move on to Hartford, Connecticut, where David makes his deepest impression so far. Of his address there, Evarts will write: "The assembly was very numerous & deeply attentive. I opened the exercises by making a statement concerning David & his family before he entered the assembly. . . . Many principal inhabitants expressed their gratification with Brown's performance. I think the occasion will be long remembered." Their take in donations is the best yet: nearly $78. In addition, they hold private meetings with prominent local families (the Wadsworths, the Terrys), and visit "several other places [where] a great interest [is] felt in them & their cause." (And this is still no more than a foretaste of what will come later on.)[52]

David returns briefly to Cornwall "with a gentleman who took him in a sleigh," and then rejoins Evarts en route to New Haven. Their arrival on December 20—"well soaked" by a sudden storm—prompts another burst of public interest and appreciation. The highlight is David's visit to the campus at Yale. There a special "convocation" has been arranged in the college chapel. The audience is "a noble one . . . [including] the Faculty & Students . . . & all the principal inhabitants of New Haven." Evarts avers that he "never saw galleries so crowded as in this instance; the aisles were crowded half way to the pulpit." Following the usual sort of introduction about his Cherokee family and background—clearly a strategy designed to build anticipation—David enters, "conducted by the President of the College—the effect . . . very fine." He is ceremoniously ushered into the pulpit, and proceeds to "deliver his address . . . [which is] rec'd in the most favorable manner." After the meeting, David is "treated with much attention and respect by the people of all classes." He and Evarts lodge overnight "at the President's," where they are lavished with numerous "other invitations." He meets with various town leaders, all of whom feel "much interested in him." (This will become a common refrain: People are "much interested," especially the "principal inhabitants." Of course, it is exactly what Evarts and others at the American Board are aiming for.)[53]

In New Haven, and elsewhere, too, David's address is shaped by a single purpose: to arouse "sympathetic feelings . . . [for] the sufferings of the original inhabitants of this country." He begins by tracing their "happy condition . . . when first visited by Europeans," then describes the impact of "European vices" upon them, "the corruption of their morals, [and] the degradation in which they have been plunged." From this misfortune came their drastic "reduction in number," a process that would be quickly accelerated by their forced involvement in colonial wars. "Repulsed from one clime to another, their coasts echoing with cries and agonies of the dying, their villages destroyed, themselves sharing a dreadful fate, the Indians were in consternation. . . . Fatal has been their doom." To be sure, Indians have themselves been guilty of "cruelties and depradations . . . against the whites." But these are as nothing when compared with the "impious and savage procedure of Europeans." Hence: "[A]s things have been in America for 300 years, better would it [have] been had the natives never seen even the shadow of a white man!" From this unhappy thought, David proceeds to a somewhat more hopeful conclusion. Certain Indian groups—Cherokees, in particular—are striving now to overcome the wrongs imposed upon them; indeed, they are making "rapid advances . . . [toward] civilization." As they proceed they have the invaluable aid of Christian missionaries. All of which leads to a final question: "[W]ho, let me ask, who will send to them missionaries, and support them? Who will obey the voice that sounds from the west for aid? Will not you, who now stand on the soil once possessed by the natives? . . . Oh, remember, remember your red brethren, the original proprietors of America." (The address is taken by hearers as a singular example of "Indian eloquence." At the same time, it is a calculated appeal to what today might be called "liberal guilt." David has found his voice—an Indian voice—and it is powerful.)[54]

From New Haven, they travel to New York City, arriving on December 27; they will stay for over a week. In the course of their visit, David will make four more public appearances. The first of these, in the large Presbyterian church on Murray Street, proves a spectacular success. Before an audience of "2000, or upwards," he speaks "with more spirit & effect than ever before." Evarts is almost beside himself with delight: "I have never known more universal satisfaction given by any performance. The grave & the gay, the religious & the worldly, the learned & the ignorant, all expressed high gratification." And the subsequent "collection" is more than twice the amount received on any previous occasion.[55]

David's other New York appearances are scarcely less remarkable.

One brings out "a large assembly," another produces a "very crowded meeting," and yet another serves as centerpiece of an anniversary celebration for the New York Female Foreign Mission School Society. At this last, David delivers "an address partly composed for the occasion, and partly extempore." In response, the society announces a special $50 gift "for the Cornwall school."[56] By now, David's journey home has the feel of a celebrity tour. Nearly everywhere, his reputation precedes him; sponsors and audiences are waiting. (Indian star power, nothing less: the allure of the exotic, perhaps also the erotic, and what the poet Pinkney has dubbed the "wild" element in native life. David is riding—is himself building—an extraordinary wave of public excitement.)

They move down through New Jersey—Newark, New Brunswick, Trenton, Princeton, Newcastle—greeted by large crowds at every stop. The pace is so rushed that David draws back a bit. At least once, according to Evarts, "I could not get him willing to pronounce more than about five minutes." Still, he soldiers on—and feels sufficiently confident that often he speaks without "having looked upon the manuscript . . . or even unrolled it." Evarts, too, has settled into the role of introducer, using it as a fine opportunity to "enlarge on general topics, such as . . . the imperious claims of the heathen world . . . [and] the magnitude of the work." The two of them have become a smoothly functioning team.[57]

In mid-January, they arrive in Philadelphia; here the tour will reach its apex. Five separate addresses have been planned in local churches, all within the span of a single week. For the first, there is "a prodigious crowd, & many hundreds could not gain admission." David's speech "was well attended to, except that the crowd about the doors was so great as to cause some interruption." At its conclusion, "to our astonishment," John Ridge suddenly appears from out of the audience. (Ridge is traveling the other way—north toward Cornwall—in order to claim the hand of Sarah Northrup.) Evarts, who knows him mostly by reputation, feels a certain wariness. "He is a fluent, forward young man, & has a great deal of Indian pride"; if only "his heart were subdued by divine grace, he might be exceedingly useful to his people." ("Indian pride" and an "unsubdued heart" make a dangerous combination. Still, he might well prove useful—not only in the long run for his fellow Cherokees but right now and right here.) With David, there is much more familiarity; he and Ridge are the same age, are fellow Cherokees and former schoolmates.[58]

Ridge is invited to join the speakers' team, on at least a temporary basis. And the following night, in a different church, things nearly get out of hand. The building is "exceedingly crowded," as are "all the neighboring streets." Those seeking entrance would be "enough . . . to fill several churches." Groups of boys and young men make "a great noise in the church yard & about all the doors." This, writes Evarts, "added to the excessive crowd, gave the whole the appearance of an exhibition rather than . . . a solemn service." (An "exhibition"? Move ahead a century or two, and you could find some equivalents: a circus performance, an evening of vaudeville, a rock concert.)[59]

Now Evarts is worried. He barely refers to David's part, and writes instead of Ridge, who "spoke extemporaneously for half an hour . . . with a good deal of conviction & force." Ridge's theme is the many "improvements" made by the Cherokees in recent years and their "perfect title to their lands"—in short, all politics, no religion. The missionary agenda has, for the moment, been eclipsed.[60]

The next evening brings another tumultuous meeting, "too much filled with women & children, the crowd excessive, the interest great." And then comes yet another, in "the largest place of worship within my knowledge" (Evarts again). "There were thought to be at least 2500 hearers"—though "boys were excluded" as too liable to create disturbance. As with the previous occasion, Ridge seems to overshadow David; he speaks in "a very bold manner . . . by recapitulating some of the most flagitious outrages upon the Indians." Evarts fears that "he would proceed too far," and is relieved when, at the end, he declares, "All this we freely forgive, in consideration of the goodwill manifested toward the Indians by the government and people of the United States." (Do his listeners seek forgiveness? To be sure, unease about Indian dispossession is part of white racial attitudes now. Perhaps, then, Ridge's speech is reassuring, even cathartic.)[61]

The following day, Ridge embarks "upon his journey," while Evarts and David hold the last of their Philadelphia meetings. Here the "noise at the door" and general commotion become so great that David is forced to stop, "and it was some time before he could . . . proceed." Afterward, he is "followed through the streets by a multitude, principally females, to his lodgings."[62] (Events have carried him a long way from their beginning in New England, two months previous, when, as he wrote then, "the people . . . seem rather shy of me." Now the opposite is true. The "multitude" is forward to a fault. "Hearers" jostle for seats in overcrowded meeting halls. "Boys" cavort noisily nearby. Groups of "females" chase him down the street. One rather remarkable Indian youth has stood a large community virtually on its head.)

Soon thereafter, still in company with Evarts, he sets out again, continuing south. In mid-February, they reach Washington, where David speaks before another "crowded audience." There, too, they encounter a delegation of Cherokee chiefs (including Major Ridge), who are just then engaged in negotiations with federal officials on urgent matters of land rights and "removal." The chiefs try to insist "upon his staying longer with them." A year before, in a quest for government support of his "further education," David had visited Washington and met with some of the same officials; now, the chiefs hope, "his acquaintance with Mr. Calhoun [secretary of war] & several members of Congress may turn to some account." But David demurs; after a few days, he and Evarts move on into Virginia. A donations list for late February mentions stops and "addresses" in Alexandria, Fredericksburg, Petersburg, and Richmond. At that point, David's conscience gets the better of him; he decides to return to the capital, after all, and take part in the negotiations there. He feels he must "do all in his power to help his people in their necessity." This means parting from Evarts, who is about to begin a far-flung tour of Cherokee and other mission sites.[63]

Back in Washington, David joins the Cherokee delegation in meetings with congressmen, Secretary Calhoun, and President Monroe (twice). David will describe all this in letters to his board sponsors. Calhoun "talked very unfavorably, & it would seem [is] unfriendly to the whole Cherokee race"; as a result, David is filled with "disgust." The president, however, "gave us some encouragement & told us that he would attend to the subject himself." Some weeks later, he writes to Evarts, describing the final part of his Washington stay: "I visited the President [again] & got acquainted with many influential members of the Union. I made an address at Georgetown to a crowded audience." (An Indian youth has direct access to the president, cabinet secretaries, and congressional leaders. How special is that? How special is David?)[64]

Just here, the record of his journey comes to an abrupt halt. The timing, and manner, of his arrival back in the Cherokee Nation is unknown. But surely it feels momentous. Six months have passed since his setting out from Cornwall, and almost four years since he left home to begin at the Mission School. It has been, in every way, an extraordinary time. And now a large swath of the country has seen at firsthand the progress of Indian "civilization."

Inevitably, following the Ridge-Northrup marriage (late January), contacts between the scholars and the surrounding community became a matter of heightened concern. Specific restrictions on such "intercourse" had been set long before; according to one young resident, scholars were "never allowed to go beyond a certain limit from the school, never into people's dwellings without an invitation, or [unless] sent for an errand from headquarters." If, however, they had "embraced Christ as their Saviour"—that is, had been baptized and admitted into the church— exceptions could be made. Then they might obtain "a written permit to go two or three miles . . . and talk with people, and tell them what Christ had done for them."[65]

But it was one thing to declare the rules, and quite another to enforce them. Whether from a liberal understanding of the "permit" exemption, or perhaps through the "errand" loophole, Mission School students and Cornwall townsfolk found ways to meet, to share, to connect. The evidence lies scattered in several directions, but it does add up.

There are the ledgers of Kellogg's General Store, which record numerous small purchases made by students (in most cases, on behalf of the school). During one randomly chosen month (September 1822), the school was charged for eleven separate transactions, with the actual buyers noted each time. The steward accounted for four of these, his kitchen assistant, Aurilla Hubbard, and his daughter, Sarah, one each. The remaining five are all noted as "per" a particular scholar. Four are listed with first names only—Thomas, Peter, David, Adin—the fifth simply as "a scholar." These are the traces of a routine practice: When butter, or eggs, or "bar soap," or "flannel," or "ribbons," or anything else, was needed for some part of school operations, a scholar might be sent to fetch it. (In fact, Kellogg's was located mere yards from the steward's residence.) The store was a hub, perhaps *the* hub, of town life. Here, then, was an open channel of contact for anyone belonging to the school.[66]

There are the "missives" penned by scholars to their patrons, in which references to individual townspeople frequently appear. A striking example is the correspondence of George "Prince" Tamoree with his initial sponsor, the New Haven minister Rev. Jedediah Morse. Tamoree's purpose was to declare his "ardent friendship" with a local youth named Ruggles Gold: "He is a person which I love . . . there is none that seems so near & dear to me." This was part of a plea for Gold's entry into the school, in preparation for joining the Hawaii mission later on. After his return home, Tamoree exchanged letters numerous times with Rev. Daggett, most of which showed strong familiarity with Cornwall's people and local culture.[67]

There are the public "occasions" at which scholars appeared and mixed with townspeople. For example, a Cornwall historian recounted the following anecdote: "At a general training [of the local militia band], Jason Cross of Cornwall had thrown every contestant in the usual wrestling of those occasions, and, [when] asked by a schoolboy if an outsider might try him, answered with a contemptuous yes . . . [whereupon] George Fox [a Seneca Indian scholar] stepped up, broad shouldered, tall, short-necked, [and] almost lifted Cross from the ground with his first movement and with the second laid him flat." (The "outsider" comment meant someone not officially a militia member.)[68]

There are the more casual encounters recorded many years later by the same historian. Thus: "Col. Pierce relates that at Bennett's Bridge, near his home, Fisk [Isaac Fisk, a Choctaw scholar] and others were swimming when the water was high; and Fisk dove off the bridge, and while they were watching for him to come up downstream, he stepped up to them from behind, having turned and gone upstream underwater." Also: "Adin Gibbs [a Delaware Indian scholar] . . . used to conduct [prayer] meetings in the Johnson Hollow schoolhouse, that Miss Hannah Harrison remembered more than a half century afterward."[69]

There are the gifts left by scholars with local residents, following their departure: for instance, an elegantly decorated strip of "cloth made from tree bark," brought from Hawaii (and known there as *tapa*), given by Hawaiian scholars to a young Cornwall woman, and then preserved to the present day by her descendants.[70]

There is, in particular, an elaborate "friendship album" made as a gift for one of Rev. Timothy Stone's children, a teenage girl nicknamed "Cherry" (sometimes "Charry"). Its contents include personal entries by no fewer than a dozen different scholars—Hawaiian, Chinese, Indian. All are handwritten; all are offered as "presents" to Cherry Stone; all express strong interest and affection. Most are of a religious nature, and many invoke the theme of remembrance. ("I will write a few lines in your book to remember me by.") The album's apparent compiler, and its largest single contributor, was Henry Martyn A'lan, "your friend [and] Chinese youth." A'lan's offerings include poetry, prayers, an elaborate acrostic built on Miss Stone's name, and handsome calligraphic drawings of birds, flowers, landscapes, and people. Some of the writing is in Mandarin characters, one of which describes the recipient as "beautiful" and "charming." (The connotations here include sexual attractiveness.) Several of A'lan's poems, when translated, prove to be unblushingly romantic. For example: "My constant heart tolerates suffering / I will never forget in my heart of hearts your beautiful face / Today I leave with this image [of you]." The last of these lines stands alongside a drawing of a handsome woman with Western features—clearly Cherry Stone herself. On the opposite page is another drawing, this of a young man with Asian features—most likely A'lan *him*self. When the book is closed and the pages meet, the two images are perfectly aligned so as press against each other, suggesting an embrace. (Perhaps a coincidence? More likely not.) What did this outpouring actually represent? Another serious courtship? A young foreigner's infatuation? A considerably overwritten tribute to a friend? We cannot say. But its repetitive nature (with numerous entries by the same person), and the fact that neither A'lan nor Cherry Stone tried to suppress it, suggest an enduring closeness between them.[71]

Entries by other scholars are less effusive but far from perfunctory. There are numerous poems, carefully chosen and handsomely inscribed. Some are almost certainly copied from elsewhere, but others may well have been original compositions. The titles include "My Friend," "The Wandering Pilgrim," "A Family Hymn," "True Happiness," and "Rejoicing in a Revival of Religion." (The last was "written by your respected friend George Fox, Native of Seneca," a fairly typical salutation.)[72]

Taken as a whole, the Stone album offers powerful testimony to this girl's many friendships with Mission School students. It is not, moreover, the only such document from Cornwall in that period. Another, quite similar volume was compiled by a young woman named Martha Day, who came to the town around 1820 to care for her "infirm" sister; the entries there encompass more than fifty different individuals—fourteen of them from the Mission School. Again, the main theme is fond feeling and shared experience.[73]

Members of the Stone family maintained an especially warm relation to the school, as evidenced by some correspondence between Mary Stone (the minister's wife) and the Hawaiian scholar William Kummooolah. Soon after Kummooolah's return home, Mrs. Stone wrote to him about "your good friend John Phelps" (another Hawaiian scholar, still in Corn-wall), who "is acting a very kind part toward us. He is taking your place in our family. As you took care of Mr. Stone (who is now recovered), so Our Dear Friend [Phelps] is taking care of our dear Pierce, who is now insane." (Pierce Stone was her son; his condition was not further explained.) The exact nature of the "care" provided by these two remains unknown. But what seems very clear is the strength and depth of their connection to the Stones, perhaps including actual residence within the household. Mrs. Stone's letter concludes: "We remember you with much affection. We can never forget you, not one of our family." A year later, another scholar, Thomas Zealand, was described by Daggett as having been "considerably in Mr. Stone's family when they have been sick. . . . He is able to do many things as a waiter . . . [and] has commended himself to them very much." Perhaps there was something of a pattern here: per-sonal service and "care-taking" by particular scholars, in exchange for the support and friendship of the Stones.[74]

Finally, there was the Sabbath—all the once-weekly occasions when school and town came together for worship in the First Church. The scholars had their own bench (perhaps more than one, if their number required) and were nothing if not conspicuous. Did they linger, after the service had finished, to chat with one or another Cornwall neighbor? Might they even have taken the opportunity to arrange more personal assignations? At the very least, a sense of familiarity must have grown—on both sides.

Years afterward, a longtime Cornwallite remembered the following about her own household: "We always laid aside all our work when the scholars came. They talked and prayed from the heart. It would revive us, so solemn and yet so joyful. It was a great wonder to them why every one in the town were not Christians, when they had heard of Jesus all their lives." Religion was the bridge to contact; but perhaps, too, there was something more. One feels an openness, an eagerness here, even a sense of delight ("so joyful"). The scholars were particularly welcome. Their arrival created great excitement. And they left behind a lasting impression.[75]

In May 1825, a young Massachusetts woman named Cynthia Thrall stopped at the school with her parents, en route to missionary work among the "western Indians." Like so many previous visitors, she was charmed by what she found there. She "conversed with youths of different nations"; all appeared "polite and manly." She watched a group "preparing for the examination next week," at which they were to enact "an Indian Council . . . [on] the subject of [removing?] the Cherokees and other tribes into the west." She was invited to the room of one of the assistant teachers, who showed her "some specimens of Chinese painting" done by the scholars; moreover, on the same occasion "a young Chinese brought in a very curious lantern of his own making . . . it is beautiful . . . of very light construction . . . [with] flowers printed on fine white cambric in imitation of chinaware." She "walked the distance of half a mile to visit the grave of Obookiah and the graves of the other heathen youths." She "received much attention from the principal of the institution." Everything seemed in order—hopeful—promising. There was no sign at all of another crisis, just then building beneath the surface, and soon to shake the school to its moral and physical foundations.[76]

The year before Cynthia Thrall's visit—and several months after the marriage of John Ridge and Sarah Northrup—a group of town leaders signed an open letter, refuting "frequent assertions . . . that there is a kind of intercourse subsisting between the families in the 'valley of Cornwall' and the 'foreign scholars' which is highly improper"; one of the signers was Col. Benjamin Gold. The letter was published in the *Connecticut Journal;* clearly, it was meant to calm a still-raging storm. But what it promised, it could not deliver. Indeed, within the Gold household itself—at that very moment—events were pointing toward a virtual repetition of the previous difficulties.[77]

The Golds were longtime, deeply devoted supporters of the school; the colonel had been directly involved from the beginning. It was he, moreover, who took the significant step of inviting the Ridge-Northrup pair into the family pew on the Sabbath immediately following their wedding. Two of his daughters had married men who were part of the school's operations—in one case an agent, in the other an assistant principal. Very likely, given this pattern of close involvement, many of the scholars were well known in the Gold household. Perhaps—as was true with the Stone family—some were guests or friends of a quite personal sort.

There were eleven surviving Gold children as of 1825. (Three others had died in childhood.) The youngest of the daughters, born in 1805, was named Harriet;* she and three of her brothers were still living at home. Years later, she would be remembered as "one of the fairest, most cultured young ladies of the place, a very pious, amiable girl, the nearest [to] perfection of any person I ever knew . . . [and] the idol of the family." Her older sisters were all "married in high rank"; now it was her turn. Family members took a lively interest in her prospects, as evidenced by the letters they wrote to (and about) her. "Poor Harriet," teased her brother-in-law Herman Vaill, "I am sorry that you are so attractive, that every old bachelor who owns land near you, & every old widower that comes along in search of minerals, should fix their eyes, on you." At that point, she seems to have had two known suitors: a much older "Colo. [colonel]" seeking "the nearest road to a Second Youth," and a certain "Mr. H. [who] . . . wished for gold to mend his fortunes." (No doubt the pun here was intended.) In spite of "poverty," the latter man apparently had an inside track. "Dost thou affection him, verilie and trulie [sic]?" Vaill asked? Then "marry him, & let others talk."[78]

But Harriet had her own plans. At some point before the date of Vaill's letter, she had formed an "attachment" to the Cherokee scholar now called Elias Boudinot. This young man, like Harriet herself, belonged to a prominent family (the Waties) within his own community. John Ridge was his first cousin; like John, he was of mixed-race heritage. He had been schooled from a young age by missionaries in the Cherokee homeland— first by Moravians at Spring Place, then by Congregationalists at Brainerd. There he was marked as "promising," even "superior"; this made his elevation to the Mission School plausible, and likely. Though initially regarded by Daggett with some skepticism, he soon gained a place among the most favored of all the scholars—both for his fine academic gifts and, at least as important, his strong "spiritual concerns." Within weeks of his arrival, he became "quite anxious for the salvation of his soul; he could not speak on the subject without tears." After much internal struggle, he achieved a full conversion and was admitted to membership in the town's First Church. At this point, he appeared "mild, gentle, and conciliatory in his manner"—in short, a model youth. Over time, the principal would come to see him as "worthy of a finished education"—meaning something more than what was offered at Cornwall. In the spring and summer of 1822, preparations were made for his transfer to the Andover

---

* Although in some sources the variant spelling "Harriett" appears, the traditional spelling, Harriet, is used here.

Theological Seminary, an important training ground for New England ministers; he went there in the early autumn. But almost immediately he was felled by illness—a "bilious complaint"—that forced his withdrawal, and then a return to his family and nation. At the end of October, he joined the travel party that included John Ridge and three others; fortunately, his health improved en route south. During a stopover in New Haven, he led a prayer meeting, after which a participant described him as "a manly, good-looking Cherokee Indian (who bears the name of his patron the immortal Boudinot)." His safe arrival home was mentioned in a Cherokee mission journal in mid-December.[79]

Elias's stay in Cornwall had been a little more than four years from start to finish. Exactly when he and Harriet began to develop their special feelings for each other is impossible to say exactly when. They seem not to have expressed themselves openly (even in private). But after Elias had gone, they kept in touch by exchanging letters, and, with the passage of time, romance blossomed. (Their letters have not survived.) Most of what is known about this largely hidden process came from Harriet's family and friends, in whom she would eventually confide. In July 1825, she allowed that "her mind had been made up for more than two years." This put the crucial moment back at least to the summer of 1823. It was then that she had received from Elias a letter containing "some things . . . that convinced her that she must stop short—or continue to correspond & be ready to meet the consequences." Apparently, this was less than a full proposal, but enough to make her "confident of his attachment." She, for her part, "knew that she should be unhappy if she stopped there"; hence "she made up her mind to marry him, should he propose it, & she did not doubt but that he would."[80]

She was not yet prepared for public disclosures, but she took the further step of asking "a good many Christian people, if they thought it could be any injury to the school, or do any hurt, in any way, if any one of the scholars (Cherokee youth) should return and marry one of our gir[ls &] they all said, no!" Perhaps these inquiries stirred curiosity—and, when set alongside her ongoing correspondence with Elias, something more. Her brother Stephen, "long before the other marriage took place . . . [had] frequently expressed his fears that sister H. would, some time or other, marry one of the Indians." Later, when "that marriage" (Ridge-Northrup) did take place, "rumours were abroad that H. had similar intentions, [and] . . . we [in the Gold family] all became somewhat suspicious." At about the same time, her brother-in-law Vaill "put the direct question . . . whether <u>she thought she should ever marry an Indian</u>; [and] she gave a direct reply, <u>I don't think I ever shall</u>." Nonetheless, according to her sister Catharine, their mother "used to tell Flora & me that she believed that Harriett loved Elias . . . [and] that she might marry him." Clearly, the members of her family felt much concerned and were pressing her hard. However, she remained unwilling to open up; hence she "did endeavor to allay all such suspicions in the minds of her relatives & friends. . . . More than once or twice she declared that people had <u>no occasion</u> to say what they did with regard to her; That <u>no indian had ever said a word on such a subject to her</u>; & That <u>she herself had never thought of such a thing</u>." (At least this was how some of her siblings remembered it—and why, later on, they would blame her for "deception.")[81]

It was not until "about 5 months after Ridge was married . . . [that] proposals were accordingly made [by Elias]. . . . [She] was then ready to answer him, & did." (This would have been June 1824.) Still, she kept matters to herself; the controversy over the first "intermarriage" was just then peaking. But when autumn came, she told her parents and asked for their consent. At first, they "gave a decided negative to it," and "brought up every argument . . . to dissuade her & prevent the connection." They had "previously felt that marriages of this kind were not sinful . . . [but] now they had a severe trial in the case of their beloved daughter." Her father wrote Elias a letter, declaring his refusal. But as winter came on, Harriet took sick; for a time, her life seemed in peril. Perhaps this was a stratagem, perhaps not. One of her brothers-in-law later accused her of "craftiness by making them [her parents] believe that she should die if she did not have her Indian." (Sarah Northrup had played a similar part the year before. And both gained the desired result.) As a consequence, her parents reconsidered, feeling that "they might be found fighting against God . . . [and] told her they should oppose her no longer." Her father sent Elias a second letter, stating his willingness "that H. should do as she pleased"; fortunately, it arrived before the first one. This, in due course, was "acknowledged with gratitude" by Elias.[82]

Harriet's parents decided not to inform others in the family so long as "H. was in a delicate state of health." They knew that her brothers and sisters "would prevent it if they could," and (as her sister Catharine subsequently wrote) that "our opposition would do no good." Suspicion, however, remained strong, and rumors continued to circulate. Some of her siblings took refuge in willful denial; Catharine remarked, "[W]e heard & saw enough to convince us of the fact [of Harriet's engagement], had we not been determined, not to believe it." Clearly, the family was suffused with worry and tension as winter yielded to spring, and spring to early summer.[83]

Finally, there came a point at which the secret could be held no longer; a series of jarring episodes in June would mark it indelibly. The first, involving Harriet's brother Stephen, was recalled years later by a young relative who helped make Harriet's wedding dress. Among all the siblings, these two were closest in age and in feeling; "what one knew, the other knew." Harriet was sure that Stephen "would feel worse over her marriage than anyone else." How, then, to tell him? She decided to write a letter revealing the truth. Then: "One evening they were as usual together in the parlor conversing when she handed him the letter; there were two doors; one she locked before they went in; she went out and locked the other, and gave the key to her mother, telling her not to let him out until he became quiet. He screamed and called 'Harriett! Harriett!' like a madman. She locked herself in her room upstairs and would not come out until he promised to behave. This was before it was publicly known." (*Locked doors, screams, a madman's reaction.* And it was only the beginning.)[84]

Apparently, Stephen was the first of the siblings to be told. Those who lived outside Cornwall received the news by letter—some from Stephen ("The dye [sic] is cast, Harriett is gone . . . "), others from Harriet herself. Their reaction ranged across a bitter gamut—from sorrow, to hurt, to shame, to fury. One of the brothers-in-law, Rev. Cornelius Everest, minister in the town of Windham, Connecticut, was particularly outraged: "We weep; we sigh; our feelings are indescribable," he wrote. "Ah, it is all to be summed up in this—our sister loves an Indian! Shame on such love." Moreover, he was quite ready to assign blame: "Sad was the day when the mission school was planted in Cornwall. What wild enthusiasm has been cherished by some in that place!" Like many others, he singled out Lydia Northrup, mother of Sarah and wife of the former steward, for special condemnation. Somehow this "Jezebel of a woman" had engineered not only her own daughter's marriage to John Ridge but the Harriet-Elias "connexion," as well. "Her art, her intrigue, her selfishness, & her deviltry" had brought "ruin" in both cases.[85]

Another brother-in-law, Daniel Brinsmade, was an agent of the Mission School; it was he who brought the matter to the attention of the full governing board. There was still no open declaration from Harriet or the family, but the rumors had become too strong to ignore. On June 7, Brinsmade "made his suspicions know[n] to the Board, and it made them (as he expressed it) 'as white as sheets.'" Timothy Stone "rose up and said it was a lie, but upon hearing Mr. B['s] reasons, his mouth was stop'd." Joseph Harvey, minister in nearby Goshen and also a school agent, was assigned to confront the Golds—parents and daughter—which he did, in a "long letter," a few days later. Harriet responded with a letter of her own, which "in full expressed her determinations." At some point, too, there was a face-to-face meeting: "[T]hey talked to her half a day, but she would argue them down. . . . She would say, 'We have vowed, and our vows are heard in Heaven; color is nothing to me; his soul is as white as mine.'" (Here was the language of race, given voice and repudiated in the same breath.) Moreover: "[H]e is a Christian; and ever since I embraced religion I have been praying that God would open a door for me to be a missionary, and this is the way." Others close to her family also sought to intervene. Some years later, she remembered, in particular, a long "conversation with Dr. [Samuel] Gold [her cousin] and how he labored with her to dissuade her from her purpose, he supposing she was going to place herself in a very unhappy situation."[86]

The following Sunday, Harvey handed her an ultimatum, "which she is to answer by next Thursday." Either the board would "publish to the world what they know and their surprise!" or Harriet would agree to break her engagement, in which case they would "enjoin secrecy." *In short: You have two alternatives. Go forward, and be exposed to public disgrace; or retreat, and we'll do our best to arrange a cover-up.*[87]

Harriet did not retreat. Thus, as promised, when the board met at the end of the week and approved its annual report, it included the following statement on the proposed marriage: "We feel ourselves bound to say, that after the unequivocal disapprobation of such connexions, expressed by the Agents, and by the Christian public universally; we regard the conduct of those who have been engaged in or accessary [*sic*] to this transaction, as criminal; as offering an insult to the known feelings of the christian community, and as sporting with the sacred interests of this charitable institution." These comments—especially the word *criminal*—would set off impassioned debate within the "christian community" throughout Connecticut, in Boston at the offices of the American Board, and well beyond. The echoes were heard as far away as the Cherokee Nation, where the wounds they caused would fester for years. Indeed, the agents went a step further. In order to disclaim any responsibility of their own, they pointed an accusing finger toward "a single individual, to whose misguided and extraordinary conduct all our troubles on this subject are justly to be ascribed." They provided no name, but didn't need to. All who read their statement would know they meant Lydia Northrup, who by this point had become something of a consensus scapegoat.[88]

Meanwhile, in Cornwall events were moving toward a dramatic culmination. The standoff between Harriet and the agents "was known far and wide, as speedily as the wings of the wind could spread it." Plans were laid for a public protest on the town "plain"—the open space directly fronting the Mission School. The time was set for Wednesday evening, June 22 (coincidentally, or not, the summer solstice). Harriet herself would leave a vivid description.[89]

The previous night, she is spirited away to a neighbor's house, "it being thought unsafe for me to stay at home." She is shown to an upstairs room, from which she has "a full prospect of the solemn transactions in our Valley." At the appointed hour, many "respectable young people, Ladies and Gentlemen" gather as a group "to witness and approve the scene & express their indignation." Most are well known to Harriet. Some are her longtime friends; one is her cherished older brother Stephen. Special staging has been prepared ahead of time, including "a painting . . . [of] a beautiful young Lady & an Indian . . . [and] also . . . a woman, as an instigator of Indian marriages." (These, of course, are meant to represent the chief targets of the meeting: Harriet, Elias Boudinot, and Lydia Northrup.) As twilight falls, church bells begin to toll—"one would conclude, speaking the departure of a soul." Two young men bring "corpses" [effigies] to simulate a funeral pyre. Stephen steps forward and ignites a "barrel of tar" as a means to consume the whole. Flames and smoke shoot skyward, reminding "some . . . of the smoke of their torment [in Hell?] which they feared would ascend forever." Watching from her hideout, Harriet is stricken: "[M]y heart truly sung with anguish at the dreadful scene." The fact that these "transactions" take place "but a few rods east of the Mission School-house" strikes her very forcibly; she takes comfort in thinking that the scholars are "in that very season . . . assembled in their Academy, praying . . . I trust earnestly & sincerely, for their enemies." (From here on, "their enemies" and hers will be the same.) Alas, these include "not . . . merely . . . the wicked world"; for "professed Christians" are present in the angry crowd and give "their approbation."[90]

Another account of the same events appears in a letter by a close eyewitness, and adds significant details. The writer, Elizabeth Pomeroy, was Rev. Bassett's sister-in-law and a member of his household. The "great commotion" of the preceding week had, she noted, created a general atmosphere of "trembling & anxiety. . . . Some of the youth and others here are determin'd she [Harriet] shall never go to the Cherokee Nation." Moreover, "a rumour had been circulated that some high fellows from Litchfield, Goshen & other towns were coming that night to burn or pull down the building belonging to the institution, & the house of Col. G[old] Father of the young lady. . . . Solemnity & consternation sat in the faces of our scholars for they expected personal assault if not death before morning." As evening came on, Miss Pomeroy—though "confined to my room" by fear—leaned out a window to speak with one of the scholars who was just then passing by; "with a pleasant smile he said . . . 'we are going to have a prayer meeting.'" This greatly affected her; "the contrast was so striking between them & our civilized heathen that I could not restrain my tears." Soon Rev. Bassett arrived and "join'd his praying flock." However, as things turned out, those assembled for the protest were a "peaceable Mob." The effigy burning was "all they did," and presently they dispersed, "saluting the school house with a few stones" as they left. The scholars felt greatly relieved; indeed, some thought "it was like one of the [Indian] Council fires, and gazed with astonishment."[91]

Now, and for months to come, Cornwall was "in great turmoil." On July 2, Everest made this assessment: "The best people here, & neighboring clergymen say that they would oppose it [Harriet's marriage] to the last moments, & that if she was a friend of theirs they would much rather follow her to the grave. We are not alone in our feelings. Nineteen-twentieths of New England view the subject just as we do." But, surely, this was an exaggeration; the people of Cornwall itself were not of one mind. Some felt especially repulsed by the notion of "burning a sister in effigy." Harriet claimed a number of "precious friends" as supporters, "but the excitement . . . is such that they dare not have it known that they are on my side." Even church routines were disrupted: "Communion is put off on account of some difficulty occasioned by the Report." Harriet had long been part of the choir, but now she was "requested to leave the singers' seat" so as not to "disgrace the rest of the girls." (Some, or all, in this group may have sympathized with her. When the minister's wife "advised [them] . . . to dress in white to-day & wear a piece of black crepe on the left arm . . . they did not.") The Northrups were in a particularly vulnerable position. In Harriet's view, they "do suffer most cruelly & unjustly"; hence they "have left Cornwall for the present—it being unsafe for her to be here." Daniel Brinsmade put their departure in a rather different light: "Mrs. N. . . . went off in the night and has not as yet return'd. . . . I shall do all in my power to prevent her getting away."⁹²

The family remained passionately engaged with what all had come to call, simply, "the subject." Some twenty of the letters that passed among them have survived to the present; individually and together, these offer vivid testimony of agonizing crisis and conflict. Most were composed during a three-month stretch between mid-June and mid-September. The writers included four of Harriet's sisters and three of the sisters' husbands. At the start, the entire group was united in opposing her plans, and hopeful of forcing a reversal. Their strategy was two-pronged: direct pleas to Harriet herself and a concerted campaign to marshal broad-gauge public resistance. Herman Vaill, husband of her sister Flora and recently an assistant principal at the Mission School, was the pivot around which much of this activity revolved. Vaill was the author of five of the letters and a recipient of fifteen. One that he sent Harriett on June 29, from his home in Millington, Connecticut, was the longest (at approximately four thousand words) and most detailed of the entire lot. In some parts lawyerly and distanced, in others passionate and personal, it encompassed all major parts of the case against her proposed "matrimonial connexions." These included "rash presumption & disobedience" in yielding to the "selfish inducement [of] love of another"; disloyalty to family, by using "gross deception & even falsehood" to conceal her plans; the likelihood that "current members of the school" would assume "license to follow the example of Ridge & Boudinot"; and the "inevitable consequences" of harm to missions everywhere and to the larger "Cause of Christ," with the eventual result that "more of the heathen will be lost." Vaill implicated Harriet's parents (his own in-laws), too; their "silent secret aid & approbation" amounted to "having knowingly disguised the truth." And he concluded with an especially bitter slap: "Will you go? If you are a hypocrite & designed for a reprobate, doubtless you will."⁹³

Harriet would later say of this letter, "[I]t cuts the hardest of anything she has ever received from anyone." There is no evidence that she replied.

Clearly, though, she showed it to several in her family. More than any
other part of their correspondence that summer, it clarified—and per-
sonalized—the issues at hand. Harriet's parents were greatly upset by the
accusations made against them. Sister Catharine wrote to Vaill that "it
is as much as ma can bear . . . to be charged of telling a falsehood; especially by her children. Pa was very much offended, he was outrageous—
he could hardly speak peacibly [sic] about you." Harriet herself lamented
the "great division of feeling among many but especially in our family. It
appears as though a house divided against itself could not stand."[94]

For a time, indeed, the family struggle only deepened. Harriet's
brothers-in-law maintained their "fix'd and unalterable . . . opposition";
in their letters to one another, they traded angry, sometimes mocking,
comments on "this business." At one point, Brinsmade asked Vaill how
well his parishioners "like the idea of having a clergyman who is brother
to an Indian." At another, he wondered facetiously why "we dont see and
feel how good and how pleasant a thing it is be kissd by an Indian—to
have black young ones & a train of evils." And Vaill went so far as to
write: "[I]f H. must die for an Indian or have him, I do say she had as
well die . . . better to die on the side of Xtian honour & Gospel sincerity
than to pine away with satisfied love, & its consequences [i.e., mixed-race
children], on the bed of Love." ("Satisfied love" and "bed of Love": This
was as close as any of them ever came to broaching the sexual aspect of
Harriet's "connexion" with Elias. But surely it was, for all, a powerful
undercurrent.) Meanwhile, too, they redoubled their efforts "to break
up the Indian wedding." In mid-August, Cornelius Everest described
to Vaill half a dozen letters he had recently sent to others; in some of
these the recipient was urged to join in creating a chain by appealing to
additional like-minded friends. In fact, Everest had written to Boudinot
himself, in hopes of administering "a damper if not a death blow to this
business." He wished "we had all written jointly week[s] ago to E.B.,"
and urged Vaill, "if it be not too late," to send off a letter of his own. Harriet's brother Stephen, for his part, "is outrageous"—so wrote one of his
friends. "For his own comfort, for the comfort of H & the whole family,
I wish something might be done to bring his feelings down where they
ought to be." He had stopped going to church, and made wild threats
against Boudinot's life.[95]

The sisters, however, were moving in the opposite direction—were
gradually changing their minds and becoming what Vaill called "turn
overs." By summer's end, all but one of them had decided to stand with

Harriet, and against their husbands. Mary Brinsmade wrote to the Vaills: "I opposed the thing till conscience repeatedly smote me & now, I must acknowledge that . . . my feelings are in unison with the multitude of my Christian friends who tell me to comfort Harriett." In fact, she added, "Harriett never appeared more interesting than she does at present." Mary was influenced by "several . . . clergymen" who had reached the same point, with some even speculating that "great good is to be brought about in these latter days by this event." (When her husband took her letter and added a few lines of "dissent" in the margins, she crossed them out before mailing it. He then sat down and wrote separately, noting her "wrathy" disposition toward him.)[96]

Eventually, feelings would soften also among the men in the family. Stephen had been from the start the most upset; but in late September, Flora Vaill could say of him: "He feels strenuously opposed to indian connections, but has given it up & sings with Harriet as usual, rides & walks with her & is as chirk [in good spirits] as ever. . . . I asked what he intended to do when E.B. came. He said he should be gone at that time." Herman Vaill, too, had begun to backtrack. He wrote to Harriet's father of his hope that "if she goes, she will . . . take such a course in going among the heathen as any good missionary would take." (His use of the conditional form perhaps expressed a lingering reservation.) To be sure, Cornelius Everest and his wife (Harriet's sister Abby) remained "more & more opposed," and considered their "dear friends in Cornwall" to be "greatly in an error." But they were standing alone now. About the rest of the clan, Flora wrote: "[I]t is a harmonious time . . . because they are all convinced it will do no good to say anything."[97]

Even as the Golds endured months of family controversy, the same matters sparked heated response in the wider world around them. Once again, Isaac Bunce, editor of nearby Litchfield's *American Eagle*, was quickly out front. His unconcealed, I-told-you-so tone meshed nicely with his basic goal of focusing blame on the mission movement as a whole. Somewhat surprisingly, this brought him to the defense of Harriet. If the *Eagle* reports can be credited, she was now widely and "wantonly" reviled with "epithets" such as "lewd, graceless, God-forsaken, loathed, disgusting, filthy female." Bunce, by contrast, considered her a "miserable victim," whose mind had been "poisoned" by years and years of missionary preaching. Around the school itself, he wrote, she heard "nothing but the praises of these youths sounded." Thus she was led to "romantic desire . . . [and] a holy zeal to evangelize the savages of the forest," and finally to the arms of "the pious and lovely young Boudinot." The school's leaders—the agents—were, in Bunce's view, the true culprits. Had they really imagined that "these pupils . . . would lose all sexual feelings by coming here?" Did they not realize that "these youths . . . would never think of going back to marry their own dirty, ignorant, and uncouth females . . . after they had learned our habits and seen the attractions of our females?" More likely, there was an actual plan to create "a nursery of Indian marriages" as a means of advancing the larger missionary cause.[98]

Newspapers elsewhere in Connecticut entered the controversy; some were openly scornful. "It appears," declared one, "that the *orthodox fair ones,* at Cornwall, have an overweening attachment to the *Indian dandies,* educated at that Mission School. Their *love-smitten hearts* are probably overcome by the *celestial charms,* which their spiritual eyes discover in the tawny sons of the forest." (And so on, at great length, with italics serving as virtual snickers.) The same element—ridicule in one form or another—appeared in much of the published commentary. Thus, for example, the *Eagle* printed a long, sardonic poem by one of its readers, entitled "Missions Unmasked." A representative verse went as follows:

> Marry Indians and the work is done!
> Or should our Mission less successful prove
> In making converts than in making love,
> Their half-breed race of mission-tinctured blood,
> On Indian ground may do the cause more good. . . .
> Boast not of modern breeds—how short they fall! . . .
> How short of that the world ere long must see,
> Of pappoose [sic] bloods, from Yankee pedigree!

Such writings reflected a steadily rising level of public fixation with the entire fraught "subject" of race mixing.[99]

Meanwhile, *Niles' Weekly Register,* a journal with a national readership, weighed in on the opposite side. "Why so much sensibility about an event of this sort?" it asked. After all, "a gentleman who was thought fit . . . for the office of president, openly and frankly recommended an incorporation of the Indian race with the citizens of the United States, by intermarriages." And "the proudest man, perhaps, in America . . . boasts of the Indian blood in his veins." (Most likely, this was Congressman

John Randolph, one of many "first family" Virginians to claim Pocahontas as an ancestor.) Yet "the rev. doctor, who is at the head of the school, rudely exposes the name of the young lady who had found pleasure in the society of an Indian youth, and makes the affair 'criminal' . . . we do not see why this fuss is made about them."[100]

Now debate would spread to other parts of the country. A "correspondent" of the *Western Recorder* (Kentucky) published a long article in support of tolerance. While acknowledging that "mixed marriages" might seem "inexpedient" to certain "parties," he insisted they were not immoral. Indeed, "these youths have the same right to marry . . . [as] any other individuals." He foresaw some "good flowing" from the current outcry, if only because it would serve to expose "how strong a prejudice exists against the Indians generally." And he "rejoiced" that "the public eye" should increasingly be drawn "to the lamentable condition and prospects of these original sovereigns of America"; he expected "the most enlightened portion of the Christian community" to respond accordingly. A writer in the *Boston Recorder and Telegraph* went much further in affirming the "benefits" to be gained from intermarriage; he included a check against the possibility of "these educated heathen youth . . . reverting back to paganism," the likelihood of "a happy moral influence upon surrounding pagan families," an encouragement to "unite the Indian tribes to the United States in bonds of permanent friendship," and the prevention of "those expensive and bloody wars which have hitherto prevailed."[101]

Indeed, such discussion could touch issues of the widest national import. The same *Boston Recorder* article declared of Indians: "This continent is their home. It is the land of their fathers. We are foreign intruders. Here they must live . . . and they cannot be kept a separate people." In the long term, therefore, they must "by intermarriages become amalgamated with the white inhabitants. . . . This, beyond all question, is the design of Providence." Moreover, the same process would serve to "remove . . . those prejudices which Indians cherish of us." For "they have their prejudices as well as we." To be sure, theirs "are more excusable. They have been cheated and demoralized by our people." Here the writer was entering some very deep waters. And he went on to specify just what he meant. "Their wives and daughters have been debased by our travellers, our fishermen, and our hunters. Sexual intercourse has been mostly illicit, and marriages [made] from motives of gain." ("Sexual intercourse" and marriage across racial lines. Thus did he bring his case clear around to engage—from the opposite, the Indian, side—the matters immediately at hand.)[102]

Nowhere was all this more keenly felt than at the offices of the American Board in Boston. An "extremely distressed" Secretary Evarts poured out his feelings in a series of letters to missionary colleagues. He wrote to one that he could not see "how the contract [between Harriet and Elias, to marry] can be proved . . . morally wrong. . . . Can it be pretended, at this age of the world, that a small variance of complexion is to present an insuperable barrier to matrimonial connexions, or that the different tribes of men are to be kept forever & entirely distinct?" He and his colleagues on the board were especially concerned lest the agents' published position "tend strongly to irritate the young men, who have been educated at Cornwall. . . . Will it not strike their minds as equivalent to a declaration that they & their people are doomed to perpetual inferiority, and that every attempt to rise to an equality with the whites is imprudent & criminal?" The letter closed with an admonition that "no measures . . . be taken to prevent fulfillment of a contract lawfully made," and that "Boudinot, should he visit Cornwall . . . be treated as becomes a Christian & civilized community to receive a youth educated among themselves & professing a faith in the Gospel of our common salvation."[103]

Hoping to head off adverse reaction among the Cherokees, in particular, Evarts wrote also to one of the missionaries at work among them. The action of the school's agents, he said, had been taken without consulting members of the board, who learned of it with "much sorrow & pain." This "should be [made] known to . . . those Cherokees who take any interest in the affair." There were, to be sure, some "extenuating circumstances," since "enemies of missions . . . had succeeded in exciting much popular feeling in that neighborhood"; hence the agents feared "that the School was in danger of suffering materially." Indeed, they "naturally partook somewhat in the excitement around them"—and thus had acted too hastily. It was, all in all, a "deplorable business." Evarts also asked that his personal regrets be conveyed directly to Elias Boudinot, "whom I love." Elias should be informed that the agents' position "is disapproved by a great majority of Christians in this part of the country"; perhaps there would be some consolation in that.[104]

As it turned out, concerns for Elias were not misplaced. Until this point, he had reportedly been "conducting well": teaching school for a time, living with his father and doing farmwork, assisting in the creation of a Cherokee census, and remaining true to his Christian faith and practice. But when news came from Cornwall of the "violent opposition" to his and Harriet's engagement—followed by "anonymous letters, filled with the most scurrilous abuse and threatening his life"—he went into a deep tailspin. According to one account, he felt "very wretched & did not care what became of him." In that frame of mind, "he went out . . . and witnessed a ball play on the Sabbath." Cherokee ball play (a direct ancestor of modern-day lacrosse) involved violent physical competition between players who were "literally naked . . . and yet a large proportion of the spectators are females"; moreover, it followed "all night dances . . . attended by wives without their husbands, and husbands without their wives . . . [with] all deeds of darkness committed." Such, at least, was the (undoubtedly skewed) picture that circulated among the missionaries, for whom ball play stood as the very epitome of "heathenish ways." That their cherished protégé, the "lovely" Elias, could have been driven to such depths—and on the Sabbath, too—was a stunning disappointment. One went so far as to say that he "has become a poor worthless Indian & has given himself up to all the foolish [illegible word] of his pagan countrymen." Others were inclined to be more charitable, noting the "cruel treatment he had received from those who would claim to be his spiritual fathers . . . [which] for a moment, darkened his eyes." (It was mentioned, too, that "the scholars at Cornwall were allowed to do this [ball play], though perhaps in a different form." However, there is no corroborating evidence from inside the school itself.)[105]

Elias himself quickly regretted his "fall." He assured Evarts, who by now had begun a new journey through the South, that "he had never done such a thing before." Moreover, "he does not justify or excuse himself"; he would try to regain his footing and move on. To that end, he decided on a forceful response to the charges leveled against him by the school's agents. He composed a letter to Timothy Stone, demanding "a public recantation . . . so far as it inculpated him, or that they should prove that his conduct was criminal." He insisted, too, that Mrs. Northrup had not "enacted any agency in promoting the match." Neither she nor her daughter Sarah had "advised him in the matter. He commenced the courtship of his own motion." (Others would later confirm this. And Sarah claimed that her mother had actually tried to dissuade Harriet on the grounds that her own marriage to John Ridge "had made so much difficulty in Cornwall.") Elias did acknowledge that "courting a lady" while still a member of the school might be "improper," but he denied "any authority of the agents" once he had left.[106]

Elsewhere in the Cherokee heartland, reaction to the events at Cornwall ranged from surprise, to bafflement, to dismay, to outrage. Sarah Ridge "could not help laughing to think how foolish they act." The elderly and much-respected Moravian missionary Rev. John Gambold "was astonished that gentlemen of intelligence, the professed friends of the Indians, should have opposed a connexion with Boudinot on the single ground that he is an Indian." (Indeed, Gambold remarked that "if . . . it should please the Lord to remove my wife," he himself would have no compunctions about "proposing matrimony . . . [to] a Cherokee woman of suitable character & attainments.") In midsummer William Chamberlain of the American Board visited Major Ridge, who confronted him with "a few plain questions . . . [to which] he wanted . . . a plain answer." In particular, "he wanted to know if my Northern friends had any grounds from scripture or anything else to justify them in their violent opposition to intermarriage with the Cherokees?" Chamberlain "could not answer for the northern people," but agreed "for my own part . . . that the young people of the different nations should marry where they pleased."[107]

In late September, David Brown wrote at length to Evarts, along very much the same lines. He began by describing the letters received by and about Elias. One, from Connecticut, declared that "if he should come to Cornwall after his intended wife, half the state would rise against him"; another stated simply, "his life would be in danger." The effigy burnings had been taken by Cherokees as "an expression of abhorrence to the Indian character." Yet, as Brown noted, many white men "have married Cherokee ladies without censure . . . so how can it be thought wicked for us to marry among them, especially if some of our white sisters are pleased with such connexions?" Such, he concluded in his typically restrained way, "are the common topics of conversation among us, & we know not how to understand them." Brown's friend and mentor, the missionary Daniel Buttrick, was not so restrained. Addressing especially the matter of death threats, he fulminated: "What? Against our dear brother Boudinot? . . . Even the heathen world blushes, and humanity sickens at the thought. . . . The tomahawk, and scalping knife, or the more polished weapons of civilized butchery, will be raised against him! The hand of the assassinating murderer, upheld by ministers, and Christians, and the gathering mob, will take away his life! All will unite in the clamorous cry, 'Let him be put to death!' . . . Where [else] . . . can such unfeeling barbarity be found?"[108]

On one point all were in full agreement: Mission work among the Cherokees was now irrevocably compromised. The "difficulties" surrounding the first "intermarriage" had left strong residues of doubt and tension. A second, very similar sequence—coming little more than a year later, and including "the publication of the Executive Committee" that used the word "criminal"—was sure to have "disastrous effects." Moreover, the widespread expressions of "harshness & cruelty . . . [toward] this promising young man [Boudinot]" only deepened the crisis. Elias himself told Evarts flatly that "the Cherokees will not send any youths to the school" in the future.[109]

At about the same time came a new round of alarming news from Cornwall. Two Choctaw scholars had been suddenly expelled and "sent off with five dollars each to find their way home, a distance of 1400 miles." En route, they "told the story of their disaster to all who befriended them," including many in the Cherokee territories. The school authorities declined to state publicly any reason for their dismissal, but Evarts's official correspondence included a brief note: "[T]he two Choctaws have been dismissed for a proposed matrimonial union." Moreover, the young Cherokee David Carter was also sent off "with censure"—probably, though not certainly, for a similar reason. (*A proposed matrimonial union?* And, possibly, two or three? Where would it end?) From the standpoint of many in Cornwall, this might well have seemed a nightmarish result of the "example" previously set by Ridge and Boudinot. For southeastern Indians, it was another kind of nightmare—a bitter confirmation of the prejudice directed against them, even by some among their erstwhile "friends."[110]

As the New Year (1826) approached, the impasse between Harriet Gold and Elias Boudinot, on one side, and the citizenry of Cornwall (and surrounding communities), on the other, seemed complete. For him to come north "after his intended wife" ought—one would imagine— to have imperiled his very life. For her to receive him as her intended husband ought to have exposed her to withering scorn from many of her neighbors. For the two of them to proceed to official marriage ought to have aroused angry, perhaps violent, local reaction.

However, none of this happened. Harriet had previously thought "she would have to leave the country and meet him [Elias] in some place agreed on," yet by winter's end she had decided "to be married in Cornwall like other folks." The initially vehement opposition of various family members had continued to weaken. Herman Vaill, for one, wrote to Harriet in early March, wishing that "you will be the instrument of accomplishing much in behalf of that People whom I suppose you now consider your Nation." He added "kind regards & best wishes, to brother Boudinott [sic], when he becomes your husband." About the attitude, just then, of others in the town and region, little can be discovered. The only surviving firsthand account—by the woman who made Harriet's wedding dress—states simply that "excitement ceased and he [Boudinot] came into town unmolested." However, residues of disaffection were undoubtedly present. Local tradition asserts that Boudinot arrived "in a disguise." And, according to a town historian writing some years after the fact, minister Timothy Stone declined to perform the wedding ceremony because this "would have exposed him to immediate . . . insult and abuse." (Stone's position was complicated and ambiguous. He was close to the Gold family and was known as "a most sincere friend" of Harriet. As an agent of the Mission School, he had developed a close relationship to Boudinot, as well. In fact, he would lose his pastorate anyway, a few years later, owing "in no small degree [to] the effect of this Indian marriage connection.")[111]

So it was that on March 28, 1826, Harriet and Elias were married by Rev. Francis Case, minister at nearby Goshen, in the parlor of the Golds' home. According to the same dressmaker's account, "they had a splendid wedding at two o'clock p.m. . . . My mother and father attended. . . . No young people were invited. Only the married friends and relatives of Harriett's parents were present." Just beforehand, there was a family breakfast, at which Stephen managed a civil greeting to the groom— "[H]ow do you do, Boudinot"—and "waited upon us, and upon Boudinot also." Again the source is the dressmaker, who was "in the room with them," and was charmed by Elias: "I almost forgot that he was an Indian; he prayed so fervently, and sang so sweetly." Stephen, however, still clung to his grievance and "could not see them married. He worked all that afternoon in the saw mill." And when the ceremony was finished, the newlyweds left town immediately, accompanied by Harriet's parents; they would spend the ensuing night at an inn in the town of Washington, Connecticut, some distance to the south. Reportedly, armed men stood ready to protect them if necessary; but the scene remained calm.[112]

The *impossible* had once again become real. That it passed without major incident this time remains, in view of all that had come before, something of a puzzle.

Coda: There is a second possibly contemporaneous source—and it is another kind of puzzle.

Buried deep in the archives of the Cornwall Historical Society lies an old, unattributed typescript fragment, which casts a strange, stark light on the Gold-Boudinot wedding. Indeed, this is no ordinary depiction; arranged as a kind of biblical allegory, it begins thus:[113]

> *Then Bennett saddled his hind horse and went to the land of Goshen and implored the Levite of that place to come with him to the house of Benjamin and join in marriage the heathen unto the daughter of Benjamin & he took with him as servants others of the sons of Ishmael. . . .* ("Bennett" would have been Bennett Roberts, an assistant teacher at the school, who was known to be a particular friend of Harriet. "Goshen" was the town adjoining Cornwall to the east. "The Levite of that place" was its minister, Rev. Case. "The house of Benjamin" was the residence of Benjamin Gold. "The heathen" was Elias Boudinot. "The daughter of Benjamin" was Harriet Gold. "The sons of Ishmael" meant other Indian youths then at the Mission School. The original Ishmael, in the Old Testament, was the unfortunate outcast son of Abraham and Hagar, of whom it was predicted [Genesis 16:12]: "[H]e will be a wild man, whose hand is against every man, and every man's hand is against him." Obliged with his mother to shift about in the wilderness, he would grow up to become "an archer." All these elements—wild man, wilderness setting, wandering life, personal estrangement, even bow-and-arrow skills—were, for white Americans of the nineteenth century, readily identified with Indians.)

A middle portion of the document describes an elaborate process of summoning guests to the wedding ceremony.

> *And Bennett . . . spake unto Erastus the Merchant & Uriah the* [illegible word], *saying . . . come I pray thee and attend the Marriage of the daughter of Benjamin with Elias, one of the sons of Ishmael, and eat of the marriage supper & drink of the wine & they said So be it. . . . Then Bennett sent messengers to John & his wife Sarah, saying . . . ye are invited to be guests at*

the wedding of Harriet the daughter of Benjamin with Elias the Ishmaelite the smell of which Ishmaelite thou loved. And Bennett also bid Abijah & his wife Lucy to the wedding, saying Come I pray thee . . . and join with those who also love the smell of the Ishmaelites at the Marriage of Elias the Ishmaelite & Harriet the daughter of Benjamin, and Abijah said So be it & his wife said seeing as thou art pleased to bid me also & as my Bowels yearn for the sons of Ishmael it shall be according to thy saying. ("Erastus the Merchant" was Erastus Swift and "Uriah" was Uriah Tucker, both longtime residents of Cornwall. "John & his wife Sarah" could perhaps have been John and Sarah [Northrup] Ridge, though their attendance at the wedding seems improbable and is otherwise undocumented. "Abijah & his wife Lucy" were a local couple surnamed Peet. The repeated mentions of "the smell of the Ishmaelites" are perplexing; possibly they have a sexual meaning, given the linked references to love and "Bowels [that] yearn for.")

Finally, the wedding itself:

Now after the Priest of the Land of Goshen had joined the Ishmaelite unto Harriet in marriage the Guests ate of the Bread & Meat & drank of the Wine that was prepared for them and made themselves merry. Each one went his way except Sarah, the Wife of John, who abode by the [illeg. word] *all night to take the smell of the Ishmaelite whom she loved so well & in the morning she departed & no one looked after her.*

The last few lines carry forward to the following day—and are especially hard to fathom.

The Ishmaelite with his wife Harriet & their kinfolks made ready their Charriotts [sic] *and journeyed to the borders of the Great River . . . saying we will go to the house of John the Duke; peradventure his heart may be softened and he will permit us to warm by his fire for it is cold; and they went in and the wrath of John the Duke was kindled and he thrust them all out of his house.* ("The Great River" was the Housatonic, Cornwall's western border. "John the Duke" cannot be identified; perhaps he was a prominent Cornwallite opposed to intermarriage.)

There remains the question of authorship. But the field of possibilities can be narrowed. It was someone fully versed in the Bible—the King James Version. It was someone intimately familiar with all the wedding details—and with the wide range of people involved. It was someone with a close emotional connection to those details and those people— hence the undercurrent of deep feeling, and the tone of mockery, maybe even self-mockery.

There is really just one person who qualifies on all counts. And that is Elias Boudinot. Almost certainly, this was a bitter send-up composed by the embattled "Ishmaelite" himself.[114]

The Cherokee Nation

Sarah (Northrup) Ridge left Cornwall for the Cherokee Nation with her husband, John, in February 1824; Harriet (Gold) Boudinot made the same trip (although by a somewhat different route) with her Elias two years later. Neither could have had any clear picture of the place to which they were headed. The land, the climate, the culture, and, most important, the people among whom they would make their home: All were blank spaces to be filled by experience.

So, too, in my own case: an equally blank space. Until I have a chance to go there.

Traveling south on the broad superhighway that crosses from southeast Tennessee into Georgia, I begin to assess the landscape. There are hilly stretches, alternating with pancake-flat plains. There are numerous streams to cross, but most so small that they can barely be seen from the road. There are areas of forest, though nothing like what must have been present two centuries ago. Much of this, in fact, is obscured behind billboards, onrushing trucks, telephone wires, and other accompaniments of modern living.

Presently, I exit the highway and turn onto a small side road. Now I'm in the north Georgia countryside; the scale of things seems greatly reduced. Approaching the town of Calhoun, I pass through a sparsely populated area, with occasional squat one-story residences, a few small chicken farms, two side-by-side auto-scrap yards, four different Baptist churches (all within the space of barely two miles), and a large fenced enclosure advertising a "Turkey Shoot." A little farther on, there is a nicely manicured golf course—and then, directly opposite, the protected historic site of the onetime Cherokee capital, New Echota.

It is still early; I have the place to myself. The land is treeless and, as one visitor wrote of it in the 1820s, "smooth as a house floor"; its color in late spring is a dusty tan. A modest office building, attached to a small museum, marks the entrance. Just inside the perimeter, the signage begins; I read that New Echota was founded in 1819, with the express purpose of creating an official center for the Cherokee Nation. It was from the start a planned community, with a carefully gridded plat of roadways, converging on a cluster of government buildings in the middle. The latter comprised a Council House, a Supreme Courthouse, and a printing office. The same 1820s visitor noted also "two or three Merchants Stores [and] about half a dozen hansom [*sic*] framed Dwelling Houses . . . which would be called respectable in Litchfield county & very decently furnished to be in any country."[1] As time passed, other residential housing would gradually fill the remaining lots.

To be sure, none of this has survived in its original form. Replicas of the three main public buildings were constructed some years ago, and may now be seen by visitors. Each is a virtual cube—two stories high, but with a remarkably small footprint (a bit more than twenty feet on a side)—raised on stone piers well above ground level, apparently to protect the base from flooding. (A good-size river, the Oostanaula, flows just to the north but isn't in view from the town itself.) The interiors of both Council House and Courthouse have elevated platforms on opposite ends—to be occupied by judges and other government officials—with benches for spectators in between; the upstairs rooms were used as conference chambers. The look of the whole is tidy, unpretentious, rather sparse, and more than a little compressed. There is one other replica to see, a "Cherokee farmstead." This includes a small dwelling made from stacked logs notched on each end so as to intersect at the corners, a boarded barn, a smokehouse, and a corncrib, set on a lot of no more than half an acre and surrounded by a split-rail fence. Presumably, this was the typical household plan when New Echota was a fully functioning unit. In my mind's eye, I correct for the passage of two centuries by imagining the presence of trees and other vegetation.

I correct also by adding a human presence; fortunately, there are period documents to help with that process. In 1819, a missionary witnessed the very first of the council meetings held here: "It was past noon, the council had convened, and a multitude of people gathered. . . . All at once a troop of horsemen were seen coming along the road . . . with a stately looking person in front. A little way from the council they alighted, [and] marched two in a file . . . with the stately person before them, whom I observed on drawing near to be the Cherokee [Major] Ridge . . . reported to be the greatest orator in the nation."[2] Another visitor described the bustle of movement and trade around New Echota: "There is much travel through [the town]. . . . Large wagons of six horses go to Augusta and bring a great load. . . . I have seen eleven of [these] . . . pass by . . . in company."[3] Nowadays, the feeling of the place is quite desolate; back then, it was anything but.

There is another part of the site that captures my attention: the lot that held the home of Elias Boudinot. It is clearly identified, but all that remains in the ground is an ancient well and a stone foundation—a rectangle of roughly sixteen feet by twelve—probably the base for a free-standing kitchen. The main residence is known to have been a substantial wood-framed building of two stories, with front and back porches and superimposed balconies, all done "according to the New England style."[4] A visitor remembered its interior as including four rooms downstairs "and three upstairs, with five closets. . . . The chimneys were of brick with large open fireplaces." On the whole, it is said to have closely resembled the only still-extant structure on the entire site, the home of the longtime missionary to the Cherokees, Rev. Samuel Worcester. (Worcester's house lies on the very fringe of town, clearly—perhaps purposefully—set apart from the rest.) The Boudinot property also included a stable, two corncribs, a smokehouse, a "turkey house," and a pair of orchards (for peaches and apples).

So here, on this exact spot, Elias and Harriet Boudinot lived for roughly a decade, beginning a year or so following their arrival from New England. Here they would birth and begin to raise their children. From here, it was just a short walk to the printing office, where Elias would hold forth as editor of the Nation's newspaper, the *Cherokee Phoenix*. And here in 1835, he and other leaders would gather in his living room to sign the famous (infamous?) Treaty of New Echota, transferring the Cherokee homeland to the federal government and presaging the migratory process that would later become known as the Trail of Tears. (But this is getting ahead of our story.)

The current reconstruction of New Echota gives no sense of the natural environment supporting the town in its heyday. For that, one must enter the surrounding woods, following a well-marked trail. It seems safe to assume that much of the vegetative life found here today would also have been present two centuries ago; indeed, period documents, by and about the Cherokees, provide good confirmation. Many of the various trees and plants can be identified with their Cherokee names and linked to a host of traditional uses.[5]

The trail parallels a small creek bed, where outsiders are believed to have set up camp while visiting New Echota; the water, though brackish now, would have been important to their stay. I pass through a grove of pines of the so-called loblolly type, common throughout the Southeast—their trunks standing straight and tall, their wide crests piercing the sky. There are also white oaks, yellow poplars, redbuds, and especially dogwoods, now bedecked with their showy springtime flowers. Before the modern era, Cherokees used the dogwood tree in multiple ways. Its blossoms were boiled in water to create a steep taken against colds or headache. Its tree bark helped make a special bath thought to cure poisons, and its root bark infused a poultice valued for healing wounds. The root might also yield a reddish dye applied to fabrics—and sometimes to human skin.

Indeed, the forest is remarkably diverse. Farther along, I see sweet gums showing their distinctive burrlike seedpods, red cedars with a berry fruit favored by birds, and hickory trees whose characteristically shaggy bark was used by the Cherokees both in basketry and in preparing a tea drink consumed by "ball game" participants in order to make their limbs more supple. There is luxuriant undergrowth everywhere: wild honeysuckle plants, ferns of many sorts, and profuse clusters of river cane. The woody stems of the cane were cut for weaving into mats, baskets, or even fences, and might also serve as arrow shafts.[6]

Of course, the forest supports a variety of wildlife (though much less now than formerly): muskrats, kingfishers, raccoons, wild turkeys, turtles, water snakes, and more. Two centuries ago there would also have been larger game: wild pig, bear, deer. In the trees are multitudes of songbirds—warblers, catbirds, yellowthroats, kingbirds—plus owls and hawks. All the different animal species would have been well known to the Cherokees. Some were hunted with arrows and guns, others taken in traps. Aside from what was consumed locally, they supported a flourishing trade—with other Indian groups, and, increasingly, with white settlers both nearby and far away. Medicinal plants were especially coveted by whites, and deerskins were carted out to colonial centers in huge quantities over the span of nearly a century.

I'm nearing the end of the nature trail now, and completing my New Echota tour. On the way out, I pass the Worcester house; it virtually shouts its "New England style." From here, in 1831, Worcester defied the Georgia law obliging white residents to leave Cherokee lands, a stance that would lead to the crucial Supreme Court case—*Worcester v. Georgia*—preceding the Nation's forced removal.

Back on the road, I head south for another several miles; my next goal is the former home of Major Ridge in the town of Rome. Now maintained as a public museum (called Chieftains), it powerfully evokes Ridge's life and times, and the community he led. Its origins and early development were unusual. The first structure on the site, dating perhaps to the 1790s, was a form known as "dog trot"—with two separate parts, aligned north and south, and joined by a covered walkway in the middle. Each part contained two single-room stories, top and bottom. A ladder on one side gave access to the upper story. Windows were two per room (just eight in all). A brick chimney climbed the south end. The walls were of hewn logs throughout, creating a strong backwoods look. As best one can tell, the second-floor rooms were used for sleeping and storage, while those on the lower level served as keeping room and kitchen.

This was the situation until the late 1820s, when the house underwent a major renovation and expansion. The original dog trot was not taken down; instead, its log walls were encased in finished siding, with the original floor plan left mostly intact. Additions were made on the east side, greatly enlarging the building's footprint. The walkway was fully enclosed so as to become a center hall, with a formal staircase ascending to the upper floor. The walls and ceilings were paneled in various hardwoods; in particular, an upstairs parlor was "finished in first-rate style."[7] And the entire design was given a new orientation by moving the front door to the south wall. The renovation also added a veranda at each end, many more windows (with shutters), two new fireplaces, a portico athwart the entrance, a balcony supported by "turned columns," and a complete weatherboard exterior painted (both then and now) a gleaming white. If this process sounds complex, so is the struggle to comprehend it. (Fortunately, the museum provides a number of helpful charts; and glassed openings afford views into the old log walls.) But the main point seems clear, and compelling: The house was transformed from "back-woods" to quite grand and genteel. The timing is also pertinent. The work was carried out within a few years following John Ridge's return from the North; he apparently played a direct, supervisory role. Thus in January 1831, he wrote, in a letter to Cornwall's Dr. Samuel Gold, "I built a fine house for my parents, which would look well even in New England, before I left them."[8] The comparison to New England brings me up short. When I stop to think about it, a New England influence could include quite a bit more in the life of the Nation—the mission-sponsored schools and churches, for example, and a certain genteel style found among its leaders. Obviously, too, there was the matter of direct support, from and by New Englanders, during the run-up to removal. (Was this outside connection held against the Cherokees by powerful southerners? Possibly including Andrew Jackson?)

With the house converted nowadays to museum format, its interior is filled with displays—standing cases and, on the walls, a large array of labeled images and text. In the period of the Ridge family's occupancy, it would, of course, have looked very different; surely, there were furnishings and other domestic appointments suited to a comfortable, even affluent, life. Much of this would be impossible to recover now. But archaeological digs near the house have unearthed a trove of ceramic and glass fragments, the residue of European-made tableware, including hand-painted china, lusterware, pearlware, mochaware, and fine crystal.[9] The most important remaining detail from the 1820s renovation is the staircase, where a gracefully sculpted railing lies atop hand-hewn pine supports. It has one peculiarity; at eighteen inches above the stair surfaces, the railing seems unusually low. According to current speculation, this was to accommodate John Ridge's congenital hip ailment; he may have gone up and down seated on his backside. (Related evidence includes a pair of shoe heel taps—made of brass, one excessively worn, the other intact—recovered from an excavation site just north of the house; these have been linked to John's chronic limp.)[10] At the turn of the staircase, a handsomely arched triple window looks out over the garden and down toward the Oostanaula River.

Today, the grounds are unprepossessing. Greatly shrunken in size, they are bordered by a much traveled highway on one side, vacant, scrub-filled lots on two others, and a patchy lawn on the slope above the river. During the Ridge years, the picture was entirely different. Close to the main house stood a group of fine old shade trees: poplars, sycamores, oaks. (One of these survived until blown down in a storm in 1977, at which point it stood nearly two hundred feet tall, with a crown one hundred feet across.) Multiple outbuildings were scattered about, serving both the domestic and "business" activities of the Ridge family. There were two freestanding kitchens close by the back door. There were corn-cribs, a stable and paddock for horses, a smokehouse, a lumber house, a henhouse, four "old round-log Negro houses," a garden for vegetables, herbs, and "11 quince trees," a stockyard for cattle (up to 150 head), and several feed lots for hogs and sheep. Farther to the south were eight crop fields (covering 280 acres) planted in cotton, tobacco, wheat, oats, indigo, potatoes, and, most especially, corn. There were, as well, large orchards, one of which contained over a thousand peach trees, the others many dozens of apple, cherry, and plum. Nearer to the house stood a paled garden, a vineyard, and a nursery for growing ornamental shrubs. The labor on all this property was performed largely by slaves—at one point said to number fifteen, at another twenty-one, at still another thirty. These, presumably, were the occupants of the aforementioned "Negro houses." (Excavation near the site of one such has uncovered traces of colonoware, a distinctive pottery type reflective of West African styles.)[11]

Two additional activities supplemented the income that Major Ridge obtained from the land. Perhaps as early as 1817, he had built a general store fifty yards directly to the north of the house. Its day-to-day operation was in the hands of a resident white trader named George M. Lavender, with Ridge as a silent partner. A stone cellar foundation is extant today; recent archaeological work around and beneath the floor has unearthed numerous "high-quality and up-to-date" ceramics produced by known English manufacturers, together with occasional shards of native cooking pots, large deposits of hog bones, suggesting the butchering and sale of meat, and several silver spoons (two of them inscribed JR, presumably for John Ridge).[12] An account of the business, written two decades later, included also "medicinal plants and roots . . . skins and venison and hams," all destined for export to white customers, and "salt, whiskey, gunpowder, calico, &c, consumed by [the Cherokees]."[13] Lavender was "said to have engaged in his service numbers of wagons transporting these commodities to Augusta, a distance of two hundred and fifty miles, and returning with goods for his store." From all this he earned, over the span of twenty years, "a large fortune," and Ridge, too, must have profited handsomely.[14]

Meanwhile, a ferry business—crossing the adjacent river—furnished still more income. Its terminus was a small dock roughly one hundred yards west of the house. From there, a simple raftlike conveyance, scarcely more than a floating bridge, would be pulled along a rope stretched between trees on opposite banks; by this means, freight as large as a wagon and team could be carried across. Evidently, this was an important service; the road on the north side ran straight through to New Echota, and the entire site was generally referred to as Ridge's Ferry. In a government-sponsored property assessment from 1836, the value of the ferry was set at $12,000, while that of everything else on the property totaled just over $10,000.[15]

Invariably, visitors came away impressed. One described the house as "an elegant painted mansion"; another compared it to "manors of old." Flanked as it was by the store and its various satellite structures, it struck a pair of touring officials as "the home of the patriarch, the scene of plenty and hospitality." Indeed, they concluded, "the Ridge . . . went forward in the march to improvement until his farm was in a higher state of cultivation and his buildings better than those of any other person in that region, the whites not excepted."[16]

Almost certainly, John Ridge and his Cornwall bride Sarah (Northrup) lived in his father's house following their arrival from the North sometime in the spring of 1824. (A contemporary source has them occupying "an apartment by themselves.")[17] This must have preceded the renovation that John would subsequently claim to have supervised "before we left them." Meanwhile, at more or less the same time, John was building his own house, roughly six miles to the northeast, beside a spring called (in Cherokee) Tanta-ta-rara or (in translation) Running Waters. The estate itself has been identified the same way, from that day to the present.

I approach it from what is now known as the Calhoun Road. It stands very much by itself and can be seen from at least a quarter of a mile away.

Its frontal presentation is not unlike that of the Major Ridge house. A wide main door, neatly framed by an overhanging porch, with paired windows on either side of the ground floor and a matching arrangement for the upper story: Here, in short, is the essence of Georgian symmetry and, at the same time, another example of "the New England style." The back includes a large L-shaped addition. There are two brick chimneys and twenty-five windows.

There is also a problem right now. The house is privately owned, and fully occupied; access is doubtful at best. My knock on the front door brings no response. I prowl somewhat furtively through the surrounding yard in order to view the building from all sides. But there is no way of gaining entrance. Instead, I must settle for the written report of a recent National Park Service site visit, with extensive photographs from both inside and out. The design of the rooms is as one might expect: front foyer, living room, dining room, den, kitchen—all on the first floor—with bedrooms overhead. There is fine detail work around the several fireplaces, handsome ceiling trim, and attractive paneling on all the doors. Taken altogether, it does seem an appropriate venue for a highly prosperous, New England–educated Cherokee chief.[18]

There are also some personal and official impressions of the house recorded not long after Ridge's own time. Here is a description left by his son, who lived at Running Waters as a child: "I remember it well—a large, two-story house, on a high hill, crowned with a fine grove of oak and hickory, a large clear spring at the foot of the hill, and an extensive farm stretching away down into the valley, with a fine orchard on the left." The son also recalled an adjacent building, "some 200 yards distant," where, at his father's invitation, a woman teacher from New England conducted school for local young-folk.[19]

This is an adequate overview, but it lacks specific details. Some of the latter can be gleaned from a different source—government documents pertaining to the process of "removal." In Ridge's case, three are of special importance. An 1832 land survey carried out by the state of Georgia—preliminary to a lottery for transferring Cherokee properties to white citizens—shows a square plat of 160 acres, plus a "field of 40 acres," all marked "John Ridges"; included in the middle is a rough sketch of a sizable residence.[20] This, however, was far from the entirety of John's holdings; a Cherokee census taken in 1835 lists a great deal more. Included there are two farms (Running Waters, and another at a place called Turkey Town, a dozen miles farther south) with 350 acres under cultivation, producing an annual yield of 6,500 bushels of corn (evidently the chief crop), plus a main house and sixteen outbuildings (kitchen, corncribs, smokehouses, chicken house, stables, and so on); five orchards containing 615 fruit trees; twenty-one slaves, housed in two separate cabins; and several additional structures at an adjacent "council ground." In addition, John owned a ferry—for crossing the Coosa River—at the second of his farms. The same section of the census shows the properties of forty-two other men living nearby; John's total far surpasses all the others.[21]

A final set of valuations, made the following year, brings the residence itself into sharper focus. Its basic shell was two stories high, built of hewn timbers, on a foundation of "neat stones," creating a footprint of fifty-one by nineteen feet, with three brick chimneys; there was also at the back a more recent single-story addition of thirty-one by twenty feet. Inside, "both floors [were] neatly laid," the upper story "ceiled," and "the whole neatly chinked and plastered." There were twenty-four "large glass windows" and six fireplaces (one with a "brick baker" [oven] attached).[22] All of this makes a close fit with what can be seen today: exactly the same footprint (including the rear addition), similar overall appearance, almost the same number of windows, and the same number of chimneys (subtracting one known to have been taken down in the mid-twentieth century).

Perhaps, too, we might try putting the Ridges—the family itself— back inside. The 1835 census records the following under "occupants." Males under eighteen, four; females under eighteen, two. These would have been the children—John Rollin, Susan, Flora, Aeneas, Herman, Andrew, in that order—their actual ages ranging from eight years to a few months. (But there should have been seven. Where was Clarinda, the Ridges' disabled daughter?) On another line just above: males over eighteen, one, and females over eighteen, one—obviously the parents, John and Sarah. A separate category, pertaining to race, mentions six "half breeds"—again the children—and one "full-blooded," which must have meant John. Sarah, evidently, was overlooked in this latter accounting, though the family total was put at "eight Cherokees." All in all, one has the sense of a snug, and still expanding, household.[23]

We have no full-on description of Sarah in these years, but about John a newspaper account from 1832 is quite specific: "J. Ridge [is] rather tall and slender in his person, erect, with a profusion of black hair, a shade less swarthy, and with less pronounced cheekbones, than our western

Indians. His voice is full and melodious, his elocution fluent, and without the least observable tincture of foreign accent or Indian."[24] There is, as well, John's portrait, painted a few years earlier by the artist Charles Bird King. He sits at a table with quill pen poised over a sheet of foolscap—this to denote his calling as a writer, a negotiator, a man of affairs. His dress matches the part: He wears a rather formal buttoned coat over a ruffled shirt with a high collar. His skin is pale, though ruddy around the cheeks. The "profusion" of his hair is evident, his lips are full and a little pinched around the edges, his nose long and straight. But it is his eyes that center the whole: They express—how to put it?—a certain distance, a wistfulness, a kind of inward resignation. Though still a quite young man (mid-twenties), he has the look of one who has experienced much, thought hard, felt deeply. It is perhaps a stretch to connect these qualities with his time in Cornwall. But they would, for certain, be needed and tested in the years that lay just ahead.[25]

~ PART FOUR ~

FINALE

CHAPTER SEVEN

American Tragedy:
Renascence and Removal

R emoval" lies at the heart of the story we commonly tell about
Indians in the nineteenth century. At first glance, removal and the
grand project of "civilizing" heathen peoples appear to be opposites. Yet
on the deepest level, they were joined—were, indeed, different expressions
of the same impulse. For the civilizing process imposed a complete
renunciation of traditional lifeways; as such, it was another form, a
cultural form, of removal. In the case of Indians, it meant essentially
this: *Let them become farmers instead of hunters, Christians instead of
pagans, cultured in the manner of white people instead of "savage." Then
maybe—just maybe—they can be absorbed into the national mainstream.*
However, by the 1820s and 1830s, many whites had already given up on
that possibility—at best it seemed impractical; at worst, dangerous—
and were coming to favor actual physical removal. *Just drive them out,
send them far away—across the Mississippi River at least—and leave them
entirely to themselves. (And then let us have their land.)*[1]

One way or another—through either kind of removal—the native
presence would be finished; hence the increasingly prevalent trope of
"the vanishing Indian." To be sure, this supposed "vanishing" was cause
for regret, even guilt, among a certain portion of whites, mostly "benevolent" reformers on or near the East Coast. Farther inland, and especially
among those living close to the frontier, neither regret nor guilt would
be much in evidence. There, the prevalent attitude could be reduced to

a single phrase: *Be gone!* That suggests another, much sharper term—drawn from our own twenty-first-century world—to replace the more neutral-sounding *removal.* In short, "ethnic cleansing."[2]

Removal—in the straightforward sense of relocation—had been part of American history from the settlement years onward. In its earliest phase, it was irregular, haphazard, ad hoc, and closely tied to warfare. Thus, in seventeenth-century Virginia, sporadic outbursts of violence (especially in 1622 and 1644) between white settlers and the so-called Powhatan Confederacy led to a treaty confining local Indians to a small part of the territory previously theirs. Farther north, in New England, a similar outcome followed the conclusion of the Pequot War (1637) and King Philip's War (1676). In Carolina, after defeat in a bloody conflict with colonists (1713), thousands of Tuscarora Indians migrated north to join the Iroquois Confederacy.[3]

As time passed, the transfer of lands and the movement of native peoples could also be accomplished peaceably, through a combination of formal purchase, negotiation, and government pressure. This was repeatedly the case, for example, in eighteenth-century Pennsylvania, where Shawnees and Delawares ceded one large tract after another, by deed or treaty, before moving on to what is now eastern Ohio. In the 1740s and 1750s, the Ohio country itself became a scene of contest between colonists and native tribes—until the Treaty of Fort Stanwix (1768) secured major Indian land cessions and established a new "line of settlement" roughly following the course of the Ohio River. Here, the Delaware (or Lenapi, as they originally called themselves) were directly involved once again. Indeed, the story of this particular group, spreading across many generations, was especially remarkable for *serial* removals. After relocating from Pennsylvania to Ohio, the Delaware would go on to Indiana (Treaty of Greenville, 1795), to Missouri (several more treaties, 1818–26), to Kansas (1829), and finally to Oklahoma (1850s and 1860s). One might well say that removal became central to their very identity.[4]

At the start of the nineteenth century, the vast territory obtained through the Louisiana Purchase appeared to open new avenues for removal. And the process itself became more organized, more systematic, with governmental authorities—at both federal and state levels—increasingly in charge. Thomas Jefferson, as president and prime mover for the Purchase, was especially active this way. In 1804, Congress formally authorized him to negotiate with "Indian tribes owning lands on the east side of the Mississippi [to] exchange lands [for] property of the United States on the west side."[5]

The results of such initiatives were profound. To the north, there began a complex process of relocating various tribes in the vicinity of the Great Lakes: Chippewa, Ottawa, Pottawattamie, Wyandotte, Menomenie, Winnebago, Sioux, Fox, Sac (among others). The overall direction of this movement was from the east side of the lakes (especially the Michigan Territory) to the west side (Wisconsin, which had also gained territorial status), and then to sites fully across the Mississippi. In the meantime, too, some native groups had moved to Wisconsin from much farther east—for example, Iroquois from upstate New York, and the Stockbridge (Massachusetts) Mahicans.[6]

But it was in the Southeast that removal would have its most dramatic enactments—and would most fully approximate ethnic cleansing. There, what were known as "the five civilized tribes"—Choctaw, Chickasaw, Creek, Seminole, and Cherokee—remained relatively well entrenched into the early nineteenth century. However, a series of treaty-based land cessions, begun long before, had eaten away much of their territorial base. Then, in the 1830s, all five were subject to federally mandated relocation in the newly designated Indian Territory (what is today the state of Oklahoma). Some ten thousand Choctaws were forced from their homes in Mississippi between 1831 and 1833. The migration of the Chickasaw from southern Alabama was spread out over a longer period, roughly 1837–50. The Creek mounted a strong resistance, but even so they were driven out (also from Alabama) during a three-year stretch, starting in 1834. The Seminole fought removal with extreme tenacity, retreating from their original settlements along the coast of Florida to its swampy interior, from where they conducted sporadic guerilla warfare against federal troops, lasting well into the 1850s. Most were eventually put to flight or killed, but enough remained to support several reservations, which are part of Florida to the present day.[7]

And then, the Cherokees—the most famously removed group of all. Considered whole, theirs is a story of remarkable, but doomed, achievement. As such, it shadows, on a vastly grander scale, that of the Foreign Mission School—high hopes, valiant effort, leading to eventual tragic defeat.

Indeed, by 1825, the Cherokees were widely considered "the most civilized tribe in America." This description included both a salute to all they had accomplished and the seeds of their destruction. "Civilization" remained the official goal. But success with the goal might undermine other interests crucially important to whites. Success would mean accepting them, on equal terms and with equal rights. Success would mean competing with them for valuable resources. Success would mean including them as partners on the route to America's "manifest destiny." Was the country at large ready for all that?

When colonial settlement began, there would have been little reason to single out Cherokees for special notice. Their interior location—on either side of the spine of the southern Appalachian Mountains—meant that contact with white newcomers did not begin until almost the end of the seventeenth century. The land they controlled was substantial, a roughly rectangular expanse of 350 by 300 miles. But their numbers were not particularly impressive—perhaps twenty thousand at that point. They differed from their nearest neighbors, the Creeks and the Choctaws, in language and lineage; they were Iroquoian (with ancestral roots far to the north), the neighbors Muskogean. Otherwise, they did not stand out.[8]

Their lifeways followed the pattern of most groups native to the region. They subsisted on a mix of hunting (deer and other wildlife), gathering (roots and berries), and hoe-based agriculture (especially corn, beans, and squash). Men were the hunters, women the farmers. They lived in largely autonomous town communities—perhaps sixty in all—each one organized around a council house and a central plot of ceremonial ground. Local populations were crosscut by the lines of seven traditional clans. Family organization, including residence and descent, followed matrilineal principles; mothers played a notably strong role. Property, especially land, was held in common. Everyday experience followed a code of cooperation and consensual decision making; group interests superseded those of the individual. Their engagement with the world around them expressed a deep and rich spirituality. Encounters with nonhuman forces, as manifest in dreams, visions, and ghostlike presences ("little people"), were expected and were accorded high value; elaborate ritual enactments (such as the annual Green Corn Festival) affirmed their links to the natural environment. It is perhaps too easy to view traditional Indian cultures as being uniquely "in balance"; but for the early Cherokees, that impression seems strong.[9]

It seems strong, at any rate, in contrast to what came next. Regular interaction with whites, starting in the 1690s, would prove fundamentally disruptive. The first of several major impacts was epidemic disease. Cherokees, like virtually every Indian group, succumbed in huge numbers to the unfamiliar microbes carried by Europeans; smallpox, typhus, measles, and other such illnesses struck them again and again, at irregular intervals. Partly from this cause, their total population shrank, over the course of a century, by at least half.[10]

Warfare had a similar effect. The French and Indian War (1755–63) found Cherokees directly engaged, first on the English side, then on the French; in response, invading armies of frontiersmen laid waste to more than a dozen of their towns. The Revolutionary War (1776–83) proved even more destructive. The Cherokees stayed loyal to the empire, preferring to take their chances with a distant monarchy rather than nearby (and increasingly hostile) white settlers. Within weeks of the war's opening, they launched a series of raids on the Carolina interior. But soon the tables were turned; "patriot" forces counterattacked and inflicted a region-wide slaughter. Even after the official Peace of Paris (1783), guerilla warfare continued in and around the Cherokee heartland. As a further result, the tribe became divided into "upper" and "lower" towns. It was the latter group that went on with the fight, until a final treaty was made in 1794.[11]

Moreover, time after time the Cherokees were obliged—cajoled, bribed, forced—to yield ground in the face of advancing white (English) settlement, part of a larger process described by historians as "settler colonialism." Some of this was formalized in negotiated land cessions (no fewer than seven within one sixteen-year period, 1768–84); the rest involved outright expropriation. The center of their remaining holdings moved unevenly toward the south and west—which meant increased proximity to Spanish and French territorial possessions. By century's end, there were European occupiers on every side.[12]

Trade with white colonists brought another kind of disruption. Cherokee hunters responded vigorously to European demand for furs and (most importantly) deerskins; in return, they received firearms, housewares, tools and other manufactured goods, textiles, liquor, and grains. The result was a growing reliance on outside sources of supply, with a corresponding decline of indigenous craft traditions. As early as 1745, a Cherokee chief lamented, "My people cannot live independent of the English. . . . The clothes we wear we cannot make ourselves. They are made for us. We use their ammunition with which to kill deer. We cannot make our guns. Every necessary of life we must have from the white people."[13]

By around 1800, Cherokee fortunes had reached a nadir. Three-quarters of their land was gone. Many of their towns lay more or less destroyed. The deerskin trade was failing (with all forms of wildlife drastically reduced by overhunting). Traditional cultural norms and sanctions lay in disarray; shamans, for example, were discredited by their inability to slow the pace of decline. Individual Cherokees would respond in different ways—some by withdrawing to remote sites (the highest of the Appalachian highlands), others by migrating far to the west (the Arkansas Territory), still others by succumbing to acute personal despair (apathy and alcoholism).[14]

Yet soon thereafter, the core population began a process of readjustment so powerful and positive that it would come to be called a "renascence." In part, this meant embracing the "civilization" policy favored by the federal government. Thus many Cherokees turned to various forms of intensive farming. For some, raising livestock became a kind of surrogate for hunting. Others stepped up their production of grains, fruits, and garden vegetables. At least a few went straight into market-based plantation agriculture, raising cotton and other cash crops with the labor of enslaved blacks. These changes meant abandoning the clustered life of their traditional towns, with households dispersing across the countryside. Families became more nuclear in structure, property holding more individualized, the cultural ethos more competitive and entrepreneurial.[15]

The process included wholesale political reorganization: first (1809) through the formation of a National Council with general oversight responsibilities, then (1817) with the creation of a three-branch system of governance, including a bicameral legislature elected on a representative basis, and, finally, the adoption (1827) of a national constitution closely modeled on that of the United States. The overall result was a far more centralized, more "republican" system than the Cherokees had known previously. Another result was a surge of ethnic pride. For, although the similarities to the pattern of the United States were immediately clear, Cherokee leaders envisioned using what they had created to promote and protect their people's interests. "Civilization" in the service of independent nationhood, "civilization" that would yet preserve their core identity: thus their ultimate goal.[16] Ultimately, their renascence might parallel—and partake of—the broader American rise to greatness. (Cherokee "exceptionalism"? Why not?)

Education was another aspect of the program, and, after about 1820, schools proliferated throughout the Cherokee country. Then, at almost the same time, came the remarkable invention of an indigenous "syllabary" (a system of figural notations to represent each of eighty-six syllabic sounds in the spoken language) by the illiterate silversmith Sequoyah. Now the large majority of Cherokees who did not speak (or read) English might avail themselves of writing; many did so within a scant few years. Scarcely less striking was the spread of Christianity—at first by way of the schools, then through the strenuous exertions of Protestant missionaries. In the 1820s, circuit-riding preachers—principally Methodists and Baptists—reached even the most remote areas of the Nation, and returned with extravagant claims of new converts.[17]

To be sure, these signs of "progress" did not go uncontested. Education and assimilation to white ways was the special province of a small minority, most of whom were of mixed-race parentage. White men had been settling among the Cherokees—marrying, buying property, starting businesses, joining in the life of the Nation—over the course of several generations. A national census from 1826 recorded the presence of 211 "intermarried whites" (within a total population of over 13,000). Estimates of "mixed-bloods" at around the same time reached into the thousands. Clearly, members of this latter group possessed important advantages in dealing with the non-native world: bilingual communication, knowledge of the market system, familiarity with mainstream (white) cultural ways—not to mention direct ties of blood and friendship. Increasingly, they assumed the status of a national bourgeoisie. Increasingly, too, they rose to positions of political leadership. But their prosperity and influence aroused resentment among the much larger mass of unassimilated "full-bloods" (whom federal agents sometimes referred to as "the real Indians"). Tensions around class and cultural difference simmered, and occasionally broke into the open. In the mid-1820s, just as the newly evolved governmental system was taking full effect, tradition-minded Cherokees mounted a vigorous pushback against the pace and direction of change. Some advocated rejection of the constitution, of Christianity, of white residents—and a return to the old tribal ways.[18]

But these internal strains were repeatedly overshadowed by struggle with outsiders. White frontiersmen pressed in on several sides; clashes with them became inevitable. Boundaries were a constant point of dispute. Young Cherokees would turn to horse stealing and cattle rustling, in a sort of counterpoint to the taking of their lands. At the same time, political leaders in states claiming sovereignty over the Nation (Georgia, in particular) pressed their case ever more stridently. The federal government was caught in the middle, tilting this way and that, searching for some middle ground. Through it all, pressure to engross additional parts of the Nation's territory grew and grew—as did Cherokee resistance.[19]

Some had already given up and joined the scattering of predecessors in Arkansas (to be known henceforth as the Western Cherokees); most were determined to stay. The choice, as presented to them in virtually continuous negotiations, amounted to this: *Cede us more of your land, or remove yourselves entirely; there is no third way.* (The hook was baited just a bit. Land cessions would be linked to equivalent territorial grants in the West—in short, would be officially part of an exchange.) In 1819, the Cherokees agreed to yield just over a quarter (four million acres) of what they still retained—this as a "guaranteed" final step. There would be no full-scale removal, and no further cessions. As described by one of the resident missionaries: "[T]his deliverance, beyond expectation, has spread joy and gladness through the nation." From now on, wrote another in a letter to a chief, "you are allowed to sit quietly around your own fires and under your own trees, and all things are . . . set before you and your children."[20]

As the Cherokee renascance went forward, American culture at large was caught in the maelstrom of the Second Great Awakening. Revivals were everywhere—in the cities, the small towns, even the villages of the rural countryside. These, in turn, lent a surge of energy to the mission movement. By 1820, no fewer than eleven different denominational and interfaith organizations were fully engaged in "the Great Cause."[21]

Within this group, the American Board of Commissioners for Foreign Missions held pride of place: more workers in the field, more sites, more schools and training grounds, more converts won (or claimed) overall. At first, the board's focus was overseas. Previous missionary efforts with the native people of America had proved disappointing; moreover, the pool of potential converts was vastly greater in "the Eastern hemisphere." Still, a case could be made the other way. "Many . . . have thought it strange," the board reflected in 1816, "that while so much has been doing for the distant heathen in India, so little should have been done for the not less destitute tribes on our continent, and within our borders." Indeed, revival activity had aroused strong feelings of guilt about dispossessing Indians. (At least this was true of a good many evangelical Christians.) A leading preacher, in an oft-reprinted sermon on missionary goals, said the following: "[W]e are living in prosperity on the very lands from which the wretched pagans have been ejected; from the recesses of whose wilderness a moving cry is heard, 'when it is well with you, think of poor Indians!'" The upshot was compromise: Missionary efforts should be directed both ways—to the domestic and foreign fields alike. The Cornwall school was itself an expression of that divided frame, with its mix of scholars from many far-flung parts of the world, alongside others from Indian groups within the territorial United States.[22]

In time, the arm of the American Board's outreach would embrace dozens of native communities, from Oneidas and Senecas east of the Great Lakes, to Ojibwa in the far north, to Choctaws and Chickasaws in the lower South, to Pawnees, Dakota Sioux, and other Plains Indians farther west. The goal was everywhere the same: "to convey to them the benefits of civilization and the blessings of Christianity." If all went according to plan, someday "the red man and the white man shall be found mingling in the same benevolent and friendly feelings, fellow citizens in the same civil and religious community, and fellow-heirs to a glorious inheritance in the kingdom of Immanuel." In short: Converting the one and reviving the other would lead to a truly biracial and bicultural consummation.[23]

There was room for debate about the most efficacious "means." Should "civilization" of the Indian precede or follow his religious conversion? Was some degree of schooling, especially the attainment of literacy, a necessary qualification for church membership? Or might "unbelief" be directly reversed without any distinct preparatory steps? Missionary groups could, and did, take different positions; the American Board, for one, generally advocated a civilization-first approach. In practice, however, both elements would usually advance together—as suggested by the wide use of the single catchall term "Christian civilization."[24]

Among the various Indian missions, the one with the Cherokees was—by the 1820s—a showpiece. It had not always been so. Throughout most of the eighteenth century, Cherokees rejected overtures from missionaries, suspecting that these folk, like other whites, were moved chiefly by greed for their land. In 1800, they did grant entrée to a small group of Moravians. And in the 1810s, they opened up to other denominations— Baptists, Methodists, Congregationalists (the American Board). Their main interest in doing so was the creation of schools; but inevitably, too, there would be growing emphasis on faith and conversion. Churches appeared in several parts of the Nation; some of the pastors were themselves Cherokee. Evangelicals all across the country (especially in New England) reacted with excitement to news of this "striking change." Tangible support, both money and goods, arrived in quantity. Visitors arrived, too—among others, President James Monroe. The 1826 census counted approximately 10 percent of Cherokees as converts; many more were said to be churchgoers, though not finally "committed." Increasingly, religion became melded with other aspects of the renascence; to be Christian was, almost by definition, to be "civilized," as well. But this alignment served to accentuate existing differences within the Nation. Again, well-to-do "mixed-bloods" proved most apt for conversion, while the vast majority of "real" Cherokees—by and large, the "full-bloods"— remained loyal to traditional belief and practice.[25]

Indeed, for all the promise of renascence, deep pools of skepticism remained among Cherokees of every background. Would white people actually accept Indians—any Indians—as "fellow citizens in the same . . . community" and "fellow heirs" to God's kingdom? Did they truly believe in the essential equality of the different races? And would they finally allow even "the most civilized tribe" to retain its own land in the heart of the rapidly expanding American republic?

It was in this doubt-filled atmosphere that members of the Nation learned of the "scandal" attending the marriages of two of their own most favored sons. And it was amid this troubled citizenry that John Ridge and Elias Boudinot would soon take up the mantle of leadership. For their compatriots who welcomed them home, as for the school that had disowned them, events were moving toward a profound denouement.

CHAPTER EIGHT

"Even the stoutest hearts
melt into tears"

As controversy swirled around the Gold-Boudinot engagement, the school entered a kind of limbo. To whatever extent possible, its leaders—the agents and principal—sought to maintain a familiar round of regular business. Rev. Bassett reported hopefully that the current scholars were busy with no fewer than a dozen academic subjects: "reading, writing, English grammar, geography, history, rhetoric, geometry, surveying, navigation, natural philosophy, and the Latin and Greek languages." To be sure, this sprawling curriculum created significant (and familiar) challenges: "[A]s but few were pursuing the same studies at the same time, the labor of instruction has ever been much greater than, in other circumstances, it would have been." There were discipline challenges, as well: Bassett noted his particular "regret . . . that some of the beneficiaries were indolent and inattentive to the regulations of the institution." Indeed, seven had been dismissed during the months of May and June alone. The ranks were further thinned by the deaths from illness of two young Hawaiians later in the summer. Others, however, were newly admitted—at least five, possibly more. On a different front, resentment flared around the old sticking point of the "preference" afforded certain scholars by gifts from private benefactors. Equality had always been a key principle of life at the school; hence the agents reemphasized that all "must conform to the regulations . . . in relation to their apparel as well as in other respects." (Those regulations were designed to minimize overt signs of difference.) Moreover, individual "donations" of spending money should be "put into a common stock," and subsequently "given to the scholar on whom bestowed . . . [only] at the discretion of the Executive Committee."[1]

But all this was beside the point—like whistling in the face of a rising wind. For the leaders of the American Board had already begun to consider permanent closure of the school. In his position as board secretary and day-to-day manager, Jeremiah Evarts was necessarily at the center of their discussion. His letters to the school's agents, while repeatedly protesting their public stance against intermarriage, also raised a different—and fundamental—question: "whether it is practicable, in the majority of cases, to take ignorant & uncivilized boys, place them in a school by themselves, & have them educated so that they will become men, capable of taking an active part in human affairs."[2]

Evarts was not alone in his concerns. At a meeting in September 1824, the American Board faced the issue of the future with unusual directness. "As the School increases in age," its leaders declared, "and [as] the more advanced students are completing the term originally fixed as the period of their education, it becomes more and more a question of delicacy and difficulty to decide whither they shall be sent, and how they shall be employed." Some—at least a few—could be "sent to their native land, and there be associated with missionaries in such . . . work as they are able to manage." However, many others "are not capable of rendering any essential service"; with these the requisite "talents, industry, self-denial, and other qualifications" were lacking. Nor were the scholars themselves entirely to blame. Their experience in the surrounding community was a bewildering mix of interest and condescension. As Lyman Beecher and others had noticed at the start, they were liable to a kind of "puffing" by outsiders of all sorts; thus there was real danger that they might come to "feel very big." At the same time, they were "treated in various respects, as though they were and must be inferior to ourselves. . . . These different kinds of treatment, which result from inquisitive curiosity, mixed with Christian benevolence on the one hand, and from established prejudices, on the other, make the young men feel as though they were *mere shows,* a feeling which is too accurate an index of their real situation."[3]

Taken together, these comments expressed a complete, and startling, turnabout. And they do suggest that the "marriage crisis" may not have been entirely unwelcome to board leaders. Even as they deplored the prejudice it called forth, they could imagine using it as a pivot for change. Operational problems had beset the school virtually from the start: problems of pedagogy, of discipline, of health, of cultural difference and personal discord. Almost nothing had gone exactly as planned—up to, and very much including, the pair of now-notorious engagements. Of course, the school had tried to shield its ongoing struggles behind a strenuous campaign of public relations. Time after time, its leaders had drawn a picture of glorious goals in process of rapid fulfillment. But their own internal records told a different story, one that was full of disappointment and frustration.

Only thus can their readiness to give up on the school be understood. How—given all they had previously claimed—might a decision to close be explained to the world at large? For a start, they could point to the matter of local opposition; Evarts, for example, noted the way "the people of Litchfield county . . . [had become] . . . more & more convinced that there were insuperable difficulties in conducting the school." With one another, they might go somewhat deeper, and fault "the character of the individuals who had been educated at the school." Evarts's reference to "ignorant & uncivilized boys" unable to "become men capable of taking an active part in human affairs" was unusually candid; the phrasing revealed an antipathy that he and his colleagues had previously sought to suppress. If the school was to go under—so they assured themselves—it would not be from mistaken premises or misdirected effort on their part. Poor "character" and lack of "capability" in the scholars could henceforth be seen as decisive factors—this, and their uncomfortable relation to the wider community. Meanwhile, the tumult around the "intermarriages" furnished a most convenient cover. Never mind what was, or wasn't, "morally wrong" here; years of practical experience provided sufficient reason to close.[4]

The actual process of closure must be managed by "orderly" means; in this, as in so much else, they were nothing if not orderly. Thus during the fall of 1825, the board appointed a special committee to consider "whether a school designed for the education of youths collected from heathen nations can be permanently supported with advantage to the cause of missions." Indeed, there were reasons to "doubt whether a sufficient number of promising youths can be obtained, and . . . restored to their respective countries greatly improved, civilized, and guarded against evil." The language here was chosen with great delicacy, but its meaning was obvious—and ominous for the school's future.[5]

In due course, the committee members "visited Cornwall & there met the Agents & very carefully investigated the condition of the Institution. . . . The question of discontinuing the School was largely discussed." Their subsequent report was a mix of temporizing and short-term compromise. They began by affirming that the school had "already answered very important purposes in promoting the interests of Christ's kingdom"; thus its numerous supporters had "no cause to regret their pious exertions & liberalities" on its behalf. At the same time, "it was evident that the relative circumstances of the Christian & heathen parts of the world have materially changed in the course of the few years . . . since the school was established . . . [and] there does not now appear . . . the same reasons for . . . [its] continuance." The committee was not yet "prepared . . . to express a decided opinion" on the matter of closure; for that, additional "inquiry & deliberation" would be needed. In the meantime, "instruction & discipline [should] be continued as formerly . . . but . . . [with] no additional pupils . . . sought for admission." If all went well, "before or during the next summer the indications of divine Providence will render the path of duty . . . clear"; the Almighty Himself would weigh in.[6]

At winter's end, the committee undertook a second round of work. The school's principal, Rev. Bassett, was asked to supply "an account of all the present members," including length of stay, academic and spiritual accomplishments to date, and likely "contribution" in the years ahead. This took until the fall; by then, a decision for "discontinuance" was widely rumored. The agents, meanwhile, scrambled to form an alternative plan: Perhaps the school might be kept open as a "mixed institution," with the training of local schoolteachers and "foreign youths" joined together? But, in fact, it was too late; as Evarts would subsequently admit, the board had made up its mind in June (but had postponed a public announcement). According to one much later account, Lyman Beecher argued vigorously for "continuance" but was outvoted by Evarts and other colleagues.[7]

In November, Evarts wrote Bassett with what amounted to a death sentence: A new committee would meet soon "to bring the concerns of the institution to a close." The idea of its continuing in "mixed" form he waved aside with a vague reference to "many obvious difficulties." His letter concluded with a brisk expression of gratitude for "the fidelity and paternal solicitude with which you [Bassett] have taught the pupils and watched over their interests," and of regret if "your private affairs have been injured & your prospects of a useful & agreeable employment interrupted." The decision was final; there would be no going back.[8]

By this time the board's overall view of missionary work had swung completely around, as evidenced (yet again) by Evarts's correspondence with colleagues and supporters. To one, he wrote that the "original design" of the school, while "most laudable" and though successful "to some extent," could henceforth "be more easily & effectually accomplished in other ways." With a second, he was more emphatic: "The fact is, the F.M. School is not answering the end of its institution. . . . We cannot be justified in keeping it up, while all the ends which it was designed to accomplish can be secured in other ways at less expense & with less hazzard [*sic*] than has attended the experiment." He reported the opinion of Rev. James Ellis, a recent visitor to Hawaii, "whom we regard as . . . very wise and judicious," that the "young men from the Sandwich Islands, had much better . . . [go] thither for an education than stay in this country." Ellis was referring to several of the scholars still enrolled at Cornwall, whose return to the islands would put them in the hands of the missionaries already at work there.[9]

As time passed, this way of thinking would come to embrace the entire missionary movement. *Instead of bringing them, the heathen—here to us, in America—for conversion and schooling, we must seek them out in their own homelands.* The point applied especially to places where missions were already ongoing. As one commentator noted, "[E]xperience seems to indicate, that youths educated upon missionary ground are more apt to be fitted for the various circumstances of a residence among their countrymen, than those who have been accustomed to a different manner of life." Put simply: Experience of America would likely reduce—not increase—their effectiveness after returning home. Here, they inevitably encountered "temptations"; here, too, a taste of "privilege" would compromise their "original hardihood," and thus unfit them for the "privations, which they must bear among their uncivilized countrymen." Better, then, to send them back, where they "can be so instructed at missionary stations as to be very useful to their countrymen." Nothing could have been more contrary to the founding principles of the Mission School.[10]

In sum: The underlying goal of worldwide "salvation" remained as before; the "ends" would be the same, but the means very different.

Within that calculus, the Mission School figured as an exemplary case—
a key "experiment" that had failed.

> Do any of them think now of the school's beginning, when its future
> seemed so uniformly bright? When they could, without hesitation, "look
> forward . . . [to] the most encouraging prospects"? When they expected,
> one and all, "to see this small stream become a river which shall make
> glad the city of God?" When, at their annual exhibition days, "a great
> concourse of people" would gather to witness a special program designed
> to present "the most gratifying . . . evidence of success in the attainments
> of the youth from various heathen lands?" When the martyred Obookiah
> set a standard of piety that would challenge the faithful across the entire
> region?
>
> And what of the midpoint, at which they could still feel enraptured by
> the way "these wild men come to our shores, and our firesides . . . [and]
> enquire for the Babe of Bethlehem . . . [and] weep for His cross"—all in
> a process so "animating . . . that the mind has almost lost the power of
> astonishment."
>
> And, finally, what about their bedrock conviction—their fount of
> inspiration, day after day, year after year—that the school "stands alone
> in the Christian world, an original essay for doing good . . . [with] not its
> like in Europe or America . . . [such that] few institutions promise more
> extensive benefit to the Church of God."
>
> All gone now?
>
> Perhaps it is hard, perhaps as their "infant institution" approaches its
> end point, they do feel a stinging disappointment. But, true to form, they
> will not acknowledge as much. Instead, they hold heads high, keep voices
> firm, and make ready to proceed as best they can "in other ways."

The school's enrollment had begun to decline as early as the winter
of 1824–25. After holding steady for several years at a level of roughly
thirty-five, the total declined to twenty-seven in February, twenty-six in
May, seventeen in October, and fifteen the following June (1826). Those
who remained would now become a source of pressing concern; Evarts,
from his vantage point at the American Board, took charge of arranging
their departure. Letters went out to ministers, college presidents, school
principals, missionary leaders—anyone who might help with developing
plans "to dispose of the young men now at Cornwall."[11]

One especially promising Indian (Oneida) scholar was accepted at Dartmouth College. Evarts sent him on his way with a comforting assurance that Rev. Tyler, the college president, "will always act the part of a kind father to you." He remained for two years, but left without receiving a degree.[12]

Five "Osage boys," apparently quite recent arrivals, would set out for the West as soon as "a careful, prudent, economical man" could be found to accompany them. The group would go "on the [Erie] Canal, to Buffalo, thence by water to Cleaveland [*sic*]"; if all went well, they might then be placed at Miami University in Oxford, Ohio. Indeed, their arrival was noted by officials of that university in the summer of 1827. None would graduate, but four of them did apparently remain enrolled for periods of up to three years.[13]

Several remaining Hawaiians were to travel home in the fall with a new contingent of missionaries. (This would be "much safer, & better for you, in all respects, than to go with the whalers.") In the meantime—as Evarts wrote to one of them, by way of a pep talk—they should read, study, pray, "learn to be industrious," find ways of "conversing with intelligent & good people," and generally make the most of "your privileges in this Christian land." As it happened, their departure was further delayed; hence in the following spring, they were parceled out, on a temporary basis, to the households of various missionary supporters. They didn't finally embark until early November 1827.[14]

Another of the scholars, "a Portuguese young man, hopefully pious," was "desirous of studying Medicine." Evarts wrote on his behalf to a minister in Pittsfield, Massachusetts, inquiring "whether there is not some respectable Physician at Pittsfield, who would instruct him gratuitously & whether some of your good people would not give him his board." With suitable training, "he might become very useful, as a Physician, in some Catholic country." Apparently, this came to nothing; a year later, however, Evarts succeeded in arranging his admission to Dartmouth.[15]

By March 1827, "all the boys, except six . . . [were] . . . provided for." This group was still in Cornwall, housed with the last of the school's stewards, a church deacon named Lorrain Loomis. Evarts requested of Loomis that they "remain . . . in your family, & under your care" for another few weeks. Clearly, the "disposing" process was dragging on longer than anyone had expected.[16]

Four of the remaining six left, by routes unknown, in the spring of 1828. Some may well have been placed with families in nearby towns

(Goshen, Milford, Winchester); in such cases, Loomis was a likely intermediary. That July, Evarts wrote to Rev. Daggett, "dissatisfied" about the two who "were not yet sent home." One was Choctaw; as for the other, "I do not recollect to what tribe . . . [he] belongs." Evarts was concerned about their prospects and hoped that the former principal might "send for them both, & give them your best counsels in regard to their leaving christian society, & commencing a residence in the wilderness." A few months later, he succeeded in arranging their departure, in the company of missionaries bound for "Buffaloe" and "thence to the Choctaw nation." They would travel through the town of Richmond, Massachusetts, where Edwin Dwight, the school's first principal, now served as minister. Evarts alerted Dwight to their arrival, noting that they were "but poorly prepared . . . [and] may need clothing & other necessaries." This was, for certain, a turning point. It had taken a good two years, but now all those who had remained after the school's closure were fully and finally "provided for."[17]

There were still some loose ends involving school properties. The schoolhouse itself reverted to town ownership and was used thereafter as a conference hall. (It would be taken down in 1873.) The steward's house was put up for sale; the board hoped it would bring "at least $750." Some of the books in the library were donated to Dartmouth "for the Indian charity school there"; others went back to a particular donor. Rev. and Mrs. Stone received "some articles . . . from the clothing &c. on hand, as a compensation for expenses incurred by them for the pupils of the school." And money previously donated "to aid in a contemplated new building" would be fully refunded.[18]

Of course, board leaders could not immediately cease thinking about the school, or about their decision for closure. At the least, they needed to reassure themselves (and one another) that they had acted correctly. Perhaps Evarts had Cornwall in mind when, during the summer of 1828, he advised a minister in North Carolina against sending a particular Indian boy away for schooling. "So far as we have had experience on the subject," he wrote, "it is not generally expedient for Indian youth to be educated in the white settlements. The notions & feelings which they acquire are not such as to fit them for usefulness among their people afterwards. The Board have educated many in this [way], & with very few exceptions they have returned to their friends & exerted a bad influence, or become wholly inefficient." Two years later, David Greene, Evarts's successor as board secretary, was even more pessimistic. "This experiment of educating unevangelized foreigners in this country, with the hope that they would return to their respective countries, and act the part of enlightened & Christian men is one among others in which much hope was placed in the earlier stages of missionary exertions, but which have been, to a greavous [*sic*] extent, failures." He noted especially that board leaders "were much discouraged by the attempts they made at the Cornwall School."[19]

These downside conclusions were based, at least in part, on reports coming in from the missionary "field"—from Hawaii, first of all. The "defection" of William Tennooe, which was noted almost immediately after the founding of the mission there, would come to seem prophetic; as time passed, concerns were raised about several others. In 1830, missionary Gerrit P. Judd wrote from Honolulu to his friend and mentor Edwin Dwight with a full account of "a number of individuals" educated at the Mission School and since returned to their homeland. The picture he gave was mixed, at best. One of the returnees had "dwindled into insignificance. We seldom see him." Another "possesses many negative qualities," and "is not depended on . . . in any important Missionary work." A third was "employed in making purchases for the chiefs . . . is quite a man of business . . . and has much money & other property in his hands. . . . We are very much in fear he may be tempted to embezzle. . . . He needs our prayer and counsel." A fourth had become "a favorite with the Gov. [of Hawaii], attends him wherever he goes, eats with him, brushes off flies while he sleeps &c &c."; as a result, he was "fast sinking into the lazy habits of a Sandwich Islander."[20]

Most distressing of all was the story of Thomas Hopoo, once a star pupil and bosom friend of the "martyred" Obookiah. According to Judd, Hopoo had begun well: "[H]e . . . spent much of his time in instructing the people" and thus became "an instrument of good." He married a native woman—his was the first wedding "ever celebrated at these islands in the manner of the christians"—and began to raise a family. But then he received a large gift of money from the Baron de Campagne (the Swiss nobleman who had previously emerged as an important benefactor of the school); unfortunately, this "wrought much evil in the heart of Thomas." Meanwhile, too, he began "to speculate & trade, got into debt & fell . . . almost to his original state of poverty & unimportance." After a year or two, he seemed to rescue himself and to behave "more in the character of a disciple of Christ." Soon, however, "our hearts were much wounded & grieved by a discovery that he was guilty of violating the 7th commandment [against adultery]"; as a result, he was "suspended from the church, put in irons, & fined according to the laws of the land." This left him "ready to sink with shame & remorse," and, after promises to repent, "he was about to be restored to the church." Then came the final act of his zigzag saga—as described, again, in Judd's own sorrowful words: "O, my Dear Sir, my heart bleeds while I relate it—the next information I had of Thomas was that he has been in the habitual practice of this sin [adultery] ever since he arrived at the islands. Mr Bishop & Thurston have heard of 20 instances or more in which either by his own confession or of others, he has been guilty." Edwin Dwight, the recipient of Judd's report, knew these "individuals" well enough; indeed, as the school's first principal, he had welcomed them to Cornwall. About Hopoo, an important figure in the famed Obookiah *Memoirs* that Dwight had ghostwritten, he must have felt especially disappointed.[21]

To be sure, the news from Hawaii was not entirely bad. Several others in the returning group had maintained a reasonably "good standing"; two, in particular, appeared to be "industrious, sober-minded young men, whose example will no doubt prove a benefit to the nation." Moreover, the fact that many of "the youths educated at the Foreign Mission School" had fallen far short of expectation "cannot . . . be attributed to any fault in that school." Instead, the problem lay with "the improper policy of the chiefs in fostering & claiming . . . [their] services"—as secretaries, linguists, business managers, and the like. (In short, these newly educated islanders possessed skills readily adapted to use by the native elite.) Judd ended with the following unhappy thought: "The change from the condition of a poor wanderer in a strange land, picked up & sent to school, to that of a favorite at court in their own native country, was too great & too sudden for them well to bear, and instead of improving on their previous advantages, they have almost without exception gradually retrograded." A year later Hiram Bingham reached the same bleak conclusion, without looking for ways to excuse those involved. In a letter to a fellow missionary, he wrote of feeling "shocked and grieved at the history of falls" of several of their Hawaiian associates, and, more generally, "at what is becoming more and more apparent of the irregularity of all the native members who were admitted in America."[22]

Almost without exception gradually retrograded. . . . The irregularity of all the native members who were admitted in America. That would, in fact, become the dominant view, one that persisted for decades. Long afterward, the author of a general history of the islands rendered the following verdict on the various "youth [sic] who had been educated at Cornwall. . . . Too much had been expected of them. . . . They were exceedingly ignorant—far more so than was imagined by their friends in the United States. . . . Many of the ideas they had gained were confused and incorrect. They were . . . miserable interpreters and very poor teachers. They were often found teaching doctrines and practices altogether opposed to the precepts of the Bible. . . . One of them [Tenooee] soon fell into sin and was excommunicated. . . . Another [Hopoo] was more correct at first but afterwards became wayward. . . . A third [Honoree] was a man naturally of weak mind and frail body and could not be of much service." So much for the first group—and those who came later "proved to be no better assistants"; indeed, "they were certainly a hindrance in the work [of the mission] rather than a help." The process of returning to their native land was more than "their weak brains and unstable minds could . . . endure." As an overall result, "they soon made shipwreck of the hopes of their friends, and it is to be feared also, in most cases, of their own souls."[23] (The metaphor of "shipwreck" seems especially resonant here. All of them had traveled to the school on long ocean voyages—with "hopes" and "souls" directly at stake.)

If the reports from Hawaii were largely unfavorable, those from the Cherokee heartland were little better. For example: "Many of the young men, on whom the missionaries bestowed unwearied pains, are great enemies to those to whom they are indebted for their instruction." In particular, it was "a painful fact, that no one of those Indians that were educated at Cornwall, from this nation, have done, or are likely to do, anything for their people, except David Brown & Steiner." Brown, of course, was the one whose speaking tour with Evarts had produced such remarkable results. His subsequent return to the Nation had raised great hopes. He had assisted the missionaries in various ways, as well as working on a project to translate the Bible into Cherokee. But later he would turn to "mercantile business," at which point (Evarts noted) "his religious state has doubtless suffered for want of congenial society & from worldly views & cares." Steiner had served for a time as a translator and occasional preacher, and seemed "a more determined opposer of vice" than any of his fellow returnees. But then he became embroiled in a jealous dispute with one of the missionaries over a certain Cherokee girl. He was said to have uttered death threats and "acted like a madman";

eventually he acknowledged as much and repented, but his "usefulness" thereafter was compromised. (Evarts charged him more than once with a conspicuous "want of zeal.")[24]

Another of the Cornwall returnees was "frequently guilty of intemperance, rarely goes to church, and will likely be excommunicated." Still another became "very cold respecting religion" and had, by some reports, engaged in even "greater evils." To all this, Elias Boudinot remained at least a partial exception. His one significant "fall"—the ball-play incident—was swiftly regretted; thereafter, he applied himself to teaching, translating work, and preaching tours.[25]

In fact, these were exactly the years of the famed Cherokee "renascence." Yet the American Board's missionaries at work in the Nation barely noticed anything of the sort; indeed, they went in the opposite direction. Stories of sin—intemperance, pride, and, above all, sexual promiscuity—filled the letters and official reports they sent to their superiors in Boston. Steiner's "madman" behavior was a case in point; discussion of that went on and on. A separate episode, recounted in detail by missionary Moody Hall, involved "criminal intercourse . . . [between] a Cherokee girl whom we had taken into our family and John Sanders [yet another Cornwall returnee]." The offending pair was removed from the family and expelled from the church; then, "to show our utter abhorrence of such crimes we had the beds whereon they laid & the cabin [in] which they slept consumed by fire." Such "decisive measures are thought necessary," Hall wrote, "because the Cherokees think so lightly of such abominable crimes." At the very least, these actions were "making much talk in the Nation"; perhaps they might yet implant the lesson that "the souls of fornicators will burn in hell." One of Hall's colleagues was led by this and similar "outrages" to conclude that "the justice of God may be more strikingly displayed in their [the Cherokees'] extermination. Certain it is that . . . [many] are ripening for destruction."[26]

These, of course, were no more than anecdotal reports of success and failure—mostly failure—involving former Cornwall scholars. It does not seem that anyone in a position of authority at the American Board thought to appraise the entire "experiment" (as they now preferred to call it). But today, even from a distance of almost two centuries, that task can be attempted by pulling together the experience of all the individuals involved. The information is incomplete, and in some cases quite fragmentary; still, it does add up.

As best one can determine, the total of scholars ever present at the Mission School was ninety-five. (There may well have been a few more, whose stay was so brief as to have left little or no trace in the surviving records.) Of this number, the largest group was composed of Native Americans: forty-two in all, representing fourteen different tribal affiliations. The second-largest was Pacific Islanders: twenty-four, including nineteen from the Hawaiian archipelago. There were also eleven from East Asia (China, India, the Malay Peninsula), five from Europe, one from Mexico, and twelve "Yankees" (white Anglo-Saxons of American birth). At the time of their arrival, they ranged in age from ten to thirty; the median age was eighteen. They are thought to have spoken a total of twenty-one different languages. Their curricular focus covered a broad span from English grammar and vocabulary to natural philosophy, geometry and trigonometry, Latin, Greek, and Hebrew, astronomy (including the calculation of lunar eclipses), and "advanced" surveying and navigation. Approximately twenty-five of them attained religious "conversion," just over one-fourth of their total number.

Comparison between the different ethnic and racial groups shows some interesting differences. First, the Native Americans were significantly younger than the Pacific Islanders and Asians. (The median ages at time of arrival were approximately fifteen versus twenty-one, respectively.) Second, by all reports the native scholars achieved the best level of academic performance. (Daggett and others repeatedly complained of the difficulties the Pacific Islanders encountered in mastering the English language. By contrast, most of the Indians arrived with at least some prior knowledge of English and thus had a good head start with the more "academical" subjects.) Third, the islanders were more than twice as likely as others to undergo a religious conversion and thus to become members of the local church. Fourth, discipline problems arose in equal measure with Native Americans and islanders—and most frequently with the East Asians. Fifth, the East Asians were least successful overall (with four out of eleven subject to expulsion). Sixth, there was no discernible difference in the matter of short-term outcomes. All groups proved disappointing in that respect, to more or less the same degree. The idea that they would go right back to their own people and become missionary workers themselves—if not actual leaders, then valuable "assistants"— simply wasn't realized on any considerable scale.

Reports about the long term would be no better. One young man from China returned home, became an "outside chop man [petty merchant]" and teacher of English, but died "a besotted heathen." Another, the Oneida Indian who attended Dartmouth for two years, went on to serve as an interpreter for several tribal chiefs; however, he became an alcoholic, abandoned his young family, went to Canada, and died there in 1837. A third, a Stockbridge Indian, was a "notorious drunkard," but then he "reformed and gave a temperance address," which was printed in the missionary press; his later doings are not known. Drink was a recurrent theme in these reports; thus, "ruined by whiskey," "died in a drunken row," "made dissolute by demon rum," and so on. To be sure, the reports themselves may be suspect, coming, as they generally did, from disappointed and disapproving missionary sources. But the same sources had some incentive also to describe the successes of former scholars—and there were at least a few of those. For example, a Delaware Indian youth concluded his four-year stay at the Mission School by going south to become a schoolmaster and occasional preacher among the Choctaws in Georgia; he was also active for many years as a speaker and fund-raiser on behalf of the American Board. And the young Portuguese scholar whom Evarts had described as "anxious to study medicine" did, in fact, go on to a long, much-appreciated career as a physician in southern Canada. (When he died in 1897, he was the last survivor among the school's former members.)[27]

Among the more meritorious post–Mission School careers was that of Photius Fisk (né Kavasales), one of the Greek boys who had arrived with such fanfare not long before the "crisis" period began. His story merits a longer telling.[28]

After Photius and his young compatriot Athanasios Karavelles are pushed out of the Mission School—where their "delicate sensibility" has rendered them "unsuitable" to continue—they are sent south to New Haven. There they are received into the homes of prominent local citizens (a Yale professor, a judge) and enrolled at the Hopkins Grammar School (then and now one of the nation's oldest private academies). After a short and relatively uneventful stay, they are transferred yet again—this time to Amherst Academy in central Massachusetts. Soon Photius falls into trouble by absenting himself without permission—something he had done previously at the Mission School—and is summarily expelled. He is "remanded to the custody of the American Board," and a decision is made "to return him to his own country." (He has, by this time, worn out his original welcome; moreover, he has not experienced, as his sponsors hoped, a religious conversion.)

In the spring of 1827, the board puts him on a ship bound for Greece. His arrival there includes a meeting with the newly installed president of the country, John Capodistrias; indeed, by some accounts, he serves briefly as the president's personal secretary. (Athanasios, meanwhile, has remained at Amherst Academy. In time, he will graduate to—and then from—Amherst College. After that, he will gain legal training, return home to Greece, and begin a law practice.)

But Greece is not where Photius wants to make his life. Thus, in short order, he begins planning a return to the United States. He takes passage on a French brig back to New York, arriving in the spring of 1828. He finds employment first in a pharmacy, then in a hardware store. He attends revival meetings, attains conversion—precisely what he never achieved at the Mission School—and joins the Congregational Church. Indeed, he decides to study for the ministry, and secures admission to a theological seminary in Auburn, New York; he completes a three-year course and is ordained in 1839. He becomes pastor of a village church in Vermont, but dislikes the cold winters there.

After another a year or two, he returns to New York, and then makes a further move to Washington, D.C. He has an entrée to political leaders, including former president John Quincy Adams, whom he had met long before as a boy newly arrived from Greece. (Two presidential connections, Greek and American, within a scant few years. How many others could claim as much?) This enables him to secure appointment as a chaplain in the U.S. Navy. His first assignment, aboard the frigate *Columbia,* takes him across the Atlantic to the coast of Africa. In the course of the voyage, he makes himself unpopular with fellow officers by openly espousing the cause of antislavery. (This will become an enduring, and deeply held, commitment. According to his biographer, "in his view, slavery was the sum of all abominations.") The return trip encompasses both South America and the Mediterranean; he takes the opportunity to visit Greece and Malta, where he renews old family connections. When finally back in Washington, he is granted shore duty. And now he has another cause in view—abolition of the practice of flogging (sailors) on ships at sea. His political contacts, especially his friendship with Adams, provide an opening for direct involvement with Congress; when, in 1850, antiflogging legislation is finally passed (after several failed efforts), he can claim at least a small part of the credit.

Eventually, he is ordered back to sea duty, serving aboard the frigate *Raritan*, headed for the Pacific. His role in the antiflogging campaign has made him especially controversial; thus "he was denounced and hated among the officers, admired and loved among the men." The *Raritan's* voyage lasts nearly three years, with stops at many South American ports. Photius has various adventures along the way, including a risky encounter with revolutionaries in Chile, and an expedition into the interior to collect rare botanical specimens for the Smithsonian Institution. (Botany is another of his interests.)

Returning home, he resumes shore duty, now in the office of the Navy Department. It is the mid-1850s, and the issue of slavery dominates public life. As his thoughts lead him in an increasingly radical direction, he wrestles with his religious faith; he concludes that if the Bible seems to sanction slavery, its authority must be rejected. He is on his way to what contemporaries call "free thought." He is transferred to Boston, where he becomes closely acquainted with abolitionist leaders William Lloyd Garrison and Wendell Phillips. He also meets John Brown, soon to lead the notorious raid on Harpers Ferry, and donates money for Brown's work in "bleeding Kansas." No longer a Christian, he must resign his chaplaincy; officially, the navy will count him as retired. Thanks to his "frugal habits" and secure investments in government bonds, he has, through many years, accumulated a considerable fortune. (One estimate puts his total wealth at between $30,000 and $40,000, the equivalent of perhaps $1 million today.) As the years pass, he extends the range of his charity, contributing to the personal upkeep of less fortunate neighbors.

He lives for a time on a farm in the Massachusetts countryside. But in the 1870s, he moves back to Boston, takes a small suite of rooms in a hotel, and begins a series of extensive travels in Europe. He continues his philanthropic efforts, now including the women's suffrage and temperance movements, colleges in the South founded for the benefit of "colored people," the Perkins School for the Blind, tornado relief in Iowa, victims of the great Chicago fire, and the poorhouse in Athens, Greece. By the 1880s, he has become "one of Boston's characters, known and loved by many." He is described as "a little old man," frequently seen "in the streets of Boston, . . . moving rapidly along with a quick, elastic step." He has "nervous gray eyes, thin face, sharp features, something between a

saffron and a bronze complexion, and long, white locks . . . drawn up on
either side over a head bald on top."[29]

   In his last years, he becomes the subject of numerous encomia—in the
public press, in official pronouncements by the many organizations he
has aided, and in personal testimonies of every sort. Said one: "He lives
not for himself, but for the cause of humanity." Said another: He is "a
true friend, a noble citizen of the world, a large-hearted philanthropist."
In December 1889, he contracts a severe case of influenza; after lingering
for several weeks, he dies in the following February. His estate of nearly
$30,000 is probated in a Boston court; his will directs it—all of it—to a
host of his favorite charities.[30]

At the opposite extreme stood the later career of George "Prince"
Tamoree.[31]

His brilliant homecoming in April 1821—including his father's effusive
welcome, his rapid assumption of power and place in island society, and
the widespread admiration he inspires in local "commoners"—casts a
glow that will rapidly dim. The missionaries, for their part, are wary of
him from the start; they are quite familiar with his erratic record at the
Mission School. (In addition, they look askance at his sudden marriage to
a virtual stranger—the "half-breed" daughter of a resident Englishman—
in a traditional native ceremony on one of the "lower" islands, even before
his arrival in Kaua'i.)

   Within scant weeks, he takes up the cultural ways of the native
people, shedding his "civilized" garments in favor of the traditional
malo (loincloth), and moving to an entirely native diet (breadfruit, poi,
raw fish); he also hosts "a native dance at his house." Though his father
expresses strong interest in the work of the mission, Humehume—his
birth name, now restored—stands apart. Business, not religion, is his
focus; in July, he writes to a Cornwall friend of having "much to do fitting
out several vessels with sandalwood."[32] He is "found in drink" with some
frequency. At one point, he makes off with a visitor's boat, which he
promptly wrecks on a reef; at another, he is suspected of setting fire to a
neighbor's house. As a result of all this, the missionaries grow more and
more disapproving; indeed, they can "scarcely suppose he had ever seen
civilized societies, much less dwelt among them." Moreover, "his conduct
of late has been such that his father has given up hope of him [and] says
he is no better than any *kanaka* [ordinary islander]."[33]

Letters from Rev. Daggett and others in Cornwall arrive for him, full of earnest moral exhortation, but are unavailing to halt his slide.[34] Meanwhile, too, he finds himself at the center of an increasingly complex political drama. His expectation of succeeding to his father's kingship runs afoul of competing claims made for a half brother who is linked on the mother's side to the island elite. (Humehume's own mother is said to be "of ordinary rank.") Within another year or two, both his father and the same half brother are married to the dowager queen of all the islands to the south. This is a matter of diplomacy, not romance; the goal is to bind Kaua'i closer to its neighbors. And it means that Humehume is marginalized even further; Hiram Bingham, leader of the missionary group, writes that he is now no more than "chief of his own little valley." In the summer of 1824, Bingham pays a personal visit and finds him "living . . . in a dingy, dirty thatched house," attended by "two or three worthless white men [renegade sailors]" and a few dozen "poor, ignorant, and comfortless . . . natives." Ominously, he voices "a restless determination to resist the ruling powers or to take revenge on some by whom he fancied . . . he had been wronged," a stance that appears to foretell open rebellion.[35] At stake now is island autonomy; his opponents wish to force Kaua'i into the same pattern of rule that prevails elsewhere in the archipelago.

That August, having gathered a small force of willing followers, Humehume plots a nighttime raid on a nearby fort where his enemies have stored a large quantity of weapons. But the attack is discovered when barely begun, and easily repulsed (at the cost of approximately a dozen lives); the defeated warriors flee in order to regroup in Humehume's own village a few miles away. He makes one final effort to rally support from local chiefs. But now the military might of all the other islands stands arrayed against him. The ensuing battle is a rout. Three hundred on his side, including many women and children, are killed; he escapes to the rain forest high in Kaua'i's remote interior. For a month, he survives alone in this wild area, eluding search parties and living off fruits and other native edibles. But finally the ordeal becomes too great, and he offers himself for surrender. With hands tied and head bowed, he is marched back down to the shoreline and ordered to undergo a speedy trial. He anticipates a death sentence—but, in the end, he is spared.[36] (Mercy shown to helpless prisoners is an island tradition.) Soon thereafter, he is relocated by the "ruling powers" to Honolulu (on Oahu, a hundred miles to the south). There he rejoins his wife and young child, and "is suffered to go at large." He seems, however, a broken man. The following year, an outbreak of influenza engulfs Oahu (one of many such epidemics that would eventually destroy some 90 percent of the native population). Humehume is among the victims; he dies quietly, and all but unnoticed, on May 3, 1826. (He is not yet thirty years old, but has seen more of the world—and known more of life's ups and downs—than all but a few of his contemporaries.) At that moment, six thousand miles to the east, the Mission School, too, is in its death throes.

Of all the school's students—and of all their life stories in the aftermath—only two achieved a high level of public significance. These were the young Cherokees John Ridge and Elias Boudinot. Both were destined for a quick rise to the forefront of their nation's leadership. Both would play a major role in galvanizing opinion and action across the full sweep of the United States. Both became closely acquainted with presidents, cabinet secretaries, congressmen, and other officials of the federal government—sometimes in friendly, but most often in oppositional, contexts. Both achieved a measure of public fame (or infamy, as the case may be). And both took with them, in their personal and public journeys, the women they had wed in Cornwall, Sarah Northrup and Harriet Gold.

Actually, John Ridge had been drawn toward public affairs while still enrolled at the Mission School. In March 1821, "at the request of my Instructor [presumably Rev. Daggett]" he composed a letter to President James Monroe. The apparent stimulus was Jedediah Morse's recent report to the federal government on the status of the country's Indians. Ridge, as well as Daggett, wished to support Morse's recommendation that (in the latter's words) "assistance may be proffered to this long neglected and despised people." Ridge's main theme was the way "my dear Nation now begin [*sic*] to peep into the privileges of civilization." He recalled how, "when I left them two years ago . . . they were at work: the tools of the whites were used, some possessed large farms—cattle—horse—hogs &c. Their women were seen at the wheel, & the weaver's shuttle was in motion." He invoked his own "dear Parents, [who are] both ignorant of the English language, but . . . exert all their power to have their Children educated like the whites." The theme of Indian—and specifically Cherokee—"improvement," of rapid progress toward "the privileges of civilization," was already well established among missionaries and others of the "benevolent" persuasion. Appropriated here in his youthful letter to an American president—he was only nineteen—it would find in Ridge its most forceful spokesman for many years to come.[37]

Almost immediately upon his leaving the school to return home, Ridge became deeply absorbed in Cherokee politics. He spent much of the year 1824 in Washington, D.C., as part of a delegation defending the Nation's territorial integrity against the threat of encroachment by the state of Georgia. While there, he helped draft memorials to Congress, attended "levees" (parties) at the White House and in the homes of cabinet secretaries, and made a generally favorable impression; Secretary of State John Quincy Adams described Ridge and his colleagues as equivalent to "well-bred country gentlemen." (It was at the end of this same trip that he traveled on to Cornwall to claim Sarah Northrup as his bride—and then was obliged to endure the bitter public reaction generated by their "intermarriage.")[38] In 1825, he made two more trips to Washington, on behalf not only of Cherokee interests but also those of the Creek Indians.[39] Meanwhile, during the intervals when he remained at home, he assumed a key role in the workings of the Nation's governing National Council.

On one of his Washington visits, he met with Albert Gallatin, former secretary of war, who had recently begun a large project to classify Indian languages and cultures. At Gallatin's request, Ridge composed "a sketch of the progress made in the civilization of the Cherokees." In fact, this was a substantial essay, touching on virtually all aspects of Cherokee life and culture. Near the end, Ridge noted the growing threat to "our national existence. . . . Strangers urge our removal. . . . We are in the paw of a Lion." His very last sentence offered a strangely ambiguous reference to interracial marriage: "In the lapse of half a Century if Cherokee blood is not destroyed it will run its courses in the veins of fair complexions who will read that their Ancestors under the Star of adversity, and curses of their enemies became a civilized Nation." In part because it was "written by a native Indian," the essay pleased Gallatin, who used it in subsequent communications with European savants, including the great German polymath Alexander von Humboldt. It was also around this time that Ridge sat for the portrait ordered by federal commissioner Thomas L. McKenney and executed by the painter Charles Bird King. This would become part of a gallery of similar works that graced McKenney's Indian Office in nearby Georgetown.[40]

Still in his early twenties, John Ridge was well on his way to forging a remarkably precocious career. Many who met him were greatly impressed; "dignified," "intelligent," "of proper manners" were among the compliments tossed his way. But inevitably, too, there were doubters. A Georgia newspaper correspondent, resentful of his effective work for the Creeks, called Ridge and his Cherokee colleague John Vann "as arrant, cunning, and mercenary diplomatists as ever graced the Council Boards." And when Jeremiah Evarts toured Cherokee missions during the spring of 1826, he reported on Ridge as follows: "I am sorry to say that his character and influence are at present very far from what we could wish them to be." This was specifically about his spiritual condition. Several years later, a missionary schoolteacher would write to her sponsors, "Do pray unceasingly for Mr. Ridge. You know his talents, intelligence, taste, & refinement; but alas, for the morals of the south, a man without religious principle is in danger at every step." His mother had converted to Christianity long before; his father, Major Ridge, would do so near the end of his life. But John himself, though outwardly respectful of the church and its doings, would never reach the same point—would never become, as his Mission School teachers had hoped, a "professor of religion."[41]

As John Ridge journeyed about on public business, his close friend and cousin Elias Boudinot struggled to find a suitable niche back in the Nation. At some point in 1823, he opened a school for Cherokee youths near the village of Haweis; a visiting missionary who spent a day there felt "very highly gratified with the appearance of it. The scholars are under excellent discipline, and are learning fast. I think there are but very few schools in New England that appear better." However, by autumn of the following year, Boudinot had moved on, and was living at his father's house in the village of Oothcaloga. For the next several months, he worked on the family farm and assisted in the taking of a Cherokee census.[42]

Meanwhile, plans were afoot to establish a national "seminary"— a school of "higher learning"—and a printing operation; Boudinot was quickly drawn in. During the summer and fall of 1825, with strong support from the Nation's leadership, he prepared to set out on a fund-raising tour through white communities in the North in order to underwrite both projects. At the same time, however, his engagement to Harriet Gold became publicly known. The resulting furor threw him badly off stride—thus his ensuing "fall" (in the eyes of his missionary sponsors) by attending a traditional ball play. Still, he seems quickly to have righted himself. His tour began in January, in the city of Charleston, South Carolina; Evarts met him there, and heard him lecture on at least two occasions. "He appeared," wrote Evarts in letters to a colleague, "to great advantage, discoursing on the benefits of a press to the Cherokees"; indeed, "very few young men could have addressed a large audience with so much propriety, & with so few mistakes in sentiment & language." Eventually, he made his way to Washington, Philadelphia, and New York (among other cities), with results that his auditors invariably found "gratifying."[43]

And now he was drawing close to Cornwall, close enough to travel there and marry his beloved Harriet. Their honeymoon—if they thought of it that way—was a continuation of the public tour. Boudinot addressed admiring audiences in churches at Boston and Salem; then, with Harriet in tow, he doubled back to Philadelphia. In that city's First Presbyterian Church, he offered what amounted to his stump speech. Its main content was a detailed description of Cherokee "progress," complete with numbers of cattle, horses, and sheep privately owned, of spinning wheels and looms, wagons and plows, gristmills and blacksmith's shops in regular operation, of schools, river ferries, "good roads," and other such marks of "civilization." Having reached this point, Boudinot explained, "the Cherokees have thought it advisable that there should be established a Printing Press and a Seminary of respectable character; and for these purposes your aid and patronage are now solicited." He concluded on a somber note, designed to touch the conscience of his audience. "I ask you, shall red men live, or shall they be swept from the earth? With you and this public at large, the decision chiefly rests. . . . Will you push them from you, or will you save them?" Published a few months later under the title *An Address to the Whites*, this would prove a remarkably valuable fund-raising tool.[44]

From Philadelphia, the Boudinot pair traveled south, through Virginia and Tennessee, and reached the Cherokee heartland late in the summer of 1826. There they were warmly received by Elias's parents and numerous younger siblings; for a time, they would stay in the "very good two-story log-house where the family now resides." Harriet wrote, in letters to her Connecticut kin, of feeling entirely accepted: "I love them all much & I may say—we love each other." This was especially true of her parents-in-law, who "frequently say that I am like an own child to them."

They gave her a Cherokee name—Kalahdee—which, she said, "already sounds natural to me." She loved the atmosphere of the household—for example, the prayer sessions "when the family are assembled [and] all are silent and attentive while Mr. Boudinot [that is, Elias] reads a portion of the Scriptures, first in English, then interprets it to father and mother. . . . I cannot but observe with what interesting earnestness the mother looks at her son when endeavoring to explain to them the word of God." She sought to make herself useful by "sewing for other people—such as making bonnets & the like." Negotiations for the press were ongoing; all sides understood that upon its arrival, Elias would be in charge. Until that time came, however, he and Harriet would feel somewhat at loose ends; according to one report, they were "poor & destitute of household furniture."[45]

A temporary solution was found by hiring them "to help conduct the school at Hightower" during the winter months. (This was one of several such schools, begun and supported by the American Board.) There they might "occupy the mission house," in which teachers and assistants lived together as a unit. The plan was that "Sister B. would take charge of the family & teach a Sabbath school." This proved a considerable challenge, inasmuch as Harriet was now chief cook for the entire group. She wrote to her sister and brother-in-law of having "not only [to] rise early enough to get my own food but sometimes for ten or fifteen besides." Still, "notwithstanding all my cares," she pronounced herself "contented." Indeed: "I . . . [have] never passed my days more pleasantly than while I have been in this Nation. . . . Nothing appears strange, but as though I had always lived here." She signed letters to her siblings back in Connecticut "your Cherokee sister." Elias, meanwhile, threw himself into teaching. He also put his language skills to good use—to "interpret on the Sabbath & at other times when necessary & attend to the translation of the New Testament." The latter project would put him in close collaboration with the missionary Samuel Worcester, who felt "more confidence in Boudinot as a translator than in any other."[46]

Likely, too, Elias was involved with John Ridge and others in planning the national "seminary." Ridge had already picked out a suitable location near the Cherokee capital and had asked another of the resident missionaries to serve as principal. Interestingly, he hoped to bring his father-in-law down from the North "to superintend the farm." He described himself as "anxious to have Mr. Northrup introduced in this nation as a missionary," a move that would reunite Sarah with her parents. Among Northrup's qualifications was his previous work as steward of the Mission School, during a period that had lasted, as Ridge put it, "until the crime was committed in the act of marriage with his daughter and myself." (This wry comment was typical of the way Ridge would refer to his enormously difficult exit from Cornwall.)[47]

The seminary plan would never come to fruition; and arrangements for the press dragged on and on. At some point in 1827, the Boudinots moved to New Echota, possibly in anticipation of the birth of their first child that May. Samuel Worcester moved his own family to the capital around the same time, and the two men continued their work together on several translation projects. Finally, at the start of the next year, the press arrived from Boston, with two sets of type, one with English characters, the other specially cast for the Cherokee syllabary. The immediate goal was publication of a newspaper, to be called the *Cherokee Phoenix,* with Boudinot serving as editor. Its content would include "the laws and public documents of the Nation," discussion of Cherokee progress in "the arts of civilized life," "interesting news of the day," and "miscellaneous articles, calculated to promote Literature, Civilization, and Religion among the Cherokees." It would appear weekly and have both English and Cherokee print, sometimes for the same material in parallel columns. The first issue appeared on February 21, 1828. As time passed, the *Phoenix* would carve a unique place in the history of journalism— the first newspaper ever published by and for an Indian community. It was very much Boudinot's personal creation—and his central preoccupation for the next five years.[48]

In the meantime, both families—Boudinots and Ridges—would be steadily enlarged by the arrival of children. Harriet Boudinot bore six and Sarah Ridge seven, all within the space of a dozen years. Reports on their domestic life reaching the North were invariably received with interest— and often enough with skepticism. According to one man living "within Twenty or twenty-five miles of Mrs. Ridge . . . her husband treats her improperly . . . [and] she is an unhappy woman." However, when Evarts visited the family in the spring of 1826, he wrote to a colleague, "As to the inquiry whether young Mrs. Ridge is contented & happy, it is certain that she often says she is, and surely she ought to know. I should think most persons believe her, but some are incredulous." That a properly raised woman from New England could live comfortably in Indian surroundings, with an Indian husband, was still hard for a good many white people to imagine. In 1836, in their *History of the Indian Tribes of North*

America, Thomas L. McKenney and James Hall praised Sarah Ridge for her "enthusiastic hope . . . [and] pious aspirations," then opined that "it must have required great strength of affection in this young lady to enable her to overcome the aversion which is usually entertained against alliances with a race so different from ourselves." Harriet, for her part, wrote unequivocally of her attachment to her husband: "[H]e is all that I could wish him to be." Indeed, she boasted that "my sisters need not think it is saying anything against their husbands to say I have excelled them all. I know they are all good <u>positively</u>, but mine <u>superlatively</u>."[49]

In 1827, the political crisis surrounding the Cherokees entered a new phase. A key development was their enactment of a full-fledged constitution, closely modeled on that of the United States. White Georgians reacted with mounting alarm; in short order, their legislature declared the state's sovereign claim to all the territory within its official boundaries, including that held by the Nation.[50] The following year brought the election as U.S. president of Andrew Jackson, who was known for favoring removal of all southeastern Indians to locations much farther west. At around the same time, the discovery of gold on Cherokee land added a new element, with miners and assorted "squatters" rushing to take advantage. Seeking to build a spirit of resistance, the National Council approved a "Blood Law," prescribing death for individuals who sold (or otherwise transferred) landed property to outsiders; both Ridges, father and son, were active in its passage. Meanwhile, occasions for violence began to multiply as bands of armed men from both sides squared off against one another; on at least one occasion, the elder Ridge led a well-organized reprisal raid on white intruders. Elias Boudinot fought the same battle in the pages of the *Phoenix*. Week after week, his passionate editorials served to rally public sentiment against removal, both within and outside the Nation. Indeed, this brought him to the attention of the Georgia Guard, which on two separate occasions summoned him for questioning about the publication of "abusive and libelous articles." (More than once, he was threatened with a flogging.)[51]

In December 1829, as part of his first presidential message, Jackson restated the case for removal and urged legislative action. Soon thereafter, a bill to achieve that goal reached the floor of both congressional houses. Several weeks of intense and bitter debate were followed by votes of approval—first, rather easily, in the Senate, then, by a narrow margin, in the House of Representatives. The Cherokees responded by sending John Ridge and two others back to Washington for further negotiations. As these dragged on, the focus shifted to the Supreme Court, where two separate cases involving the Cherokees were being readied for trial. In December 1831, Ridge and Boudinot set out on a new speaking tour through northern cities, hoping to rally white supporters of the Cherokee position. Each of their several appearances drew an enthusiastic reception. Each elicited participation by civic and religious leaders; in Boston, for example, Lyman Beecher—erstwhile agent of the Mission School— joined Ridge and Boudinot on the speakers' platform. And each yielded "a collection [of money] to assist the Cherokees in maintaining their cause before the Supreme Court."[52]

The tour did much to enhance the reputation of the two young leaders on whom the fate of all Cherokees would increasingly depend. Press coverage was mostly positive. Catherine Beecher, daughter of the minister and herself on the way to a significant career as a writer, wrote of the two visitors in the *Boston Courier:* "No person can be in their society without being struck with their appropriate use of language, their extent of information, and readiness of expression"; Ridge, in particular, she praised for "his thrilling and unpremeditated eloquence." (Other news accounts noted his "loftiness of mind, decision of purpose . . . keenness of wit, and strength of argument; his manner was a rare combination of dignity and ease.") At one point, Boudinot paid a visit to the American Antiquarian Society in Worcester, and was favorably appraised by a local dignitary: "He is a full blooded Cherokee, and was educated . . . at Cornwall, Con. He is about 35, of pleasing and gentlemanly manners, and speaks English as fluently as tho a native. . . . I asked him a great many questions concerning the ancient history of his nation, and he answered all my enquiries readily and sensibly." He did, however, seem extraordinarily sensitive "when anything was said touching the present controversy between the people of Georgia and the Cherokees . . . [and] intimated his belief that the nation would soon be exterminated, unless the General Government should interpose its arm and shield them from the sword of the Georgians."[53]

In late March, the Supreme Court rendered its verdict in the second, and most crucial, of the Cherokee cases—*Worcester v. Georgia*—rejecting any right in the individual states to supersede federal authority over Indian tribes; no longer could Georgia, on its own, set limits to Cherokee sovereignty and governance. John Ridge wrote to a cousin, "It has been a day of rejoicing with patriots of our country." Still, he noted, "the contest is not over. . . . The chicken snake General Jackson has time to crawl and hide in the luxuriant grass of his nefarious hypocrasy [*sic*]." Events would soon confirm Ridge's fears. The Jackson administration refused to involve itself in enforcing this decision, and Cherokee hopes were dashed once more.[54]

In fact, both John Ridge and Elias Boudinot had already begun to doubt the wisdom of further opposition to removal. According to a somewhat later account, they had "intimated" to others a sense that "the case was hopeless" even as they toured the country that spring. Soon after the *Worcester* decision, Ridge obtained an interview with Jackson in order to learn the president's views firsthand. Reportedly, he left with "a melancholy feeling . . . convinced that the only alternative to save his people from moral and physical death was to make the best terms they could with the government, and remove out of the limits of the States." Gradually, in the months that followed, he made his new position known to close friends and colleagues within the Nation, while not as yet revealing it more widely. Boudinot went through a similar transition. And Major Ridge, too, was brought around—albeit with great reluctance. Meanwhile, white supporters of the Cherokee cause, including many in government, were reaching the same conclusion, urging the Nation to accept removal and focus henceforth on securing the most favorable possible "conditions."[55]

From this point forward, the Nation was convulsed by bitter controversy and dissension. With his views finally out in the open, John Ridge became the acknowledged leader of a faction favoring emigration. On the other side stood a much larger number, led by principal chief John Ross, who remained doubtful, or fully opposed. The issue was argued back and forth at every level—from individual firesides to the National Council. The *Phoenix* was, necessarily, in the thick of it; but since he was now on the minority side, Boudinot was obliged to resign as editor. Ridge and Ross would travel again and again to Washington to meet with federal officials, sometimes together and sometimes as heads of separate (and rival) delegations. The animus between the two men, personal as well as political, grew more and more intense. At the same time, Ridge and Jackson forged an unlikely alliance (sufficiently close for Ridge to name his last child after the president). Meanwhile, Georgia authorities were enacting specific measures aimed at removal: surveying Cherokee lands for transfer to whites, holding a lottery among would-be owners, and harassing resisters with arrest or other legal action. Moreover, the problem of white intruders—squatters and vigilantes—had by now touched all corners of the Nation; in many cases, individual Cherokees were forced off their property by actual or threatened violence. A jaunty, and cynical, bit of doggerel, sweeping through the South's white population, captured the spirit of the moment: "All I ask in this creation / is a pretty little wife and a big plantation / way up yonder in the Cherokee nation."[56]

In the fall of 1834, John Ridge, his father, and other advocates of removal convened a special council at John's home (Running Waters). Its members decided to send a memorial to Congress, explicitly signaling their willingness to leave. At the same time, they appointed yet another delegation to go to Washington for a new round of negotiations, with a removal treaty as the presumed object; John Ridge would be its leader and Boudinot a fellow participant. The eventual result was a package of proposals featuring a vast territorial swap—most Cherokee land in the Southeast for a large federal grant in Arkansas and Oklahoma, plus a onetime payment of $4.5 million by the federal government to the Nation. (Later that sum would be raised to an even $5 million, and later still to nearly $7 million.) Following their return to the Nation, Ridge, Boudinot, and their allies held additional meetings at Running Waters to explain, and justify, these terms. But interest was low and attendance poor. And even as they met, unidentified men wrapped in blankets were seen lurking menacingly on the edge of the property. Clearly, most Cherokees remained opposed, and many felt cruelly betrayed. Both then and later on, treaty supporters might be waylaid and beaten. Several were murdered; direct threats were made on the life of John Ridge himself. Both Ridges—and Boudinot, too—were suspected of receiving secret payoffs from the federal government in exchange for their pro-removal advocacy. That idea would persist for decades, though bitterly denied by all three men and never substantiated with any hard evidence.[57]

Month by month in the following year (1835), events approached a point of culmination. In December, a rump gathering of Cherokee leaders met in New Echota with federal commissioner John Schermerhorn for formal consideration of a treaty that largely reinstated the previous removal proposals. John Ridge was still away in Washington, but his father was present and spoke in favor. The treaty was approved on the twenty-eighth of that month, and signed in the parlor of Boudinot's house the following day. Upon affixing his mark, Major Ridge reportedly said, "I have signed my death warrant." John would add his own signature—with a similar sense of foreboding—a few weeks later; indeed, he would tell others that he was quite ready for death if it came. Elias, for his part, told the assembled group, "I know that I take my life in my hand. . . . But Oh! What is a man worth who will not dare to die for his people?" Finally, the treaty was sent on to Washington for consideration by the U.S. Senate. There it occasioned renewed, and intense, debate—with some supporters of the Nation pronouncing it an outright "fraud"—before gaining passage by a single vote.[58]

While these public events moved inexorably along, life inside the Ridge and Boudinot households traced its own, more intimate patterns. About the former, the evidence is limited. In January 1831, John Ridge wrote to Samuel Gold, the doctor who had cared for him a decade before in Cornwall: "My health has improved, but I am not altogether well. I limp a little in my gait in walking, occasioned, as you know, by the disease of my hip. My wife Sarah is the happy mother of three Indian children, two girls, and one boy named John Rollin. They are all well. I have eighteen servants, stock of horses and cattle, etc., and a delightful place six miles from father's, which I calculate to improve. . . . My wife is very good to me and I love her dearly. She is a good wife." (His "servants" were actually slaves. Did anyone note the bitter irony that Indian victims of the color line in Cornwall were now enforcing, and profiting from, a related line drawn around dark-skinned African Americans?) There is also one brief comment by a near contemporary, the daughter of a Cornwall friend: "She [Sarah] remained at home, taking care of her servants, for she had thirty living in the back yard. She simply said to this one, go, and he goeth, and to another, come, and he did so. She dressed in silk every day." She was also said to have had a "fine carriage" at her beck and call.[59] Considered all around, hers was the life of an affluent plantation mistress.

In contrast, many of Harriet's letters to her Connecticut kin—some including a page or two added by her husband—have survived. And they open a wide window on the Boudinot family's everyday doings.

Often there are details of domestic activities: "I am baking rice pudding for dinner today." Or: "Today our people have had a corn husking & I have had a quilting." There are references to Elias's work: "He has just finished a tract the translation of which is entirely his own work. I will send you a copy of it." Occasionally, Harriet sends a special request to one or another of her relatives: "If you are disposed to send a box . . . any kind of clothing would be very acceptable." Sometimes she writes about the weather: "It has been snowing most of the day—seems quite like New England." Their children are a particular focus: "Eleanor [the eldest daughter] is a great girl now—begins to talk smartly. . . . Mary [second daughter] has real black Indian eyes. . . . William Penn [eldest son] goes to school & he & little Br[other] Charles are beginning to read." (At one point, Harriet sends her parents several locks of Eleanor's and Mary's hair. Preserved to the present at the Cornwall Historical Society, they are straight, fine, and somewhat blond.) They speak also of each other, with Elias referring playfully to "Harriet my squaw," and her describing him as "truly worthy of my warmest affections—my tenderest love."

From time to time, Harriet expresses a wistful nostalgia for all she left behind: "I have thought much of my Father's family of late, & especially my Sisters. I suppose you sometimes get together. Let Harriet be remembered, though absent, I sometimes very much wish to compose one of your circle again." In particular, she mourns a continuing breach with her sister Abby "whom I tenderly loved. Does she ever talk about Harriet with affection? Or are the feelings she cherished two years ago, still unalterable?" (Abby and her husband, Cornelius Everest, have remained the most vehemently opposed, among all the family, to Harriet's "intermarriage"; there is no evidence they ever became reconciled to it.) She might also reverse the direction of her longings: "I wish . . . you could just step in, & sit . . . with us this evening. Susan [an unidentified housemate] sits in one corner, mending her stockings, and I in the other writing this letter—while the children are all a bed & asleep." She mentions visitors, including Sarah Ridge: "Last week, I had a very unexpected visit from Cousin Sarah. . . . Her husband . . . sent her in their Coach with a driver & little black girl to take care of Clarinda." (Because their husbands are cousins, Harriet and Sarah now consider themselves related. Clarinda is Sarah and John Ridge's infant daughter. The black girl is one of their slaves.) She makes scattered references to religion and missionary goals: "Pray for the Cherokees that they may all be brought to truth." She regrets public ignorance of Cherokee ways: "I wish you to see how Indians can live—how families, & how a nation of Indians can live." Her wedding anniversary moves her to a more extended reflection: "[I]t is this day 6 years since I received the hand of Mr. Boudinott & gave my own in the covenant of marriage. . . . I am thankful. I remember the

trials I had to encounter—the thorny path I had to tread, the bitter cup
I had to drink—but a consciousness of doing right—a kind affectionate
devoted Husband, together with many other blessings, have made amends
for all."⁶⁰

On both sides—the elder Golds in Cornwall, the Boudinots in New
Echota—there was talk of arranging visits in one place or the other.
Then, in September 1829 the Golds began a journey, in their own horse
and carriage, southward to the Nation. Benjamin (Harriet's father)
would describe their experience to relatives back in Connecticut. They
were "47 days on the road . . . [but] upheld & preserved all the way in
good health & free from any material harm." As they went along, they
felt themselves to be "on Harriotts [*sic*] track"; indeed, they "heard of
her & her husband often in many places where the people appeared to
remember them with much interest & told us many interesting things
about them." When at length they reached their destination and "met
our Dear children & friends in health," they experienced "feelings of Joy
that may be better conceived than expressed."⁶¹

They would remain for just over six months; by all accounts, the visit
was an unqualified success. They took the opportunity to visit other
parts of the Nation, including three different missionary stations. Benjamin's letters were full of praise for all he observed: "I find the families
very polite & agreeable & pleasant & fit associates for any country. . . . In
their Council and Court are Quite a number of learned pollished [*sic*] &
well Qualified Gentlemen fit to appear in any place in Connecticut." He
was especially pleased by his "beautiful and interesting" grandchildren,
who might "pass in company for full blooded Yankees." When safely
back in Cornwall, the Golds regaled neighbors with details of life in the
Boudinot household. According to one, "Mrs. Gold told me . . . that she
never had such a store of provisions (and Col. Gold was wealthy and a
good provider). In one room upstairs was a barrel of coffee; a barrel of
sugar; and everything good they needed: a kind, good husband, and the
smartest grandchildren we ever had. Harriett had married as well as any
of our children, and you know that our children have married well."⁶²

There would be other visits in the years ahead. In the spring of 1832,
Elias stopped to see his in-laws in Cornwall, in the midst of his speak-
ing tour with John Ridge. And during the winter of 1833–34, the entire
Boudinot family traveled north for a more extended stay in Cornwall.
This visit is largely undocumented, but a Litchfield resident who passed

through New York in early January wrote of seeing "Boudinot (Cherokee) & his sister & his wife (formerly Miss Gold of Cornwall) & their
children. They will probably be in Litchfield on their way to Cornwall."[63]

As the years passed, the removal crisis closed in, step by step, on both
the Ridges and the Boudinots; Harriet's letters told the story. In January
1831, there was still room for hope; thus she could write, "We know not
what is before us. Sometimes I fear the Cherokees will see evil days—but
I think they will come off victorious in the end." Six months later, Elias
was much more pessimistic: "[W]e have been in hot water ever since
our last to you . . . we have hardly known which way to turn. Trouble
upon trouble, vexation upon vexation." He complained, too, about "our
friends at the north . . . [who] appear to be so careless. Do they not
know that a piece of great wickedness is in a course of perpetration?"
Harriet agreed; decrying the "apathy which prevails in the States," she
asked, "How are the American people ever to atone for the injuries
done the original inhabitants of this Country?" (She seems by now to
have considered "the States" a foreign land, and herself an expatriate.)
By 1833, with the Nation divided within itself, she told her sister that
"our Nation are [sic] in great trouble—and will no doubt feel themselves
forced to give up their country to the white people. . . . Poor Indians,
above all people, are most forcibly reminded that the world is not their
home." And two years further along, with removal a definite prospect,
she wrote, "Our situation is becoming truly desperate. . . . I look upon
this pleasant land . . . as no longer a home for ourselves or our children.
Even should the Nation choose to remain, and meet the consequences,
we have no idea that we shall do so." Though many other Cherokees
continued to hold fast—no matter what—the Boudinots had become
firmly committed to leave.[64]

But Harriet would not be part of the actual removal. In May 1836, as
the family was making preparations for the journey, she delivered her
sixth child, a boy she and Elias named Franklin Brinsmade Boudinot.
(The middle name invoked her sister Mary, whose husband, Gen. Daniel Brinsmade, had been an agent of the Mission School. Indeed, it was
Brinsmade who, at a crucial moment ten years before, broke the news
of Harriet and Elias's engagement to the rest of the school's leadership.)
Soon after giving birth, Harriet contracted what Elias described as "a
dangerous illness," and following some weeks of acute struggle, she died

on August 15. The details were presented in a long, grief-filled letter from the widower to her parents. The letter would, in turn, be published a few months later in the *New York Observer,* then reprinted in other newspapers around the country.[65]

Quite rapidly, the "Last Hours of Mrs. Boudinott"—a title supplied by the *Observer*—would gain a place in the lore of evangelical spirituality. In many ways, it mirrored accounts of Obookiah's passing at the Mission School two decades earlier. Its focus was Harriet's "religious exercises" as the end drew near; she was the center—the star—of an engrossing drama. Along with "extreme bodily suffering," she endured deep anxiety about "the state of her soul." As the days passed, she listened attentively while others read Scripture passages or sang hymns by her bedside. When her condition permitted, she exhorted her husband and weeping children to live "according to the rule of Christ." At one point, she sent for a Cherokee neighbor and counseled him, through an interpreter, on "the importance of religion." Friends came to pray with her—most notably John and Sarah Ridge, and Sarah's parents (just then on a visit from New England). Eventually, she seemed to gain "assurance," and said "her darkness was removed . . . that there was then a clear sky between her & her Redeemer." Near the moment of death, Elias observed "a benignity and smile about her countenance that I had never noticed before."[66]

Elias felt utterly devastated by his loss; as he wrote to one of his wife's sisters and her husband, "All my plans are now disconcerted. I really do not know what to do. You cannot imagine the extent of my bereavement." Still, he needed to act without delay to provide for his children (none older than ten); thus within days of their mother's death, he put them in the care of a missionary family at a "station" some distance to the west of New Echota. He considered sending several of them "to the north"—that is, to their Connecticut aunts and uncles—but changed his mind when, the following spring, he made a new marriage to a New England woman working in the Nation as a schoolteacher. All the while, he remained in affectionate contact with Harriet's parents, continuing to address them in letters as "Father and Mother," and assuring them, about his second wife, that "your dear grand children could never expect a better friend, a better mother."[67]

By this time, too, he was heavily involved—along with John Ridge— in the procedural side of removal. The two of them were part of an "Indian Committee" that assisted federal commissioners in resolving the claims of pro-removal Cherokees for compensation on their land and other properties. In November 1836, John wrote to one of his Northrup sisters-in-law about his own claims. "My place here [Running Waters] was valued at six thousand & seven hundred dollars"; additional sums for his crops, hogs, thirteen horses, ferry service, "other improvements," and a second house in Alabama would raise the total to over $20,000. At the same time, he was "engaged in business in settling the affairs of the Nation as President of the National Com[mittee]." Finally, he was making his own preparations to leave: "We will send all blacks & horses to Arkansas under the conduct of Mr. [illegible name] except Maria which we will retain to cook for us, & Henry to drive our carriage & wait on us, and Mary to take care of the children." (Undoubtedly, the last three named were slaves. There was, in addition, a pony named Dick, "which Rollin [his eldest son] will not allow to leave him.") He wrote, too, of his father, who had prepared "a carriage for his negroes & a large wagon & a coach for himself." It was clear that both families would travel in what (for the time and place) was comfortable style—in sturdy conveyances, and with slaves to look after their personal needs.[68]

Major Ridge, his wife, and their little retinue left in March 1837. Their journey was not uneventful, but—contrary to the usual pattern with Indian removals—no lives were lost, and, after about a month, it ended as planned in the territory that would henceforth be known as "Cherokee Nation West" (or, in some other renderings, "New Cherokee Nation"). In short order, Major Ridge purchased land and "improvements" for his own household at a place called Honey Creek (near the point at which the borders of the present-day states of Missouri, Arkansas, and Oklahoma are joined). There, with the labor of his eighteen slaves, he would soon build a handsome farm.[69]

John Ridge remained in the East throughout the summer, for one last round of dealings with federal commissioners sent to supervise removal. When, in late September, he resigned his position on the Indian Committee, the commissioners paid him strong tribute for his "lofty efforts . . . [as] the leader and guide of a whole nation," compelled by circumstance to "sacrifice . . . the beloved land of his birth and that of his fathers for generations past." Free at last of public responsibilities, he and Boudinot, with their respective families, set out for the West early in October. They chose a route, through parts of Alabama, Tennessee, Kentucky, southern Illinois, and Missouri, and reached their destination after a journey of roughly seven weeks. (They made a stop en route at the Hermitage, home of Andrew Jackson, and were warmly received by the recently retired president. If John remembered at all his previous view of Jackson as a "chicken snake," he gave no sign.) John chose to settle near his father, on land he described as "superior to any country I ever saw in the U.S."[70] His first concern was to build shelter for his family—what he would later describe as "a good double-log house." His business records show an entry, dated December 21, for "eight hands to raise the house, $1 each." A few weeks later, he paid $75 "for house carpenter work," including "flooring, ceiling, 2 doors, 5 window frames, 72 sash lights [window panes], 1 table, shelves." These details suggest a much less grand place than his Running Waters residence back in Georgia; perhaps he saw it as no more than temporary quarters. He began to farm; the same accounts include "hogs and the hire of two hands to drive them," plus the purchase of a "new prairie plough." And he joined Major Ridge in opening a large general store on Honey Creek.[71]

He was eager to see other parts of the Nation's new home, and soon after his arrival spent several weeks traveling here and there. Then, the following spring, he and his wife undertook a much longer journey to New York and New England, leaving their children in the care of the Connecticut woman who ran a school on their property. It was, in part, a business trip; John needed to arrange the purchase and shipment of supplies for the store—foodstuffs, clothing, leatherwork, tools, hardware of many kinds, and more. But they seized the chance also to visit Sarah's family in South Lee, Massachusetts. Unfortunately, John took sick while there, and, in a strange reprise of his experience at the Mission School long before, had to spend several months convalescing under the Northrups' roof. Sarah, meanwhile, returned alone to Honey Creek to be with their children.[72]

By the time John got back, the major phase of removal was fully under way. In sharp contrast to his own experience the previous year, it was cause for enormous sorrow and suffering—on what has been known ever since as the Trail of Tears. The headlines are familiar and haunt us still.[73]

First, the "round up": federal soldiers evicting thousands of Cherokee families from their land and other property.

Then: the incarceration of these thousands in "stockades" for weeks or months at a time, during which they endured extreme drought, rampant disease, and arbitrary, sometimes openly cruel, treatment by guards and other government officials.

Next: forced embarkation for the trip west. Wrote one missionary who stood by as they left: "It is mournful to see how these people go away—even the stoutest hearts melt into tears when they turn their faces toward the setting sun."[74]

Followed by: additional months of laborious, often lethal, journeying, some by boat, some by railway, some on horseback, some by horse-drawn wagon, and, in by far the largest number of cases, on foot. Many Cherokees walked the entire way, covering distances of a thousand miles or more. And all this went on in the face of harsh weather conditions (summertime heat, followed by bitter winter cold), grossly inadequate provisioning, recurrent bouts of disease, and callous treatment by whites encountered along the way. A traveler from New England described one large detachment trudging through Kentucky: "Some carry a downcast dejected look bordering upon the appearance of despair; others a wild frantic appearance as if about to burst the bonds of nature." Death repeatedly stalked their ranks; according to the most reliable estimates four thousand lives were lost, either during the initial roundup or on the route west, out of the approximately fifteen thousand directly involved.[75]

Finally: their arrival in the "Indian Territory"—that part of it specifically allotted to the Nation, in what is today northeastern Oklahoma—with its manifold challenges of practical and emotional adjustment: unfamiliar landscapes; uncertain reception by those already present (including the "Old Settlers," Cherokees who had voluntarily removed themselves years, or decades, earlier); procedural confusion around every aspect of resettlement (obtaining land, building houses, putting in crops, and acquiring livestock, tools, and other necessities); and, not least, the toll taken by exposure and fatigue on their already weakened bodies and souls.[76]

Exactly when John Ridge returned from Massachusetts to confront this hugely forbidding prospect is unclear; pertinent letters and other evidence have not survived. We do know that he sought to assist new arrivals—and to capitalize on their needs—through his and his father's general store. Business records reflect both the extent and the range of its offerings. When John left on a second buying trip to New York and New Orleans in March 1839, he had with him money orders, "drafts," and cash totaling almost $17,000 (the equivalent of roughly $400,000 today); some was borrowed from his father, his brother, "Mr. Boudinot," and Rev. Worcester. He returned with large quantities of corn, pork, salt, chickens, calico and other cloth, ribbon, and boots. His records also show "money loaned the emigrants"; in short, the store doubled as a bank. He planned to rebuild his life as a plantation owner, but was a business-man, too. He was no longer directly involved in public life, and it seems he wanted it that way. When he stopped in Washington during the second of his trips east and encountered his old negotiating partner, federal commissioner John Schermerhorn, he spoke of their joint service in the past tense: "My brother, we have been laboring long together . . . [for] the salvation and happiness of the Cherokees. You for what you have done, have been abused, misrepresented and slandered by your countrymen; and I might yet someday die by the hand of some poor infatuated Indian, deluded by the counsels of Ross and his minions; but we have this to console us, we shall have suffered and died in a good cause. My people are now free and happy in their new homes, and I am resigned to my fate, whatever it might be."[77]

The idea that his fellow citizens were "free and happy" was, however, wildly off the mark—perhaps a form of willful denial. Most were struggling, with great difficulty, to make a new start. And many continued to think of both Ridges, father and son, as perpetrators of an unforgivable crime against the Nation. One immediate and vexing problem was meshing the "Late Immigrants" (as the newest arrivals were called) with the lives and political practice of the Old Settlers. A large majority of the Late Immigrants were committed to the leadership of principal chief John Ross; moreover, prior to removal they had bound themselves to continue the Nation's established pattern of governance in the West. But the Old Settlers clung to their own system—a more austere and traditional version of conciliar rule—and hoped that it could work for all. In this configuration, the so-called Treaty Party, consisting of the two Ridges, Boudinot, and their followers, was more or less the odd man out.[78]

With the aim of resolving differences and creating a formal union, the various factions met in council in June 1839. Major Ridge, John Ridge, and Elias Boudinot proposed to attend simply as onlookers, but when their presence aroused resentment among others of the Late Immigrants, they decided to leave. The meeting broke up without an agreement, and feeling on all sides sharpened ominously. The followers of Ross suspected that the Ridges and Boudinot had colluded with the Old Settlers to foment disunion. Although Ross publicly urged forbearance, a band of his followers met secretly and formed plans to invoke the Nation's "Blood Law" against leaders of the Treaty Party. Its key provision, now held up as a kind of sacred commitment, read as follows: "[I]f any citizen

or citizens of this nation should treat and dispose of any lands belonging
to this nation without special permission from the national authorities,
he or they shall suffer death." (Did the plotters pause to recall that it was
John Ridge himself who had put the law into writing a decade before?)[79]

As the sun began to rise over Honey Creek in the early morning of
Saturday, June 22, a team of twenty-five armed men quietly surrounded
the John Ridge house. Three who had been officially designated "exe-
cutioners" approached the door, forced it open, stole upstairs, found John
still asleep, dragged him outside, stabbed him repeatedly with knives,
and stamped on his bleeding body one by one "as they marched over it
single file." Sarah ran to him, whereupon "he raised himself on his elbow
and tried to speak, but the blood flowed into his mouth and prevented
him. In a few moments more he died, without speaking that last word
he wished to say." His shocked children watched from inside the house
as his killers galloped off. Years later, one of his sons would compose a
vivid remembrance of the scene that immediately followed. "In a room
prepared for the purpose lay pale in death the man whose voice had been
listened to with awe and admiration in the councils of his Nation, and
whose fame had passed to the remotest of the United States, the blood
oozing through his winding sheet and falling drop by drop on the floor.
By his side sat my mother, with hands clasped, and in speechless agony—
she who had given him her heart in the days of her youth and beauty, left
the home of her parents, and followed the husband of her choice to a wild
and distant land. And bending over him was his own afflicted mother,
with her long, white hair flung loose over her shoulders, crying to the
Great Spirit to sustain her in that dreadful hour."[80]

On the same morning, fifty miles to the south, a similar drama was
unfolding in the village of Park Hill, where Elias Boudinot had decided
to resettle his family. Elias was at that point living temporarily in the
home of Rev. Samuel Worcester, his missionary friend and collaborator,
since the building of his own house a short distance away was not yet
finished. As Worcester would write a few days later to one of his colleagues at the American Board, "Last Saturday a horrid deed was done
almost at our very door, and most afflictive to us all. Mr. Boudinot is
murdered . . . by the hands of assassins." That was the headline; details
followed. "He went to his house . . . a quarter of a mile distant. There
some Cherokee men came up, inquiring for medicine, and Mr. Boudinot

set out with two of them to come and get it. He had walked but a few rods when his shriek was heard by his hired men, who ran to his help; but before they could come up the deed was done. A stab in the back with a knife, and seven gashes in the head with a hatchet, did the bloody work. He lived a few minutes, till we had time to arrive at the spot, and see him breathe his last, his wife among the rest, but was speechless and insensible to surrounding objects. The murderers ran a short distance into the woods, joined a company of armed men on horseback, and made their escape."[81]

There would be still more killing that day. Major Ridge had left Honey Creek the previous afternoon to check on one of his slaves who had been hired out to a planter across the Arkansas border and now lay ill; he stayed overnight and then headed home. Another band of anti-treaty partisans learned of his plans and set an ambush alongside a creek. When he rode up at midmorning and stopped to water his horse, he was felled by a volley of rifle shots and died almost instantly.[82]

Three men down within the space of a few hours. Families ripped apart. Cleavage within the Nation driven so deep that vengeance murders would go on for decades. In retrospect, the events of June 22, 1839, might well be viewed as state executions. But why, then, their stealthy enactment? And what to make of the weapons used—traditional native hatchets and knives in two cases, the white man's firearms in the third? And where to fit the ritual stomping ("single file") of Ridge's dying body? This mix of elements hints at the hybrid, in-between status of the Cherokees—too "civilized" to be fully "Indian," too "Indian" to live in white-controlled Georgia.

How had the two Ridges and Boudinot become leading advocates of removal in the first place—knowing, as they did, the grave risk they incurred? Their position was not lightly taken. Indeed, it had required a complete reversal of their earlier views. Yet once they switched, they never wavered.

To the Cherokee public, they stressed the immediate difficulties—the impossibility, as they saw it—of staying put. The pressure of white settlers, of squatters and other intruders, had become overwhelming. The state of Georgia was adamant in declaring its sovereignty over the Nation's land and citizens. The federal government was unwilling to enforce the mandates of the Supreme Court. There continued to be many in the North who supported the Cherokee cause, but even these seemed more and more to accept the necessity of removal. When Boudinot looked back on the treaty making from two years later on, he commented, "Instead of contending uselessly against superior power, the only course left was to yield to circumstances over which [we] . . . had no control."[83]

When, however, they wrote in private channels to known friends and sympathizers—to the missionary leaders in Boston, for example—they struck a different note. In that context, they would advance what was essentially a cultural argument. Their central point, repeated over and over, was the danger of "degradation" and "pollution" of Cherokee lifeways from the malign influence of whites intruding on the Nation. Ridge, in a letter to David Greene (at the American Board), offered an especially powerful statement: "I hope we shall still do well, if we can only induce our Indians to abandon the land of whiskey kegs & bottles, the vile corruptions of the whites, where our poor women are contaminated to become wretches, in the land where they once enjoyed peace & respectability." In direct contrast, opponents of the treaty preferred to "amalgamate with [our] oppressors . . . [rather than] leave their nation to reunite with those who have gone before & and now enjoy liberty in the west." Ridge found this possibility deeply repugnant: "[T]he thought of amalgamating our people to such creatures under such unfortunate circumstances, is too horrid for sober consideration." For Ridge, whose calm judgment and mental balance were widely acknowledged by whites and Cherokees alike, these were extraordinarily strong words.[84]

Boudinot's views were exactly of a piece, and no less forcefully expressed. He, too, stressed the matter of degradation owing to "the promiscuous settlement of whites among the Cherokees." He elaborated on the same point in a bitterly reproachful letter to chief Ross: "I notice you say little or nothing about the moral condition of this [Cherokee] people. . . . [Instead] you seem to be absorbed altogether in the pecuniary aspects. . . . But look, my dear sir, around you and see the progress that vice and immorality have already made." He noted especially "the spread of intemperance and the wretchedness and misery it has already occasioned . . . [and] the slow but sure insinuation of the lower vices into our female population." Hence: "[I]t is not to be denied that, as a people, we are making rapid tendency to a general . . . debasement." The previous rise of the Cherokees from "a savage state" to "civilization" was now gravely imperiled.[85]

The moral aspect of this viewpoint—its language and tone—

distinctly recalled the attitudes of the missionaries among whom Ridge and Boudinot had once been schooled. And some of their statements in defense of removal offered a grateful bow in that very direction. Ridge, for example, praised the efforts of the American Board, without which "the U States would not have a white spot on which the blackness of infamy could make any shade. . . . I know there is a good spirit in the Christians of America. I know it dwells in New England, because I have seen it."[86]

If mission work in general retained value for these two, what of the Foreign Mission School in particular? Their writings made no mention of it. However, their intense concern with *degradation, contamination,* and *pollution* through contact with racial and cultural others—together with the danger posed by actual, or potential, *amalgamation*—seems, at the least, highly suggestive. In fact, the same concern was widely prevalent among "benevolent" white advocates for Indians, especially those who had come around to supporting removal. But with Ridge and Boudinot it touched a special, acutely sensitive nerve. For it reinvoked the struggle they had personally endured when, a decade before, they had taken to wife two "fair flowers" of white womanhood. The removal crisis framed a similar struggle—in reverse. Now it was the Nation that would try to hold the line for "civilization" against "savage" and dissolute intruders pressing in on every side. Even the color imagery was turned around. In Ridge's pungent phrasing, the "U States" encompassed "the blackness of infamy"; hence, by implication, the Cherokees were whitened.

As time passed, the pragmatic ground for favoring removal seemed more and more solid; if the Cherokees tried to hold on in Georgia, their odds of survival were bleak. Both Ridge and Boudinot acknowledged this, accepted it, and voiced it fervently; reason and judgment allowed no other conclusion. But their fervency, too, demands attention, and leads to a crucial question. Might they not have retained, at some level, a dark lesson from their time at the school—nothing less than a profound default of trust? Surely they remembered what they had felt at the time; perhaps it went something like this: *We acted unfailingly to reach the goals that our teachers and sponsors set for us. We were model "scholars"; we were drawn as well to Christian faith and practice.* (Elias had quickly become a convert and a member of Cornwall's First Church; John had approached, without quite reaching, the same point.) *For these reasons, we enjoyed widespread, apparently genuine, approval. Even our engagements might have been viewed in a similar light. That a pair of previously "heathen" youths should court and win the hearts of two fine local women: What better evidence of our progress toward "civilization"? But no; for most white Americans, "intermarriage" is a different thing entirely, a red flag of transgression. And so they abandoned us—excoriated us—humiliated us—cast us out.*

Their experience as Cherokee leaders would follow a parallel course. Both began by defending the Nation's ancient territorial rights in whatever way they could—Ridge as a principal negotiator with federal authorities, Boudinot through his editorials in the pages of the *Phoenix*. Both counted on the ultimate goodwill and good sense of the white public, as represented by its leaders in government. However, these hopeful expectations were cruelly upended—first by congressional passage of the 1830 Removal Act, then by the Jackson administration's refusal to enforce the Supreme Court decision in *Worcester v. Georgia*. At that point, they swung completely around; from then on, they insisted that emigration was the only possible course. *Another desertion, another betrayal: We have seen this script before. Nothing more heard from white leaders can be trusted. Better, then, to go—to take our people as far away as possible. Amalgamation? Never! That way lies "degradation" and disaster.*

Thus removal, their their own journey west, resettlement in the Indian Territory, the hope for renewed prosperity, and, finally, on a languid summer morning, fulfillment of the Blood Law . . . and violent death.

As summer moved along, news of the assassinations traveled across the entire country. Press coverage traced a widening set of concentric circles—from nearby Little Rock, Arkansas, where a "rumor" arrived within two days, to major urban centers, to towns and villages in the rural countryside. As was typical of that era, the means of transmission were personal: "by a gentleman who arrived here [Alexandria, Virginia] Monday evening from the West," or "by a letter received in this city [Charleston, South Carolina] yesterday from one of our citizens at Fort Gibson, Arkansas," or "by passengers who arrived here [Philadelphia] in the *Cinderelle* [apparently a steamship] on Sunday last." Literally hundreds of local newspapers would, sooner or later, receive and print reports. Their titles ran a considerable gamut: "Murder of Ridge and Boudinot," "The Cherokee War," "Trouble Among the Cherokees," "Outrages Among the Cherokee Indians," "Indian Murders" were among the favorites. Most commentary was favorable to the deceased. John Ridge was praised for his "gentlemanly bearing and stirring eloquence. . . . He was fond of distinction, wealth, and power, pleased with rich apparel and ornaments, jealous of his supposed rights, and seemed to be an affectionate husband and father." Major Ridge, "formerly one of the principal chiefs of his nation . . . was altogether a man of strong and discriminating mind." Boudinot had become "a distinguished leader . . . [who] as editor of the Cherokee Phoenix, displayed talents of no ordinary character." Some accounts mentioned the connection to the Mission School, an "institution established . . . something like fifteen years since . . . by the exertions and munificence of a number of philanthropic individuals, at Cornwall, Connecticut." One that was widely reprinted, under the title "The Cherokee and His Beautiful Bride," retold the story of the Boudinot-Gold courtship and marriage, including "incidents . . . that partake somewhat of the romantic." Of Harriet, it said this: Having "bade farewell . . . to the holy ties that bound her to all that was lovely and sacred to her on earth . . . [she] with her youthful forest lord pushed afar off to her wigwam home in the lone forests of the Cherokee land. . . . She was represented as appearing contented and happy with her lot, in the midst of her little family of half-papoose, half-Yankee urchins." (A "romantic" picture indeed!)[87]

Harriet, of course, was not present to witness the shattering events of June 22, 1839. And it fell to Elias's second wife, Delight (Sargent) Boudinot, to arrange for the disposition of their six children. Their friend and neighbor, Rev. Worcester, wrote as follows to some of the Gold in-laws in Connecticut: "Mr. Boudinot had requested his wife, if he should be taken away, to go with the children to their friends and hers in New England, which she intends to [do] as soon as circumstances allow." At first, she was so stricken by "the circumstances of my dear husband's death, and the . . . alarming scenes that followed" as to feel "unfit to perform almost any duty." Within a month, however, she was "recovering . . . strength" and making plans to travel north; the children, ranging in age from three to twelve, would accompany her.[88]

They set out in the fall. Delight Boudinot had been born and raised in Manchester, Vermont, and returned there now. On the way, she stopped in Washington, Connecticut, to leave two of her stepdaughters with their aunt Mary (Gold) Brinsmade, who would care for them thereafter. The rest went on with her to Manchester. Some years later, one of the sons was apprenticed to an engraver in Philadelphia, and a second to a civil engineer in Vermont. As time passed, the Boudinot and Brinsmade households remained in close touch, with the Boudinot siblings paying frequent visits back and forth. There was also regular communication and visiting between the children and their Gold grandparents in Cornwall. For example, in August 1845, William Penn Boudinot (the eldest of the sons) wrote in loving tones to his "dear Grandma & Grandpa . . . who have in solicitude for me taken the place of my own father & mother." And the following month his sister Mary sent a letter of her own to "my dear grandparents," providing the latest news of "our little family"— her stepmother and two brothers—in Vermont. Mary also mentioned a lapse in communication with "our Arkansas relatives for a long time." She meant the Cherokee branch of the family—her "Uncle Stand" [Stand Watie, her father's brother] and various cousins, for whom, evidently, she yet retained warm feelings of connection.[89]

The later lives of these second-generation Boudinots would go in various directions. Two of the sons made their way back to the Indian Territory, reclaimed their Cherokee roots, and sought to play a role in the Nation's affairs; one was a lawyer and businessman, the other a lawyer, writer, and editor. The third became an actor and operatic performer in New York City, enlisted in the Union army during the Civil War, and died while in service of a fall from a horse. (Other family members fought on the opposite side; for example, "Uncle Stand" Watie became a Confederate army general.) Their descendants have carried the Boudinot name, and a sense of Cherokee identity, to the present day. Of Elias and Harriet's daughters, one died in childhood, while the other two remained in New England, found "Yankee" husbands, and left little trace behind them. Presumably they, with their children and grandchildren, passed quietly into the white community.[90]

In the immediate aftermath of the killings, Sarah Ridge faced her own set of terrible challenges. A friend described her as "sinking under the weight of sorrow," and overwhelmed by "fearful apprehensions & undecided anxieties"; one of her sons feared "that she would not live under it." Indeed, so long as she remained at Honey Creek, she expected "every night that our sufferings would be terminated by assassination from the murderers of my husband." After several days, "interested persons" persuaded her that she must pull together and leave without further delay, considering the "danger . . . [to] herself & children." Thus on July 1, she gathered the family together and traveled some fifty miles to the town of Fayetteville, Arkansas. There she bought a "dog-trot" log house reminiscent of a traditional Cherokee style. (Later she would expand it into a two-story "salt box" dwelling with clapboard exterior; it remains today the oldest still-standing house in Fayetteville.) For months more, she remained "overwhelmed by grief . . . [and] complained . . . that her faculties were destroyed, that she could not remember common things, that she should never be able to take care of her family." Yet eventually "skillful physicians . . . & the tender & judicious sympathy of some friends did much to bring her back." In the mid-1840s, she moved to the village of Osage Prairie (later Bentonville) in Benton County, but she returned to her Fayetteville home in 1853. She struggled through years of court proceedings concerning the settlement of her husband's estate; at one point, some of her Cherokee in-laws brought suit to deny her (and her children's) inheritance rights entirely, since she was "a white lady and had no clan." She obtained income from hiring out her slaves. By some accounts, she never recovered fully from the trauma of John's death; as one put it, "she bore a dead heart in a living bosom." Still, when she died in 1856, she was said to be "very highly esteemed by the best people" of Fayetteville.[91]

It is not clear that she ever revisited Honey Creek. In any case, the Ridge farm was despoiled soon after her departure. As she wrote later, with evident bitterness, "The Indians considered my property as public plunder and immediately commenced their depredations on whatever they could find. They destroyed or stole my poultry, killed my cattle and hogs, and not satisfied with camping in my fields and eating just what they wanted, they turned their horses into the fields, evidently designing to destroy all the corn in their power." This description was part of a plea she made to the federal government for financial assistance. In 1846, she received "an appropriation" of $5,000, ratified by the U.S. Senate, "as compensation for the losses sustained by the family of John Ridge, in consequence of his death and the subsequent confusion into which his affairs were thrown."[92]

Her children would grow to adulthood around her in Arkansas. Two of her daughters married and raised a family there; the third was "feeble-minded" (as they said in those days) and died at a relatively young age. Among her sons, the eldest, John Rollin Ridge, would have a particularly colorful and consequential life. He began by venturing back to Honey Creek and purchasing a farm there. However, he was soon embroiled with followers of Ross, his father's enemies, one of whom he shot and killed in the course of a personal quarrel. Anxious to avoid prosecution—and urged by his mother to leave the Nation forever—he set out for California at the time of the gold rush, and began a career as a writer and editor. He worked for a Know-Nothing newspaper and inveighed against Mormons and abolitionists; he was also a vocal supporter of the Democratic Party and a sympathizer with the South during the Civil War. Under the pen name Yellow Bird, he wrote poems and a popular romance based on the life of a notorious Mexican-American bandit. (Reputedly, this was the first novel published in California; it brought its author a measure of fame.) He took up the cause of California Indians, the so-called Diggers, adapting his family's long-standing goal of "civilization" to their particular circumstances. He never returned to the Nation, but remained passionately concerned with its affairs, scheming at several points to avenge his father's death. Shortly after the Civil War, he went to Washington with a delegation of "Southern Cherokees" (legatees of the old Treaty Party) for negotiations to close the still-festering cleavage within the Nation. He died in 1868 of "brain fever" (apparently a form of encephalitis); the obituaries were long and laudatory.[93]

Of the other sons, one—named Herman Daggett Ridge, after the Mission School principal—had a farm near Fayetteville, "cultivated by his negroes"; later he was killed fighting for the Confederacy. A second went for a few years to California, returned, took ill, and died in his twenties. The youngest studied law, moved briefly to Texas and then to California, where he began a long career as an attorney. Like later generations of Boudinots, Ridge descendants are today scattered across the country, many of them successful professionals and businesspeople.[94]

It is impossible to know in detail how news of the 1839 assassinations was received in Cornwall. Some in the town must have read the several accounts published in the new county newspaper, the *Litchfield Enquirer*—beginning with "Outrage Among the Cherokee Indians Near Fort Gibson," on July 25. Surely, a good many remembered John Ridge and Elias Boudinot in quite specific, even personal, ways. But most of those who had been closest to them were gone by now. Herman Daggett, the intrepid, ever-hopeful (but unsmiling) principal, had died in 1832, and Jeremiah Evarts, corresponding secretary of the American Board, the year before. Timothy Stone, onetime agent and devoted supporter of the school, was forced from his ministry in the First Church (1826), apparently as part of the fallout from the "intermarriage" crisis (even though he had declined to perform either of the actual wedding ceremonies). Lyman Beecher had moved on from Litchfield to bigger things: a pastorate in Boston (1826), another in Cincinnati (1834), the presidency of the Lane Theological Seminary (also 1834), and a leadership role in the Second Great Awakening.[95]

Meanwhile, memory of the school itself had begun to fade. From its original position as "an institution . . . famous throughout the country," "an experiment . . . [that] stands alone in the Christian world . . . [with] not its like in Europe or America," "a school [that] had a celebrity beyond all expectation, and [made] the vale of Cornwall . . . known in almost all the world," its public reputation would shrink and recede as the years went by, until, finally, it became *just a piece of local history.*[96]

Epilogue

Throughout the nineteenth century, the story of Henry Obookiah remained alive and vibrant. The famous *Memoirs* were reissued again and again, informing new generations of his conversion to Christianity and "civilized" ways, and his tragic, yet transfiguring, early death. This was especially true in Hawaii itself, where missionaries regularly invoked his example for their native charges. His status as the islands' "first Christian" was widely acknowledged and celebrated.

The same pattern continued into the twentieth century. Moreover, with long-distance travel becoming faster and easier to manage, Hawaiian Protestants began appearing at Cornwall as pilgrims bent on honoring Obookiah in more personal ways. Often they would bring seashells, bottles filled with island soil, or other Hawaii-related artifacts, to festoon his grave site.[1]

In 1968, on the 150th anniversary of his death, a semiofficial delegation from the Hawaiian Christian community came to conduct a prayer service at the grave (and to spread dozens of decorative leis alongside). At the same moment, in carefully coordinated fashion, thousands of worshipers gathered at two different sites in the islands—one group at the first mission church in Honolulu, the other on the bay shore at Napo'opo'o, from where Obookiah had originally set out. In addition, the Hawaiian

Tourist Bureau donated a special "warrior marker" for his grave in Cornwall; this "coveted honor . . . [was] the only one of its kind to be granted outside of the islands." (In fact, the marker would quickly be removed to the local Historical Society for safekeeping, and has remained there ever since.)[2]

The 175th anniversary, in February 1993, brought another ceremonial round of "remembrance and celebration." Once again, planners organized simultaneous events in both Cornwall and Hawaii. By then, moreover, a group of Obookiah's kinfolk had incorporated themselves to promote "the return [of] his remains to his homeland." Together, they raised money (upward of $25,000) from both private and foundation sources, and secured the approval of Cornwall authorities. In truth, some in the town were reluctant about this. An "informational meeting" at the First Church considered all sides, but in the end most agreed that "the family's wishes" should trump other concerns. Obookiah's place in Cornwall's history would not be compromised, remarked one resident, for "part of him will always be with us." The process that followed took a month to complete, with several intervening stages. In effect, it reversed the arc of Obookiah's own life—by moving from essentially Christian (and "white American") elements to others rooted in native Hawaiian tradition.[3]

On July 12, 1993, the grave was opened for exhumation. As curious onlookers gathered around, Connecticut's state archaeologist and half a dozen assistants carefully removed the facing on top, then worked down through several inches of topsoil, a layer of flat stones, and a large quantity of sand—to find, at a depth of nearly five feet, a fully intact skeleton. The original coffin, though decayed, had left a clear imprint in the sand. Most striking of all was an assemblage of brass tacks in what would have been the chest area, formed in the shape of a heart and enclosing the initials *H* and *O* and the number 26 (Obookiah's presumed age at the time of death). There was also a scattering of glass shards, apparently the remnants of a viewing window placed at head level. Each of these features—the stones, the glass, the tacks—was unusual in grave-site construction; taken together, they implied a high degree of care and interest.[4]

The remains, when removed, were wrapped in cloth and placed in a new casket made from Hawaiian koa wood. On the second Sunday following, the church held a ceremony of "homegoing." Close to two hundred worshipers attended, including native Hawaiians from various parts of the country, some of whom claimed kinship to Obookiah. Two who were Protestant ministers led prayers and songs in both English and Hawaiian. According to a subsequent account, "everyone wore a colorful lei entwined with Hawaiian tea leaves."[5]

A day later, the casket, now in the hands of the kinfolk, was flown to Honolulu. There it was conveyed to a succession of island sites—two schools and at least seven churches—for religious services and other expressions of public respect. The conclusion of this tour was set in and around the great bay with the *heiau* at which Obookiah had spent most of his later childhood. From here on, every step (as reported in local newspapers) was carefully choreographed to represent significant aspects of his life—especially his Hawaiian origins. The casket was carried to the shore from the sea in a large canoe. There was a "symbolic swim" by one of the relatives "out to where the ship *Triumph* was anchored in 1808." Finally, on August 15, came the moment of reinterment. The proceedings featured a native ceremony called *ka oha ola hou* (meaning "the bamboo lives again"). At the close, U.S. senator Daniel Akaka offered remarks; Obookiah, he said, was "one who positively altered the course of a people, a state, and a nation." Then came a procession to the grave— a handsome vault raised somewhat above ground level and capped by a stele with commemorative inscriptions. Marchers passed "between a human chain of women dressed in full-length black gowns carrying in their hands bright orange feather leis that resembled torches." As the casket was lowered, and emotion crested, "observers noted a break in the darkened sky, when the sun peered out and the storm clouds dissipated." The day concluded with a luau—a feast of traditional foods— with music from ukeleles and "hand-made acoustical instruments," and hula performances. Through it all, participants kept repeating, "Praise God, Henry's home."[6]

And so he was.

There are more burials to mention. In north Georgia, on a gentle knoll not far from the original Cherokee capital of New Echota, lies a rough square of embedded stones, shaded by tall trees and enclosing a tiny graveyard. In the middle stands a plain limestone slab with the following inscription:[7]

To
the memory of
HARRIET RUGGLES
wife of
MR ELIAS BOUDINOT
She was the daughter of
Col Benjamin Gold
of Cornwall Con
where she was born
June 1805
And died at New Echota
Cherokee Nation
Aug 15 1836
Aged 31
We seek a rest beyond the skies

Her beginning and her end: born in Cornwall, died in the Cherokee Nation, resting now beyond the skies. But the stone gives no hint of how much lay in between. Her growing-up as "one of the fairest, most cultured ladies of the place [Cornwall]." Her status as "the idol of her family." The gradual, intensely private ripening of her attachment to Elias, and of his to her. Their eventual acknowledgment—first to each other, then to her family, finally to the world at large. The agonizing rift with her siblings, and the "great turmoil" that followed, both locally and far beyond. Her determination to proceed, against the "fix'd & unalterable" opposition of so many around her. The terrible night of public repudiation on the town green, as she watched from a hiding place in a nearby house while her effigy burned in a fire lit by her closest brother. The shocked resentment among Cherokees about such overt prejudice, together with the indignant response of some (not all) missionary leaders. The wound felt by Elias, prompting his temporary "fall" from Christian ways—and the bitterness of his "Ishmaelite" writing. And yet, when feelings had finally cooled, their "splendid wedding" in her parents' home, with Elias so fully accepted that some who were present "almost forgot . . . he was an Indian."

All of it leading, after many years had passed, to exactly here.

.   .   .

Finally: what's called the Polson Cemetery, in the northeast tip of Oklahoma, a mile or so from the border with Missouri. Here one finds the graves of several Ridge family members. It's a two-acre plot, with a framed sign at the entrance reading RIDGE-WATIE and an American flag flying alongside.

Today it's surrounded by hay fields, part of a larger area known as Peter's Prairie. (Peter was one of Major Ridge's slaves; why the land was named for him is unknown.) The site of John Ridge's house, long since destroyed, was about two hundred yards to the northeast. On the other side, the land slopes down toward Honey Creek, a clear, gently flowing stream that seems to have been part of what attracted the Ridges to this spot in the first place. There are remains of some old barns, perhaps from the time of the family's settlement here. Major Ridge's widow, Susannah Wickett, returned to the property some years after the murders; following her death, ownership passed to a grandson. Except for one brief interval, it has remained in the hands of descendants ever since. Local belief held that Major Ridge and John had buried money near their houses; and, in the late nineteenth century, people from the surrounding towns would dig at likely spots in search of it. (Nothing was ever found.)[8]

John Ridge was buried here immediately following his death, but with no marker at all for more than a century. As long as bitter feeling about removal remained abroad in the Nation, there was reason to fear that any public memorial to the leader of the Treaty Party would invite desecration. Finally, in the 1960s a modest stone was set alongside one for his father; it reads as follows:

JOHN RIDGE

CHEROKEE LEADER

BORN ROME, GA. 1802

ASSASSINATED HERE

JUNE 22, 1839

Even more than in the case of Harriet Gold Boudinot, this stone seems to beg for additional information. His life, after all, made an astonishing story of movement and change, of accomplishment and defeat. Born and raised in the Cherokee Nation, the son of a widely admired chief. Spirited away by missionaries to a completely different life in the world of white people. Revealed there as a quick study, who would make the most of his special educational opportunities. Half of a notorious love match across racial lines; target from then on of racist intolerance. Thrust into leadership roles at an early age. Eloquent speaker, gifted writer, passionate defender of Cherokee rights and interests. Colleague, opponent, and friend of U.S. presidents, cabinet secretaries, congressmen, and other figures of prominence. Obliged by his own best instincts and judgment to reverse course and embrace—albeit reluctantly—the necessity of removal. Successful planter and businessman, slave owner, husband, father of seven. And victim, finally, of a bitter internecine struggle.

So: three grave sites to consider. Together, they evoke the sweep of the heathen school story: its geographic range, its remarkable cast of characters, its violent twists and turns, its emotional depth, its eventual, conclusive finality. As well, they disclose its interior meanings, including:

The bedrock ambition to make the world a better place—and, in that regard, something intrinsic to American culture and history.

The challenge posed by human difference—pointing, then, toward the diverse, multicultural people we have become today.

The hubris of overreaching—and the harsh reality of failure.

But the story will not quite rest there. In the summer of 2010, the Cornwall Historical Society mounted an elegant little exhibition on the school, including artifacts from its heyday, maps, images of individual scholars, helpful descriptive information, and lectures by historians with knowledge of one or another pertinent topic. Special guests included half a dozen descendants of John Ridge and Elias Boudinot; some came from as far away as Oklahoma and California. There were also Hawaiian visitors, collaterally related to Henry Obookiah, one of whom traveled to Cornwall by motorcycle from Michigan. The atmosphere was pleasant, friendly, animated—with just a hint in the air of the troubled history that had led to this point.

As the absolute finale, resident members of the Gold family hosted a dinner for the visiting Ridge and Boudinot kin. No others were invited, only the descendants on both sides. The hosts commented afterward on "the normalcy of the evening." Conversation flowed easily around current lives and interests. At some point, it was decided to show how everyone present was related. To this end, the group created a large genealogical chart, showing all manner of cousin connections. Otherwise, history was not invoked. "The past was what it was," remarked one participant. "It was just nice to catch up and learn about another part of the family."[9]

Perhaps for them, this was closure at last. But what about other participants in the story? Certainly, nothing closed for the Protestant missionary movement as a whole. Its leaders did make one important, strategic adjustment—at least in part as a result of the Cornwall experience. From then on, there would be no more concerted efforts to bring "wild men ... to our shores" for religious conversion and training; instead, "the Great Cause" would be centered in foreign lands. This would avert the danger that more "innocent maids" might someday be lured to join Sarah Northrup and Harriet Gold in crossing the race line. Indeed, missionary work would grow and flourish in its redirected mode. And its part in the collective life of a "redeemer nation" would become ever more conspicuous. The American Board of Commissioners for Foreign Missions would sponsor projects in dozens of different countries. (The spirit of all this would remain unchanged: Both then and thereafter the "heathen" must be saved from their own "gross errors" and wickedness.)

Nor would closure come to the places from which the original scholars had been drawn. Hawaii would pass through a tumultuous, and searing, process of change, one that continues to the present day. The native population would be steadily cut down by disease and other causes. White immigrants from the U.S. mainland would arrive in ever-larger numbers (followed by many others from Japan, Southeast Asia, and some parts of Europe). Large-scale plantation agriculture (sugarcane, rice, pineapples, coffee) would reshape the local economy, while reducing indigenous workers to a state of virtual peonage. Political power would pass to a new—mostly white—elite. Traditional culture would be shunted aside. And eventually the islands would become one with the larger United States, first through an imposed annexation, then with the granting of full statehood. (The missionaries and their descendants were deeply involved in these transformations. And Henry Obookiah himself could be seen as a source point for some of them.)

American Indians, too, were subject to a grinding sequence of change, without closure. Cherokee removal became the starting point for generations of conflict both inside and outside the Nation. As such, it was a prototype for the dislocations forced upon many different Indian groups for decades to come. (As architects of removal, John Ridge and Elias

Boudinot would be long remembered—sometimes admired, more often vilified. Even today they remain highly controversial figures.)

None of this, of course, was solely attributable to the Mission School; much the same would have happened without its influence. The school was one link among countless others in a many-stranded chain that has no end.

And what, finally, of closure for an author and his readers? We can close a book—the physical object—but not the thoughts and feelings it evokes. We can bid good-bye to its principal characters—in this case, Obookiah, Boudinot, Ridge, Sarah Northrup, Harriet Gold, Herman Daggett, Jeremiah Evarts—but their stories linger. We can travel back from "history" to our present lives—known people, familiar places, established routines—but the journey has left its mark. Would we have it otherwise?

Acknowledgments

My helpers with this book have been many, their contributions extraordinary. My research began at the Public Library in Cornwall, Connecticut, where Virginia Potter pointed me toward a valuable archive on Mission School history. Created some years before by the late Michael Gannett (and since relocated to the Cornwall Historical Society), this material got me off and running. Mr. Gannett would quickly become a major source of advice and counsel on all things Cornwall; I very much regret that he won't see the completion of the project. Early on I was put in touch with Ann Schillinger, another in the town's sturdy band of local historians. For long stretches Ann became virtually a collaborator—running down sources on my behalf, answering my many inquiries about matters both large and small, and providing exactly the sort of encouragement every historian/author yearns for. Jeremy Brecher was my tour guide through the visible landscape; his deep knowledge directly informed the writing of my "interlude" on Cornwall. Charles and Barbara Gold shared with me pertinent details of their family's history, up to and including the poignant meeting described at the end of that same interlude.

Another of the interludes concerns Hawaii. My visit there was facilitated by Barbara Anderson, Barbara Lee, and, most of all, Marie Delores Strazar and Louis Doody. The latter pair drove me all over the Big Island, hosted me at their hillside cabin, and offered valuable insights into Hawaiian history and culture. While in Honolulu I had a long and useful discussion with Douglas Warne, whose work in reconstructing the lives of Hawaii-born "scholars" at the Mission School is unmatched. After my return I profited from several e-mail exchanges with Fred Hoxie (himself Hawaii-born).

The third, and last, of the interludes is about the original territories of the Cherokee Nation (especially what is today north Georgia). In touring that region I was fortunate to have the company of Bob Morrissey; his reactions enlarged and enhanced my own. The proprietors of the Chieftains Museum (Rome, Georgia), once the home of Major Ridge, gave me a cordial reception. And W. Jeff Bishop enabled me to read the results of a careful site evaluation carried out by the National Park Service on the home built and occupied by John Ridge (Calhoun, Georgia). I learned about Ridge home sites in Oklahoma from Nancy Brown, a direct descendant of Major Ridge and John, and the current owner/occupant of those properties.

In addition to all that I found in Cornwall, archival holdings at the following institutions proved essential: Houghton Library (Harvard University), current custodian of the original records of the American Board of Commissioners for Foreign Missions; Sterling Library (Yale University), repository of important papers from the Gold, Morse, and other mission-connected families; the Connecticut Historical Society (Hartford); the American Antiquarian Society (Worcester, Massachusetts); the local historical societies of Litchfield, Woodbury, and Torrington, Connecticut; the Norman Rockwell Museum (Stockbridge, Massachusetts); the Huntington Library (Pasadena, California); the Arkansas Historical Commission (Little Rock); and the Mission Houses Museum (Honolulu, Hawaii). Staff at each of these places afforded me unfailing courtesies.

In gathering the illustrations I received valuable assistance (and, in some cases, permissions) from William Reese, James Boudinot, Alec C. Frost, Raechel Guest, and others at the Cornwall Historical Society, the New Echota Historic Site (Calhoun, Georgia), Chieftains Museum, and, most especially, Mark Chiusano.

My project was supported by fellowships from the Radcliffe Institute for Advanced Study and the American Antiquarian Society, and by a grant from the provost's office at Yale University. While at the Antiquarian Society I was fortunate to have Mark Mulligan working as my research assistant.

Many scholars responded helpfully to my requests for comment on specific issues and questions, among them, John Harley Warner, Jean O'Brien, Theda Perdue, Bill Hutchison, Peter Wood, Tom McCarthy, Gary Nash, Emily Conroy-Krutz, and Harry Stout.

This long list must particularly include the readers of my various written drafts, friends and colleagues without whose help the book would have been a much lesser thing. Aaron Sachs and Jane Kamensky, two of the finest writers I know, provided exhaustive, page-by-page responses to the whole manuscript version; their advice was crucial throughout. Other readers of the whole included Wendy Warren, my editor Andrew Miller, and members of the Historians and Writers group at Cornell University; all made valuable suggestions. Individual chapters were read and critiqued by Dawn Peterson, Richard D. Brown, Jill Lepore, Peter Silver, Daniel Mandell, Ann Marie Plane, Robert Johnston, Jim Sleeper, Maura Fitzgerald, and workshop gatherings at Rutgers, Princeton, and Yale Universities and the Huntington Library.

Editorial staff at Alfred A. Knopf skillfully steered the book toward publication, especially Andrew Miller and Mark Chiusano. Carol Edwards did remarkable, and much-needed, work as copy editor. Closer to home, Gary Harrington smoothed my sometimes troubled relations with my word processor. And closest of all to home, Virginia Demos endured the many years of the project's life, and offered repeated infusions of comment, suggestion, and hope.

I offer great thanks to all these people and institutions, while at the same time clearing them of responsibility for any of the book's inevitable shortcomings.

Notes

There are two archives in particular that are cited repeatedly in the notes. These are identified by call number or folder number, but the repositories listed below are not repeated in individual notes.

American Board of Commissioners for Foreign Missions ms. archive, Houghton Library, Harvard University, Cambridge, MA. There are four record sets, each with its own call number:

ABC 1.01
ABC 11
ABC 12.1
ABC 18.3.1

Foreign Mission School Archive (FMS), Cornwall Historical Society, Cornwall, CT. The records are filed in sixty-one folders.

Prologue

1. At the time of deciding to pursue this topic, previous writing about it included the following: Edward C. Starr, *A History of Cornwall, Connecticut: A Typical New England Town* (New Haven, CT, 1926), 136–57; Paul H. Chamberlain, "The Foreign Mission School" (typescript pamphlet, Cornwall, CT, 1968); John Andrew, "Educating the Heathen: the Foreign Mission School Controversy and American Ideals," *Journal of American Studies* 12 (1978): 331–42; John Andrew, *Rebuilding the Christian Commonwealth: New England Congregationalists and Foreign Missions* (Lexington, KY, 1976), chapter 9; Ralph Gabriel, *Elias Boudinot, Cherokee, and His America* (Norman, OK, 1941), part 2; Thurman Wilkins, *Cherokee Tragedy: The Ridge Family and the Decimation of a People* (Norman, OK, 1970), chapter 6. In the years since, the Foreign Mission School and, in particular, its two leading

members, Elias Boudinot and John Ridge, have drawn attention from literature scholars. See, for example, Theresa Strouth Gaul, ed., *To Marry an Indian: The Marriage of Harriett Gold & Elias Boudinot in Letters, 1823–1839* (Chapel Hill, NC, 2005); Karen Woods Weierman, *One Nation, One Blood: Interracial Marriage in American Fiction, Scandal, and Law, 1820–1870* (Amherst, MA, 2005), chapter 1; Maureen Konkle, *Writing Indian Nations: Native Intellectuals and the Politics of Historiography, 1827–1863* (Chapel Hill, NC, 2004), chapter 1; Hilary E. Wyss, *English Letters and Indian Literacies: Reading, Writing, and New England Missionary Schools, 1750–1830* (Philadelphia, 2012), chapter 4.

2. Recent discussions of the theme of American exceptionalism include, for example, Ted Widmer, *Ark of the Liberties: America and the World* (New York, 2007), and Godfrey Hodgson, *The Myth of American Exceptionalism* (New Haven, CT, 2009). See also Ernest Lee Tuveson, *Redeemer Nation: The Idea of America's Millennial Role* (Chicago, 1968).

3. Tzvetan Todorov, *The Conquest of America*, trans. Richard Howard (New York, 1984), 3.

4. Samuel Beckett, *Worstward Ho* (New York, 1983), 7. I am grateful to Adrienne Miesmer for calling this comment to my attention.

CHAPTER ONE *American Outreach: The China Trade*

1. James R. Gibson, *Otter Skins, Boston Ships, and China Goods: The Maritime Fur Trade of the Northwest Coast, 1785–1841* (Montreal, 1992), 12–35.

2. Ibid., 36–61, 292–95. The literature on the China Trade is vast. The most recent book-length account is Eric Jay Dolan, *When America First Met China: An Exotic History of Tea, Drugs, and Money in the Age of Sail* (New York, 2012). For a good short introduction, see James Kirker, *Adventures to China: Americans in the Southern Ocean* (New York, 1970). Perhaps the fullest account of the Chinese end of the trade is Jacques Downs, *The Golden Ghetto: The American Commercial Community of Canton and the Shaping of American China Policy, 1784–1844* (Bethlehem, PA, 1997). A somewhat older book, Foster Rhea Dulles, *The Old China Trade* (New York, 1970), is still useful. See also Henry Trubner and William Jay Rathbun, *China's Influence on American Culture in the 18th and 19th Centuries* (New York, 1976); Philip Chadwick Foster, *The Empress of China* (Philadelphia, 1984); Margaret Christman, *Adventurous Pursuits: Americans and the China Trade, 1784–1844* (Washington, D.C., 1984); John Rogers Haddad, *The Romance of China: Excursions to China in U.S. Culture, 1778–1876* (New York, 2008), especially chapters 1–3. For more specialized studies, see David Sanctuary Howard, *New York and the China Trade* (New York, 1984); Jean Gordon Lee, *Philadelphians and the China Trade* (Philadelphia, 1984). On the economic importance of transpacific trade (including trade with China), see James R. Fichter, *So Great a Profit: How the East India Trade Transformed American Capitalism* (Cambridge, MA, 2010). On the material side of the trade, see the handsome exhibition catalog by Thomas Vaughan and Bill Holm, *Soft Gold: The Fur Trade and Cultural Exchange on the Northwest Coast of America*, rev. ed. (Portland, OR, 1989); Carl L. Crossman, *The Decorative Arts of the China Trade: Paintings, Furnishings, and Exotic Curiosities* (Woodbridge, CT, 1991); China Trade Issue, *Historic Deerfield* 6 (2005).

3. On the Boston Exchange Coffee House, see the superb work by Jane Kamensky,

The Exchange Artist: A Tale of High-Flying Speculation and America's First Banking Collapse (New York, 2008).

4. Gibson, *Otter Skins, Boston Ships, and China Goods,* 32–35, 41–42; Kirker, *Adventures to China,* 24–34.

5. Kirker, *Adventures to China,* 20–23, 35–49. See also Briton Cooper Busch, *The War Against the Seals: A History of the North American Seal Fishery* (Kingston, ON, 1985), chapters 1–2.

6. Kirker, *Adventures to China,* 65–81.

7. Ibid., 118–43; Gibson, *Otter Skins, Boston Ships, and China Goods,* 253–54.

8. Gibson, *Otter Skins, Boston Ships, and China Goods,* 6–11, 57–60, 110–36, 176–77.

9. Ibid., 50–56, 84–104, 188–203, 294–95; Kirker, *Adventures to China,* 161–75; Crossman, *The Decorative Arts of the China Trade;* Howard, *New York and the China Trade;* Lee, *Philadelphians and the China Trade.*

10. Downs, *The Golden Ghetto,* 67–72; Gibson, *Otter Skins, Boston Ships, and China Goods,* 92–93, 99–100.

11. John Meares, *Voyages Made in the Years 1788 and 1789, from China to the Northwest Coast of America* (London, 1790), quoted in Gibson, *Otter Skins, Boston Ships, and China Goods,* 44; "Shadows of Destiny: A French Navigator's View of the Hawaiian Kingdom and Its Government in 1828," *Hawaiian Journal of History* 17 (1983): 28, quoted ibid.; J. C. Beaglehole, ed., *The Journals of Captain James Cook on His Voyages of Discovery,* 5 vols. (Cambridge, 1955–1974), vol. 3, 1083–85, quoted ibid., 48.

12. Amasa Delano, *A Narrative of Voyages and Travels in the Northern and Southern Hemispheres* (Boston, 1817), 542, quoted in Kirker, *Adventures to China,* 4.

13. Kirker, *Adventures to China,* 150–54. See also Gibson, *Otter Skins, Boston Ships, and China Goods,* 51–52, 151–52, 279–80, 289–91.

14. See David A. Chappell, *Double Ghosts: Oceanian Voyagers on Euroamerican Ships* (Armonk, NY, 1997). By some estimates, Pacific Islanders—especially Hawaiians—would eventually compose a quarter of the crew members on ships involved in this transoceanic trade.

CHAPTER TWO *"Providence unquestionably cast them on our shores"*

1. See *A Narrative of Five Youth from the Sandwich Islands, Now Receiving an Education in This Country* (New York, 1816), 9.

2. Ibid. See also E. W. Dwight, *Memoirs of Henry Obookiah, a Native of the Sandwich Islands, Who Died at Cornwall, Connecticut, February 17, 1818, Aged 26* (New Haven, CT, 1818), 22–23. For a later account of these same events, see Thomas C. Richards, *Samuel J. Mills: Missionary, Pathfinder, Pioneer, and Promoter* (Boston, 1906), 16, quoted in Thomas E. French, *The Missionary Whaleship* (New York, 1961), 20.

3. Dwight, *Memoirs of Henry Obookiah,* 17.

4. Ibid., 21, 25.

5. On the life and career of Timothy Dwight, see Kenneth Silverman, *Timothy Dwight* (New York, 1969); John R. Fitzmeir, *New England's Moral Legislator: Timothy Dwight, 1752–1817* (Bloomington, IN, 1998); Stephen E. Berk, *Calvinism Versus Democracy: Timothy Dwight and the Origins of American Evangelical Orthodoxy* (Hamden, CT, 1974). For photographs of the president's house (long since

destroyed), see the Dana Scrapbook Collection, vol. 13, 106, 108, Whitney Library, New Haven Museum, New Haven, CT.

6. Dwight, *Memoirs of Henry Obookiah*, 4–5, 8.

7. On the place and year of Obookiah's birth, see Albert S. Baker to Librarian, Public Library, Cornwall, CT, July 23, 1941, in FMS Archive, folder 31. See also Baker to Emily Marsh, September 11, 1941, in FMS Archive, folder 31. Until the excellent work of Baker, a missionary and careful genealogist, the generally accepted year for Obookiah's birth was 1792.

8. There are numerous histories in which these events are described. See, for example, Ralph S. Kuykendall and A. Grove Day, *Hawaii: A History from Polynesian Kingdom to American State* (Englewood Cliffs, NJ, 1976), chapter 3.

9. Ibid., 5–8. See also Baker to Librarian, July 23, 1941. The identity of Obookiah's uncle has been clearly established: one of his mother's older brothers, named Pahua. This man was indeed a *kahuna* (high priest) at the famous *heiau* (temple) known as Hikiau, near Napo'opo'o, on the shore of Kealakekua Bay. He remained active for many years after Obookiah's departure, and was visited in the 1820s by several members of the newly founded Protestant mission.

10. Kuykendall and Day, *Hawaii*, 9.

11. The fullest account of the plan for Obookiah and Hopoo to chaperone the prince on a voyage to America appears in "Memoirs of Thomas Hopoo," reprinted in *Hawaiian Journal of History* 2 (1968): 42–54. (The manuscript original of this document is at the Andover Newton Theological School, Newton Center, MA.) See also *A Narrative of Five Youth*, 7; Dwight, *Memoirs of Henry Obookiah*, 10–12.

12. Dwight, *Memoirs of Henry Obookiah*, 12.

13. Ibid., 15, 14; *A Narrative of Five Youth*, 19.

14. Dwight, *Memoirs of Henry Obookiah*, 16. On April 8, 1809, the *Connecticut Herald* carried the following notice: "The ship Triumph (Captain Caleb Brintnall), belonging to this port, has arrived at New York City, in 5 months from Canton."

15. Gardner J. Spring, *Memoirs of the Rev. Samuel J. Mills* (New York, 1820), 47; Samuel J. Mills to Gordon Hall, December 20, 1809, ibid., 49; Dwight, *Memoirs of Henry Obookiah*, 23; *Daily Herald* (West Winsted, CT), October 25, 1894.

16. Dwight, *Memoirs of Henry Obookiah*, 23; Letter from the Rev. Mr. Mills, quoted ibid., 24.

17. Dwight, *Memoirs of Henry Obookiah*, 25, 27, 28. See also *The Religious Intelligencer*, vol. 1 (1816–17), 13.

18. Dwight, *Memoirs of Henry Obookiah*, 32.

19. Ibid., 36–37.

20. *A Narrative of Five Youth*, 10.

21. Dwight, *Memoirs of Henry Obookiah*, 39, 90–91, 37.

22. On Eleazer Williams, see John Demos, *The Unredeemed Captive: A Family Story from Early America* (New York, 1994), epilogue. Samuel J. Mills to the Prudential Committee, American Board of Commissioners for Foreign Missions, March 14, 1814, ABC 12.1, vol. 2, no. 2; William Bartlett, S. Spring, and Samuel Worcester to the Prudential Committee, American Board of Commissioners for Foreign Missions, March 18, 1814, ABC 12.1, vol. 2, no. 1

23. Lyman Beecher, *A Sermon Delivered at the Funeral of Henry Obookiah* (New Haven, CT, 1818), reprinted in Dwight, *Memoirs of Henry Obookiah*, 29, at back of volume.

24. Dwight, *Memoirs of Henry Obookiah*, 38, 23.

25. Ibid., 43.

26. Ibid., 44.

27. For numerous examples of letters by Obookiah and other scholars, see Dwight, *Memoirs of Henry Obookiah,* and *The Religious Intelligencer,* vols. 1–3. The quoted passages in this paragraph are found in Dwight, *Memoirs of Henry Obookiah,* 46, 52, 49, 66, 62, 66–67, 55, 26.

28. Henry Obookiah to A Christian Friend, December 15, 1812, in *A Narrative of Five Youth,* 13; Dwight, *Memoirs of Henry Obookiah,* 40.

29. Dwight, *Memoirs of Henry Obookiah,* 91, 42, 48, 93.

30. Ibid., 32; Cyrus Franklin Burge to E. C. Starr, February 22, 1899, in FMS Archive, folder 31.

31. Dwight, *Memoirs of Henry Obookiah,* 89; letter of J. P. Stone, quoted in A. C. Thompson, *A Commemorative Address . . . at the Semi-Centenary of the Ordination of the First Missionaries to the Sandwich Islands* (Boston, 1869), 15n.

32. Dwight, *Memoirs of Henry Obookiah,* 89–93.

33. Ibid., 41, 96.

34. *A Narrative of Five Youth,* 19, 26, 29. On Honoree's experience, in particular, see also *The Panoplist and Missionary Magazine,* vol. 13 (1817), 43.

35. *A Narrative of Five Youth,* 30–35; *The Religious Intelligencer,* vol. 1 (1816–17), 446–47. See *The Religious Intelligencer,* vol. 1 (1816–17), 142, 334–35, 414; *The Panoplist and Missionary Magazine,* vol. 13 (1817), 44.

36. *A Narrative of Five Youth,* 32, 38, 28.

37. W. Safford to Jeremiah Evarts, May 13, 1816, ABC 12.1, vol. 2, no. 3.

38. *The Religious Intelligencer,* vol. 1 (1816–17), 14, 174.

39. Charles Prentice, James Harvey, and James Morris to the American Board of Commissioners for Foreign Missions, August 20, 1816, ABC 12.1, vol. 2, no. 8.

40. Ibid.

41. Ibid.

42. *The Religious Intelligencer,* vol. 1 (1816–17), 439–40. Leaders of the American Bible Society announced similar ambitions with a similar time line. In 1833, the Society's Virginia chapter resolved "that the world shall be supplied with the Holy Scriptures within twenty years." See American Bible Society, *Resolutions of the American Bible Society, and an Address to the Christian Public, on the Subject of Supplying the Whole World with the Sacred Scriptures, Within a Definite Period* (New York, 1833), vol. 1, 5, quoted in Richard D. Brown, *The Strength of a People: The Idea of an Informed Citizenry in America, 1650–1870* (Chapel Hill, NC, 1996), 112.

43. The School's constitution is published in *A Narrative of Five Youth,* 41–42.

44. Ibid., 42.

45. Ibid., 43–44.

46. Ibid., 44.

47. Edwin W. Dwight to Abigail Welles Dwight, April 1, 1817, Dwight Collection, vol. 11, 43, Norman Rockwell Museum, Stockbridge, MA; *The Religious Intelligencer,* vol. 1 (1816–17), 14; James Morris to Jedediah Morse, November 25, 1816, ABC 12.1, vol. 2, no. 40. In midwinter, the American Board reimbursed Pettingill for charges incurred in "boarding and instructing the Owhyhean youths to Jan. 31st [1817]"; see Charlestown to Rev. Amos Pettingill, February 24, 1817, ABC 1.01, vol. 2, no. 63. See also *A Narrative of Five Youth,* 30; "Recollections of Mrs. Cowles of Morris," ms. notes, FMS Archive, folder 10.

48. George Prince Tamoree to unidentified correspondent, November 20, 1816, in *The Religious Intelligencer,* vol. 1 (1816–17), 335.

49. Lyman Beecher to Elias Cornelius, December 5, 1816, Morse Family Papers, folder 006-0176, Manuscripts and Archives Division, Sterling Memorial Library, Yale University, New Haven, CT.
50. *The Religious Intelligencer,* vol. 1 (1816–17), 487; *A Narrative of Five Youth,* 5. On the rise in annual donations to the ABCFM, see John A. Andrew, *Rebuilding the Christian Commonwealth: New England Congregationalists and Foreign Missions, 1800–1830* (Lexington, KY, 1976), 91. I am indebted also to Gretchen Heefner's unpublished essay "Salvable Savages: The Nineteenth-Century Missionary Construction of Hawaii" (Yale University, 2003).
51. Joseph Harvey to Samuel Worcester, October 12, 1817, ABC 12.1, vol. 2, no. 10; Prudential Committee, American Board of Commissioners for Foreign Missions to James Morris et al., November 15, 1816, ABC 1.01, vol. 2, nos. 17–19; Dwight, *Memoirs of Henry Obookiah,* 91; N. Perkins, Jr., to unidentified recipient, January 21, 1817, in *Memoirs of Henry Obookiah,* edition published by the Women's Board of Missions for the Pacific Islands (Honolulu, 1990), 106.
52. *Memoirs of Henry Obookiah* (1990 edition), 84, 80–81.
53. Ibid., 85.
54. James Harvey to Samuel Worcester, October 30, 1816, ABC 12.1, vol. 2, no. 12; James Morris to Jedediah Morse, November 20, 1816, ABC 12.1, vol. 2, no. 40. On details of the buildings, see Morris to Worcester, December 9, 1816, ABC 12.1, vol. 2, no. 41; James Morris, Report of the Visiting Committee to the Foreign Mission School, September 2, 1817, ABC 12.1, vol. 2, no. 44. See also *The Panoplist and Missionary Magazine,* vol. 13 (1817), 324, 344. Copies of the deeds transferring land "with an academy standing on the premises" are in FMS Archive, folder 18. The grant was to last "so long as the American Board of Commissioners for Foreign Missions shall want the same for said school."
55. James Morris to Samuel Worcester, December 9, 1816, ABC 12.1, vol. 2, no. 41. For the school's petition to the General Assembly, together with the latter's response, see Connecticut Archives, Ecclesiastical Affairs, 2d series, vol. 6 (Missions: Miscellaneous), 1a–5b, Connecticut State Library, Hartford, CT.
56. Jonathan Miller to Dr. Ebenezer Porter, November 15, 1816, ABC 12.1, vol. 2, no. 177.
57. George Prince Tamoree to Kummoree, October 19, 1816, in *The Religious Intelligencer,* vol. 1 (1816–17), 446–47; George Prince Tamoree to Capt. Cotting, January 2, 1817, ABC 12.1, vol. 2, no. 168.
58. These arrangements are summarized in *The Panoplist and Missionary Magazine,* vol. 13 (1817), 339. See also *The Religious Intelligencer,* vol. 2 (1817–18), 487.
59. The information and quoted passages in this paragraph are taken from "Rev. Edwin Welles Dwight's Life," *Springfield Republican,* January 23, 1910 (photocopy), and "Sketch of Edwin Welles Dwight," *Berkshire Courier,* January 31, 1907 (photocopy), both in FMS Archive, folder 31. See also Franklin Bowditch Dexter, *Biographical Sketches of the Graduates of Yale College,* vol. 6 (New Haven, CT, 1912), 247–49.
60. Edwin W. Dwight to Abigail Welles Dwight, April 1, 1817, Dwight Collection, vol. 11, 75, Norman Rockwell Museum, Stockbridge, MA.

INTERLUDE *Hawaii*

1. The name Opukaha'ia is said to mean "stomach slashed open" or "disemboweled." According to long-standing tradition, a "high chiefess of the family" had

died in childbirth, and "her husband saved the baby by opening his wife's stomach to remove the child." Then, "in honor of this unusual birth . . . he was named Opukaha'ia because of the cutting of the stomach. . . . The two births occurred around the same time." Although this account is somewhat confusing as written, it appears that Opukaha'ia was not the child actually born in such an unusual way, but, rather, a relative. The story appeared first in a Hawaiian translation of Edwin W. Dwight's *Memoirs of Henry Obookiah* and is included in Wayne H. Brumaghim, "The Life and Legacy of Heneri Opukaha'ia, Hawaii's Prodigal Son" (M.A. thesis, University of Hawaii, 2011), 33–34. For elaborate genealogical tracings of Opukaha'ia's past and present kin, see ibid., 19–36. His ancestors included "the progenitor of a great family of chiefs from Hilo, Hawaii," the "principal chief of the Ka'u district on Hawaii island," and other figures of importance; in short, they were not "commoners" (as stated in the *Memoirs*). Most of his (collateral) descendants would derive from one of his uncles (his mother's older brother). There was much intermarriage with white settlers; the result today is a large kin group of mixed race, including some of the island's most prominent families.

2. William Ellis, *A Narrative of an 1823 Tour Through Hawaii, or Owhyhee, with Remarks on the History, Traditions, Manners, Customs, and Language of the Inhabitants of the Sandwich Islands* (New York, 1825; reprint, Honolulu, HI, 2004), 200–201.

3. Ibid.

4. On the environment and settlement patterns of the Ka'u district, see Ross Cordy, *Exalted Sits the Chief: The Ancient History of Hawaii Island* (Honolulu, 2000), 24–25, 45–46. On traditional Hawaiian house forms, see David Malo, *Hawaiian Antiquities,* trans. Nathaniel B. Emerson, 2d ed. (Honolulu, 1951), chapter 23; Glen Grant, *Ancient Hawaiian Civilization* (Honolulu, 1999), chapter 6; Patrick Vinton Kirch, *Feathered Gods and Fishhooks: An Introduction to Hawaiian Archaeology and Prehistory* (Honolulu, 1985), 4, 252, 259–65. For a period description of housing, see Ellis, *A Narrative of an 1823 Tour Through Hawaii,* 313–20. On *heiau* construction, see Kirch, *Feathered Gods and Fishhooks,* 259–65.

5. On land distribution and farming practices, see Kirch, *Feathered Gods and Fishhooks,* chapter 9; Malo, *Hawaiian Antiquities,* chapter 39; Grant, *Ancient Hawaiian Civilization,* chapter 10; Valerio Valeri, *Kingship and Sacrifice: Ritual and Society in Ancient Hawaii,* trans. Paula Wissing (Chicago, 1985), 154–55. On labor use, see Kirch, *Feathered Gods and Fishhooks,* 289–90. On local trails and communication, see ibid., 266–70.

6. On food and diet, see Malo, *Hawaiian Antiquities,* chapters 14–15; Cordy, *Exalted Sits the Chief,* 34–40. On fishing, see Malo, *Hawaiian Antiquities,* chapter 40; Kirch, *Feathered Gods and Fishhooks,* chapter 8.

7. On many aspects of traditional Hawaiian religious belief and practice, see Valeri, *Kingship and Sacrifice.* See also Malo, *Hawaiian Antiquities,* chapter 23; Cordy, *Exalted Sits the Chief,* 59–62. On ritual sacrifice, see Valeri, *Kingship and Sacrifice,* chapter 2.

8. On *kapu,* see Valeri, *Kingship and Sacrifice,* 85–95, 124–27; Malo, *Hawaiian Antiquities,* chapter 11. On social gradation, see Malo, *Hawaiian Antiquities,* chapter 18; Cordy, *Exalted Sits the Chief,* 50–59; Kirch, *Feathered Gods and Fishhooks,* 6–7, 294–95; Valeri, *Kingship and Sacrifice,* 147–48.

9. On gender segregation, see Valeri, *Kingship and Sacrifice,* 111–24, and Malo, *Hawaiian Antiquities,* chapter 11.

10. There is a large literature describing, and interpreting, Cook's murder. See, for example, Anne Salmond, *The Trial of the Cannibal Dog: The Remarkable Story of Captain Cook's Encounters in the South Seas* (New Haven, CT, 2003), 409–16.

11. James Cook and James King, *A Voyage to the Pacific Ocean in the Years 1776, 1777, 1778, 1779, and 1780,* 4 vols. (London, 1784), vol. 3, 152–53.

12. E. W. Dwight, *Memoirs of Henry Obookiah, a Native of the Sandwich Isles, Who Died at Cornwall, Connecticut, February 17, 1818, Aged 26* (New Haven, CT, 1818), 5.

13. Cook and King, *A Voyage to the Pacific Ocean,* 152–53; John Ledyard, *Journal of Captain Cook's Last Voyage,* ed. John Kenneth Munford (Corvallis, OR, 1963), 110.

14. Dwight, *Memoirs of Henry Obookiah,* 9, 45.

CHAPTER THREE *American Mission: The World Savers*

1. Norman Cohn, *The Pursuit of the Millennium* (London, 1957); Marjorie Richards, *The Influence of Prophecy in the Later Middle Ages* (Oxford, 1969). See also Ruth Bloch, *Visionary Republic: Millennial Themes in American Thought* (Cambridge, 1985), preface. The best short summary of the world-saving theme in American history is Bernd Engler, Joerg O. Fichte, and Oliver Scheiding, "Transformations in Millennial Thought in America, 1630–1860," in *Millennial Thought in America: Historical and Intellectual Contexts, 1630–1860* ed. Engler, Fichte, and Scheiding (Tubingen, 2002).

2. Louis B. Wright, *The Dream of Prosperity in Colonial America* (New York, 1965); Bernard McGinn, *Visions of the End: Apocalyptic Traditions in the Middle Ages* (New York, 1979); J. H. Elliott, *The Old World and the New, 1492–1650* (Cambridge, 1970), chapter 1; Howard Mumford Jones, *O Strange New World: American Culture: The Formative Years* (New York, 1952); Henri Baudet, *Paradise on Earth: Some Thoughts on European Images of Non-European Man* (London, 1965); Charles L. Sanford, *The Quest for Paradise: Europe and the American Moral Imagination* (Urbana, IL, 1961).

3. Ernest Lee Tuveson, *Redeemer Nation: The Idea of America's Millennial Role* (Chicago, 1968), chapter 1.

4. Bloch, *Visionary Republic,* chapters 1–2; B. W. Ball, *A Great Expectation: Eschatological Thought in English Protestantism* (Leiden, 1988); James Holstun, *A Rational Millennium: Puritan Utopias of Seventeenth-Century England and America* (New York, 1987); Katherine Firth, *The Apocalyptic Tradition in Reformation Britain, 1530–1645* (New York, 1979). See also Ernest Lee Tuveson, *Millennium and Utopia: A Study in the Background of the Idea of Progress* (Berkeley, 1949), chapters 2–4; David D. Hall, *A Reforming People: Puritanism and the Transformation of Public Life in New England* (New York, 2011), chapter 3.

5. Perry Miller, *Errand into the Wilderness* (Cambridge, MA, 1956), chapter 1; J. F. Maclear, "New England and the Fifth Monarchy: The Quest for the Millennium in Early American Puritanism," *William and Mary Quarterly,* 3d series, 32 (1975): 3–32; Tuveson, *Redeemer Nation,* 97ff.; Cushing Strout, *The New Heavens and the New Earth: Political Religion in America* (New York, 1975); Sacvan Bercovitch, *The American Jeremiad* (Madison, WI, 1978), especially introduction and chapter 4; Avihu Zakai, *Exile and the Kingdom: History and the Apocalypse in the Puritan Migration to America* (Cambridge, 1992), especially chapter 1. To be sure, the idea of a central Puritan "errand" has been challenged; for counterviews, see Andrew

Delbanco, "The Puritan Errand Re-viewed," *Journal of American Studies* 18 (1984): 343–60; Theodore Dwight Bozeman, "The Puritans' 'Errand into the Wilderness' Reconsidered," *New England Quarterly* 59 (1986): 231–51. Perhaps the strongest contribution to this debate is Reiner Smolinski, "*Israel Redivivus*: The Eschatological Limits of Puritan Typology in New England," *New England Quarterly* 63 (1990): 357–95. It is Smolinski's view that the "errand" was somewhat diffuse and disorganized during the first phase of New England history but became sharper and more American-centered in the late seventeenth century; from then on it "played a central role in nurturing a uniquely American identity that came to full flower in the nineteenth century" (359). On this point, see also Oliver Scheiding, "Samuel Sewall and the Americanization of the Millennium," in *Millennial Thought in America*, ed. Engler, Fichte, and Scheiding, 165–85.

6. Cotton Mather, *Magnalia Christi Americana* (London, 1702; reprint, ed. Thomas Robbins, 2 vols., Boston, 1853–55), vol. 1, 1. On declension, see Perry Miller, "Declension in a Bible Commonwealth," *Proceedings of the American Antiquarian Society* 51 (1941): 37–94; Robert G. Pope, *The Half-Way Covenant: Church Membership in Puritan New England* (Princeton, NJ, 1969).

7. *The Testimony and Advice of an Assembly of Pastors*, quoted in Nathan Hatch, *The Sacred Cause of Liberty: Republican Thought and the Millennium in Revolutionary New England* (New Haven, CT, 1977), 29; Samuel Finley, *Christ Triumphing, and Satan Raging* (Philadelphia, 1741), 26, quoted in Bloch, *Visionary Republic*, 16; Jonathan Edwards, "Some Thoughts Concerning the Present Revivals," in *The Great Awakening*, ed. C. C. Goen (New Haven, CT, 1972), 353–58, quoted in William R. Hutchison, *Errand to the World: American Protestant Thought and Foreign Missions* (Chicago, 1987), 41.

8. Tuveson, *Redeemer Nation*, 101; Bloch, *Visionary Republic*, 48; Hatch, *The Sacred Cause of Liberty*, 4.

9. For an image of the Massachusetts Bay Colony seal, see John Demos, *Remarkable Providences: Readings on Early American History*, rev. ed. (Boston, 1991), 11. On the "praying towns," see Richard Cogley, *John Eliot's Mission to the Indians Before King Philip's War* (Cambridge, MA, 1999). See also Neal Salisbury, "Red Puritans: The 'Praying Indians' of Massachusetts Bay and John Eliot," *William and Mary Quarterly*, 3d series, 31 (1974): 27–54; Kristina Bross, "The Mission Upon a Hill: New England Evangelism, 1643–1653," in *Millennial Thought in America*, ed. Engler, Fichte, and Scheiding, 133–64; Holstun, *A Rational Millennium*, chapter 3; Dane Morrison, *A Praying People: Massachusetts Acculturation and the Failure of the Puritan Mission, 1600–1690* (New York, 1995); Jean M. O'Brien, *Dispossession by Degrees: Indian Land and Identity in Natick, Massachusetts, 1650–1790* (Lincoln, NE, 1997). On eighteenth-century schools for Indians, see Margaret Szasz, *Indian Education in the American Colonies* (Albuquerque, 1988). On Indians at Harvard College, see Samuel Eliot Morison, *Harvard College in the Seventeenth Century* (Cambridge, MA, 1936).

10. Hutchison, *Errand to the World*, 39ff. See also Szasz, *Indian Education in the American Colonies*.

11. Judah Champion, *A Brief View of the Distresses, Hardships, and Dangers Our Ancestors Encounter'd in Settling New England . . .* (Hartford, 1770), 6, 28–29, quoted in Hatch, *The Sacred Cause of Liberty*, 79; Samuel Baldwin, *The Duty of Rejoicing under Calamities and Afflictions* (Boston, 1776), 38, quoted ibid., 88.

12. Philip Freneau and Hugh Henry Breckinridge, *A Poem on the Rising Glory*

of America (Philadelphia, 1772), 25, quoted in Bloch, *Visionary Republic*, 71; John Adams, *Letters of John Adams, Addressed to His Wife*, ed. Charles Francis Adams (Boston, 1841), 82–83, quoted ibid., 94–95; John Adams, *The Works of John Adams*, ed. C. F. Adams, 10 vols. (Boston, 1850–56), vol. 3, 452, quoted ibid., 71; David Ramsay, *Oration on the Advantages of American Independence* (Charleston, SC, 1778), 17, quoted ibid., 84; *New Jersey Journal* (Chatham), March 29, 1780, quoted in Charles Royster, *A Revolutionary People at War: The Continental Army and American Character, 1775–1783* (Chapel Hill, NC, 1979), 6. On the general theme of millennialism and the American Revolution, see Royster, *A Revolutionary People at War*, 152–59; Bercovitch, *The American Jeremiad*, chapter 4.

13. The citations and quotations in this paragraph are taken from Tuveson, *Redeemer Nation*, 103–12. On the life and career of Timothy Dwight, see Kenneth Silverman, *Timothy Dwight* (New York, 1969). Dwight's poetic and patriotic writings can be found in *A Selection of American Poetry, from Various Authors of Established Reputation* (New York, 1794).

14. See Bloch, *Visionary Republic*, 102–15,

15. Ibid., 131ff., 154ff. See also Bercovitch, *The American Jeremiad*, chapter 4.

16. John A. Andrew III, *Rebuilding the Christian Commonwealth: New England Congregationalists & Foreign Missions, 1800–1830* (Lexington, KY, 1976), chapter 1. On the impact of the Second Great Awakening in the general vicinity of the Foreign Mission School, see David W. Kling, *A Field of Divine Wonders: The New Divinity and Village Revivals in Northwestern Connecticut, 1792–1822* (University Park, PA, 1993). See also Paul William Harris, *Nothing but Christ: Rufus Anderson and the Ideology of Protestant Foreign Missions* (New York, 1999), and John A. Andrew, *From Revivals to Removal: Jeremiah Evarts, the Cherokee Nation, and the Search for the Soul of America* (Athens, GA, 1992).

17. Julian Mellen, *A Sermon Delivered Before His Excellency the Governor* (Boston, 1797), quoted in Hatch, *The Sacred Cause of Liberty*, 156; Lyman Beecher, "A Plea for the West," in *God's New Israel: Interpretations of America's Destiny*, ed. Conrad Cherry (Englewood Cliffs, NJ, 1971), quoted in Hatch, *The Sacred Cause of Liberty*, 173; Nathaniel Emmons, "God Never Forsakes His People," in *Works of Nathaniel Emmons*, 6 vols. (Boston, 1826), vol. 5, 179–80, quoted in Hutchison, *Errand to the World*, 61.

18. Clifton Jackson Phillips, *Protestant America and the Pagan World: The First Half Century of the American Board of Commissioners for Foreign Missions, 1810–1860* (Cambridge, MA, 1969); Andrew, *From Revivals to Removal*, chapters 1–2; Sereno Edwards Dwight, *Thy Kingdom Come: A Sermon Delivered in the Old South Church, Boston, Before the Foreign Mission Society of Boston, and the Vicinity, January 3, 1820* (Boston, 1820), 7.

19. Dwight, *Thy Kingdom Come*, 13–15, 27–28; Francis Wayland, *The Moral Dignity of the Missionary Enterprise: A Sermon Delivered Before the Boston Baptist Foreign Missionary Society . . . November 4, 1823* (Boston, 1824), 20.

20. Auxiliary Foreign Mission Society of Essex County, *Proceedings at the Fourth Annual Meeting, Held at Andover, April 14, 1830* (Salem, MA, 1831), quoted in Andrew, *From Revivals to Removal*, 150.

21. Edward Dorr Griffin, *A Sermon Preached October 20, 1813, at Sandwich, Massachusetts . . .* (Boston, 1813), 33, quoted in Hutchison, *Errand to the World*, 56.

CHAPTER FOUR *"A seminary for the education of heathen youth"*

1. This and the following descriptive summary of Cornwall's early history is based primarily on E. C. Starr, *A History of Cornwall, Connecticut: A Typical New England Town* (New Haven, CT, 1926).

2. For a full account of Cornwall's churches in these years, see ibid., chapter 3. On revivalism, see David W. Kling, *A Field of Divine Wonders: The New Divinity and Village Revivals in Northwestern Connecticut, 1792–1822* (University Park, PA, 1993).

3. This language was attached to a particularly generous donation to the school. See *The Missionary Herald,* vol. 17 (1821), 362.

4. These arrangements are described in James Morris to Samuel Worcester, December 9, 1816, ABC 12.1, vol. 2, no. 41. See also Morris to American Board, September 2, 1817, ABC 12.1, vol. 2, no. 44. A typescript copy of the deed that conveyed the Academy property to the school is in FMS Archive, folder 18.

5. James Morris to Samuel Worcester, December 9, 1816, ABC 12.1, vol. 2, no. 41.

6. Ibid. For a description of the school's physical plant a few years later on (1820), see *The Missionary Herald,* vol. 17 (1821), 2.

7. James Morris reported that "sundry towns in this County offered more than two thousand dollars to have the School established in their town"; see Morris to Jedediah Morse, November 25, 1816, ABC 12.1, vol. 2, no. 40. See also chapter 2 (above).

8. On plans to open the school "by the beginning of May," see James Morris to Samuel Worcester, December 9, 1816, ABC 12.1, vol. 2, no. 41.

9. See ibid.

10. *Hartford Courant,* May 13, 1817.

11. The steward's official duties were described as follows: "to superintend the business and prepare the food for the students . . . and [provide] washing and ordinary mending for each student"; see Report of the Visiting Committee to the Foreign Mission School, September 2, 1817, ABC 12.1, vol. 2, no. 44. On the admission of Ruggles and Ely, "two young men of our own nation," see ibid. and ms. letter, Herman Daggett to the American Board, September 1, 1818, ABC 12.1, vol. 2, nos. 96–97. For the descriptive comments on other students, see James Morris to Jeremiah Evarts, November 11, 1818, ABC 12.1, vol. 2, no. 55 (Kummooolah); Herman Daggett to Rev. Walter Harris (extract), November 22, 1820, FMS Archive, folder 16 (Sandwich); Morris to Evarts, November 11, 1818, ABC 12.1, vol. 2, no. 55 (Annance); Morris to Evarts (Windall).

12. Johnson's remarkable story is included in "Report of the Visiting Committee of the American Board . . . ," *The Religious Intelligencer,* vol. 2 (1817–18), 524.

13. Henry Obookiah to Samuel Wells, June 16, 1817, Division of Manuscripts and Archives, Sterling Memorial Library, Yale University, New Haven, CT.

14. *The Missionary Spelling Book and Reader, Prepared at the Foreign Mission School, Cornwall, Conn., and Designed Especially for Its Use* (Hartford, CT, 1822), 32–34.

15. Extracts from the Report of the Agents of the Foreign Mission School, in *The Religious Intelligencer,* vol. 2 (1817–18), 522–25.

16. Joseph Hawley to Samuel Worcester, October 12, 1816, ABC 12.1, vol. 2, no. 10; *The Religious Intelligencer,* vol. 1 (1816–17), 494; *The Missionary Herald,* vol. 17 (1821), 86.

17. The following entries are selected somewhat randomly from archival records of the Mission School, ABC 12.1, vol. 2, and from the published volumes of *The*

Religious Intelligencer and *The Missionary Herald*. See also a detailed summary of donations in the manuscript notes of the Cornwall historian E. C. Starr, FMS Archive, folder 10.

18. *The Religious Intelligencer*, vol. 5 (1820–21), 575, 126.

19. One of these sermons (from a few years later on) was criticized by an auditor for being "too long and diffuse." The point, he said, "was not to be instructed in a whole system of theology, but to be interested and aroused on the subject which peculiarly characterizes the institution"; see *The Religious Intelligencer*, vol. 7 (1822–23), 365. For the description of the students' part, see Mrs. Eunice (Wadsworth) Taylor, "Recollection," in Starr, *A History of Cornwall, Connecticut*, 155. On the reactions of Gallaudet and Treadwell, see Hiram Bingham to Samuel Worcester, May 11, 1819, Bingham Family Papers, Division of Manuscripts and Archives, Sterling Memorial Library, Yale University, New Haven, CT.

20. "Report of the Visiting Committee of the American Board . . . ," *The Religious Intelligencer*, vol. 2 (1817–18), 525. See also Jedediah Morse to Susannah Morse, September 19, 1817, in Morse Family Papers, Division of Manuscripts and Archives, Sterling Memorial Library, Yale University, New Haven, CT.

21. "Report of the Visiting Committee of the American Board . . . ," *The Religious Intelligencer*, vol. 2 (1817–18), 525.

22. See "Extract from Report of ABCFM," reverse of ms. letter from Rev. Jedediah Morse to Elizabeth Morse, September 19, 1817, Morse Family Papers, Division of Manuscripts and Archives, Sterling Memorial Library, Yale University, New Haven, CT.

23. Ibid.

24. James Morris to Samuel Worcester, January 25, 1817, ABC 12.1, vol. 2, no. 42.

25. E. W. Dwight, *Memoirs of Henry Obookiah, a Native of the Sandwich Isles, Who Died at Cornwall, Connecticut, February 17, 1818, Aged 26* (New Haven, CT, 1818), 101.

26. Herman Daggett to Henry Obookiah, January 12, 1818 (photocopy), FMS Archive, folder 36.

27. The most detailed account of Obookiah's illness and death is in Dwight, *Memoirs of Henry Obookiah*, 100–109. Numerous, slightly different versions appeared in the missionary press. See also the manuscript letter by an unidentified female eyewitness to Obookiah's funeral, n.d. (photocopy), FMS archive, folder 34. The costs of Obookiah's treatment and funeral were substantial. Rev. Stone sent a bill "for nursing, house room, fuel, candles, & c. & c. and funeral expenses" totaling $51.67. The bill from "Dr. Calhoun" added another $36.84. See James Harvey to American Board, December 28, 1818, ABC 12.1, vol. 2, no. 18.

28. Within less than a week of Obookiah's death, James Morris wrote to the headquarters of the American Board that "some memoirs of his life & death will shortly be given to the public"; see James Morris to Jeremiah Evarts, February 28, 1818, ABC 12.1, vol. 2, no. 46. See also note 29.

29. According to one eyewitness, the mourners made "a numerous congregation of people from Cornwall and the surrounding towns"; see James Morris to Jeremiah Evarts, February 23, 1818, ABC 12.1, vol. 2, no. 46. On Lyman Beecher and the "new divinity," see Kling, *A Field of Divine Wonders*.

30. Lyman Beecher, *A Sermon Delivered at the Funeral of Henry Obookiah* (New Haven, CT, 1818), reprinted in Dwight, *Memoirs of Henry Obookiah*, 1–34 (at back of volume).

31. These details are reported in a ms. letter by an unidentified woman who was present at the funeral; see FMS Archive, folder 34.

32. On the matter of expense, see James Harvey to American Board, December 28, 1818, ABC, 12.1, vol. 2, no. 18. The grave-marker inscription can be viewed in the town cemetery, Cornwall, CT. The pattern of pilgrimage, begun in the immediate aftermath of Obookiah's death, has continued to the present day. For one randomly chosen and relatively recent example, see "Pilgrimage to Wintry Cornwall," in *The Friend* (a publication of the Hawaii Conference of the United Church of Christ), vol. 19, no. 2, 1ff. For a full treatment of these matters, see the epilogue on page 266.

33. See, for example, the obituary notices in *The Religious Intelligencer,* vol. 2 (1817–18), 640; *The Boston Recorder,* March 10, 1818. The poem referenced here was by John Catlin, a student in Cornwall some years later on. Entitled "Thoughts at the Grave of Henry Obookiah," it was published in *The Religious Intelligencer* in 1835; a copy is included in FMS Archive, folder 46. For another such poem, see "Obookiah's Grave," reprinted from *The Connecticut Mirror,* in *The Religious Intelligencer,* vol. 2 (1817–18), 640. On the rapid development of plans to publish a memoir, see James Morris to Jeremiah Evarts, February 23, 1818, ABC 12.1, vol. 2, no. 46. On the wax figure exhibition, see *Connecticut Herald* (New Haven), May 4, 1824.

34. See Albertine Loomis, *Grapes of Canaan* (Hawaii, 1820), 120. On expectations that sales of the *Memoirs* would "relieve the treasury of the Mission School," see James Harvey to Jeremiah Evarts, October 23, 1818, ABC 12.1, vol. 2, no. 16. When, in January 1820, a new edition of the book appeared, it was frankly stated that "the profits of this work are to aid the funds of the Foreign Mission School." Moreover, the same report noted the example of a "legacy" of $500 from a certain "Col. Williams of Greenwich, Mass . . . [who] a few days before he made his will had been reading the Life of Obookiah . . . it is in consequence of the interest excited by that little book that the legacy was inserted in his will"; see *The Religious Intelligencer,* vol. 6 (1821–22), 708–9. The gift from the Baron de Campagne (Switzerland) stated: "I have been sensibly affected [by] . . . intelligence of the death of young Obookiah"; see *The Religious Intelligencer,* vol. 6 (1821–22), 790. Additional references to the effect of the *Memoirs* on readers can be found in the Morse Family Papers, Division of Manuscripts and Archives, Sterling Memorial Library, Yale University, New Haven, CT. For a recent appraisal of the impact of the *Memoirs,* see Jeffrey K. Lyons, "Memoirs of Henry Obookiah: A Rhetorical History," *Hawaiian Journal of History* 38 (2004): 35–57.

35. James Morris to Samuel Worcester, March 16, 1818, ABC 12.1, vol. 2, no. 47; J. L. Hale to James Robbins, January 28, 1819, Beebe Collection, Litchfield Historical Society, Litchfield, CT; James Harvey, *The Banner of Christ Set Up* (New Haven, CT, 1818), reprinted in Dwight, *Memoirs of Henry Obookiah,* 14 (at back of volume).

36. Quoted in Oscar P. Bollmann, "The Foreign Mission School of Cornwall, Connecticut," M.A. thesis, Divinity School of Yale University, 46. Original source not given.

37. "Extract of a Letter from Rev. Chauncy Lee . . . ," May 12, 1818, reprinted in *Connecticut Courant,* June 30, 1818; *The Religious Intelligencer,* vol. 2 (1817–18), 827; *The Missionary Herald,* vol. 14 (1818), 264–65, quoted in E. C. Starr, "Outlines of the Story of the Pupils of the Foreign Mission School, at Cornwall, Collected and Pre-

sented to the Cornwall Library Association, by E. C. Starr (1895)," 205, Cornwall Historical Society, Cornwall, CT.

38. Harvey, *The Banner of Christ Set Up,* reprinted in Dwight, *Memoirs of Henry Obookiah,* 3, 4, 8, 29 (at back of volume).

39. Herman Daggett, *An Inauguration Address Delivered at the Opening of the Foreign Mission School, May 6, 1818* (New Haven, CT, 1818), reprinted in Dwight, *Memoirs of Henry Obookiah,* 1–10 (at back of volume).

40. "Extract of a Letter from Rev. Chauncy Lee . . ." (May 12, 1818); see note 37 for reprint information.

41. For an example of the recruitment network in full operation, see the case of Aaron Johnson, a Tuscarora youth "who came very highly recommended by the Rev. M. Crane, by the chief Sacharissa, and by the male members of the church among the Tuscarora Indians"; see Herman Daggett to Samuel Worcester, February 6, 1820, ABC 12.1, vol. 2, no. 114. Another example, from the following year, was described as follows: "Four youths from the Sandwich Islands have lately been offered for admission to the Foreign Mission School, one by Mr. Phelps of Brookfield, two by Capt. Brintnall, recently arrived, and [the last] from Albany, recently arrived. They will probably be admitted as they are all spoken of as promising"; see Joseph Harvey to Jeremiah Evarts, July 11, 1821, ABC 12.1, vol. 2, no. 30. The same network could assist students leaving the school. Thus when Arnold Krygsman (originally from Malaya) was expelled for stabbing another student, he was "taken up by Mr. Fenn, a young clergyman from Ohio . . . who has placed him with an uncle of his in Milford, a farmer and excellent Christian man"; see Herman Daggett to Samuel Worcester, August 5, 1820, ABC 12.1, vol. 2, no. 116. On the troubled post–Mission School life of John Johnson, see James Morris to Samuel Worcester, March 16, 1818, ABC 12.1, vol. 2, no. 47; Samuel B. Ingersoll to Samuel Worcester, December 4, 1818, ABC 12.1, vol. 2, no. 176.

42. James Morris to Samuel Worcester, March 16, 1818, ABC 12.1, vol. 2, no. 47; James Morris to Jeremiah Evarts, November 11, 1818, ABC 12.1, vol. 2, no. 55; Herman Daggett to American Board, September 1, 1818, ABC 12.1, vol. 2, nos. 96–97.

43. On the arrival of the southeastern Indians at the school, see Herman Daggett to American Board, September 1, 1818, ABC 12.1, vol. 2, nos. 96–97. On the founding of the Moravian school at Spring Place, see Thurman Wilkins, *Cherokee Tragedy: The Ridge Family and the Decimation of a People,* 2d ed. (Norman, OK, 1986), 100–101 passim. See also Edmund Schwartze, *History of the Moravian Missions Among the Southern Indian Tribes of the United States* (Bethlehem, PA, 1923). On the life and career of David Brainerd, see Philip E. Howard, Jr., ed., *The Life and Diary of David Brainerd* (Chicago, 1949).

44. On the recruitment and subsequent experience of Cherokee students, see Jeremiah Evarts to Rev. Ard Hoyt, September 26, 1818, ABC 1.01, vol. 2, nos. 170–71; Jeremiah Evarts to Messrs. Dodge and Sayre, October 29, 1819, ABC 1.01, vol. 2, no. 194; Jeremiah Evarts to Herman Daggett, November 19, 1818, ABC 1.01, vol. 2, nos. 209–10. On Cherokee discussions about the wisdom of sending students to the Mission School, see "Journal of the Mission to the Cherokees," ABC 18.3.1, vol. 2, no. 84; see also ABC 18.3.1, vol. 2, no. 116. On the plan for a layered system of missionary-sponsored education, see Jeremiah Evarts to General Calvin Jones, January 8, 1819, ABC 1.01, vol. 2, nos. 248–50.

45. Herman Daggett to the American Board, September 1, 1818, ABC 12.1, vol. 2, nos. 96–97; James Morris to Jeremiah Evarts, November 11, 1818, ABC 12.1, vol. 2,

no. 55; *The Religious Intelligencer,* vol. 2 (1817–18), 252. See also Herman Daggett to Samuel Worcester, December 18, 1818, ABC 12.1, vol. 2, no. 101.

46. Samuel Worcester to Rev. Ard Hoyt, November 11, 1818, ABC 12.1, vol. 2, nos. 99–100.

47. On preparations for the Sandwich Islands mission, see, for example, Herman Daggett to Samuel Worcester, September 1 and 27, 1819, ABC 12.1, vol. 2, nos. 107–8. On fears of Tamoree absconding, see Herman Daggett to Samuel Worcester, February 6, 1819, ABC 12.1, vol. 2, no. 102.

48. *The Religious Intelligencer,* vol. 3 (1818–19), 240–41; Herman Daggett to Samuel Worcester, November 14, 1818, ABC 12.1, vol. 2, no. 100.

49. Jeremiah Evarts to Levi Hoyt, Esq., August 21, 1818, ABC 1.01, vol. 2, nos. 166–67; Jeremiah Evarts to Herman Daggett, August 21, 1818, ABC 1.01, vol. 2, nos. 167–68.

50. Jeremiah Evarts to Herman Daggett, August 21, 1818, ABC 1.01, vol. 2, nos. 167–68; James Morris to Jeremiah Evarts, September 7, 1818, ABC 12.1, vol. 2, no. 52.

51. Herman Daggett to Samuel Worcester, December 18, 1818, ABC 12.1, vol. 2, no. 101; Herman Daggett to Rev. Jedediah Morse, January 6, 1819, in Morse Family Papers, Division of Manuscripts and Archives, Sterling Memorial Library, Yale University, New Haven, CT.

52. Herman Daggett to Samuel Worcester, September 1, 1819, ABC 12.1, vol. 2, no. 107.

53. Herman Daggett to Samuel Worcester, November 14, 1818, ABC 12.1, vol. 2, no. 100. On this "danger," see also Herman Daggett to Jeremiah Evarts, August 6, 1821, ABC 12.1, vol. 2, no. 129; Herman Daggett to Jeremiah Evarts, August 14, 1822, ABC 12.1, vol. 2, no. 138; Herman Daggett to Jeremiah Evarts, November 11, 1822, ABC 12.1, vol. 2, no. 142.

54. Herman Daggett to Samuel Worcester, September 1, 1819, ABC 12.1, vol. 2, no. 107; Herman Daggett to Samuel Worcester, February 6, 1819, ABC 12.1, vol. 2, no. 102; Rev. James Harvey to Jeremiah Evarts, October 5, 1819, ABC 12.1, vol. 2, no. 25.

55. Rev. James Harvey to Jeremiah Evarts, October 5, 1819, ABC 12.1, vol. 2, no. 25; Herman Daggett to Samuel Worcester, September 27, 1819, ABC 12.1, vol. 2, no. 108; Herman Daggett to Samuel Worcester, September 1, 1819, ABC 12.1, vol. 2, no. 107.

56. Hiram Bingham to Samuel Worcester, July 18, 1819, Bingham Family Papers, Division of Manuscripts and Archives, Sterling Memorial Library, Yale University, New Haven, CT. For more discussion of the "Anglo-Americans" chosen for the Sandwich Islands mission, see John Prentice to Samuel Worcester, June 7, 1819, ABC 12.1, vol. 2, no. 58.

57. James Morris to Rev. James Harvey, September 10, 1818, ABC 12.1, vol. 2, no. 53; Herman Daggett to Jeremiah Evarts, October 7, 1819, ABC 12.1, vol. 2, no. 111.

58. Evidently, the Morse painting has not survived. On the use of prints made from it, see *The Missionary Herald,* vol. 18 (1822), 399. From time to time, gifts would reach the school from "the avails of the sale of prints of the Owhyhean youth"; see *The Missionary Herald,* vol. 21 (1825), 230.

59. *The Missionary Herald,* vol. 15 (1819), 262.

60. Ibid.

61. The event is fully described in *The Religious Intelligencer,* vol. 4 (1819–20), 74–75. The sermon was subsequently published; see David Perry, *The Spiritual Temple: A Sermon Delivered at the Annual Examination of the Foreign Mission School in Cornwall May 17, 1820* (Hartford, CT, 1820).

62. Ibid.
63. *The Religious Intelligencer,* vol. 4 (1819–20), 74–75.
64. *The Religious Intelligencer,* vol. 3 (1818–19), 120–22.
65. David Brown to Catharine Brown, January 25, 1821, FMS Archive, folder 16; Herman Daggett to Jeremiah Evarts, September 8, 1823, ABC 12.1, vol. 2, no. 71.
66. David Brown to Rev. William Chamberlain, July 24, 1820, and David Brown to Catharine Brown, January 25, 1821 (ms. copies of the originals made by Herman Daggett), FMS Archive, folder 16; David Brown to Jeremiah Evarts, March 5, 1822, ABC 12.1, vol. 2, no. 133.
67. *The Religious Intelligencer,* vol. 7 (1822–23), 688. On the negotiations around the renaming of John Irepoah, see extract of a letter from Rev. Walter Harris to Herman Daggett, November 23, 1820, and Herman Daggett to Rev. Walter Harris, January 19, 1821 (ms. copies of the originals made by Daggett), FMS Archive, folder 16. The practice of renaming converts (or would-be converts) was widely adopted by missionaries at work inside "heathen nations." For a general discussion of this matter, see *The Missionary Herald,* vol. 19 (1823), 64. For specific examples at the Choctaw mission in Alabama, see *The Missionary Herald,* vol. 18 (1822), 180–81. For examples in Hawaii, see *The Missionary Herald,* vol. 18 (1822), 182. In one rather special case, an unidentified New England woman donated money to a mission in Ceylon "toward the support of two heathen children . . . to be named for my two eldest children." This, she hoped, would benefit both pairs—her own children, in particular, by "exciting in their tender breasts compassion for the heathen." See *The Missionary Herald,* vol. 18 (1822), 232.
68. The specific comments included in this description of life at the Mission School are found in letters from David Brown to his sister Catharine (July 22, 1820, and January 25, 1821) and to Rev. William Chamberlain (July 24, 1820), ms. copies of the originals made by Herman Daggett, FMS Archive, folder 16.
69. John Prentice to Jeremiah Evarts, July 29, 1822, ABC 12.1, v. 2, no. 68; Herman Daggett to Jeremiah Evarts, August 6, 1823, ABC 12.1, vol. 2, no. 148; David Brown to Catharine Brown, July 22, 1820 (ms. copy of the original made by Daggett), FMS Archive, folder 16.
70. Thomas Hopkins Gallaudet, "The Language of Signs Auxiliary to the Christian Missionary," *The Christian Observer,* vol. 26 (1826), 593; Hiram Bingham to Samuel Worcester, May 11, 1819, Bingham Family Papers, Division of Manuscripts and Archives, Sterling Memorial Library, Yale University, New Haven, CT. See also *The New Hampshire Repository* (Concord), April 7, 1823.
71. Adam Hodgson, *Letters from North America . . .* , 2 vols. (London, 1824), vol. 2, 295–97.
72. James Harvey to Jeremiah Evarts, January 20, 1821, ABC 12.1, vol. 2, no. 28. For particular examples of letters written by scholars, see *The Missionary Herald,* vol. 17 (1821), 256–59.
73. The quotations in this and the preceding paragraphs are from the *American Eagle* (Litchfield, CT), April 24 and 26, 1824, October 4 and 17, 1824, and November 22, 1824, as well as *The Pilot* (New Haven, CT), June 22, 1824, and *The New Hampshire Observer,* February 14, 1825. Other issues of the *American Eagle* also contain pertinent information. Additional newspapers expressing anti-mission attitudes include *Plain Truth* (Rochester, NY, 1828–29), *Priestcraft Exposed and Primitive Christianity Defended* (Lockport, NY, 1828–30), and *The Telescope* (New York, NY, 1825–30).

74. Rev. T. Blumhardt to Jeremiah Evarts, July 16, 1820, in *The Religious Intelligencer,* vol. 6 (1821–22), 603–4; Herman Daggett to Jeremiah Evarts, February 3, 1823, ABC 12.1, vol. 2, no. 143. (The books mentioned in this letter would become the foundation of what the school's leadership called "the Campagnean Library"; see *The Religious Intelligencer,* vol. 7 [1822–23], 90.) James Harvey to Jeremiah Evarts, January 20, 1821, ABC 12.1, vol. 2, no. 28; *The Religious Intelligencer,* vol. 6 (1821–22), 605; Herman Daggett to Jeremiah Evarts, April 6, 1821, ABC 12.1, vol. 2, no. 123. Gifts to the school by supporters are frequently noted in *The Religious Intelligencer* and *The Missionary Herald.*

75. James Harvey to Jeremiah Evarts, November 14, 1821, ABC 12.1, vol. 2, no. 32; see also James Harvey to Jeremiah Evarts, October 22, 1821, ABC 12.1, vol. 2, no. 33. A collection box, in original condition and carrying the inscription "For the Mission School Cornwall" is among the holdings of the Litchfield Historical Society, Litchfield, CT. For an example of a "concert of prayer," see *The Missionary Herald,* vol. 20 (1824), 21.

76. *The Religious Intelligencer,* vol. 5 (1820–21), 722; *The Missionary Herald,* vol. 17 (1821), 122, 114.

77. See, for example, *The Missionary Herald,* vol. 16 (1820), 168, and vol. 17 (1821), 114; see also vol. 21 (1825), 140. In the case of the scholar who destroyed a group of "stone gods," see *The Missionary Herald,* vol. 20 (1824), 282. In the case of the scholar who approached several "huge stones," see *The Missionary Herald,* vol. 21 (1845), 140.

78. *The Missionary Herald,* vol. 17 (1821), 124, 217; George Prince Tamoree to Herman Daggett, July 25, 1820, with addendum by Herman Daggett, ABC 12.1, vol. 2, 125.

79. Herman Daggett to George P. Tamoree, June 21, 1821, FMS Archive, folder 16. See also Herman Daggett to Jeremiah Evarts, May 18, 1821, ABC 12.1, vol. 2, no. 125; *The Religious Intelligencer,* vol. 6 (1821–22), 607. Idols were a special focus of reports from the Hawaii mission. For example: "In the windward part of Owhyhee 102 idols were committed to the flames in one day"; see *The Missionary Herald,* vol. 19 (1823), 100.

80. The quoted sentences are from Rev. A. C. Thompson, *Commemorative Address . . . at the Semi-Centenary of the Ordination of the First Missionaries to the Sandwich Islands* (Boston, 1869), 29. Consider, too, the attitude of disgust implicit in the following comment by one of the missionaries upon the moment of his arrival in the islands. "A first sight of these degraded creatures was almost overwhelming: their naked figures, wild expression of countenance, their black hair streaming in the wind as they hurried their canoes over the water with all the eager action and muscular power of savages, their rapid and unintelligible exclamations, and whole exhibition of uncivilized nature, gave to them the appearance of being half-man and half-beast, and irresistibly pressed on the thoughts the query—*can they be men?—can they be women?—do they not form a link in creation connecting man with the brute?*" (Italics in original.) See Charles Samuel Stewart, *A Residence in the Sandwich Islands* (Boston, 1839), 70.

81. The quoted passages in this and the preceding paragraphs are from *The Religious Intelligencer,* vol. 5 (1820–1821), 770–72, and vol. 6 (1821–22), 17–20. See also *The Missionary Herald,* vol. 17 (1821), 112, 169; George P. Tamoree to Herman Daggett, July 25, 1820, ABC 12.1, vol. 2, no. 125.

82. *The Missionary Herald,* vol. 17 (1821), 241. See also *The Missionary Herald,* vol. 17 (1821), 122, and vol. 18 (1822), 324; *The Religious Intelligencer,* vol. 5 (1820–21), 726,

and vol. 7 (1822–23), 310–11. At the time of Tennooe's "defection," Hiram Bingham sent him a very stern letter, officially severing his connection to the mission church. See Hiram Bingham to William Tennooe, July 23, 1820, Bingham Family Papers, Division of Manuscripts and Archives, Sterling Memorial Library, Yale University, New Haven, CT.

83. *The Missionary Herald,* vol. 17 (1821), 172, 247–49.

84. Ibid., vol. 18 (1822), 214; *The Religious Intelligencer,* vol. 5 (1820–21), 748.

85. John Prentice to Jeremiah Evarts, July 24, 1822, ABC 12.1, vol. 2, no. 68. See also John Prentice to Jeremiah Evarts, September 18, 1820, ABC 12.1, vol. 2, no. 66, and Herman Daggett to Jeremiah Evarts, May 7, 1821, ABC 12.1, vol. 2, no. 124.

86. *The Religious Intelligencer,* vol. 7 (1822–23), 445–46.

87. Ibid.

88. Ibid., 186–87; Rev. T. Blumhardt to Jeremiah Evarts, in *The Religious Intelligencer,* vol. 6 (1821–22), 603–4.

89. Semi-Annual Report of the Foreign Mission School (Litchfield, CT, June 1825), 5.

90. Herman Daggett to Jeremiah Evarts, May 18, 1822, and October 8, 1819, ABC 12.1, vol. 2, nos. 134, 112.

91. Ibid.; Herman Daggett to Jeremiah Evarts, August 22, 1822, and August 6, 1823, ABC 12.1, vol. 2, nos. 139, 148. On the same topic, see also Herman Daggett to Jeremiah Evarts, July 21, 1823, and January 2, 1824, ABC 12.1, vol. 2, nos. 149, 154. Actual examples of such placement are noted in *The Missionary Herald,* vol. 18 (1822), 20.

92. Herman Daggett to Samuel Worcester, November 6, 1819, ABC 12.1, vol. 2, no. 113; Herman Daggett to Jeremiah Evarts, January 2, 1824, ABC 12.1, vol. 2, no. 154; Herman Daggett to Jeremiah Evarts, September 11, 1822, ABC 12.1, vol. 2, no. 140; Herman Daggett to Jeremiah Evarts, January 2, 1824, ABC 12.1, vol. 2, no. 154; Herman Daggett to Samuel Worcester, August 5, 1820, ABC 12.1, vol. 2, no. 116; Herman Daggett to Jeremiah Evarts, August 22, 1822, ABC 12.1, vol. 2, no. 139; John Prentice to Samuel Worcester, September 2, 1819, ABC 12.1, vol. 2, nos. 60–63.

93. Timothy Stone to Jeremiah Evarts, November 16, 1823, ABC 12.1, vol. 2, no. 78; Herman Daggett to Jeremiah Evarts, April 6, 1821, ABC 12.1, vol. 2, no. 123; Herman Daggett to Jeremiah Evarts, August 22, 1822, ABC 12.1, vol. 2, no. 139; Herman Daggett to Jeremiah Evarts, November 11, 1822, ABC 12.1, vol. 2, no. 142; Timothy Stone to Jeremiah Evarts, November 16, 1823, ABC 12.1, vol. 2, no. 78.

94. James Harvey to Jeremiah Evarts, July 26, 1823, ABC 12.1, vol. 2, no. 38.

95. Herman Daggett to Jeremiah Evarts, October 7, 1819, ABC 12.1, vol. 2, no. 111; Herman Daggett to Jeremiah Evarts, June 5, 1821, ABC 12.1, vol. 2, no. 126; Herman Daggett to Samuel Worcester, February 6, 1819, ABC 12.1, vol. 2, no. 102; Herman Daggett to Jeremiah Evarts, October 8, 1819, ABC 12.1, vol. 2, no. 112; Herman Daggett to Jeremiah Evarts, December 18, 1819, ABC 12.1, vol. 2, no. 83; Herman Daggett to Jeremiah Evarts, October 7, 1819, ABC 12.1, vol. 2, no. 111; Herman Daggett to Samuel Worcester, August 5, 1820, ABC 12.1, vol. 2, no. 116; George Whitefield to Rev. Amos Bassett, n.d., ms. archive, Litchfield County Historical Society, Litchfield, CT; Herman Daggett to Jeremiah Evarts, November 11, 1822, ABC 12.1, vol. 2, no. 142; Herman Daggett to Samuel Worcester, August 6, 1819, ABC 12.1, vol. 2, no. 106.

96. Herman Daggett to Jeremiah Evarts, December 23, 1823, ABC 12.1, vol. 2, no. 153; Herman Daggett to Jeremiah Evarts, February 3, 1824, ABC 12.1, vol. 2, no. 143.

97. Herman Daggett to Jeremiah Evarts, April 8, 1819, ABC 12.1, vol. 2, no. 103; Henry Hart to Jeremiah Evarts, March 25, 1820, ABC 12.1, vol. 2, no. 86.

98. Herman Daggett to Jeremiah Evarts, July 21, 1823, ABC 12.1, vol. 2, no. 149; Jonas Abrahams to Herman Daggett, with addendum by Daggett, February 11, 1823, ABC 12.1, vol. 2, no. 144.

99. Herman Daggett to Jeremiah Evarts, May 7, 1819, ABC 12.1, vol. 2, no. 103, and Herman Daggett to Samuel Worcester, February 6, 1819, ABC 12.1, vol. 2, no. 102; *Semi-Annual Report of the Foreign Mission School* (Litchfield, CT, June 1825), 6–7.

100. "An Indian School," *Hartford Courant*, August 29, 1900.

INTERLUDE *Cornwall*

1. Personal conversation with Jeremy Brecher, March 23, 2011. I offer special thanks to Ben Gray, the current owner and occupant of what was formerly the Northrup residence, and Mary Sams, owner today of the former Gold house. Both gave me full access to these historically significant buildings.

CHAPTER FIVE *American Paradox: The Indelible Color Line*

1. Letter of John Rolfe to Sir Thomas Dale, in Lyon G. Tyler, ed., *Narratives of Early Virginia* (New York, 1907), 239–44. On Virginians claiming descent from the Rolfe-Pocahontas marriage, see Bernard W. Sheehan, *Seeds of Extinction: Jeffersonian Philanthropy and the American Indian* (Chapel Hill, NC, 1973), 175; Richard Beale Davis, *Intellectual Life in Jefferson's Virginia, 1790–1839* (Chapel Hill, NC, 1964), 313–19.

2. On ethnocentric attitudes among early modern Englishmen, see Winthrop D. Jordan, *White Over Black: American Attitudes Toward the Negro, 1550–1812* (Chapel Hill, NC, 1968), 3–43, 85–90.

3. On the "noble savage" concept, see Sheehan, *Seeds of Extinction,* chapter 4; Robert E. Berkhofer, *The White Man's Indian: Images of the American Indian from Columbus to the Present* (New York, 1979), 74–80. On colonists' first impressions of Indian physique, see Karen Kupperman, *Indians and English: Facing Off in Early America* (New York, 2000), chapters 1–2; Alden Vaughan, *Roots of American Racism* (New York, 1995), chapter 1. On perceptions of Indians' color, see Vaughan, *Roots of American Racism,* chapter 1; Nancy Shoemaker, *A Strange Likeness: Becoming Red and White in Eighteenth-Century America* (New York, 2004), chapter 6; Kupperman, *Indians and English,* chapter 2; Elise Lemire, *"Miscegenation": Making Race in America* (Philadelphia, 2002), 37ff. On ideas about Indian governance, see Kupperman, *Indians and English,* chapters 1, 3; Shoemaker, *A Strange Likeness,* chapter 2. On views of Indian religion, see Kupperman, *Indians and English,* chapter 4.

4. On colonists' views of Indians as educable, see Kupperman, *Indians and English,* chapter 2; Vaughan, *Roots of American Racism,* chapters 1–2.

5. Sheehan, *Seeds of Extinction,* 23–26; Anthony F. C. Wallace, *Jefferson and the Indians: The Tragic Fate of the First Americans* (Cambridge, MA, 1999), 95ff. On "monogenesis" and colonists' theories about Indian origins, see Berkhofer, *The*

White Man's Indian, 35–36, 39–40. See also Arthur O. Lovejoy, The Great *Chain of Being: A Study of the History of an Idea* (Cambridge, MA, 1936).

6. The comments by Byrd and Beverley are quoted in Sheehan, *Seeds of Extinction,* 177. The most careful studies of colonial attitudes toward racial intermarriage are David D. Smits, "'We Are Not to Grow Wild': Seventeenth-Century New England's Repudiation of Anglo-Indian Intermarriage," *American Indian Culture and Research Journal* 13 (1987): 1–32; Smits, "'Abominable Mixture': Toward the Repudiation of Anglo-Indian Intermarriage in Seventeenth-Century Virginia," *The Virginia Magazine of History and Biography* 500 (1987): 157–92.

7. Colonists frequently noted Indian "nakedness," a line of comment that seemingly reflected a sexual interest; see Kupperman, *Indians and English,* chapter 2. See also Theda Perdue, *Mixed Blood Indians: Racial Construction in the Early South* (Athens, GA, 2003), 8ff., and June Namias, *White Captives: Gender and Ethnicity on the American Frontier* (Chapel Hill, NC, 1993). For occasional examples of interracial sexual contact (and marriage), see Ann Marie Plane, *Colonial Intimacies: Indian Marriage in Early New England* (Ithaca, NY, 2000), 35–36, 81–82. See also Smits, "'We Are Not to Grow Wild,'" 8–11, 15–17. The comment about settlers departing to "take up their abode with the Indians" is from J. H. Trumbull and C. J. Hoadly, eds., *Public Records of the Colony of Connecticut,* 15 vols. (Hartford, CT, 1850–90), vol. 1, 8, quoted in Smits, "'We Are Not to Grow Wild,'" 16. On the life of Eunice Williams, see John Demos, *The Unredeemed Captive: A Family Story from Early America* (New York, 1994).

8. On changing perceptions of Indians' color, see Vaughan, *Roots of American Racism,* chapter 1; Shoemaker, *A Strange Likeness,* chapter 6.

9. Lemire, *"Miscegenation,"* 48ff. There is some debate among historians as to when the term *red* applied to Indian skin color became a pejorative. For a summary of this, see Vaughn, *Roots of American Racism,* 158 n. 37.

10. The historical literature on frontier warfare, and its relation to Indian hating, is vast. See, for example, Peter Silver, *Our Savage Neighbors: How Indian War Transformed Early America* (New York, 2008); Kevin Kenny, *Peaceable Kingdom Lost: The Paxton Boys and the Destruction of William Penn's Holy Experiment* (New York, 2009); Sheehan, *Seeds of Extinction,* 265ff. The quote from Johnson can be found in Vaughan, *Roots of American Racism,* 20.

11. Thomas Ingersoll, *To Intermix with Our White Brothers: Indian Mixed Bloods in the United States from Earliest Times to the Indian Removals* (Albuquerque, NM, 2005), chapters 1–2; Perdue, *Mixed Blood Indians,* chapter 1; Richard Godbeer, "Eroticizing the Middle Ground: Anglo-Indian Sexual Relations Along the Eighteenth-Century Frontier," in *Sex, Love, Race: Crossing Boundaries in North American History,* ed. Martha Hodes (New York, 1999), 91–111. For firsthand observation, see John Lawson, *A New Voyage to Carolina,* ed. Hugh T. Lefler (Chapel Hill, NC, 1967), 24ff.

12. See Gregory Evans Dowd, *A Spirited Resistance: The North American Indian Struggle for Unity, 1745–1815* (Baltimore, 1992).

13. Sheehan, *Seeds of Extinction;* Vaughan, *Roots of American Racism,* chapter 1; Lemire, *"Miscegenation,"* 14–18. On Jefferson's central role in the "civilization" policy, see Wallace, *Jefferson and the Indians,* 223ff., 277ff. For a succinct summary of Secretary Knox's program in his own words, see ibid., 168. See also Reginald Horsman, "The Indian Policy of an 'Empire for Liberty,'" in *Native Americans and the Early Republic,* ed. Frederick E. Hoxie, Ronald Hoffman, and Peter J. Albert

(Charlottesville, VA, 1999), 37–61; Berkhofer, *The White Man's Indian*, 142–44. On Indians as farmers, see Daniel Usner, "Iroquois Livelihood and Jeffersonian Agrarianism," in *Native Americans and the Early Republic*, ed. Hoxie, Hoffman, and Albert, 200–225.

14. Sheehan, *Seeds of Extinction*, chapter 5; Perdue, *Mixed Blood Indians*, 51ff., 74ff.; Wallace, *Jefferson and the Indians*, 203ff. On the founding of schools, see Wallace, *Jefferson and the Indians*, 277ff.; Sheehan, *Seeds of Extinction*, 129ff.; Ingersoll, *To Intermix with Our White Brothers*, 138–39. On missionary projects in the Southeast and elsewhere see Wallace, *Jefferson and the Indians*, 188ff.; Sheehan, *Seeds of Extinction*, 130–34.

15. The sentences quoted here, from the writings of Jefferson, can be found in Horsman, "The Indian Policy of an 'Empire for Liberty,'" 50; William G. McLoughlin, *Cherokee Renascence in the New Republic* (Princeton, NJ, 1986), 33; Wallace, *Jefferson and the Indians*, 223.

16. On "amalgamation" (and the later creation of the word *miscegenation*), see Lemire, "*Miscegenation*," 4; Perdue, *Mixed Blood Indians*, 75ff. The comments by Rush and Morse are quoted in Sheehan, *Seeds of Extinction*, 177. On Hawkins's plan to promote intermarriage, see Perdue, *Mixed Blood Indians*, 76ff.

17. On Patrick Henry's legislative proposal, see Sheehan, *Seeds of Extinction*, 175. On Knox's idea of offering bounties, see Horsman, "The Indian Policy of an 'Empire for Liberty,'" 46. See also Robert E. Bieder, "Scientific Attitudes Toward Indian Mixed Bloods in Early Nineteenth-Century America," *The Journal of Ethnic Studies* 8 (1980): 17–30.

18. On Jefferson's defense of Indians, against European theories of American "degeneracy," see Wallace, *Jefferson and the Indians*, chapter 3. (His comment to Chastellux is quoted on p. 77.) See also Sheehan, *Seeds of Extinction*, chapters 3–4.

19. On the threat of extermination, see Wallace, *Jefferson and the Indians*, 11ff.; Ingersoll, *To Intermix with Our White Brothers*, 169ff.

20. On the perception of Indians as childlike, see Sheehan, *Seeds of Extinction*, 153; Richard White, "The Fictions of Patriarchy: Indians and Whites in the Early Republic," in *Native Americans and the Early Republic*, ed. Hoxie, Hoffman, and Albert, 83.

21. For a detailed account of Jefferson's involvement in land speculation, see Wallace, *Jefferson and the Indians*, chapter 1. (Jefferson's comment to Hawkins is quoted in Horsman, "The Indian Policy of an 'Empire for Liberty,'" 51.)

22. Vaughan, *Roots of American Racism*, chapter 1; Sheehan, *Seeds of Extinction*, chapter 7; Reginald Horsman, *Race and Manifest Destiny: The Origins of American Racial Anglo-Saxonism* (Cambridge, MA, 1981), chapter 6. The comment on "rancorous antipathy" is from John F. D. Smyth, *A Tour of the United States of America*, 2 vols. (London, 1784), vol. 1, 345–46, quoted in Vaughan, *Roots of American Racism*, 24.

23. The comment by McKenney is quoted in Wallace, *Jefferson and the Indians*, 19. For a rather critical appraisal of McKenney's career as an Indian agent, see Richard Drinnon, *Facing West: The Metaphysics of Indian-Hating and Empire Building* (Norman, OK, 1980), 170ff. On the alleged propensity of Indians for violence (including the comments quoted here), see Sheehan, *Seeds of Extinction*, 189ff.

24. Colin G. Calloway, "The Continuing Revolution in Indian Country," in *Native Americans and the Early Republic*, ed. Hoxie, Hoffman, and Albert, 3–33; Horsman, "The Indian Policy of an 'Empire for Liberty.'" See also Sheehan, *Seeds of Extinction*, 207ff.

25. See Laura Mielke, *Moving Encounters: Sympathy and the Indian Question in Antebellum Literature* (Amherst, MA, 2008).

26. On these points, see Ingersoll, *To Intermix with Our White Brothers,* chapter 5; Perdue, *Mixed Blood Indians,* 80ff.; Lemire, "*Miscegenation,*" 48–49; Berkhofer, *The White Man's Indian,* 56–57. For an especially authoritative discussion of "scientific racism," see Horsman, *Race and Manifest Destiny,* chapter 7. The passage on Indian inferiority is from Samuel George Morton, *Crania Americana: or, a Comparative View of the Skulls of Various Aboriginal Nations of North and South America* (Philadelphia, 1839), 81–82, quoted in Horsman, *Race and Manifest Destiny,* 127.

27. Berkhofer, *The White Man's Indian,* 33ff. See also Ingersoll, *To Intermix with Our White Brothers,* 170–72. The statement by President Monroe is quoted ibid., xx. The statement about a "mongrel population" is from "The Report of the Committee on the State of the Republic," *Augusta [GA] Chronicle and Advertiser,* November 17, 1830, quoted in Watson W. Jennison, *Cultivating Race: The Expansion of Slavery in Georgia, 1750–1860* (Lexington, KY, 2012), 208.

28. For useful overviews of Indians' experience in early New England, see Kathleen Bragdon, *Native People of Southern New England, 1650–1775* (Norman, OK, 2009); Daniel R. Mandell, *Behind the Frontier: Indians in Eighteenth-Century Eastern Massachusetts* (Lincoln, NE, 1996); William S. Simmons, *Spirit of the New England Tribes: Indian History and Folklore, 1620–1984* (Hanover, NH, 1986). See also the essays included in several anthologies: Robert S. Grumet, ed., *Northeastern Indian Lives, 1632–1816* (Amherst, MA, 1996); Colin G. Calloway and Neal Salisbury, eds., *Reinterpreting New England Indians and the Colonial Experience* (Charlottesville, VA, 2003); Colin G. Calloway, ed., *After King Philip's War: Presence and Persistence in Indian New England* (Hanover, NH, 1997); Peter Benes, ed., *Algonkians of New England: Past and Present* (Boston, 1993); Laurie Weinstein, ed., *Enduring Traditions: The Native Peoples of New England* (Westport, CT, 1994). For an extended history of a single group, see Jean O'Brien, *Dispossession by Degrees: Indian Land and Identity in Natick, Massachusetts, 1650–1790* (Lincoln, NE, 1997). On the governance of Indian "reserves" (and the role of white "guardians"), see, especially, Mandell, *Behind the Frontier,* 117–63.

29. On Indians' work as whalemen and mariners, see Daniel Vickers, "The First Whalemen of Nantucket," in *After King Philip's War,* ed. Calloway, 90–113. On Indian women as healers, see Bunny McBride and Harald E. L. Prins, "Walking the Medicine Line: Molly Ockett, a Pigwacket Doctor," *Northeastern Indian Lives,* ed. Grumet. On Indian basket making, see Mandell, *Behind the Frontier,* 31ff.; Nan Wolverton, "'A Precarious Living': Basket-Making and Related Crafts Among New England Indians," in *Reinterpreting New England Indians and the Colonial Experience,* ed. Calloway and Salisbury, 341–68; and, most especially, Russell G. Handsman and Ann McMullen, *A Key to the Language of Woodsplint Baskets* (Washington, CT, 1987).

30. On the blurring of racial distinctions between blacks and Indians, see Mandell, *Behind the Frontier,* 35ff.; specifically for Rhode Island, see Ruth Wallis Herndon and Ella Wilcox Sekatau, "Colonizing the Children: Indian Youngsters in Servitude in Early Rhode Island," in *Reinterpreting New England Indians and the Colonial Experience,* ed. Calloway and Salisbury, 137–73. On problems created by black/Indian intermarriage, see David Silverman, "The Church in New England Indian Community Life," in *Reinterpreting New England Indians,* ed. Calloway

and Salisbury, 264–98, (especially 279–80); Daniel R. Mandell, "The Saga of Sarah Muckamugg: Indian and African American Intermarriage in Colonial New England," in *Sex, Love, Race,* ed. Hodes, 72–90. The comments reflecting scornful attitudes toward Indians are quoted in Mandell, *Behind the Frontier,* 34, 144, 36. For the comment on "a miserable remnant," see John W. DeForest, *History of the Indians of Connecticut* (1851; reprint, Hamden, CT, 1964), 446. For a particularly shocking instance of anti-Indian prejudice, see Daniel R. Mandell, "*The Indian's Pedigree* (1794): Indians, Folklore, and Race in Southern New England," *William and Mary Quarterly,* 3d series, 61 (2004): 521–38. On the alleged "vanishing" of Indians, see Daniel R. Mandell, *Tribe, Race, History: Native Americans in Southern New England, 1780–1880* (Baltimore, 2008); Jean M. O'Brien, *Firsting and Lasting: Writing Indians out of Existence in New England* (Minneapolis, 2010), especially chapters 3–4. On local "last Indian" stories, see Mandell, *Tribe, Race, History,* 179–83.

31. Barry O'Connell, ed., *On Our Own Ground: The Complete Writings of William Apess, a Pequot* (Amherst, MA, 1992). For thoughtful discussion of Apess's life and writings, see Lisa Brooks, *The Common Pot: The Recovery of Native Space in the Northeast* (Minneapolis, 2008), chapters 4–5.

32. The firsthand comments are quoted in O'Connell, ed., *On Our Own Ground,* lxv, lvii, lxii, lxviii–lxix.

33. Quoted ibid., xlvi.

34. Quoted in O'Brien, *Firsting and Lasting,* 205.

CHAPTER SIX *"So much excitement and disgust throughout our country"*

1. See Edward C. Starr, *A History of Cornwall, Connecticut: A Typical New England Town* (New Haven, CT, 1926), 402, 521.

2. See A. Judd Northrup, *The Northrup-Northrop Genealogy* (New York, 1910), 26–27, 60–61, 142, 266; *New Haven Historical Society Papers,* vol. 1, 117–18; vol. 2, 378–80.

3. On the steward's regular duties, see John Prentice to Samuel Worcester, June 23, 1817, ABC 12.1, vol. 2, no. 59; Report of the Visiting Committee to the Foreign Mission School, September 2, 1817, ABC 12.1, vol. 2, no. 44.

4. *Cartersville [GA] Courant,* March 19, 1885, quoted in Thurman Wilkins, *Cherokee Tragedy: The Ridge Family and the Decimation of a People,* 2d ed. (Norman, OK, 1986), 132.

5. The best single account of the life of Major Ridge is in Wilkins, *Cherokee Tragedy.* The tribute noted here is by Judge J. W. H. Underwood, *Cartersville [GA] Courant,* April 2, 1885, quoted in Wilkins, *Cherokee Tragedy,* 15.

6. See Wilkins, *Cherokee Tragedy.*

7. Ard Hoyt to Jeremiah Evarts, August 7, 1823, ABC 18.3.1 (1st series), vol. 3, no. 107.

8. On these parts of Major Ridge's career, see Wilkins, *Cherokee Tragedy,* especially chapters 2–4.

9. Wilkins, *Cherokee Tragedy,* 100–110.

10. Journal of the Mission to the Cherokees (Brainerd), July 4, 1817, ABC 18.3.1, (1st series), vol. 2, no. 2.

11. Ard Hoyt to Samuel Worcester, September 25, 1818, ABC 18.3.1 (1st series), vol. 2, no. 116. Herman Daggett to Samuel Worcester, December 18, 1818, ABC 12.1, vol. 2, no. 101. For thoughtful discussion of John Ridge's ownership of a watch, see Hil-

ary Wyss, *English Letters and Indian Literacies: Reading, Writing, and New England Missionary Schools, 1750–1830* (Philadelphia, 2012), 150–57.

12. Herman Daggett to Samuel Worcester, December 18, 1818, ABC 12.1, vol. 2, no. 101.

13. Mrs. Eunice (Wadsworth) Taylor, "Recollection" ("written by Mrs. Ellen Gibbs, Crystal Lake, Illinois"), March 1, 1910. (The original manuscript of this document has been lost. A typescript copy was made for the Dwight Collection, then housed in Boston; this copy is currently at the Norman Rockwell Museum, Stockbridge, MA. A duplicate was sent to the Cornwall Historical Society, Cornwall, CT; see FMS Archive, folder 19. The entire document is published in Starr, *A History of Cornwall, Connecticut,* 154–57.) As a child, Mrs. Taylor had lived in Cornwall "and was familiar with the following transactions"; these included the Ridge-Northrup wedding. Wherever possible, details of the document have been checked against other evidence; inaccuracies have been found in only one or two minor instances. Mrs. Gibbs, the transcriber, was Mrs. Taylor's daughter.

14. John Howard Payne Papers, vol. 8, 63–102, Newberry Library, Chicago, IL.

15. The comments on John Ridge's declining health are, successively, in Herman Daggett to Jeremiah Evarts, December 16, 1820, April 6, 1821, June 5, 1821, July 11, 1821, August 6, 1821, ABC 12.1, vol. 2, nos. 123, 126, 128, 129. The order for crutches appears in the account book of C. and F. Kellogg, 59, Cornwall Historical Society, Cornwall, CT.

16. Mrs. Eunice (Wadsworth) Taylor, "Recollection," in Starr, *A History of Cornwall, Connecticut,* 155; C. E. B. (Catherine E. Beecher), *Boston Courier,* March 15, 1832; T. S. Gold, *Historical Records of the Town of Cornwall, Litchfield County, Connecticut* (Litchfield, CT, 1904), 351. The Cherokee council pipe is currently in the possession of Charles Gold (Cornwall, CT), who kindly allowed the author to examine it.

17. Herman Daggett to Jeremiah Evarts, September 22, 1822, ABC 12.1, vol. 2, no. 141.

18. Mrs. Eunice (Wadsworth) Taylor, "Recollection," in Starr, *A History of Cornwall, Connecticut,* 154. The italicized passages are direct quotes from the Taylor account. The description of the reactions of Major Ridge and Susanna is based on an article in *The Religious Intelligencer,* vol. 10 (1825–26), 280, as noted in Wilkins, *Cherokee Tragedy,* 133.

19. Herman Daggett to Jeremiah Evarts, September 22, 1822, ABC 12.1, vol. 2, no. 141.

20. "Visit of Indian Young Men at Charleston, S.C.," *The Missionary Herald,* vol. 19 (1823), 29–30.

21. *The Religious Intelligencer,* vol. 7 (1822–23), 446; *Cartersville* [GA] *Courant,* March 19, 1885, quoted in Wilkins, *Cherokee Tragedy,* 137.

22. Emily Fox, "The Indian Song, Sarah and John," in Gold, *Historical Records of the Town of Cornwall,* 32. Reportedly, this poem "once had a considerable local fame"; indeed, according to Gold, "there are many among our aged readers who will remember having read it."

23. *The Christian Herald,* vol. 10 (1823), 48.

24. A copy of the marriage certificate of John Ridge and Sarah Northrup is in the files of the Cornwall Historical Society, Cornwall, CT. There were many announcements in newspapers; see, for example, *Connecticut Courant,* February 10, 1824, and *Connecticut Mirror,* February 16, 1824.

25. A report of these events was authored by a local resident identified only as "A.B., Cornwall, June 7, 1824," as noted in E. C. Starr, "Outlines of the Story of the Pupils of the Foreign Mission School, at Cornwall, Collected and Presented to the

Cornwall Library Association, by E. C. Starr (1895)," Cornwall Historical Society, Cornwall, CT.

26. On the recollections of John and Sarah (Northrup) Ridge, see "Then and Now," *Fort Smith* [AR] *Herald,* May 21, 1870. Additional details quoted in this paragraph are from *American Eagle* (Litchfield, CT), March 1, 1824.

27. See *American Eagle* (Litchfield, CT), February 23, 1824; April 19, 1824; February 2, 1824; March 1, 1824. See also the article entitled "Married," *Massachusetts Spy* (Worcester), February 25, 1824, and *Litchfield Gazette,* reprinted in *Nantucket Inquirer,* February 23, 1824.

28. *American Eagle* (Litchfield, CT), May 31, 1824; August 8, 1824; May 31, 1824; February 2, 1824.

29. See *The Pilot* (New Haven, CT), February 17, 1824.

30. For the comment on romantic competition, see ibid. The poem "The Indian Song, Sarah and John" quoted here is by Emily Fox. See Gold, *Historical Records of the Town of Cornwall,* 32.

31. *American Eagle* (Litchfield, CT), September 27, 1824, February 23, 1824.

32. The school's defense of its own position was part of a "Letter of the Executive Committee to Mr. Charles Sherman, March 9, 1824," published in *Connecticut Courant,* March 23, 1824.

33. Daniel Buttrick to Jeremiah Evarts, November 4–7, 1824, ABC 18.3.1 (1st series), vol. 4, no. 5; Moody Hall to Jeremiah Evarts, September 18, 1824, ABC 18.3.1 (1st series), vol. 5, no. 328.

34. Edward Coote Pinkney, "The Indian's Bride," in Thomas Olive Mabbott and Frank Leslie Pleadwell, eds., *The Life and Works of Edward Coote Pinkney* (New York, 1926), 95–99.

35. Silas Hurlbut McAlpine, "To the Indians of Cornwall"; see Gold, *Historical Records of the Town of Cornwall,* 31–32.

36. Daniel Buttrick to Jeremiah Evarts, October 12, 1824, ABC 18.3.1 (1st series), vol. 4, no. 2.

37. *American Eagle* (Litchfield, CT), June 7, 1824, April 19, 1824.

38. William Chamberlain to Jeremiah Evarts, July 30, 1824, ABC 18.3.1 (1st series), vol. 4, no. 37; Moody Hall to Jeremiah Evarts, April 5, 1825, ABC 18.3.1 (1st series), vol. 5 (part 2), no. 333.

39. *Foreign Mission Society of Litchfield County, Annual Meeting, 9 February 1825,* 3. (Pamphlet with no place or date of publication. Copy seen at the Torringford [CT] Public Library.)

40. "Visit of Indian Young Men at Charleston, S.C.," *The Missionary Herald,* vol. 19 (1823), 29–30.

41. The donation totals presented here, and the accompanying quotation, appear in *Foreign Mission Society of Litchfield County [CT], Annual Meeting, 9 February 1826,* 4–5. (Copy seen at the Torringford [CT] Public Library.) The figures for the ABCFM as a whole are in S. A. Howland (attrib.), *The History of American Missions to the Heathen, from Their Commencement to the Present Time* (Worcester, MA, 1840), 110–13.

42. Summary of the meeting of the American Board of Commissioners for Foreign Missions, Hartford (CT), September 15–17, quoted in Howland (attrib.), *The History of American Missions to the Heathen,* 125.

43. *Quarterly Report of the Foreign Mission School, 1 June 1824.* (Copy seen at the Torringford [CT] Public Library.)

44. Herman Daggett to Jeremiah Evarts, January 2, 1824, Herman Daggett to Jeremiah Evarts, July 21, 1823, Herman Daggett to Jeremiah Evarts, September 4, 1823, Herman Daggett to Jeremiah Evarts, September 25, 1823, and Herman Daggett to Jeremiah Evarts, May 26, 1824, ABC 12.1, vol. 2, nos. 154, 149, 150, 151, 155.

45. Herman Daggett to Jeremiah Evarts, January 2, 1824, ABC 12.1, vol. 5, no. 154.

46. Information on these arrivals is scattered through ABC 12.1, vol. 2, and ABC 11, vol. 1. For Patoo, see also Harlan Page, *Memoir of Thomas H. Patoo, a Native of the Marquesas Islands* (New York, 1840); for A'lan and Alum, *The Farmer's Cabinet* (Amherst, NH), July 19, 1823, and Carl T. Smith, *Chinese Christians: Elites, Middlemen, and the Church in Hong Kong*, 2d ed. (Hong Kong, 2005), 56–57; for Abrahams, *Israel's Advocate*, vol. 1 (December 1823), and *Quarterly Report of the Foreign Mission School in Cornwall, Connecticut, for June 1, 1824*, 6–11; for Kavasales and Karavelles, *Boston Daily Advertiser*, March 5, 1823, and Luther Hodge, *Photius Fisk: A Biography* (Boston, 1891); for Carter, "The Captives," *St. Albans* [VT] *Messenger*, April 19, 1846, and Starr, *A History of Cornwall, Connecticut*, 286–87.

47. Herman Daggett to Jeremiah Evarts, January 2, 1824, ABC 12.1, vol. 2, no. 154.

48. Jeremiah Evarts to Rufus Anderson, December 18, 1823, ABC 11, vol. 1, no. 245.

49. For a brief summary of the life and career of David Brown, see Starr, *A History of Cornwall, Connecticut*, 279–80. Brown's sister Catharine achieved considerable fame in her own right by qualifying as "the first, who was hopefully converted from among the Indians, by means of the missionaries sent out by the American Board of Missions." See Rufus Anderson, *Memoir of Catharine Brown, a Christian Indian of the Cherokee Nation* (Boston, 1825), 26.

50. *New Hampshire Repository* (Concord, NH), January 5, 1824; *Haverhill* [MA] *Gazette*, November 15, 1823; *The Farmer's Cabinet* (Amherst, NH), November 8, 1823.

51. David Brown to Rev. Elias Cornelius, December 1, 1823, ABC 18.3.1 (1st series), vol. 1, no. 89.

52. Jeremiah Evarts to Rufus Anderson, December 17, 1823, ABC 11, vol. 1, no. 244.

53. Jeremiah Evarts to Henry Hill, December 15, 1823, ABC 11, vol. 1, no. 243; Jeremiah Evarts to Rufus Anderson, December 20, 1823, ABC 11, vol. 1, no. 247; Jeremiah Evarts to Rufus Anderson, December 27, 1823, ABC 11, vol. 1, no. 250.

54. "Indian Eloquence," *Haverhill* [MA] *Gazette*, November 29, 1823.

55. Jeremiah Evarts to Henry Hill, January 2, 1824, ABC 11, vol. 1, no. 255.

56. Ibid.; Jeremiah Evarts to Henry Hill, January 9, 1824, ABC 11, vol. 1, no. 258; Jeremiah Evarts to Henry Hill, January 6, 1824, ABC 11, vol. 1, no. 254.

57. Jeremiah Evarts to Henry Hill, January 16, 1824, ABC 11, vol. 1, no. 261.

58. Jeremiah Evarts to Henry Hill, January 20, 1824, ABC 11, vol. 1, no. 264.

59. Ibid.

60. Ibid.

61. Ibid.; Jeremiah Evarts to Henry Hill, January 22, 1824, ABC 11, vol. 1, no. 265.

62. Ibid.

63. David Brown to Jeremiah Evarts, March 15, 1824, ABC 18.3.1 (1st series), vol. 1, no. 92; Jeremiah Evarts to S. A. Worcester, February 14, 1824, ABC 11, vol. 1, no. 275; David Brown to Jeremiah Evarts, April 21, 1823, ABC 18.3.1 (1st series), vol. 1, no. 87; Jeremiah Evarts to Henry Hill, February 25, 1824, ABC 11, vol. 1, nos. 283–84.

64. David Brown to Jeremiah Evarts, March 15, 1824, ABC 18.3.1 (1st series), vol. 1, no. 92; David Brown to Jeremiah Evarts, April 19, 1824, ABC 18.3.1 (1st series), vol. 1, no. 93.

65. Mrs. Eunice (Wadsworth) Taylor, "Recollection," in Starr, *A History of Cornwall, Connecticut*, 155.

66. See the account book of C. and F. Kellogg, Cornwall Historical Society, Cornwall, CT.

67. George "Prince" Tamoree to Herman Daggett, July 25, 1820, ABC 12.1, vol. 2, no. 125; George "Prince" Tamoree to Rev. Jedediah Morse, January 21, 1819, Morse Family Papers, Division of Manuscripts and Archives, Sterling Memorial Library, Yale University, New Haven, CT. See also Rev. Timothy Stone to Rev. Jedediah Morse, January 22, 1819, Morse Family Papers.

68. This anecdote was attributed to Col. D. W. Pierce; see Starr, *A History of Cornwall, Connecticut*, 150.

69. Ibid., 148.

70. A strip of cloth, "made from tree bark by the Hawaiians," is in the collections of the Cornwall Historical Society, Cornwall, CT; correspondence about its provenance is in FMS Archive, folder 48. This may be the same piece reported elsewhere as given by Henry Obookiah "to the Miner family of South Canaan"; see Starr, "Outlines of the Story of the Pupils of the Foreign Mission School," 179.

71. Friendship album of Miss Cherry Stone, FMS Archive, folder 52. For detailed analysis of this document, including translation of the entries in Mandarin, see Karen Sánchez-Eppler, "Copying and Conversion: An 1824 Friendship Album 'From a Chinese Youth,'" in *Asian Americans in New England: Culture and Community*, ed. Monica Chiu (Lebanon, NH, 2009).

72. Ibid.

73. Friendship album of Martha Day, Waterbury Historical Society, Waterbury, CT.

74. Mary Stone to William Kummooolah, n.d., addendum to letter from John Eliot Phelps to William Kummooolah, n.d., Archives of the Mission Houses Museum, Honolulu, HI; Herman Daggett to Rev. Elias Cornelius, September 25, 1823, ABC 12.1, vol. 2, no. 151.

75. Mrs. Eunice (Wadsworth) Taylor, "Recollection," in Starr, *A History of Cornwall, Connecticut*, 155.

76. In the spring of 1825, Cynthia Thrall traveled with her parents to the Dwight mission among the Cherokees in Arkansas. En route they visited the Foreign Mission School, about which Cynthia wrote at some length to an unidentified friend. The original of this letter, dated May 12, 1825 (Goshen, CT), cannot be located today, but it was seen as recently as 1954. A long passage from it was quoted in Mrs. Carrie McKendrick to Emily Marsh, January 15, 1954; see FMS Archive, folder 48.

77. *Connecticut Journal*, August 10, 1824.

78. Mrs. Eunice (Wadsworth) Taylor, "Recollection," in Starr, *A History of Cornwall, Connecticut*, 155; Herman Vaill to Harriet Gold, April 22, 1823, in Theresa Strouth Gaul, ed., *To Marry an Indian: The Marriage of Harriett Gold & Elias Boudinot in Letters, 1823–1839* (Chapel Hill, NC, 2005), 79–80.

79. See Ralph Henry Gabriel, *Elias Boudinot, Cherokee, & His America* (Norman, OK, 1941). The comments by Daggett on school performance are found in the files of the American Board of Commissioners for Foreign Missions, Houghton Library, Harvard University, Cambridge, MA. For the description of Boudinot's visit to New Haven, see *The Religious Intelligencer*, vol. 7 (1822–23), 556.

80. Catharine Gold to Herman and Flora (Gold) Vaill, July 18, 1825, in Gaul, ed., *To Marry an Indian*, 110.

81. Ibid. Herman Vaill to Mary (Gold) Brinsmade, August 2, 1825, in Gaul, ed., *To Marry an Indian*, 118–20.
82. Daniel Brinsmade to Herman and Flora (Gold) Vaill, June 29, 1825, in Gaul, ed., *To Marry an Indian*, 89; Mary (Gold) Brinsmade to Herman and Flora (Gold) Vaill, July 14, 1825, ibid., 105–6; Catharine Gold to Herman and Flora (Gold) Vaill, July 18, 1825, ibid., 111.
83. Catherine Gold to Herman and Flora (Gold) Vaill, July 18, 1825, in Gaul, ed., *To Marry an Indian*, 110; Mary (Gold) Brinsmade to Herman and Flora (Gold) Vaill, July 14, 1825, ibid., 106; Catharine Gold to Herman and Flora (Gold) Vaill, July 18, 1825, ibid., 110.
84. Mrs. Eunice (Wadsworth) Taylor, "Recollection," in Starr, *A History of Cornwall, Connecticut*, 156.
85. Stephen Gold to Herman and Flora (Gold) Vaill, June 11, 1825, in Gaul, ed., *To Marry an Indian*, 81; Cornelius Everest to Stephen Gold, July 2, 1825, ibid., 103–4.
86. Stephen Gold to Herman and Flora (Gold) Vaill, June 11, 1825, in Gaul, ed., *To Marry an Indian*, 81; Harriet Gold to Herman and Flora (Gold) Vaill and Catharine Gold, June 25, 1825, ibid., 84; Benjamin Gold to Hezekiah Gold, December 8, 1829, quoted in Mary Brinsmade Church, "Elias Boudinot: An Account of His Life by His Grand-daughter," Town History Papers of the Woman's Club of Washington, Conn. (1913), typescript copy, FMS Archive, folder 61.
87. Stephen Gold to Herman and Flora (Gold) Vaill, June 11, 1825, in Gaul, ed., *To Marry an Indian*, 81–82.
88. "Special communication to the public," in *Semi-Annual Report of the Foreign Mission School, for June 1825*, June 17, 1825. (Pamphlet with no date or place of publication. Copy seen at the Torringford [CT] Public Library.)
89. Harriet Gold to Herman and Flora (Gold) Vaill and Catharine Gold, June 25, 1825, in Gaul, ed., *To Marry an Indian*, 84.
90. Ibid.
91. Elizabeth Pomeroy to Mrs. Abigail Gillett, June 25, 1825; see Barbara Austen, "Marrying Red: Indian/White Relations in the Case of Elias Boudinot and Harriet Gold," *Connecticut History* 45 (2006): 256–60.
92. Daniel Brinsmade to Herman and Flora (Gold) Vaill, June 29, 1825, in Gaul, ed., *To Marry an Indian*, 89; Cornelius Everest to Stephen Gold, July 2, 1825, ibid., 104; Harriet Gold to Herman and Flora (Gold) Vaill and Catharine Gold, July 25, 1825, ibid., 83–87.
93. Herman Vaill to Harriet Gold, June 29, 1825, in Gaul, ed., *To Marry an Indian*, 90–101.
94. Flora (Gold) Vaill to Herman Vaill, September 19, 1825, in Gaul, ed., *To Marry an Indian*, 135; Catharine Gold to Herman Vaill and Flora (Gold) Vaill, July 18, 1825, ibid., 109; Harriet Gold to Herman and Flora (Gold) Vaill and Catharine Gold, July 25, 1825, ibid., 84.
95. Daniel Brinsmade to Herman Vaill, July 14, 1825, in Gaul, ed., *To Marry an Indian*, 107–8; Herman Vaill to Mary (Gold) Brinsmade, August 2, 1825, ibid., 121–22; Cornelius Everett to Herman and Flora (Gold) Vaill, August 10, 1825, ibid., 123; Bennett Roberts to Herman Vaill, August 1, 1825, ibid., 115.
96. Mary (Gold) Brinsmade to Herman and Flora (Gold) Vaill, July 14, 1825, in Gaul, ed., *To Marry an Indian*, 105; Daniel Brinsmade to Herman and Flora (Gold) Vaill, July 14, 1825, ibid., 107.

97. Flora (Gold) Vaill to Herman Vaill, September 17, 1825, in Gaul, ed., *To Marry an Indian,* 135; Herman Vaill to Col. Benjamin Gold, September 5, 1825, ibid., 131; Abbey (Gold) Everest to Herman and Flora (Gold) Vaill, September 5, 1825, ibid., 133.
98. *American Eagle* (Litchfield, CT), August 29, 1825.
99. Ibid., October 8, 1825.
100. *Niles' Weekly Register,* July 9, 1825.
101. *Western Recorder,* October 4, 1825; *Boston Recorder and Telegraph,* August 26, 1825.
102. *Boston Recorder and Telegraph,* August 26, 1825.
103. Jeremiah Evarts to Rev. Dr. Chapin, July 5, 1825, ABC 1.01, vol. 5, nos. 326–27; Jeremiah Evarts to Rev. T. Stone, August 26, 1825, ABC 1.01, vol. 5, nos. 359–61.
104. Jeremiah Evarts to Rev. William Chamberlain, September 16, 1825, ABC 1.01, vol. 5, nos. 387–88; Jeremiah Evarts to Rev. Daniel Buttrick, September 16, 1825, ABC 1.01, vol. 5, nos. 388–89.
105. Jeremiah Evarts to Henry Hill, January 23, 1826, ABC 11, vol. 2, no. 26; Jeremiah Evarts to Henry Hill, February 9, 1826, ABC 11, vol. 5, no. 31; Isaac Proctor to Jeremiah Evarts, December 11, 1827, ABC 18.3.1 (1st series), vol. 4, no. 189; Rev. Daniel Buttrick to Henry Hill and Jeremiah Evarts, December 13, 1825, ABC 18.3.1 (1st series), vol. 5, no. 386. See also *American Eagle* (Litchfield, CT), August 29, 1825. For a "personal observation" of Cherokee ball play by a contemporary, see J. P. Evans, untitled typescript, in the John Howard Payne Papers, vol. 6, no. 689, Newberry Library, Chicago, IL. According to this source, participants were not "literally naked," as the missionaries alleged; instead, after "stripping" off their regular garb, they wore "a short covering around the loins."
106. Jeremiah Evarts to Henry Hill, February 9, 1826, ABC 11, vol. 2, no. 30; Jeremiah Evarts to Henry Hill, April 2, 1826, ABC 11, vol. 2, no. 41.
107. Jeremiah Evarts to Henry Hill, April 2, 1826, ABC 11, vol. 2, no. 41; Rev. William Chamberlain to Jeremiah Evarts, August 29, 1825, ABC 18.3.1 (1st series), vol. 4, no. 43.
108. David Brown to Jeremiah Evarts, September 29, 1825, ABC 18.3.1 (1st series), vol. 5 (part 2), no. 285; Rev. Daniel Buttrick to Jeremiah Evarts, September 17, 1825, ABC 18.3.1 (1st series), vol. 4, no. 18.
109. Jeremiah Evarts to Rev. Charles Prentice, July 26, 1825, ABC 8.6, vol. 5, nos. 29–31; Jeremiah Evarts to Rev. Dr. Chapin, July 5, 1825, ABC 1.01, vol. 5, nos. 326–27; Jeremiah Evarts to Henry Hill, February 9, 1826, ABC 11, vol. 2, no. 31.
110. Jeremiah Evarts to Henry Hill, February 9, 1826, ABC 11, vol. 2, no. 31; Starr, "Outlines of the Story of the Pupils of the Foreign Mission School," 91.
111. Bennett Roberts to Herman Vaill, August 1, 1825, in Gaul, ed., *To Marry an Indian,* 115; Herman Vaill to Harriet Gold, ibid., 141–42; Mrs. Eunice (Wadsworth) Taylor, "Recollection," in Starr, *A History of Cornwall, Connecticut,* 155; T. S. Gold, *Historical Records of the Town of Cornwall,* 85–86.
112. Mrs. Eunice (Wadsworth) Taylor, "Recollection," in Starr, *A History of Cornwall, Connecticut,* 155; Church, "Elias Boudinot," FMS Archive, folder 61.
113. "Ishmaelite" document (typescript), FMS Archive, folder 17. Italicized words in the text are direct quotes from this document. The ms. original cannot be located, but it was apparently seen by researchers in the early twentieth century. The latter included E. E. Dale, whose book *Cherokee Cavaliers: Forty Years of Cherokee History as Told in the Correspondence of the Ridge-Watie-Boudinot Family* (Norman, OK, 1939) includes a mention of it.

114. E. E. Dale reached the same conclusion as to Boudinot's authorship; see Dale to Emily Marsh, February 12, 1938, FMS Archive, folder 32.

INTERLUDE *The Cherokee Nation*

1. Benjamin Gold to Herman and Flora (Gold) Vaill, October 29, 1829, in Theresa Strouth Gaul, ed., *To Marry an Indian: The Marriage of Harriett Gold & Elias Boudinot in Letters, 1823–1839* (Chapel Hill, NC, 2005), 166.
2. Abraham Steiner to John Heckwelder, March 6, 1820, Vaux Family Papers, Pennsylvania Historical Society, Philadelphia; quoted in Thurman Wilkins, *Cherokee Tragedy: The Ridge Family and the Decimation of a People*, 2d ed. (Norman, OK, 1986), 142.
3. Benjamin Gold to Hezekiah Gold, December 8, 1829, quoted in Mary Brinsmade Church, "Elias Boudinot: An Account of His Life by His Grand-daughter," Town History Papers of the Woman's Club of Washington, Connecticut (1913), typescript copy, FMS Archive, folder 61.
4. *Atlanta Constitution*, December 1, 1889, quoted in Wilkins, *Cherokee Tragedy*, 196. Harriet's father described the Boudinot residence as "a large and convenient framed house, two stories, 30 by 40 feet on the ground, well off and well furnished with the comforts of life." See Benjamin Gold to Hezekiah Gold, December 8, 1829, quoted in Church, "Elias Boudinot."
5. For much valuable information on these matters, see William H. Banks, *Plants of the Cherokee* (Gatlinburg, TN, 2004). On both flora and fauna, with special attention to the period of Cherokee occupancy, see Gary C. Goodwin, *Cherokees in Transition: A Study of Changing Culture and Environment Prior to 1775* (Chicago, 1977). Signage along the nature trail at the New Echota Historic Site is also very useful.
6. See Goodwin, *Cherokees in Transition*.
7. Valuations in Floyd County, Georgia, by Agents Hemphill and Liddell, appraised September 20, 1836, 12–13; quoted in Don L. Shadburn, *Cherokee Planters in Georgia, 1832–1838: Historical Essays on Eleven Counties in the Cherokee Nation of Georgia* (Cumming, GA, 1900), 128.
8. John Ridge to Dr. Samuel Gold, January 2, 1831, quoted in T. S. Gold, *Historical Records of the Town of Cornwall, Litchfield County, Connecticut* (Hartford, CT, 1904), 350.
9. See Patrick H. Garrow, *The Chieftains Excavations, 1969–1971* (Rome, GA, 2010), chapter 5.
10. Ibid., 73. John Ridge's letter to Dr. Samuel Gold (cited in note 8) noted the "limp . . . in my gait in walking, occasioned, as you know, by the disease of my hip."
11. Garrow, *The Chieftains Excavations*, 18; Wilkins, *Cherokee Tragedy*, 188; Shadburn, *Cherokee Planters in Georgia, 1832–1838*, 127–28.
12. Garrow, *The Chieftains Excavations*, 53, 55–56, 88, 94–95, 98 passim.
13. Robert Battey, "Remarks Upon the Medicinal Plants of Cherokee Georgia," *American Journal of Pharmacy* 29, no. 5 (1857): 59, quoted in Garrow, *The Chieftains Excavations*, chapter 17.
14. Garrow, *The Chieftains Excavations*, chapter 17.
15. Valuations in Floyd County, Georgia . . . September 20, 1836, pp. 12–13, quoted in Shadburn, *Cherokee Planters in Georgia*, 126.

16. Thomas L. McKenney and James Hall, *History of the Indian Tribes of North America with Biographical Sketches and Anecdotes of the Principal Chiefs,* ed. F. W. Hodge, 3 vols. (Edinburgh, 1933), vol. 1, 305.

17. *The Religious Intelligencer,* vol. 10 (1825–26), 280–81, quoted in Wilkins, *Cherokee Tragedy,* 170.

18. On details of the John Ridge residence, see W. Jeff Bishop, *Running Waters* (report under the sponsorship of the National Park Service and Chieftains Museum, 2008). There is, to be sure, some controversy about the matter of origins. The present-day occupants—a family named Rush—believe that the house was constructed by an ancestor of theirs around 1840, after the original John Ridge residence was taken down. But the close correspondence of the current structure with all the period evidence suggests otherwise. (What sense would it make to destroy a handsome, capacious building, then almost immediately construct another to nearly identical specifications?) The authors of the National Park Service report decided, after careful consideration, to reject the Rush attribution and confirm the link to the original Running Waters.

19. John R. Ridge, *Poems* (San Francisco, 1868), 6.

20. Shadburn, *Cherokee Planters in Georgia,* 130.

21. Ibid., 129–31.

22. Ibid., 129.

23. Census of Cherokees in the Limits of Georgia in 1835, as Taken by Geo. W. Underwood, Esq. (copy seen at Chieftains Museum, Rome, GA).

24. *Poulson's American Daily Advertiser,* vol. 41, February 6, 1832, quoted in Bishop, *Running Waters,* 14.

25. The painting was done at the direction of the Federal Indian agent Thomas McKenney, to hang alongside portraits of other native leaders in the Indian Office in Georgetown. It was McKenney's practice to have copies made for the sitters; this was done in Ridge's case. At some point, the original passed to the Smithsonian Institution, where it was destroyed in a fire in 1865. The copy is said to have hung in an upstairs room at Running Waters, John Ridge's house on the Calhoun Road. Subsequently, it descended through several generations of his family, and was recently consigned to auction. It is currently in a private collection. A lithograph made from the original was published in McKenney and Hall, *History of the Indian Tribes of North America;* see the image of this in Wilkins, *Cherokee Tragedy,* 176.

CHAPTER SEVEN *American Tragedy: Renascence and Removal*

1. Bernard W. Sheehan, *Seeds of Extinction: Jeffersonian Philanthropy and the American Indian* (New York, 1974).

2. Ibid. For an overview of the politics and ideology of removal, see Reginald Horsman, *The Origins of Indian Removal, 1815–1824* (East Lansing, MI, 1970). See also Ronald Satz, *American Indian Policy in the Jacksonian Era* (Norman, OK, 2002), especially chapter 1. On the trope of the "vanishing Indian," see Daniel Mandell, *Tribe, Race, History: Native Americans in Southern New England, 1780–1880* (Baltimore, 2008), 145–46, 178–89, and Jean M. O'Brien, *Firsting and Lasting: Writing Indians Out of Existence in New England* (Minneapolis, 2010).

3. David W. Miller, *The Taking of American Indian Lands in the Southeast: A History*

of Territorial Cessions and Forced Removals, 1607–1840 (Jefferson, NC, 2011), chapters 2–3.

4. See David W. Miller, *Forced Removal of American Indians from the Northeast: A History of Territorial Cessions and Relocations, 1620–1854* (Jefferson, NC, 2011).

5. *United States Statutes at Large*, vol. 2, 227, quoted in Grant Foreman, *Indians and Pioneers*, rev. ed. (Norman, OK, 1936), 11–12.

6. Miller, *Forced Removal of American Indians from the Northeast*, chapter 33.

7. Miller, *The Taking of American Indian Lands in the Southeast*, chapters 27–30.

8. On Cherokee population size at the time of first contact with Europeans, see Russell Thornton, *The Cherokees: A Population History* (Lincoln, NE, 1990), 16–18.

9. For a fine summary of the Cherokee way of life in the colonial era, see William G. McLoughlin, *Cherokee Renascence in the New Republic* (Princeton, NJ, 1986), chapter 1. See also David Corkran, *The Cherokee Frontier, 1740–1762* (Norman, OK, 1962), chapter 1; Charles M. Hudson, *The Southeastern Indians* (Knoxville, TN, 1976); Grace Steele Woodward, *The Cherokees* (Norman, OK, 1963), chapter 3.

10. Thornton, *The Cherokees*, chapter 2; Gary C. Goodwin, *Cherokees in Transition: A Study of Changing Culture and Environment Prior to 1775* (Chicago, 1977), 105–49.

11. Goodwin, *Cherokees in Transition*, 105–49; See also McLoughlin, *Cherokee Renascence in the New Republic*, 18–22; Woodward, *The Cherokees*, chapter 5; and Corkran, *The Cherokee Frontier*, chapters 10–15.

12. For a detailed picture of Cherokee land cessions, see Charles Royce, *The Cherokee Nation of Indians* (Chicago, 1975), especially the table on p. 256. See also the map in McLoughlin, *Cherokee Renascence in the New Republic*, 27.

13. Chief Skiagunsta to the governor of South Carolina, "Indian Books of South Carolina," vol. 3, 321, quoted in Corkran, *The Cherokee Frontier*, 14.

14. See McLoughlin, *Cherokee Renascence in the New Republic*, 25–32, 55–57.

15. Ibid., chapter 14; McLoughlin, "Who Civilized the Cherokees?" *Journal of Cherokee Studies* 13 (1988): 55–81. On changing settlement patterns, see Goodwin, *Cherokees in Transition*, chapters 3 and 6. See also Theda Perdue and Michael D. Green, *The Cherokee Nation and the Trail of Tears* (New York, 2007), chapter 2.

16. Perdue and Green, *The Cherokee Nation and the Trail of Tears*, passim.

17. On schools for the Cherokees, see Robert F. Berkhofer, Jr., *Salvation and the Savage: An Analysis of Protestant Missions and American Indian Response, 1787–1862* (New York, 1976), chapter 2; McLoughlin, *Cherokee Renascence in the New Republic*, 72–76, 173–74. On religious proselytizing among the Cherokees, see William G. McLoughlin, *Cherokees and Missionaries* (New Haven, CT, 1984); Meg Devlin O'Sullivan, "A Family Affair: Cherokee Conversion to American Board Churches, 1817–1839," *Tennessee Historical Quarterly* 36 (2005): 264–83.

18. On intermarriage between Cherokees and whites, see Thornton, *The Cherokees*, 52–53, and McLoughlin, *Cherokee Renascence in the New Republic*, 69–70, 169–71. On Cherokee concepts of citizenship, as relating to intermarriage with whites, see Fay A. Yarborough, *Race and the Cherokee Nation: Sovereignty in the Nineteenth Century* (Philadelphia, 2008), especially chapter 1. On internal divisions among the Cherokees, see McLoughlin, *Cherokee Renascence in the New Republic*, chapter 16; McLoughlin, *Cherokees and Missionaries*, chapter 6.

19. For a summary of these events, see Perdue and Green, *The Cherokee Nation and the Trail of Tears*, 54–59. On Georgia's part, in particular, see McLoughlin, "Georgia's Role in Instigating Compulsory Indian Removal," *Georgia Historical Quarterly*,

70 (1986): 605–32, and Mary Young, "The Exercise of Sovereignty in Cherokee Georgia," *Journal of the Early Republic* 10 (1990): 43–63.

20. Ard Hoyt to Samuel A. Worcester, April 10, 1819, and Samuel A. Worcester to Charles Hicks, March 4, 1819, both quoted in McLoughlin, *Cherokee Renascence in the New Republic,* 258.

21. For a brief overview of the Second Great Awakening, with special attention to mission work, see John A. Andrew, *Rebuilding the Christian Commonwealth: New England Congregationalists and Foreign Missions, 1800–1830* (Lexington, KY, 1976), chapter 1.

22. *Seventh Annual Report, American Board of Commissioners for Foreign Missions,* (Boston, 1823), 10, quoted in Oscar P. Bollman, "The Foreign Mission School of Cornwall, Connecticut," Master of Sacred Theology thesis, Yale University Divinity School (1939), 57; Edward Dorr Griffin, *The Kingdom of Christ* (Philadelphia, 1805), 27. See also Clifton Jackson Phillips, *Protestant America and the Pagan World: The First Half-Century of the American Board of Commissioners for Foreign Missions, 1810–1860* (Cambridge, MA, 1969).

23. *Missionary Herald,* vol. 29 (1828), 193–94.

24. On the question of whether "civilization" (including formal education) was a necessary precondition of conversion, see Paul William Harris, *Nothing but Christ: Rufus Anderson and the Ideology of Protestant Foreign Missions* (New York, 1999), 20–23. For discussion of this matter within the leadership of the American Board, see Jeremiah Evarts to Rev. J. E. Darneille, July 28, 1826, ABC 1.01, vol. 6, nos. 220–22.

25. See McLoughlin, *Cherokees and Missionaries.* See also O'Sullivan, "A Family Affair," 264–83.

CHAPTER EIGHT *"Even the stoutest hearts melt into tears"*

1. *Sixteenth Annual Report, American Board of Commissioners for Foreign Missions* (Boston, 1825), 96; Rufus Anderson to Jeremiah Evarts, July 19, 1825, ABC 1.01, vol. 5, no. 332; *Semi-Annual Report of Donations to the Foreign Mission School, June 1825* (Boston, 1825), 7.

2. Jeremiah Evarts to Rev. T. Stone, August 26, 1825, ABC 1.01, vol. 5, nos. 359–61.

3. *Fifteenth Annual Report, American Board of Commissioners for Foreign Missions* (Boston, 1824), 131; *Seventeenth Annual Report, American Board of Commissioners for Foreign Missions* (Boston, 1826), 106.

4. Jeremiah Evarts to Amos Bassett, November 10, 1826, ABC 1.01, vol. 6, no. 349.

5. See *The Religious Intelligencer,* vol. 10 (1825–26), 610.

6. Report of the Prudential Committee, October 26, 1825, Evarts Family Papers, box 4, folder 158, Division of Manuscripts and Archives, Sterling Memorial Library, Yale University, New Haven, CT.

7. Jeremiah Evarts to Amos Bassett, October 7, 1826, ABC 1.01, vol. 6, no. 309. See also Edward C. Starr, *A History of Cornwall, Connecticut: A Typical New England Town* (New Haven, CT, 1926), 137.

8. Jeremiah Evarts to Amos Bassett, November 10, 1821, ABC 1.01, vol. 6, nos. 347–49; Jeremiah Evarts to Rev. Timothy Stone, October 7, 1826, ABC 1.01, vol. 6, nos. 310–11; and Jeremiah Evarts to Revs. R. Emerson and H. Hudson, November 8, 1826 (typescript copy), FMS Archive, folder 17.

9. Jeremiah Evarts to Rev. Charles A. Boardman, October 10, 1826, ABC 1.01, vol. 6, nos. 318–19; Jeremiah Evarts to Rev. Charles A. Boardman, October 7, 1826, ABC 1.01, vol. 6, nos. 308–9; Jeremiah Evarts to Rev. T. Smith, August 26, 1825, ABC 1.01, vol. 5, nos. 359–61.
10. *Fifteenth Annual Report, American Board of Commissioners for Foreign Missions* (Boston, 1824), 130; *Sixteenth Annual Report, American Board of Commissioners for Foreign Missions* (Boston, 1825), 97.
11. On efforts to place departing scholars, see, for example, Jeremiah Evarts to Rev. Bennet Tyler, October 7, 1826, ABC 1.01, vol. 6, nos. 316–17; Jeremiah Evarts to Deacon L. Loomis, May 4, 1827, ABC 1.01, vol. 7, nos. 93–94.
12. Jeremiah Evarts to Rev. Dr. Tyler, November 11, 1826, ABC 1.01, vol. 6, no. 359; Jeremiah Evarts to Augustine N. Hooker, May 1, 1827, ABC 1.01, vol. 7, nos. 170–71.
13. Jeremiah Evarts to Deacon L. Loomis, May 4, 1827, ABC 1.01, vol. 7, nos. 93–94.
14. Jeremiah Evarts to John E. Phelps, May 26, 1827, ABC 1.01, vol. 7, nos. 165–67.
15. Jeremiah Evarts to Rev. Rufus W. Bailey, n.d., ABC 1.01, vol. 6, nos. 311–12. See also David Greene to Rev. Bennet Tyler, August 29, 1827, ABC 1.01, vol. 7, no. 399.
16. Jeremiah Evarts to Deacon L. Loomis, March 28, 1827, ABC 1.01, vol. 7, nos. 50–52.
17. Jeremiah Evarts to Rev. Herman Daggett, July 21, 1828, ABC 1.01, vol. 8, nos. 428–29; Jeremiah Evarts to Deacon L. Loomis, September 5, 1828, ABC 1.01, vol. 8, nos. 544–45; Jeremiah Evarts to Edwin Dwight, September 17, 1828, ABC 1.01, vol. 8, nos. 560–61.
18. Jeremiah Evarts to Elisha Stearns, May 25, 1827, ABC 1.01, vol. 7, no. 158; Jeremiah Evarts to Philo Swift, July 19, 1827, ABC 1.01, vol. 7, nos. 307–8; *Connecticut Herald*, December 5, 1826. See also Jeremiah Evarts to Rev. Timothy Stone, September 6, 1827, ABC 1.01, vol. 7, no. 427.
19. Jeremiah Evarts to Rev. E. W. Caruthers, August 26, 1828, ABC 1.01, vol. 8, nos. 516–17; David Greene to Rev. Heman Humphrey, June 20, 1830, ABC 1.01, vol. 10, nos. 67–68; David Greene to Rev. Hiram Smith, March 30, 1830, ABC 1.01, vol. 10, nos. 57–59.
20. On Tennooe's "defection," see chapter 4. The letter from Gerrit P. Judd to Edwin Dwight, September 27, 1830 (typescript copy) is in FMS Archive, folder 36. (The original is in the Dwight Collection, Norman Rockwell Museum, Stockbridge, MA.)
21. On Hopoo's work, and also his sexual transgressions, see Gerrit P. Judd to Edwin Dwight, September 27, 1830. On his marriage, see *New-York Commercial Advertiser*, September 23, 1823.
22. Gerrit P. Judd to Edwin Dwight, September 27, 1830 (typescript copy), FMS Archive, folder 36; Hiram Bingham to E. W. Clark, February 22, 1831, Bingham Family Papers, Division of Manuscripts and Archives, Sterling Memorial Library, Yale University, New Haven, CT.
23. Sheldon Dibble, *A History of the Sandwich Islands* (Honolulu, 1909), 148–49.
24. Moody Hall to Jeremiah Evarts, April 5, 1825, ABC 18.3.1 (part 2), vol. 5, no. 333; Moody Hall to Jeremiah Evarts, August 20, 1825, ABC 18.3.1 (part 2), vol. 5, no. 338; David Brown to Jeremiah Evarts, July 11, 1826, ABC 18.3.1 (part 2), vol. 6, no. 290; Jeremiah Evarts to Henry Hill, March 4, 1826, ABC 11, vol. 2, no. 37; Jeremiah Evarts to Rufus Anderson, March 13, 1826, ABC 11, vol. 2, no. 39; William Manwaring to Jeremiah Evarts, August 9, 1825, ABC 11, vol. 5, no. 346.
25. Samuel Worcester to Jeremiah Evarts, July 28, 1826, ABC 11, vol. 5, no. 231; Samuel Worcester to Jeremiah Evarts, May 29, 1827, ABC 11, vol. 5, no. 235.

26. Moody Hall to Jeremiah Evarts, September 18, 1824, ABC 11, vol. 5, no. 333; William Manwaring to Jeremiah Evarts, August 9, 1825, ABC 11, vol. 5, no. 346.
27. "One young man from China" (Henry Martyn Alan): See Carl T. Smith, *Chinese Christians: Elites, Middle Men, and the Church in Hong Kong*, 2d ed. (Hong Kong, 2005), 56–58. "An Oneida Indian" (Peter Augustine Hooker): See H. K. Cooper to Rev. E. C. Starr, January 5, 1899, FMS Archive, folder 43. "A Stockbridge Indian" (John Newcombe Chicks): See *The Missionary Herald*, vol. 29 (1833), 25. "A Delaware Indian" (Adin Gibbs): See Adin Gibbs to the Gentlemen of the Prudential Committee, June 20, 1822, ABC 12.1, vol. 2, no. 135. "A young man of Portuguese extraction" (Joseph J. Loy): See obituary in *Daily Witness* (Montreal, Canada), March 27, 1897 (photocopy), FMS Archive, folder 54.
28. This account of Fisk's life is based largely on Lyman F. Hodge, *Photius Fisk: A Biography* (Boston, 1891). On his experiences soon after leaving the Mission School, see also Rufus Anderson to Rev. Daniel Temple, June 25, 1827, ABC 1.01, vol. 7, nos. 248–52.
29. *The Commonwealth* (Boston), March 31, 1883, quoted in Hodge, *Photius Fisk*, 183.
30. *Lowell Vox Populi*, n.p., quoted in Hodge, *Photius Fisk*, 188; Susan H. Mixon, quoted ibid., 199.
31. Douglas Warne, *Humehume of Kaua'i: A Boy's Journey to America, An Ali'i's Return Home* (Honolulu, 2008).
32. George "Prince" Tamoree to Benjamin Gold, July 29, 1820 (photocopy), FMS Archive, folder 36.
33. Mercy Whitney's Journal, vol. 1 (1821–27), quoted in Warne, *Humehume of Kaua'i*, 156.
34. See, for example, Herman Daggett to George P. Tamoree, November 14, 1820 (photocopy), FMS Archive, folder 16. See also Herman Daggett to George P. Tamoree, December 1, 1825 (photocopy), FMS Archive, folder 16. In this letter, the principal deplores Tamoree's "unhappy interference with government." (This refers to his leadership of an ill-advised rebellion.)
35. Bingham's comments are quoted in Warne, *Humehume of Kaua'i*, 181, 184.
36. On Tamoree's leadership of the Kaua'i rebellion of 1824 and its aftermath, see Warne, *Humehume of Kaua'i*, 185–205. See also Catherine Stauder, "George Prince of Hawaii," *Hawaiian Journal of History* 6 (1972): 28–44; Anne Harding Spoehr, "George Prince Tamoree: Heir Apparent of Kaua'i and Niihau," *Hawaiian Journal of History* 15 (1981): 73–88. For contemporary accounts of these events, see *Connecticut Courant* (Hartford), March 22, 1825, and *The Missionary Herald*, vol. 21 (1825), 123–24.
37. John Ridge to President James Monroe, March 8, 1821, John Howard Payne Papers, no. 761, Newberry Library, Chicago, IL. On John Ridge's role (and also Elias Boudinot's) in making the case for Cherokee "improvement," see Maureen Konkle, *Writing Indian Nations: Native Intellectuals and the Politics of Historiography, 1827–1863* (Chapel Hill, NC, 2004), chapter 1; Hilary Wyss, *English Letters and Indian Literacies: Reading, Writing, and New England Missionary Schools, 1750–1830* (Philadelphia, 2012), 171–78.
38. Wyss, *English Letters and Indian Literacies*, 154–60.
39. Ibid., 161–85. (The quote from the Creek citation is on p. 180.)
40. The full text of Ridge's "sketch" can be found in William C. Sturtevant, ed., "John Ridge on Cherokee Civilization in 1826," *Journal of Cherokee Studies* 6 (1981): 79–91. On the portrait by Charles Bird King, see p. 206 (and note 25 on p. 309).

41. *Savannah Georgian,* June 3, 1826, quoted in Thurman Wilkins, *Cherokee Tragedy: The Ridge Family and the Decimation of a People,* 2d ed. (Norman, OK, 1986), 177n; Jeremiah Evarts to Henry Hill, April 1826, ABC 11, vol. 2, no. 41; Sophia Sawyer to David Greene, August 28, 1834, ABC 18.3.1 (part 2), vol. 8, no. 183.

42. *The Missionary Herald,* vol. 20 (1824), 348. See also Jeremiah Evarts to Henry Hill, January 23, 1826, ABC 11, vol. 2, no. 26.

43. On plans for the fund-raising tour, see Jeremiah Evarts to Henry Hill, January 23, 1826, ABC 11, vol. 2, no. 26; Wilkins, *Cherokee Tragedy,* 193ff. On Boudinot's success as a speaker, see Jeremiah Evarts to Henry Hill, February 9, 1826, ABC 11, vol. 2, no. 30. See also Jeremiah Evarts to Henry Hill, February 3, 1826, ABC 11, vol. 2, no. 29.

44. The full text appears in Theda Perdue, ed., *Cherokee Editor: The Writings of Elias Boudinot* (Athens, GA, 1996), 68–79.

45. Jeremiah Evarts to Henry Hill, March 22, 1826, ABC 11, vol. 2, no. 40; Harriet (Gold) Boudinot to Herman and Flora (Gold) Vaill, January 5, 1827, in Theresa Strouth Gaul, ed., *To Marry an Indian: The Marriage of Harriett Gold & Elias Boudinot in Letters, 1823–1839* (Chapel Hill, NC, 2005), 154–55; Harriet (Gold) Boudinot to Benjamin and Eleanor Gold, July 17, 1826. (The original of this letter has apparently been lost; the quote beginning "when the family are all assembled" appears in Mary Brinsmade Church, "Elias Boudinot: An Account of His Life by His Grand-daughter," Town History Papers of the Woman's Club of Washington, Conn. (1913), typescript copy, FMS Archive, folder 61. See also Daniel Buttrick to Jeremiah Evarts, October 7, 1826, ABC 18.3.1 (part 2), vol. 4, no. 25.

46. Daniel Buttrick to Jeremiah Evarts, October 7, 1826, ABC 18.3.1 (part 2), vol. 4, no. 25; Elias and Harriet (Gold) Boudinot to Herman and Flora (Gold) Vaill, January 5, 1827, in Gaul, ed., *To Marry an Indian,* 153–57; Samuel Worcester to Jeremiah Evarts, January 8, 1827, ABC 18.3.1 (part 2), vol. 5, no. 234.

47. John Ridge to E. Butler, July 7, 1826, ABC 18.3.1 (part 2), vol. 4, no. 69.

48. See Perdue, ed., *Cherokee Editor,* 90 passim; Ralph Henry Gabriel, *Elias Boudinot, Cherokee, & His America* (Norman, OK, 1941), especially chapters 14–15.

49. Morris Woodruff to Candace Woodruff, February 26, 1827, Woodruff Collection, Litchfield County Historical Society, Litchfield, CT; Jeremiah Evarts to Henry Hill, April 2, 1826, ABC 11, vol. 2, no. 41; Thomas L. McKenney and James Hall, *History of the Indian Tribes of North America with Biographical Sketches and Anecdotes of the Principal Chiefs,* ed. F. W. Hodge, 3 vols. (Edinburgh, 1933), vol. 1, 327–28; Church, "Elias Boudinot." For a further opinion on the Ridge marriage, see Daniel Buttrick to Jeremiah Evarts, October 12, 1824, ABC 18.3.1 (part 2), vol. 4, no. 2.

50. The account presented here of Cherokee removal—with special attention to the participation of John Ridge and Elias Boudinot—draws heavily on Wilkins, *Cherokee Tragedy.* The scholarly literature on removal is vast, extending from the classic work of Grant Foreman, *Indian Removal: The Emigration of the Five Civilized Tribes of Indians* (Norman, OK, 1934) to, most recently, Theda Perdue and Michael Green, *The Cherokee Nation and the Trail of Tears* (New York, 2007). Other important works include Marion Starkey, *The Cherokee Nation* (New York, 1946); John Ehle, *Trail of Tears: The Rise and Fall of the Cherokee Nation* (New York, 1988); William G. McLoughlin, *Cherokee Renascence in the New Republic* (Princeton, NJ, 1986). See also Ronald N. Satz, *American Indian Policy in the Jacksonian Era*

(Lincoln, NE, 1974), and William G. McLoughlin, *After the Trail of Tears: The Cherokees' Struggle for Sovereignty, 1839–1880* (Chapel Hill, NC, 1993).

51. See Wilkins, *Cherokee Tragedy,* chapter 8. On harassment of Boudinot, see Perdue, ed., *Cherokee Editor,* 226.

52. "Indian Rights," *Haverhill* [MA] *Gazette,* March 17, 1832.

53. C. E. B. (Catherine E. Beecher), *Boston Courier,* March 15, 1832; "Indian Rights," *Haverhill* [MA] *Gazette,* March 17, 1832; Jack Larkin and Caroline Sloat, eds., "A Place in My Chronicle," *A New Edition of the Diary of Christopher Columbus Baldwin, 1829–1835* (Worcester, MA, 2010), 115.

54. John Ridge to Stand Watie, April 6, 1832, in *Cherokee Cavaliers: Forty Years of Cherokee History as Told in the Correspondence of the Ridge-Watie-Boudinot Family* ed. Edward E. Dale and Gaston Little (Norman, OK, 1939), 7–8.

55. "The Cherokees," *New York Journal of Commerce,* July 22, 1839; Amos Kendall, quoted in Wilkins, *Cherokee Tragedy,* 237.

56. See Wilkins, *Cherokee Tragedy,* chapter 10.

57. Ibid., chapter 11. On threats against Ridge, see, for example, Sophia Sawyer to David Greene, June 15, 1835, ABC 18.3.1 (part 2), vol. 8, no. 186. On suspicion that leaders of the Treaty Party had personally profited from removal, see Wilkins, *Cherokee Tragedy,* 251n. For Boudinot's denial, see Perdue, ed., *Cherokee Editor,* 201.

58. See Wilkins, *Cherokee Tragedy,* chapter 12. The treaty signing was witnessed by a white man, J. W. H. Underwood; see *Cartersville* [GA] *Courant,* March 26, 1885, quoted in Perdue, ed., *Cherokee Editor,* 27.

59. John Ridge to Doctor Sam'l W. Gold, January 2, 1831; see T. S. Gold, *Historical Records of the Town of Cornwall, Litchfield County, Connecticut,* 2d ed. (Hartford, CT, 1927), 350–51; Mrs. Eunice (Wadsworth) Taylor, "Recollection," in E. C. Starr, *A History of Cornwall, Connecticut: A Typical New England Town* (New Haven, CT, 1926), 155.

60. These quoted comments are taken from several of Harriet's letters to her parents and siblings in Connecticut, written between January 5, 1827, and May 27, 1833; see Gaul, ed., *To Marry an Indian,* 153–63, 170–83, and FMS Archive, folders 14–15. The locks of the children's hair are in FMS Archive, folder 15.

61. Benjamin Gold to Herman and Flora (Gold) Vaill, October 29, 1829, in Gaul, ed., *To Marry an Indian,* 164; Benjamin Gold to Hezekiah Gold, December 8, 1829, quoted in T. S. Gold, *Historical Records of the Town of Cornwall* 38; *The Ohio Star* (Ravenna), August 4, 1830.

62. Benjamin Gold to Hezekiah Gold, December 8, 1829, quoted in Gold, *Historical Records of the Town of Cornwall* (1904), 38; *The Ohio Star* (Ravenna), August 4, 1830.

63. Lewis B. Woodruff to George C. Woodruff, February 7, 1834, Woodruff Collection, Litchfield Historical Society, Litchfield, CT.

64. Harriett (Gold) Boudinot to Herman and Flora (Gold) Vaill, January 7, 1831, in Gaul, ed., *To Marry an Indian,* 173; Elias and Harriett (Gold) Boudinot to Herman and Flora (Gold) Vaill, July 1, 1831, ibid., 175, 177; Harriet (Gold)Boudinot to Sarah (Gold) Hopkins (letter fragment), n.d. (typescript copy), FMS Archive, folder 14.

65. Elias Boudinot to Benjamin and Eleanor Gold, August 16, 1836, in Gaul, ed., *To Marry an Indian,* 183–90. For the *New York Observer* version, republished with editorial notes, see *Journal of Cherokee Studies* 4 (1979): 102–7.

66. *Journal of Cherokee Studies* 4 (1979): 102–7.

67. Elias Boudinot to Herman and Flora (Gold) Vaill, August 28, 1836, in Gaul, ed., *To Marry an Indian*, 195; Elias Boudinot to Job Swift Gold, October 26, 1836, ibid., 197; Elias Boudinot to David Greene, April 14, 1837, ABC 18.3.1 (part 2), vol. 8, no. 217; Elias Boudinot to Benjamin and Eleanor Gold, May 20, 1837, in Gaul, *To Marry an Indian*, 200.

68. John Ridge to Eliza Northrup, November 1, 1836 (typescript copy), FMS Archive, folder 19.

69. For a firsthand account of the emigrant party that included Major Ridge and family, see Grant Foreman, ed., "Journey of a Party of Cherokee Emigrants," *Mississippi Valley Historical Review* 18 (1931): 232–45. See also Wilkins, *Cherokee Tragedy*, 304–7. The newspaper report quoted here came from the *Jonesboro* [TN] *Sentinel*, April 19, 1837, as reprinted in the *Times-Picayune* (New Orleans), May 8, 1837.

70. Statement of U.S. Commissioners, June 27, 1837, quoted in Wilkins, *Cherokee Tragedy*, 308; John Ridge to Col. John Kennedy et al., January 16, 1838 (photocopy), Ridge Family File, VFHC 5176–77, Manuscripts Division, Arkansas History Commission, Little Rock, AR.

71. Indian Pioneer Historical Project, Oklahoma Historical Society, vol. 75, 388; Ridge accounts, HM 1730, Henry E. Huntington Library, Pasadena, CA.

72. John Ridge to Col. John Kennedy et al., January 16, 1838 (photocopy), Ridge Family File, VFHC 5176–77.

73. For overviews of the removal process, see Perdue and Green, *The Cherokee Nation and the Trail of Tears;* Ehle, *Trail of Tears.* For an especially vivid eyewitness account, see *Cherokee Removal: The Journal of Rev. Daniel S. Butrick, May 19, 1838–April 1, 1839* (Park Hill, OK, 1998).

74. H. G. Clauder to Theodore Schultz, March 17, 1837, quoted in Wilkins, *Cherokee Tragedy*, 322.

75. *New York Observer*, January 26, 1839, quoted in Perdue and Green, *The Cherokee Nation and the Trail of Tears*, 134. For a useful summary of efforts to calculate the total of deaths in the removal process, see Russell Thornton, *The Cherokees: A Population History* (Lincoln, NE, 1990), 73–76.

76. See Perdue and Green, *The Cherokee Nation and the Trail of Tears*, chapter 7.

77. Ridge accounts, HM 1730, Henry E. Huntington Library, Pasadena, CA; *Arkansas Gazette* (Little Rock), October 2, 1839, quoted in Wilkins, *Cherokee Tragedy*, 328.

78. See Wilkins, *Cherokee Tragedy*, 329–34.

79. Ibid. See also Samuel Worcester to David Greene, July 17, 1839, ABC 18.3.1 (part 2), vol. 10, no. 137; John Howard Payne Papers, vol. 6, 199, Newberry Library, Chicago, quoted in Wilkins, *Cherokee Tragedy*, 209.

80. *Niles' National Register*, August 3, 1839, quoted in Wilkins, *Cherokee Tragedy*, 335–36; John Rollin Ridge, *Poems* (San Francisco, 1868), 7–8.

81. Samuel Worcester to David Greene, June 26, 1839, ABC 18.3.1 (part 2), vol. 10, no. 136. A similar account of Boudinot's murder appears in Samuel Worcester to Daniel Brinsmade, June 26, 1839 (typescript copy), FMS Archive, folder 14.

82. Joan Gilbert, "Death in Arkansas," *Rural Arkansas*, October 1987, 4–5.

83. Elias Boudinot, *Letters and Other Papers Relating to Cherokee Affairs: Being a Reply to Sundry Publications Authorized by John Ross* (Athens, GA, 1837), reprinted in Perdue, ed., *Cherokee Editor*, 160.

84. John Ridge to David Greene, July 24, 1834, ABC 18.3.1 (part 2), vol. 8, no. 213.

85. Elias Boudinot to David Greene, April 14, 1837, ABC 18.3.1 (part 2), vol. 8, no. 218;

Boudinot, *Letters and Other Papers Relating to Cherokee Affairs,* reprinted in Perdue, ed., *Cherokee Editor,* 222–25.

86. John Ridge to David Greene, May 17, 1837, ABC 18.3.1 (part 2), vol. 8, no. 215.

87. For extensive coverage of the Ridge and Boudinot assassinations, see *New York Journal of Commerce,* July 17, 18, 22, 30, and 31, 1839. See also *Little Rock* [AR] *Gazette,* July 17, 1839; *The Daily Picayune* (New Orleans), July 18, 1839; *Houston Telegraph and Texas Register,* September 18, 1839; *Connecticut Courant,* August 3, 1839; *New York Commercial Advertiser,* August 17, 1839; *New Hampshire Sentinel,* August 14, 1839; *New Bedford* [MA] *Mercury,* August 9, 1839; *The Farmer's Cabinet* (Amherst, NH), July 26 and August 9, 1839. The comment on John Ridge appears in the *Portsmouth* [NH] *Journal of Literature and Politics,* August 3, 1839. The comment on Major Ridge is in the *Houston Telegraph and Texas Register,* September 18, 1839. The comment on Elias Boudinot and the quoted reference to the Foreign Mission School appear in "The Cherokee and His Beautiful Bride," *The Cabinet* (Schenectady, NY), August 6, 1839.

88. Samuel Worcester to Daniel B. Brinsmade, June 26, 1839, FMS Archive, folder 14; Delight Sargent Boudinot to Mr. & Mrs. Brinsmade, July 18, 1839, FMS Archive, folder 14.

89. On the apprenticeship arrangements for the Boudinot sons, see A. E. W. Robertson to Rev. E. C. Starr, February 21, 1896 (typescript copy), FMS Archive, folder 19. The family letters quoted here are William P. Boudinot to Colonel Benjamin Gold, August 26, 1845, FMS Archive, folder 14; Mary H. Boudinot to Col. Benjamin Gold, September 24, 1845, FMS Archive, folder 14.

90. On the careers of the Boudinot children, see, for example, the obituary for Elias C. Boudinot, *The Evening Call* (Woonsocket, RI), September 2, 1890 (photocopy), in FMS Archive, folder 12; A. E. W. Robertson to E. C. Starr, February 21, 1896 (typescript copy), FMS Archive, folder 19.

91. Sophia Sawyer to David Greene, October 10, 1839, ABC 18.3.1 (part 2), vol. 8, no. 322; John Rollin Ridge to David Greene, December 7, 1839, ABC 18.3.1 (part 2), vol. 8, no. 323; S. B. N. Ridge to John Spencer, Secretary of War, June 7, 1842 (photocopy), Ridge Family File, VFHC 5176–77; Jack Straight, "The Ridge House: A Preliminary Report" (typescript) Ridge Family File, VFHC 5176–77; "Fayetteville's Oldest Home" (typescript), Ridge Family File, VFHC 5176–77; obituary of Mrs. Sarah B. N. Ridge (typescript copy), Ridge Family File, VFHC 5176–77; A. E. W. Robertson to Rev. E. C. Starr, February 21, 1896 (typescript copy), FMS Archive, folder 19. Numerous papers relating to various Ridge properties, and efforts to contest Sarah Ridge's inheritance rights, are in Ridge Family File, VFHC 5176–77.

92. S. B. N. Ridge to John Spencer, Secretary of War, June 7, 1842 (photocopy), Ridge Family File, VFHC 5176–77; Sarah B. N. Ridge et al. to William Medill, Commissioner of Indian Affairs, November 28, 1846, Ridge Family File, VFHC 5176–77.

93. See James W. Parins, *John Rollin Ridge: His Life & Works* (Lincoln, NE, 1991). On his career as a writer, see Franklin Walker, *San Francisco's Literary Frontier* (New York, 1939).

94. Sarah B. N. Ridge to Eliza Northrup, n.d. (typescript copy), FMS Archive, folder 19. For information on the children of John and Sarah (Northrup) Ridge, see also Ridge Family File, VFHC 5176–77.

95. *Litchfield Enquirer,* July 25, 1839. See also *Litchfield Enquirer,* August 15, September 5, and September 26, 1839.

96. Church, "Elias Boudinot"; David Perry, *The Spiritual Temple: A Sermon Delivered*

at . . . (Hartford, CT, 1820), FMS Archive, folder 16; Gold, *Historical Records of the Town of Cornwall* (1904), 40.

Epilogue

1. The grave is in the southeast corner of Cornwall's town cemetery, adjacent to U.S. Route 4. It is easily recognized by its large tablet-style marker.
2. *New York Times,* April 12, 1993.
3. On the process of arranging the return of Obookiah's remains to Hawaii, see *Lakeville* [CT] *Journal,* July 5, 1993; *Torrington* [CT] *Register Citizen,* February 17, 1993.
4. *Torrington* [CT] *Register Citizen,* July 14, 1993; *Lakeville* [CT] *Journal,* July 13, 1993. See also *United Church News,* CONNtact edition 9 (September 1993), 1–3. For a full account of the exhumation process, see Nicholas Bellantoni, Roger Thompson, David Cooke, Michael Park, and Cynthia Trayling, "The Life, Death, Archaeological Exhumation and Re-interment of Opukaha'ia (Henry Obookiah)," *Connecticut History,* 46 (2007): 206–26.
5. *Torrington* [CT] *Register Citizen,* July 26, 1993.
6. *United Church News,* CONNtact edition 9 (September 1993).
7. The stone that stands in the cemetery today is a reproduction; the original is in the collections of the New Echota Historic Site (Rome, GA). The inscription "We seek a rest beyond the skies" is from a hymn that Harriet favored; according to her husband she asked that it be sung by her bedside during her last days See Theresa Strouth Gaul, ed., *To Marry an Indian: The Marriage of Harriett Gold & Elias Boudinot in Letters, 1823–1839* (Chapel Hill, NC, 2005), 185.
8. Details of the layout of the Polson Cemetery are principally from Nancy Brown, personal communications to author, 2012–13. On the ownership history of the Ridge properties at Honey Creek, see Ridge Family File, VHFC, 5166–67, Manuscripts Division, Arkansas History Commission, Little Rock, AR.
9. Personal communication, Charles Gold to author, January 15, 2013.

Index

Boudinot-Gold intermarriage scandal
  (continued)
  Harriet Gold seen as "victim" in, 185–6
  initial secrecy in, 177–80, 183
  public effigy burning in protest of,
    181–2, 190, 269
  public outrage in, 180–3, 185–6, 189,
    190–2, 239–40, 260, 269
  wedding in, 192, 193–5, 269
  white support and defenders in, 182,
    185, 186–7, 190
Bradford Academy, 23
Brainerd (mission school), 88–9, 99, 147,
  176
Brecher, Jeremy, 297n
Breckenridge, Hugh Henry, 61
Brinsmade, Daniel, 179–80, 183, 184, 250
Brinsmade, Mary Gold, 185, 250, 261–2
Brintnall, Caleb, 16, 17, 20, 21–2, 50, 292n
Brown, Catharine, 304n
Brown, David, 99–102, 164–71, 190
  celebrity and reputation of, 168,
    169–70
  in return to Cherokee Nation, 229
  speaking tours of, 164–70, 229
Brown, John, 234
Brumaghim, Wayne H., 285n
Bunce, Isaac, 154, 155–6, 159, 185–6
Buttrick, Daniel, 190–1
Byrd, William, 131

Calhoun, Ga., 196–7
California Indians (Diggers), 264
Campagne, Baron de, 105, 113, 227,
  291n
Campbell, Archibald, 92–3
Campbell, Mrs., 92, 93
Canada, 24, 71, 232
Canton, 10, 11, 12, 13, 14, 21, 88
Capodistrias, John, 233
Carhooa, Benjamin, 31
Carter, David, 164, 191
Case, Francis, 192, 193
Catholicism, Catholics, 59, 131
Catlin, John, 291n
Ceylon, 64, 294n
Chamberlain, William, 190
Charleston, S.C., 76, 90, 151, 240, 260
Charleston Navy Yard, 31

Cherokee Nation, 100, 133, 145, 149, 151,
  153, 155, 164, 166, 169, 182, 211–16, 262,
  264, 269, 270
  as aiding in white military conflicts,
    146, 167, 213, 262, 264
  anti-mission sentiment in, 160, 188, 191,
    217–18
  author's visit to, 196–206
  ball play in, 189, 199, 230, 240, 307n
  bitter dissension over removal
    controversy in, 245–6, 250, 255–6,
    257, 258, 264, 270, 272
  "Blood Law" of, 243, 255–6, 260
  Boudinot-Gold's married life in,
    198–9, 239, 240–1, 242, 243, 247–9,
    250, 261, 308n
  census of, 189, 204–5, 239
  Chieftains Museum of, 200–2, 309n
  Christian conversions in, 215, 218, 239,
    259
  "civilization" policies embraced by,
    167, 211–12, 214–15, 237–8, 240, 242,
    257, 258
  class and cultural tensions in, 215
  D.C. delegations of, 170, 238, 244, 245,
    246, 264
  declining population of, 213, 254
  displacement and forced-removal crisis
    of, 3–4, 175, 198–9, 200, 201, 204, 211,
    213, 214, 216, 238, 243–4, 245–7, 250,
    251–5, 257–60, 271, 272–3, 314n
  education and schools in, 88–9, 99, 147,
    176, 201, 215, 218, 237, 239, 240, 241
  epidemic disease and impact on, 213,
    253, 254
  extermination threat to, 230, 244,
    259
  family organization in, 212
  farming and agriculture in, 145, 147,
    189, 197, 202, 204–5, 212, 214, 237, 239,
    241, 252, 253
  FMS recruitment network in, 88–91,
    147, 176
  FMS scholars from, 90, 91, 98, 99–101,
    111, 114–15, 147–8, 151, 160, 164, 170,
    176
  FMS scholars in homecomings to, 111,
    164, 170–1, 177, 229–30, 240
  forests and trees of, 199, 202

Georgia sovereignty controversy
and, 200, 216, 238, 243, 244–5, 257,
260
Gold family's visit to, 249
homesteads on, 197, 200–2, 203–5, 262,
308*n*, 309*n*
hunting by, 200, 212, 213
"Indian Committee" of, 251–2
intermarriage scandal "outrage" and
reaction of, 180–1, 188, 190, 191, 269
interracial marriage in, 126, 135, 150,
157, 190, 191, 215, 238
John Ridge's estate claimed by, 263
John Ridge's leadership role in, 151–2,
206, 218, 237, 238, 243, 244, 245, 246,
252, 256, 260, 271
land cessions to U.S. government by,
198–9, 204, 211, 213, 214, 216, 245–7,
251–2
Late Immigrants–Old Settlers tensions
in, 255–6
missionary presence in, 88–90, 99, 147,
150, 157, 159, 167, 170, 176, 177, 188, 189,
190, 198, 201, 215, 217–18, 229–30, 239,
241–2, 248, 249, 251, 305*n*, 307*n*
National Council of, 198, 214, 238, 243,
245, 252
national "seminary" project in, 239,
240, 241–2
New Echota as onetime capital of,
197–200, 268, 318*n*
political organization in, 214–15, 243,
255
printing press project in, 239, 240, 241,
242
resistance to white encroachment in,
145, 213, 215–16, 243, 245, 246, 250
Ridge and Boudinot's advocacy for
removal of, 3–4, 198–9, 245, 246,
251–3, 255, 257–60, 271, 272–3, 314*n*
Ridge-Boudinot assassinations in,
256–7, 260–1, 264
Ridge family farmland and business
holdings in, 202–3, 204–5, 247, 252,
253, 254–5, 263, 271
Ridge-Northrup's domestic life in, 203,
205, 242–3, 247, 248, 253
slave ownership in, 145, 146, 159, 202,
205, 247, 248, 252, 257, 270, 271

traditional culture and lifestyle of, 212,
214
Trail of Tears and, 4, 199, 253–4
in treaty negotiations with U.S.
government, 146, 170, 198–9, 211, 213,
244, 245, 246–7, 258, 260, 264
in violent clashes with white settlers,
215–16, 243
western Indian Territory resettlement
of, 211, 216, 252–3, 254–7, 260, 262,
270
white influence and decline of
indigenous traditions in, 213–14,
258–9
white supporters of, 245, 247, 257–8, 259
white trade with, 200, 203, 213–14
Cherokee Phoenix, 198, 242, 243, 245, 260,
261
Cherokee Tragedy (Wilkins), 308*n*
Chickasaw Indians, 133, 211, 217
Chieftains Museum, 200–2, 309*n*
Chile, 13, 234
China, 3, 11, 13, 14, 21, 33, 88, 92
FMS scholars from, 173, 175, 231, 232
China Trade, 9–14, 16, 20, 21, 29, 70, 88,
107, 163
goods exchanged in, 10–11, 12–13, 21
Hawaii as central crossroads in, 13–14
outposts and targets of, 10–14
regulation and protocol of, 12
Chippewa Indians, 115, 211
Choctaw Indians, 88, 90, 91, 111, 133, 135,
155, 164, 172, 191, 211, 212, 217, 226,
232, 294*n*
Christian conversions, 32, 70, 71–2, 88,
106–7, 151, 160, 163, 209, 217, 233, 248,
272, 304*n*
of American Indians, 60, 91, 129, 140,
176, 215, 218, 239, 259, 304*n*
failed efforts in, 132, 218, 233, 239
"falls" and reversions in wake of, 110,
189, 227–8, 229, 230, 234, 240, 269
of FMS scholars, 73, 163, 171, 176, 231
FMS's main focus on, 3, 33, 34–5, 36,
38–9, 69, 73, 165, 171, 231, 239
as fundamental concern of
millennialism, 60, 62–3
Hawaii mission's accomplishment in,
106–7

Gold family, 125, 175–6, 180, 192, 249
  Boudinot children taken in by, 261–2
  descendants of, 149, 271–2
  reaction to Boudinot-Gold marriage
    in, 177–9, 181, 183–5, 192, 248
Golitsyn, Aleksandr, 84
Goshen, Conn., 29, 30, 31, 35, 42, 96, 160,
    182, 192, 193, 194, 226
Grapes of Canaan (Loomis), 291*n*
Gray, Ben, 297*n*
Great Awakening, 59
Great Britain, 9, 60, 136, 137, 146, 164
  colonization by, 57–8, 129
  foreign missions established by, 64
Greece, 6, 64, 164, 232, 233, 234
Greek War of Independence, 164
Greene, David, 226–7, 258
Grenada, 71
Griffin, Edward Dorr, 64

Hall, James, 243
Hall, Moody, 230
Harris, Walter, 294*n*
Harrison, Hannah, 172
Hart, Henry, 70, 117
Hartford Courant, 70
Hartford Deaf and Dumb Asylum, 77,
    102
Harvey, James, 70
Harvey, Joseph, 35, 40, 42, 80, 85, 86, 180
Hawaii, Hawaiian islands, 3, 14–15, 30,
    41, 44–53, 69, 81, 82, 92, 102, 163, 172,
    223, 272
  author's journey to retrace Obookiah's
    childhood in, 45–53
  as central crossroads in China Trade,
    13–14
  civil wars in, 18–19, 49, 236
  declining native population of, 272
  destruction of "idols" on, 107, 295*n*
  diet of, 14, 44, 48
  export trade of, 50
  farming and agriculture in, 44, 47–8,
    50, 52, 272
  FMS scholars from, 3, 37, 43, 45, 69, 70,
    72, 85, 86, 87, 93, 100, 115, 172, 173–4,
    225, 231, 292*n*
  gender segregation in, 49
  geography of, 45–6, 47–8, 50, 52, 53

indigenous religious practices of, 17,
    19–20, 21, 44, 46, 47, 48–9, 50–1, 52,
    107, 108, 268
  Ka'u district of, 19, 45–50, 285*n*
  Morse's written accounts on, 44–5
  Obookiah's childhood in, 18–20, 47, 48,
    49–50, 51–2, 268
  Obookiah's departure from, 20–1, 50
  Obookiah's life as continuously
    celebrated in, 15, 266–8
  Obookiah's remains returned to, 267–8
  overturning of traditional culture and
    religion in, 20, 106, 107, 272, 295*n*
  paradise-like atmosphere of, 13–14
  "Prince" George's homecoming to,
    109–10, 235
  social hierarchy in, 49
  statehood granted to, 272
  trade ships in hiring natives of, 14, 20,
    21, 29, 30, 31, 70, 163
  volcanoes in, 46, 48, 50, 53
Hawaiian Tourist Bureau, 266–7
Hawaii mission, 13, 32, 46, 51, 93, 97–8,
    106–11, 112, 164, 172, 223, 225, 266,
    282*n*
  curriculum at, 94
  defections of scholars from, 110, 227,
    229, 296*n*
  disappointing reports on former
    scholars at, 110, 227–9, 235–7
  final sendoff for staff of, 96–7
  first year accomplishments of, 106–7,
    109–11
  FMS's plans for, 32, 86, 91
  fund-raising and donations for, 91,
    94–5, 97
  King Tamoree as key benefactor to,
    109, 110
  native culture as negatively viewed by,
    108, 295*n*
  in overturning of traditional culture
    and religion, 106–7, 295*n*
  planning and preparations for, 91–2,
    93–7
  religious "falls" and disappointing
    performances of scholars at, 227–9
  special "Owhyhean book" created for,
    94
  staffing of, 95–6

ALSO BY

JOHN DEMOS

THE UNREDEEMED CAPTIVE
A Family Story from Early America

The setting for this haunting and encyclopedically re-
searched work of history is colonial Massachusetts, where
English Puritans first endeavoured to "civilize" a "savage"
native populace. There, in February 1704, a French and
Indian war party descended on the village of Deerfield,
abducting a Puritan minister and his children. Although
John Williams was eventually released, his daughter horrified the family by staying with her captors and marrying a
Mohawk husband. Out of this incident, the Bancroft Prize–
winning historian John Demos has constructed a gripping
narrative that opens a window into North America, where
English, French, and Native Americans faced one another
across gulfs of culture and belief—and sometimes crossed
over.

American History

Printed in the United States
by Baker & Taylor Publisher Services